Twenty-First Century Color Lines

Twenty-First Century Color Lines

Multiracial Change in Contemporary America

Edited by

ANDREW GRANT-THOMAS AND GARY ORFIELD

Foreword by

CHRISTOPHER EDLEY JR.

TEMPLE UNIVERSITY PRESS
Philadelphia

TEMPLE UNIVERSITY PRESS
1601 North Broad Street
Philadelphia PA 19122
www.temple.edu/tempress

⊗ The paper used in this publication meets the requirements of the American National Standard for Information Sciences—Permanence of Paper for Printed Library Materials, ANSI Z39.48-1992

Library of Congress Cataloging-in-Publication Data

Twenty-first century color lines : multiracial change in contemporary America / edited by Andrew Grant-Thomas and Gary Orfield ; with a foreword by Christopher Edley, Jr.
   p. cm.
Includes bibliographical references and index.
ISBN 978-1-59213-691-9 (cloth : alk. paper)
ISBN 978-1-59213-692-6 (pbk. : alk. paper)
1. United States—Race relations. 2. United States—Ethnic relations. 3. Pluralism (Social sciences)—United States. 4. Ethnicity—United States. 5. Social change—United States. I. Grant-Thomas, Andrew, 1965– II. Orfield, Gary.

E184.A1T94 2008
305.800973—dc22   2008011773

2 4 6 8 9 7 5 3 1

Contents

Foreword

CHRISTOPHER EDLEY JR.

This volume is about the future of integration and inclusion in a multiracial America where aspirations of equal opportunity are at war with endemic civil rights fatigue.

Separate and unequal schools were one of the central elements of the system of Jim Crow laws that defined and enforced the color lines of racial caste in America, and this arena produced some of the most dramatic litigation victories of the modern civil rights movement. The struggle for educational equality has been perhaps a bellwether, and when the Supreme Court began its turn away from court-ordered school desegregation in 1973, there soon followed more backward-leaning decisions in voting and employment, as well. While some of those decisions could be and were ameliorated by congressional action, overall there was a marked deceleration of progress toward thoroughgoing racial reconstruction. In 1996, the Fifth Circuit Court of Appeals ruled in *Hopwood v. State of Texas* that public universities in Texas, Louisiana, and Mississippi could not consider race when making admissions decisions in order to pursue voluntarily the goal of racial diversity. The court's reasoning was read by many as a sweeping attack on not just the means but even the value of pursuing racial inclusion. The genesis of this volume resides in that decision.

Hopwood served as a clarion call for many in the civil rights community who saw in the court's reasoning not merely another conservative decision erecting another procedural hurdle or substantive speed bump but, rather, the threatened demolition of an important vehicle—voluntary affirmative action—in a critical gateway institution, selective higher education. Within weeks of the ruling, I joined with my colleague Gary Orfield to convene an emergency meeting of university presidents, scholars, and rights leaders to discuss our response. What we discovered dismayed us: there was virtually no research base to demonstrate the value of diversity in education. All of us at the table that day assumed that the benefits of maintaining racially diverse campuses were obvious and apparent. We possessed plenty of anecdotal evidence, lofty theories, and intentions. But, as we quickly realized, none of these carried much weight with skeptical judges insisting on "hard" data, or with segments of the public that had been fed a steady stream of distortions and manipulations about racial quotas, fairness, and "color-blind" admission policies.

Our distress accelerated when we inventoried the existing scholarship—or lack thereof—on other contemporary civil rights issues. We identified major research gaps on college access and opportunity, on K–12 education, housing, transportation, criminal justice, health care, employment, and hiring. In fact, on virtually every issue facing the civil rights community, the academy was missing in action, and had been for almost two decades.

The knowledge gaps were made all the more glaring by the massive demographic transformation that had taken place since the last wave of major civil rights research was produced. Four decades ago, at the start of the civil rights movement, our nation was 90 percent white. African Americans, our only significant racial minority, were concentrated largely in the rural South and urban North. Today, Latinos and Asians represent our fastest-growing racial minorities. They are settling in the suburbs in the West and Southwest. We will be a nation without a racial majority in less than fifty years. Our schools will be the first institutions to experience this dramatic transformation; indeed, in several states, they already have. Yet incredibly, we had no language, no framework, and no forums for discussing the implications of these sweeping changes to our schools, our businesses, our politics, our neighborhoods, our interactions, and our governments. The research that did exist chronicled an America that had largely disappeared.

New scholarship was also desperately needed to ground a racial-justice agenda that had slowed or stalled completely on several fronts. Fifty years after *Brown v. Board of Education* legally abolished "separate but equal," our nation's schools and neighborhoods remained stubbornly segregated. Access to quality education and to health care were still color-coded propositions. Twenty years into a school-reform movement, the achievement gap continued to confound educators, policymakers, and civil rights leaders. Only half of our nation's black and Latino students were graduating on time from high school, compared with over three-quarters of whites. Disproportionate numbers of black and brown men, and, increasingly, women, were filling up our nation's swelling prisons. The median net worth for white families was ten to thirty times greater than for black and Latino families. The reasons for these continued inequalities were complex, difficult to discern, and frequently disputed. But they could rarely be explained away completely by overt discrimination or racism, although those certainly played a role.

Put simply, the quest for racial justice in this country could no longer be viewed within a black and white context, literally, figuratively, or metaphorically. A new generation of research was urgently needed to jumpstart a second civil rights movement—one with a decidedly multiracial focus. It was this realization that prompted Gary and me to found the Civil Rights Project at Harvard University in 1996. Our vision was ambitious but relatively simple: leverage the Harvard name and our own networks and decades of experience to recruit leading and talented scholars throughout the country to build a critical mass of new data and knowledge that could be linked quickly to the lawyers and activists who were waging legislative, legal, and public battles on the ground.

During the early years, most of our efforts were directed toward responding to immediate crises in affirmative action and K–12 education. But we also envisioned the Civil Rights Project as a think/action tank that could create forums for exploring the issues that lay "over the horizon." The Color Lines conference was born out of this dream. We wanted to bring together the best, most creative, and most rigorous minds in the country to present new data, ideas, and frameworks for addressing the critical questions no one else had the time, wherewithal, or resources to ask: how do we think about race in light of today's realities? Does the integration ideal still resonate? If so, what is blocking us from achieving this ideal? If not, what replaces it? What do we need to know in order to get to the kind of society we hope to become? What future do we want, and how do we shape it? What public policies and private practices are most promising?

Did we succeed? I know that we tapped into a powerful current running through the country. Between August 30 and September 1, 2003, almost 1,200 researchers, civic leaders, journalists, activists, and policymakers came to Cambridge over Labor Day weekend. Fully one-third of them were students. We turned away another two hundred people for lack of space. The discussions between panelists and audience members were unfailingly vibrant and instructive, if also occasionally testy and confrontational. This was not a conference consisting only of academics debating the fine points of methodology—although there was some of that. We put leading scholars in rooms filled with passionate activists, idealistic students, seasoned lawyers, skeptical journalists, and wary policymakers. We wanted to vet and strengthen the research through contact with those working in the trenches who were most in need of new intellectual capital.

This volume represents some of the best thinking that came out of that conference. Some of the chapters were first presented as papers there, some were not. But they all illuminate aspects of the themes we identified and debated over that Labor Day weekend. Perhaps most critically, the authors of these studies begin to provide the framework and the language for addressing our multicultural, multiracial future. They not only feature the range of major racial and ethnic groups, but they begin to examine complex multiracial dynamics that are both underexposed and misunderstood. For example, in many communities "interminority" relations are now higher on the agenda than white–minority relationships. Unfortunately, while such interactions now dominate life in many communities, truly interracial analyses are still rare.

And with very few exceptions, the essays in this anthology represent original contributions that advance our understanding of fundamental concepts of racial dynamics. Anthony Kwame Harrison, for example, suggests that the simultaneous appeals to colorblindness and claims of ethnic distinctiveness that typify the underground San Francisco Bay Area hip hop scene will increasingly mark other multiracial venues in the United States. Andrew Grant-Thomas and john powell offer a new framework for distinguishing structural racism from institutional racism, with which it is typically conflated. Nilanjana Dasgupta's important essay illuminates the prevalence and widespread impact of implicit racial bias. All of these help us to achieve a more precise understanding of the barriers—often subtle and almost invisible—that continue to impede racial progress, and therefore to shape more effective policy responses to combat these.

The first landmark civil-rights decision of Chief Justice Roberts's tenure on the U.S. Supreme Court came in the June 2007 school-integration cases from Seattle and Louisville. The sharply divided court could not even find common ground on whether society has a compelling interest in promoting racial diversity in public K–12 education—a proposition sustained by only the barest majority. Indeed, that slender moral victory was accompanied by nearly crippling limitations on the means that might be pursued by school boards interested in voluntary integration. It seems a world gone mad, where the courts that were for too brief a time indispensable instruments in the dismantling of Jim Crow are now flirting with blatant obstructionism on the path toward multiracial equality. This can only have developed because too many judges, like so many of the rest of us, have come to believe that America's color lines are innocuous, immutable, or both.

W. E. B. Du Bois was right when he predicted in 1903 that the color line would continue to vex us through the twentieth century. The vexation continues, to our collective frustration and even shame. We have at best a shaky grasp on the policies required to create a truly just multiracial society. Progress will be limited if we remain ambivalent about confronting the realities of race relations across various sectors and, indeed, within each of us.

An integrationists' creed today might be this: the myriad social and economic challenges America faces cannot be met if we remain so divided by color and class, with both mutual misunderstanding and individual opportunity color-coded and poisoned by Jim Crow's long reach through time. And further: to bridge and ultimately erase the color lines dividing us will require relentless teaching, study, and struggle, together with imaginative policy engineering and moral resolve. Too little progress will come by accident, by the unassisted operation of human goodness, or by the natural workings of the market or even democracy.

Today, notwithstanding the talent and dedication of many, one is hard put to discern a movement equal to the task. An honest and rigorous inventory of the state of racial inequality in this country represents the essential first step toward reinvigorating a new civil rights movement—one aimed at both completing the agenda set forth in the 1960s and at identifying a new set of priorities brought on by the changing nature of our increasingly multiracial society. Its success will depend on whether the foot soldiers in the new movement—lawyers, elected officials, journalists, academics, business leaders, artists, educators, and everyone else—are armed with the information, data, and understanding they need to make their case compellingly and effectively. We hope this volume will be of value in defining and succeeding at the struggles ahead.

Twenty-First Century Color Lines

INTRODUCTION

The Past as Racial Prologue?

ANDREW GRANT-THOMAS

> *The past is never dead. It's not even past.*
> —WILLIAM FAULKNER, *REQUIEM FOR A NUN*

The routine and explicit appearances of race and ethnicity in our national discourse tend to be either celebratory (for example, the recognition of national heritage or history months, acclamations of "multiculturalism" and "diversity") or sensationalistic (for example, the O. J. Simpson and Wen Ho Lee cases or, more recently, the Jena 6).[1] Serious and thoughtful engagements with issues of race and ethnicity are rare.

The 1992 Los Angeles riots riveted the country's attention on issues of race and poverty only briefly. President Clinton's Initiative on Race, the most recent deliberate attempt to promote a broad national dialogue on race, left scarcely a ripple on the national consciousness as the furor over the president's impeachment consumed any possible attention to the Initiative advisory board's final report (Kim 2000). The dialogue prompted by the University of Michigan affirmative action cases decided by the Supreme Court in 2003 largely skirted the old, but still deeply relevant questions of racial equity in favor of newer questions about the contribution of campus diversity to students' cultural competence. Partisans of the current immigration debate variously insist that the *real* issue is undocumented immigration, or economic competition, or national security. We have yet to collectively engage with the profound ways in which racial considerations condition public attitudes and opinions in each of these three important arenas.

Many observers hoped that the disastrous aftermath of hurricanes Katrina and Rita throughout the Gulf Coast would finally force a probing evaluation of the continuing centrality of race, and of the intertwining of race and class, in American life. That hope goes unfulfilled at the time of this writing. That the congruence of blackness, poverty, and vulnerability, particularly in New Orleans, was greeted as a revelation by the media and much of the U.S. public speaks loudly to our national ignorance of, or indifference to, these issues.

A range of factors helps account for our generally patchy knowledge and superficial explorations of race in the United States. For one, many Americans believe that racial identity now has only marginal effects on a person's social interactions or access to social opportunities, and therefore conclude that "race talk" and racial inquiry are superfluous (Bonilla-Silva 2003; Schuman et al. 1997). Some advocates for a "colorblind" discourse go further. More than superfluous, they say, race talk of any kind is inherently divisive. It is clear that race talk and progressive racial advocacy often trigger deep anxieties and resentments—especially among whites, but among many non-whites as well. As a result, even people who know that race remains a powerful shaper of social opportunity sometimes complain of "race fatigue."

Then, too, maybe the problem extends beyond denial or lack of interest to the need for new conceptual tools to make sense of our changing conditions. What does "integration" look like in a society where Latinos now outnumber African Americans, where Asian Americans are a faster-growing population, proportionately, than either, and where people with multiracial identities comprise an ever larger part? What is "unity" in a multicultural nation of 300 million, and what are its foundations? Over the last three or four decades the United States (and the world) has changed in ways that not only shape how we experience race at the national level, but also create dramatic variations in the experience of race at the level of schools, neighborhoods, metropolitan areas, states, and national regions. Much of the cross-talk around race in the United States may be due to the speed, scope and variability of racial change on the ground, to the fact that we have many stories to tell, rather than only one.

With *Twenty-First Century Color Lines* we hope to help meet the need for fresh information and insight in a society marked by racial transformation. We want to engage skeptical, skittish, fatigued, and confounded readers and contribute to more nuanced and incisive scholarly and public debates on race and ethnicity in the United States. From a range of disciplinary and methodological perspectives, the contributors to this volume provide compelling, if necessarily contingent, answers to fundamental questions about the present and future of multiracialism in the United States: How can we understand the production and reproduction of racial and ethnic inequality in the twenty-first century? How are racial and ethnic identities promoted and defended across a range of social, geopolitical and cultural contexts, and what stakes are implicated in the process? What do two generations of demographic and social shifts around race look like on the ground? And what do the answers to these questions portend for our inescapably multiracial future?

Engagements with multiracialism, including the present volume, usually take as their primary point of departure two generations of dramatic *change—*

in demography, racial ideology and opportunity structures, the rules of ethno-racial identity formation, intra-group diversity, and more—that have destabilized a racial landscape many thought more or less settled after the civil rights reforms of the 1950s and 1960s. The centrality of change to present racial realities and discourses makes it easy to miss or discount the ways in which patterns and structures rooted in the past combine with more recent developments to shape our ongoing possibilities. In the remainder of this introduction I elaborate this argument with reference to the critical case of racial inequality, still the nation's most vexing "changing same." I close with a brief summary of each chapter.

Contemporary Racial Inequality and the Sediment of History

Racial hierarchy endures. Whites still predominate in terms of population and influence, comprising huge majorities of the nation's homeowners, business and political elites, and opinion leaders (for an overview, see McArdle, this volume). In 2004, black, Latino, and Native American poverty rates all exceeded the non-Hispanic white rate by a factor of three (DeNavas-Walt et al. 2005, table 4). Half a century after *Brown v. Board of Education,* many black and Latino students remain consigned to separate and unequal schools. In the resurgence of white supremacist groups, ambivalence about racial integration, and bitter disputes about immigration, affirmative action, bilingual education, racial profiling, Indian casinos, and anti-Muslim detentions we see signs of continuing racial fracture. Many of the largest gaps in U.S. public opinion pertain to race, form along racial lines, or both.[2]

Americans often draw a sharp line between the nation's past and its racial present. For many, the civil rights era marks the critical transition point, our moment of racial paradigmatic shift. According to this narrative, before the 1950s we had slavery, Native American genocide and land seizure, Jim Crow, *Plessy v. Ferguson,* anti-Asian immigration reform, the eugenics movement, Japanese American internment, and Bull Connor.[3] Since then, and here the narrative turns celebratory, we have had *Brown,* the Civil Rights, Voting Rights and Fair Housing acts of the 1960s, affirmative action, "fourth wave" immigration, and the enlightenment of white racial attitudes. Racism posed a major obstacle to the upward social mobility of people of color until the civil rights era, especially in the South, but then widespread policy and attitudinal change leveled the social and economic playing field. If anything, affirmative action policies and liberal white guilt have tilted the field in favor of racial minorities. Racial inequality may persist in the twenty-first century, the narrative concludes, but not for reasons rooted in the past (Gilliam 2006, 8).

I argue that, in fact, historically inscribed patterns and structures *can* and *do* imprint on current social and institutional practices, though their apparent naturalness may mask their continuing impact. The analytical eye is not readily drawn to "sameness" or to temporally remote causes. And yet, with respect to present-day inequalities, disregarding the past can lead to sins of explanatory omission; restricting the scope of our inquiry encourages sins of explanatory commission as well.[4] With reference to wealth, education, and political empowerment, in the pages that follow I offer a few examples of decisions made and practices entrenched—before we moved to "level the playing field"—that remain powerfully implicated in producing inequality today. In much of what follows, the long history of black Americans as the country's predominant racial minority group, and the paucity of historical data on other groups, leads me to focus at times on black-white dynamics. While this emphasis does not fully reflect the reality of racial inequality demographically, it does capture the imbalance of privilege between whites and non-whites.

Wealth Inequality

According to Amartya Sen, we "generally have excellent reasons for wanting more income or wealth. This is not because income and wealth are desirable for their own sake, but because they are admirable general-purpose means for having more freedom to lead the kind of lives we have reason to value" (Sen 1999, 14). Wealthier people can buy rather than rent their homes; live in safer neighborhoods with better schools, public services, and richer social networks; weather unexpected financial strain due to joblessness, prolonged family illness, or other factors; create new business and other opportunities; save for and enjoy retirement (without worrying about the future of Social Security); and, generally, create more attractive options for themselves. The road to security, prosperity, and influence—even to health and a longer life (Bond Huie et al. 2003)—is paved largely by wealth.

Importantly, more affluent people pass these advantages on to their children in the form of a quality high school education, college tuition help, a first car, down payment assistance for a home, a job in the family business, cash gifts, bequests, or other unearned advantages. Financial or other material transfers from relatives account for as much as 80 percent of lifetime wealth accumulation (Conley 1999; Shapiro 2004). Racial gaps in wealth transfers are enormous: four times as many white (28 percent) as black families (7.7 percent) inherit money, with black beneficiaries receiving about 40 cents per dollar inherited by whites (Shapiro 2004, 63). In addition, about half of white families provide substantial *in vivo* financial assistance to young adult members, roughly twice the proportion of black families able to do so.

As a partial consequence of this discrepancy in intergenerational giving, non-Hispanic white households enjoyed a median net worth of $88,700 in 2002, *eleven times* the net worth of Latino households and *fourteen times* the net worth of African American households (Kochhar 2004, 2). Thirty-two percent of black households had zero or negative net worth in 2002, as did 26 percent of Latino households and 13 percent of white households. (Unfortunately, we have little data about the financial assets of Asian Americans and still less about those of

Native Americans, especially the roughly half who live in Indian country.[5]) White households at every income level enjoyed much more wealth than did African American and Latino households at similar incomes (Orzechowski and Sepielli 2003, 13).

The roots of current wealth inequalities lie substantially in historical public sector policies and practices that created wealth for many whites while denying it to non-whites. The value of land, labor and other resources expropriated from or unfairly denied non-white peoples over the centuries is incalculable, but some of the key plot lines are clear, if not widely familiar. In the case of Native Americans they include hundreds of treaties and laws that sanctioned the forcible removal of hundreds of thousands of Indians from their homelands and made their land available to white settlers or the U.S. government. By 1900, white settlers had filed claims for 80 million acres of "unappropriated public lands" under the Homestead Act, displacing many tribes in Kansas, Colorado, Nebraska and Wyoming. In 1891 alone, the "Indian Commissioner sold off one-seventh of all Indian lands in the United States to white settlers, over 17.4 million acres" (Anderson et al. 2006, 44, 46).

With respect to Latinos, the wealth transfer story includes the 1848 Treaty of Guadalupe Hidalgo, under which the interim government of an occupied Mexico transferred roughly half of its land mass—the present-day states of California, Nevada, and Utah, as well as parts of Arizona, Colorado, and New Mexico—for $15 million (Anderson et al. 2006). The 1853 Gadsden Purchase secured the rest of Arizona and New Mexico for the United States. The story also highlights the Bracero program, which brought millions of laborers from Mexico, Latin America, and the Caribbean into the United States during and after World War II to work for paltry wages. Chinese immigrants attracted to the California Gold Rush paid the Foreign Miners Tax, but the services the tax paid for went exclusively to whites. The 1924 Alien Land Act excluded non-citizens from land ownership. Facing imminent internment by the federal government in World War II, Japanese Americans, many of them citizens, "sold" their properties to whites at exploitative prices.[6]

The African American story begins with two hundred fifty years of chattel slavery, during which slaves were legally forbidden from owning anything, including their labor, and includes anti-miscegenation laws and the "one drop rule" of African American descent, which made most children of white men and black women both black-identified and ineligible to inherit any part of their father's wealth. It extends through the broken promise of "40 acres and a mule" made at the end of the Civil War, and on to a viciously exploitative sharecropping system that doomed blacks to perpetual debt. The story also must refer to the terrorism visited on the few blacks who managed to prosper, such as the burning of the "Black Wall Street" in Tulsa, Oklahoma by whites on June 21, 1921. Hundreds of black businesses and homes, and many lives, were lost (Tulsa Race Riot 2001).

The political scientist Ira Katznelson traces much of the current wealth gap, especially between whites and African Americans, to the starkly different treatment afforded whites and non-whites under the major social welfare programs of the 1930s and 1940s (Katznelson 2005). For example, the initial exclusion of domestic and agricultural workers from the Social Security, Fair Labor Standards, and Wagner Acts meant that most African Americans and many Latinos were denied pensions, minimum wage protections, unemployment insurance and access to labor unions. Sixty-five percent of African Americans, including three in four black Southerners, fell into those two occupational categories, as did roughly 40 percent of whites nationwide (Katznelson 2005, 43).

The GI Bill, which invested $95 billion between 1944 and 1971 in young veterans returning from World War II, deserves special mention. GI Bill provisions helped millions of young Americans to attend college, find jobs, buy homes, and start businesses. "Through these opportunities, and by advancing the momentum toward suburban living, mass consumption, and the creation of wealth and economic security, this legislation created middle-class America. No other instrument was nearly as important" (Katznelson 2005, 113). However, the discriminatory administration of the bill's key programs meant that benefits accrued mainly to whites. Two of 3,200 loans for homes, businesses and farms guaranteed by the GI Bill in Mississippi in 1947 went to black veterans; in New York and northern New Jersey, fewer than 100 of 67,000 home mortgages insured by the GI Bill went to non-whites (Katznelson 2005, 140). All but shut out of "white" colleges and universities by formal and informal segregationist policies, thousands of black veterans armed with GI Bill vouchers in turn were also denied entry to historically black colleges and universities too small and too poor to accommodate them. The middle class made possible by this unprecedented government largesse was essentially all white.

Homeownership is the main source of wealth accumulation in the United States today. In 2000, home equity comprised three-fourths of the median net worth of U.S. households, and more than 80 percent of the median wealth of Latino and black households (Orzechowski and Sepielli 2003, 14). However, whereas three in four white families owned their homes in 2006, only half of black and Latino families did (U.S. Bureau of the Census 2007, 8), and those homes held much less value than homes owned by whites.[7] These racial differences in home values and ownership rates account for much of the racial wealth gap (Charles 2003; Oliver and Shapiro 1995). Accordingly, no story is more instructive about the historically racialized acquisition and transfer of wealth than that of homeownership.

The federal government first opened up the suburbs to whites under the National Housing Act of 1934 (Cashin 2004). The law created the Home Owners' Loan Corporation, later renamed the Federal Housing Administration (FHA), which subsidized home mortgages for whites in the suburbs. Until then, few families could afford homes because of the requirement that the down payment comprise a third or more of the purchase price. FHA subsidies enabled millions of families to buy homes and build equity. Again, whites benefited from this generosity almost exclusively. The FHA-funded sales in racially homogeneous white neighborhoods and favored the purchase of homes in the suburbs. The underwriting manual for home mortgage insurance disseminated by the federal government was forthrightly racist.[8] The federal government also pushed home buyers to adopt covenants that precluded the sale of subsidized homes to non-whites (Massey and Denton 1993). While both racial covenants and racist mortgage insurance policies were declared unconstitutional in 1948, their legacy prompted private companies to engage in redlining practices that continue to shape housing market outcomes (Cashin 2004, 112).

The implications of the foregoing observations for the reproduction of racial inequality deserve underlining. It is not simply that blacks, Native Americans, Latinos and Asian Americans have lost or been refused their fair share of the nation's wealth and therefore had relatively little to pass on to their children. It is also that white Americans sometimes have gained in direct proportion to the deliberate and race-conscious deprivation of non-whites (slavery, under which whites had exclusive extractive rights to black bodies and labor, being the quintessential case). As a result, even if racial discrimination ended today, inequalities grounded in historically rooted disparities in wealth accumulation and intergenerational transfers would persist.

Educational Inequality

The structure of educational opportunity offers another instructive example of how historical legacies continue to benefit whites disproportionately. Education not only generates knowledge, skills, and other kinds of social capital, but also powerfully shapes outcomes in other key arenas as well, including employment, occupation and job satisfaction, income, wealth, health, and criminal justice (Children's Defense Fund 2005; *The Condition of Education 2006* 2006; Wolfe and Haveman 2001). Chief Justice Earl Warren's observation on behalf of a unanimous Supreme Court in *Brown v. Board of Education* rings even more true today: "in these days, it is doubtful that any child may reasonably be expected to succeed in life if he is denied the opportunity of an education" (Children's Defense Fund 2005, 88). Racial gaps in educational attainment have narrowed in the half century since *Brown*. However, whether with respect to standardized test scores, high school dropout rates, college graduation rates, and many other important measures, wide gaps remain (McArdle, this volume; Mickelson 2003).

Trend data on educational attainment by race highlight immediate instances in which the pre-civil rights past casts its shadow on the racial present. For example, constrained to separate and unequal schools, in 1960 only 39 percent of African Americans ages 25–29 had completed high school or more (*Digest of Education Statistics 2005* 2006, table 8). Sixty-four percent of same-age whites had done so. By 2005, that twenty-five–point gap had closed to six.[9] However, the human capital shortfalls imposed on older generations of African Americans, of which that twenty-five–point high school completion gap is but one indicator, continue to exert a drag on the fortunes of the African American community today.[10]

Among today's school-age children, educational achievement owes to a range of factors, many of them, like family background and neighborhood characteristics, widely considered outside the purview of schools. But school resources—teachers, facilities, curricular materials, and much more—also matter a great deal, as does the funding required to secure them (Mickelson 2003). Black, Latino, and poor students suffer by comparison to their white and affluent counterparts on all of these dimensions.[11] Bearing in mind the strong link between school poverty rates and the quantity and quality of school resources (Orfield and Lee 2005), consider that half of black and Latino public school students, but only 5 percent of white students, attend schools where at least 75 percent of the student body is poor (Children's Defense Fund 2005, 94).

The funding field tilts against poor and minority students at the interstate, inter-district *and* intra-district levels. African Americans and Latinos together were 40 percent or more of public school students in eight states in the 2003–2004 school year. All but one of those states (Maryland) ranked below the national average in per pupil funding, and five (Texas, Florida, Louisiana, Arizona and New Mexico) ranked in the bottom third of states (U.S. Bureau of the Census 2006, table 11). Within states, affluent districts with strong tax bases can lend more support to their neighborhood schools than can poorer districts, which tend to have more black and Latino students. As a result, in twenty-eight states "high-minority districts receive less state and local money for each child than low-minority districts. . . . Across the country, $908 less per student is spent on students in the districts educating the most students of color, as compared to the districts educating the fewest" (Education Trust 2006, 6).

Finally, we see racially inequitable funding even across schools in the same districts, largely the result of "intradistrict funding formulas that allocate positions, rather than dollars, to schools, and teacher sorting patterns that allow higher paid [and more qualified] teachers to systematically opt into lower-need schools" (Rubenstein et al. 2006, 11; see also Thomas B. Fordham Institute 2006, 15). These absolute comparisons actually understate the inequity of current funding patterns. Minority students typically enter schools with greater needs than white students: 35 percent of black, 28 percent of Latino, and 29 percent of American Indian children, but only 10 percent of white children, lived in poor families in 2005 (Fass and Cauthen 2006). Under these circumstances, the equal distribution of monies and resources across schools often segregated by race and class would not signify their equitable distribution, a point recognized and reflected in the educational equity movement. In practice, most schools and districts serving large racial minority student populations would be pleased to achieve resource parity with their more well-to-do peers.

The historical narrative of inequitable public school funding builds on the twin pillars of federalism and segregated schooling. The primacy of state and local governments in public education has its roots in the early nineteenth century outside the South and late in the century in the South, after the post–Reconstruction disenfranchisement of black Americans made it politically feasible for whites to channel the bulk of education dollars toward their own children (Walters 2001, 40). More than one hundred years later. the historical trend is away from state and local control: between 1920 and 2004, the federal share of public school funding crept from less than 1 percent to 9 percent, and most federal monies come with directives attached (Howell 2005, 4; *The Condition of Education 2007* 2007, Table 37-1).[12] That said, as William Howell observes of local school boards, "once a political entity has been granted certain powers, it is extremely difficult to reclaim them" (Howell 2005, 7). When those entities also have the political and financial clout to underwrite their historical prerogatives, as local and state governments do in the education arena, we might suspect that rumors of their demise have been exaggerated.[13]

The record of recent court decisions around funding equalization is instructive in this regard. Citing the work of Sean Corcoran and colleagues on "The Changing Distribution of Education Finance: 1972–1997," Pamela Barnhouse Walters concludes that, although "the Supreme Courts in almost twenty states have issued decisions ordering school finance reform, in no state has the degree of resource equalization ordered by the Courts been realized, and levels of resource inequality between affluent and poor districts remain high" (Walters 2007, 24). By the end of 2005, when plaintiffs had filed cases in forty-five of fifty states and won about half the judgments, the verdict remained roughly the same. In many of those "wins," legislatures and state officials have resisted implementing remedies or have reallocated funds in ways that reflect "the balance of political power, usually heavily weighted in favor of suburban school districts" (Hunter 2005). In the end, a federal government that spends less than one in ten education dollars is no match for politically savvy schools and districts, mostly affluent and white, able to use their superior political access and clout to secure favorable judgments from key decision makers.

Of course, the different abilities of rich and poor districts to channel resources to "their" schools would have less racial significance if not for the persistence of segregated housing patterns. School and residential segregation are deeply linked, both because parents with housing options typically weigh school quality heavily in making their decisions and because most children attend neighborhood schools. (About 10 percent of K–12 students attended private schools in 2000.[14]) The racial makeup of neighborhoods thus becomes the main determinant of the racial makeup of the schools within them. "In the absence of effective school desegregation policies, location is destiny, and segregated housing for families, reinforced by differential use of private schools, produces education that is starkly polarized" (Orfield and McArdle 2006, 4–5). Like local and state control over education, housing segregation today is partly rooted in history.

Between 1860 and 1940, African American segregation from whites increased dramatically (Massey and Denton 1993, 21, 47). The rise of hyper-segregated "ghettos," especially in the large metropolitan areas of the Northeast and Midwest, was facilitated by the "Great Migration" of blacks to the North during the first half of the twentieth century but caused by decades of discriminatory policies such as the mortgage practices noted above; violence directed against blacks; "urban renewal" projects that moved many blacks to marginal neighborhoods; federal pubic housing programs that isolated black residents in high-poverty neighborhoods; and the growth of the interstate highway system, which fuelled "white flight" and suburbanization (Cashin 2004; Massey and Denton 1993; powell 2000). These developments inscribed a housing landscape defined by racial isolation, economic polarization, and considerable overlap between the two. Such a landscape will tend to perpetuate itself in the absence of remedies as forceful as those that created it in the first place. But "America has never undertaken any serious effort to reverse its nefarious role in creating such residential misery" (Cashin 2004, 242).

Residential segregation concentrates socioeconomic advantage and disadvantage and, through processes of wealth accumulation, differentially allows more and less affluent groups to expand the residential choices of future generations. Especially in the context of virulent employment discrimination, blacks confined to the large urban ghettos of the mid-twentieth century were hard-pressed to accumulate the human, material and social capital required for social mobility—their own or their children's (Massey and Denton 1993). Conversely, segregation created well-defined "white neighborhoods" that sustained considerable advantages in terms of incomes, property values, education, employment and social networks (Roithmayr 2004). The twenty-five–point gap in high school completion rates between young blacks and whites in 1960, noted earlier, was one outcome of this divergence in opportunity. The legacy of unequal wealth accumulation produced by several generations of enforced social and economic isolation explains some part of blacks' residential outcomes today (Charles 2003).

By constraining economic opportunities for African Americans, segregation also regenerates itself by "produc[ing] interracial economic disparities that incite further discrimination and more segregation" (Massey 2001, 419). The fundamental attribution error is at work here. Many Americans attribute the "pathological" behaviors associated with urban blackness to biological or cultural predisposition rather than to the structural impacts of institutional discrimination, concentrated poverty, and social isolation (Loury 2002). The error reinforces prejudice, negative stereotypes, and anti-black stigma, which prompt further discrimination in and beyond housing markets. A large body of research finds that many white Americans express a low tolerance for black neighbors and that housing market discrimination remains a major cause of residential segregation today (Charles 2003).[15]

Political Inequality

Formal politics is yet another arena in which current racial inequalities can be traced in part to historical sources. Racial minorities lag far behind whites with respect to their descriptive and substantive representation in the country's political life. In 2000, much more was said about the fact that Latinos had become the nation's largest minority group than about the reality that, comprising one quarter of the country's population, blacks and Latinos also comprised less than 10 percent of our elected officials and held no governorships or U.S. Senate seats (Amy et al. 2000). By 2003, African Americans, Latinos, and Asian Americans were a mere 15 percent of the membership of the U.S. House of Representatives and 2 percent of Senate members (*Statistical Abstract of the United States: 2006* 2005, table 395). This pattern of minority under-representation repeats itself at the state and local levels.

It is also true that the candidates supported by blacks and Latinos are elected less often than those endorsed by whites. In seven of nine presidential elections held since 1972, for example, large majorities of African Americans and Latinos voted for the Democratic candidate while smaller majorities of whites supported the Republican candidate.[16] The candidate favored by white voters won six of those seven elections (Jimmy Carter's 1976 victory over Gerald Ford being the exception; 47 percent of whites supported Carter while 52 percent supported Ford).

The research on whose substantive preferences are realized in the policy arena suggests that people of color do not enjoy the level of political representation that whites do. For example, in their analysis of the correspondence between the policy preferences of African Americans and whites, and the roll call votes of their U.S. Senators from 1989 to 2002, Griffin and Newman found that "African Americans are severely underrepresented across the broad range of Senators' voting behavior" (Griffin and Newman 2004, 28).[17] Similarly, using two thousand survey questions on policies proposed between 1981 and 2002, Martin Gilens found that "when Americans with different income levels differ in their policy preferences, actual policy outcomes strongly reflect the preferences of the more affluent but bear virtually no relationship to the preferences of poor or middle-income Americans" (Gilens 2005, 778). Given that blacks and Latinos are much more likely than whites to have low or moderate incomes, Gilens's finding suggests that they also are less likely to prevail when group preferences clash.

The disparities in political representation captured in these and similar outcomes have many sources, several of which have received considerable attention in the wake of the contested 2000 presidential election results. I focus on just two here: the dominance of non-Hispanic "whites" among the U.S. resident population and the fact that whites vote at much higher rates than non-whites do. Both factors have deep historical roots, none of them "natural" or inevitable.

It is impossible to understand the emergence of the United State as a predominantly "white" nation without appreciating the political and historical contexts for contested *decisions* about how to classify people racially in the first place. From 1850 to 1910, census enumerators used categories like Mulatto, Quadroon and Octoroon to distinguish among blacks. By 1920, however, the "principle of hypodescent as practiced in Jim Crow legislation made such distinctions superfluous" and they were dropped altogether (Snipp 2003, 567). The move from racial designation by the census enumerator to racial self-identification by the respondent in the 1960 census led to a 48 percent "increase" of the American Indian population between 1950 and 1960 (Snipp 2003, 569–570). The strategic assimilation of various European immigrant groups into "whiteness" in the United State during the nineteenth and early twentieth centuries was similarly episodic and contingent (Ignatiev 1995; Jacobson 1998; Roediger 1991).

Put differently, the very existence of "non-Hispanic whites" as a politically salient category composed of German, Irish, Italian Americans, and so on, owes largely to historical circumstance. What if these large ethnic subdivisions of whiteness instead were racialized, as they once were to varying degrees, and as "African Americans" and "Asian Americans" are today?[18] What if pollsters regularly reported public support for policies and candidates in terms of ethnic rather than racial categories? What if national politicians vied not for the black, white, or Latino vote, but for the German, African, Italian, Irish and Mexican American votes? When we add to the fact of historically contingent racial classification a record of public policy decisions about war, annexation, birth control, medical care, and the flow of peoples across national borders—many of those decisions expressly intended to promote white racial dominance and supremacy—it becomes clear that the topography of our current racial landscape and the present political dominance of "whites" are as socially and historically constructed as race itself.

In the case of African Americans, felony disfranchisement is the major legal obstacle to voting. Roughly 5.3 million U.S. citizens in forty-eight states and the District of Columbia cannot vote because they have felony convictions.[19] Two million African Americans, most of them *former* prisoners, are temporarily or permanently denied the vote. Felony convictions disenfranchise 13 percent of black men nationwide; one in four is permanently disenfranchised in the five states that deny the vote to former offenders.[20] Had current imprisonment rates held in 1960, John F. Kennedy might not have been elected president (Uggen and Manza 2002). Conversely, had voting rights been granted to any category of disenfranchised felons in 2000, Al Gore would surely have won the presidency. To put U.S. disenfranchisement practices in international perspective, no country in the European Union bars former convicts from voting and many allow some (Austria, Belgium, France, Germany, Italy, and Norway) or all (Australia, South Africa, Greece, Poland Spain, and Sweden) current prisoners to vote (Uggen and Manza 2002).

The majority of disfranchisement laws, including the most stringent ones, can be traced directly to post–Civil War statutes aimed at diluting the voting strength of newly empowered black Americans (Behrens et al. 2003). To whet the racial edge of the legislation, lawmakers in the South linked "the loss of voting rights to crimes alleged to be committed primarily by blacks while excluding offenses held to be committed by whites" (Mauer 2004, 16). In 1850, roughly one in three states disenfranchised ex-felons; by 1920, three in four did, at which time literacy tests, poll taxes, white-only primaries and other pointedly discriminatory measures had also been enacted. Many states restored voting rights to some categories of former felons in the 1960s and 1970s and recent years have seen further liberalization across the country (Behrens et al. 2003). Still, with the explosion of the prison population during the last three decades of the twentieth century, the impact of century-old disenfranchisement laws on the voting strength of people of color, especially African Americans, has never been more devastating.

For many Asians and Latinos in the United States, non-citizenship represents the most serious legal obstacle to voting. Six in ten Latinos and Asians, compared with 35 percent of blacks and 25 percent of whites, could not register to vote in 2000 because they were not U.S. citizens or were too young (Passel 2004). The Constitution does not prelude non-citizens from voting and, for the first century of the country's history, eligibility to vote depended more on race, gender, and property ownership holdings than on citizenship status (Harper-Ho 2000). Indeed, until the War of 1812, voting by white male immigrant property owners was common. By 1875, twenty-two states and federal territories had extended the suffrage to non-citizens, first on the basis of "no taxation without representation," and later in the hope of attracting settlers to the South and West after the Civil War.

The subsequent sharp retrenchment of "alien suffrage" shadowed a marked shift in the geographic origins and racial/ethnic makeup of the U.S. immigrant population. Where once the franchise had been offered as a carrot for immigrants hailing primarily from Northern Europe, its rapid withdrawal around the turn of the century was a stick meant to moderate the new wave of racially and politically suspect immigrants from Central, Southern, and Eastern Europe and the Mediterranean (Harper-Ho 2000; Hayduk 2004). By 1900, only eleven states granted non-citizens the franchise at any level; by 1928, none did. As with ex-felon disfranchisement, recent years have seen more and more insistent calls for extending voting rights to non-citizens, as well as some marginal gains. Six towns in Maryland now permit non-citizen voting in local elections, and non-citizens vote in school board elections in Chicago, as they did for thirty years in New York City until the dissolution of school boards in 2002.

Would U.S. legislatures have imposed non-citizen and felon disfranchisement laws in the post-civil rights period were they not already in place? We cannot know. We can say that these laws have now assumed a taken-for-granted quality that makes it difficult to bring the serious questions of racial impact and democratic fairness they raise to the national policy debate, much less to change policy and practice on a meaningful scale. Commanding few votes, non-citizens, prisoners and former felons lack the social and political capital needed to organize themselves, forge strong political coalitions, or attract influential policy champions. As a result, even in the case of ex-felon disfranchisement, which four in five Americans oppose, progressive reformers continue to push against the heavy weight of our historical inheritance.

Why Deny History?

The study of history offers more than a baseline against which to celebrate the nation's egalitarian racial turn or source material for "specious" minority claims to victimization, as some would have us believe.[21] The general failure to recognize the causal links between historically grounded arrangements and present inequalities is due to several factors. For one, many people, especially white Americans, mistakenly believe that racial equality has already been achieved not only in terms of the law and popular sensibilities, but in terms of group outcomes as well.[22] If equality of outcomes is the reality then there is no need to search for the roots of inequality in the past or anywhere else. Even among people aware that deep inequalities persist, the growth of the black, brown, and Asian American middle classes, and the many examples of prominent non-whites, is often taken as evidence of the irrelevance of past practices.[23]

Another reason to deny the links between past and present in this context is strategic: to agree that historical legacies help shape present-day outcomes plausibly shifts the burden of responsibility for remedial action onto society as a whole, and perhaps onto whites in particular. White racial resentment has been well documented (Kinder and Sanders 1996; Swain 2002). Many whites believe that affirmative action policies already serve as sufficient, even excessive, compensation for historical racial wrongs. As one white man put it in response to a question about slavery reparations, "I think they've gotten enough" (Bonilla-Silva 2003, 159). When the belief that racial minorities have "gotten enough" is wedded to the belief that group welfare is inherently a competitive, zero-sum game—"My [white] friend did not get a job because a black man got it" (Bonilla-Silva 2003, 159)— whites' incentive to delineate between past and present becomes stronger still.

Perhaps the biggest reason for past-present myopia in this context is the one highlighted by the structural racism framework: the overly narrow construction of racism that sets the terms of the debate about inequality in the United States (Grant-Thomas and powell, this volume). If we insist that racism attaches only to people, policies and practices that discriminate intentionally on the basis of race, then, indeed, with the passing of Jim Crow laws the links between the pre–civil rights era past and current inequality are few and largely symbolic.[24] If instead we recognize racial inequality as the result of cultural and institutional dynamics unfolding over time and across domains, the notion of intentionality itself loses meaning, and we are compelled to consider racism, and history, in new ways.

Plan of the Book

We can understand that the past is "not even past" without resigning ourselves to a future that recapitulates its most dreadful racialist features. James Baldwin nicely captured the insight: "I am what time, circumstance, and history have made of me, certainly. But I am so much more than that. We all are."[25] Beyond the certainty of its multiracial character, few among us believe that the future of race in America is preordained. The future we shape for ourselves and generations to come will largely depend on our ability to recognize the nature and enormity of our racial challenges and opportunities, and on the insights, intention and creativity we bring to them. The essays in this book are presented in the spirit of that conviction.

The fact of our nation's rapidly increasing racial and ethnic diversity is widely known, hailed by newspaper headlines, political and civic leaders, and researchers alike. What that diversity looks like on the ground and the challenges and opportunities it entails are less widely appreciated. In her chapter "Color Lines in a Multiracial Nation," Nancy McArdle begins to answer those questions with a detailed demographic and institutional overview that provides the backdrop for the theoretical and empirical analyses that make up the remainder of the volume. McArdle begins by documenting "the changing face of the nation" at the national, regional, city, and suburban levels, with attention to the dynamics that propel the differential growth of racial and ethnic populations. She then examines how these large-scale transformations manifest in the institutional spaces where our lives unfold, from families, schools and places of worship to workplaces and the political arena. Her analysis affirms that fifty years of transformation have moderated racial inequality and "blurred" the color line in America but hardly erased it.

While the view that racial inequality in the twenty-first–century United States owes largely to old-fashioned "racism" has its adherents, the stance is one that increasingly prompts eye-rolling both within and outside racially liberal circles. In our post–civil rights era, many whites, in particular, assign primary responsibility for persistent inequality to the cultural and personal failings of those at the lower rungs of the social hierarchy, with poor and working-class African Americans bearing the brunt of criticism (Brown et al. 2005). In Part I, "Foundations of Multiracial Inequality," Nilanjana Dasgupta, Andrew Grant-Thomas, and john powell present emerging critiques of racial inequality that bridge this interpretive disconnect by recognizing the subordinate status of nonwhites as more than the product of self-inflicted injuries or due only to expressly prejudicial attitudes and behaviors.

Dasgupta draws on two decades of psychological research showing that even people who consciously and sincerely hold tolerant racial attitudes nonetheless often harbor *implicit* or *unconscious* biases. Moreover, Dasgupta documents how unconscious biases inform behavior, with implications for a wide range of racial outcomes. Her chapter closes with practical suggestions for undermining implicit bias.

Grant-Thomas and powell similarly argue that explicitly racist attitudes and behaviors are just part of the process that allows the privileges attaching to whiteness and the disadvantages associated with color to endure and adapt over time. Working at a level of analysis complementary to Dasgupta's, they articulate the ways that social institutions interact to organize or "structure" critical opportunities and outcomes in racially distinctive ways. In particular, they emphasize how interactions across social institutions and patterns of resource distribution can racialize the distribution of opportunity with or without the involvement of "racist" individuals.

If race is socially constructed, a foundational assertion of contemporary race theory, then racial inequality is as well. In this respect, engagements with the nature and meanings of racial identity logically supersede disputes about the causes and severity of racial inequality even as questions of inequality and identity rival each other as the main flashpoints of our racial politics. Many observers already regard Latinos, the nation's largest racial or ethnic minority community and predicted to comprise one in four U.S. residents by midcentury, as the country's key electoral swing group. As Christina Gómez notes in her chapter, the first in Part II, "Ambiguities of Racial and Ethnic Identity," how members of this diverse population choose to exercise the identity options afforded them in the decades to come will have enormous social, economic, and cultural, as well as political, ramifications for the country as a whole. Gomez outlines the factors likely to inform those judgments, not least among them the distinct understandings of race that Latino immigrants bring with them.

Like Gómez, co-authors Anayra O. Santory-Jorge, Luis A. Avilés, Juan Carlos Martínez-Cruzado, and Doris Ramírez see identity choices as politically strategic moves with both practical and symbolic consequences. In their study of racial self-identification among Puerto Ricans on the island, Santory-Jorge and her colleagues take as their point of departure the huge gaps between how Puerto Ricans identified themselves racially in the 2000 U.S. Census and in a representative, island-wide survey conducted just three years later. The authors argue that the variability of Puerto Rican identity claims are comprehensible in light of respondents' very different political and ideological relationships with their interlocutors in each case—the federal government, on one hand, and the University of Puerto Rico, on the other.

As the incorporation of Latinos arguably now substitutes for that of African Americans as the critical test of the inclusiveness of U.S. racial democracy, the relative success of Asian Americans, as a group, is often promoted as its primary defense. Among the mostly educational and economic indicia of the group's status, for some, as the nation's "model minority," the significant number of Asian children adopted into white Americans families in recent decades has been heralded as an especially poignant sign of the liberalization of white racial attitudes and the nation's fading color line. Jiannbin Lee Shiao and Mia H. Tuan draw on the experiences of a generation of Korean children adopted by white parents to probe the terms of their integration into these families. While recognizing the variety of approaches the parents used to manage adoptive, cultural and racial differences, the authors find that, for many, practicing "colorblindness" actually meant integrating their children into whiteness.

Moving our research and analyses "beyond the black-white paradigm" requires more than expanding the corpus of group-specific work to include more attention to Asian Americans, Latinos, and Native Americans, or extending race relations work to examine dyads other than the familiar blacks and whites. Our research efforts will remain of limited application until they more often reflect the fact that local racial politics are now often triadic or still more complex, and that interactions between communities of color now often assume a higher priority than those between minorities and whites. The contributors to Part III, "Negotiating Change: Group Interaction on the Ground," engage such irreducibly multiracial dynamics in a range of arenas and places.

Anthony Kwame Harrison's work examines the tension between the color-blindness that professedly marks the politically progressive, racially diverse San Francisco Bay Area hip hop scene and the pervasive inclination toward strong ethnic identification he sees among hip hop participants. He argues that this tendency to toggle between the assumption of racial sameness and assertions of racial distinction, all within a normative black–white hierarchical framework, increasingly characterizes a range of urban sociocultural spaces in the United States. Similarly presenting arts and cultural practice as a crucial site for multiracial community building, Maria Rosario Jackson contends that multiracial *and* separatist spaces are both necessary conditions for realizing a cultural commons that supports genuine racial and ethnic diversity. Jackson closes her survey of arts and cultural practices with several suggestions for urban planners and policymakers concerned with fostering healthy diversity in U.S. communities.

Convinced that the kind of cosmopolitan, multidirectional vision of integration flagged by Harrison and Jackson must increasingly accompany our growing diversity, Patricia Gurin, Gerald Gurin, John Matlock, and Katrina Wade-Golden ask whether and how young adults' perceptions of common "core values" with other groups shape their orientation toward this more dynamic vision of integration. They find that, on the whole, perceptions of commonality have powerful implications for the degree to which young white, black, Latino and Asian American adults move in integrated settings, seek to bridge racial differences, and adopt a structural or individualistic view of racial inequality. In these results the authors see the seeds for multiracial political coalitions that are both more *and* less progressive.

With reference to electoral politics in New York City and Los Angeles, John Mollenkopf examines how demographic change at the neighborhood level is generating new political coalitions as well as new kinds of competition. Where activists once fought to wrest from whites a measure of political power for native-born minorities, Mollenkopf notes that the growth of immigrant populations has transformed the contest into one that often find immigrants challenging both whites and native minorities, especially in our large urban centers.

Finally, in his brief piece in Part IV, "The Road Ahead?" David Roediger tries to divine the future course of the Du Boisian "color line" in the twenty-first-century United States. Taking the public, media, and governmental responses to the September 11, 2001, attacks on the World Trade Center and the Pentagon and the devastation punctuated by Hurricane Katrina on the Gulf Coast in 2005 as his points of departure, Roediger anticipates that color lines are very likely to persist, but in ever more globalized forms. In particular, he argues, these two signature national events of the young century "point to a world in which racial positions are multiple and show that global and local realities mix promiscuously in determining where color-lines will be drawn." Gary Orfield concludes the volume with reflections on the role of scholars in the project of racial transformation.

Notes

1. The Jena 6 refers to six black students charged with assaulting a white classmate at Jena High School in Jena, Louisiana, on December 4, 2006. The six were initially charged with attempted second degree murder and conspiracy to commit second degree murder. Supporters of the Jena 6 contend that the charges were excessive and racially discriminatory. Moreover, they note that three white students who hung nooses from a tree on school grounds, after several black students expressed their intention to sit under the tree, had been merely suspended, rather than expelled, from school. The case has sparked protests in Jena and across the country: See "Thousands 'March for Justice' in Jena, Court Orders Hearing on Teen," available online at http://www.cnn.com/2007/US/law/09/20/jena.six/index.html.

2. Vincent Hutchings and Nick Valentino note that significant black–white preference gaps emerge with respect to race-targeted policies (e.g., affirmative action and school segregation), nonracial policies (e.g., levels of government spending on education and poverty relief), and "values" issues (e.g., egalitarianism, the fairness of the U.S. political system), and that "these disparities have persisted over time and easily exceed differences across gender, class, and religion" (Hutchings and Valentino 2004, 389).

3. To be sure, even on the question of race the pre–civil-rights-era narrative also includes some powerful, mitigating strands—the enduring belief that Lincoln waged the Civil War "to free the slaves," for example, or the perception of the United States as a "nation of immigrants" that has enabled many generations of multihued newcomers to advance as far as their hard work could take them. But even for those who would defend the country's racial history on the (contested) grounds that the United States has treated its minorities better than many other countries have, or that its march toward racial justice has been steady, Indian genocide, slavery, and Jim Crow are undeniable stains on that pre-1960s history.

4. For example, many Americans understand racial inequality as a function of bad choices impelled by pathological group cultures (Brown et al. 2005). In my view, this inordinate attention to putative "cultural pathologies" constitutes such a sin of commission.

5. One study of Asian American wealth using data from the Survey of Income and Program Participation estimated that in 2000 Asian American households had a median net worth of $73,600, $28,100 less than the median net worth of non-Hispanic white families. This was true even though Asian American families enjoyed slightly higher median incomes than did white families (Ong and Patraporn 2006).

6. The 1988 Civil Liberties Act authorized a payment of $20,000 to the victims of internment, an important gesture of recognition but one that hardly fairly compensated most victims for their actual property loss (Hollinger 2003).

7. The median value for white homeowners in 2002 was $81,200, compared with $49,800 and $40,700 for Latino and black owners, respectively (Kochhar 2004, 17).

8. "Areas surrounding a location are [to be] investigated to determine whether incompatible racial and social groups are present, for the purpose of making a prediction regard-

ing the probability of the location being invaded by such groups. If a neighborhood is to retain stability, it is necessary that properties shall continue to be occupied by the same social and racial classes. A change in social or racial occupancy generally contributes to instability and a decline in values" (McKenzie 1994, 65).

9. At the same time, in those forty-five years, during which labor market success has increasingly required a college degree rather than a high school diploma, the gap favoring whites age twenty-five to twenty-nine in the attainment of a bachelor's degree (or higher) has grown from 6 to 16 points (*Digest of Educational Statistics 2005* 2006, table 8). The corresponding gap favoring whites over Hispanics grew from 15 points in 1975, the first year for which the *Digest of Educational Statistics* presented data on Hispanic achievement, to 23 points in 2005.

10. It was not until 1968 that blacks in the South were provided universal secondary schooling (Walters 2001).

11. On the correspondence between high-minority and high-poverty schools, see Orfield and Lee 2005. On the distribution of high-quality teachers and principals, see Clotfelter et al. 2007; Darling-Hammond 2004. On school quality, see Dinkes 2006; Mayer et al. 2000.

12. In the 2003–2004 school year, 44 percent of the $462 billion dollars allocated to U.S. public schools had local sources, most of it in the form of property tax revenue (*The Condition of Education 2007* 2007, table 37-1). Another 47 percent came from the states. Note that federal funds are intended only to supplement, not to replace, state and local funds. "Unfortunately, some states and districts game the system, perhaps unknowingly, by lowering their own allocations to schools catering to needy children because they know these schools will receive federal funds" (Thomas B. Fordham Institute 2006, 19). Perversely, federal Title I monies, meant to supplement state and local funds in states with large numbers of poor children, instead disproportionately go to wealthier states (Education Trust 2006, 2–3).

13. William Howell reports that when a recent Gallup poll asked, "Who should have the greatest influence in deciding what is taught in the public schools?" 61 percent of respondents "selected the local school board, while 22 percent chose the state government and just 15 percent chose the federal government" (Howell 2005, 8–9). Howell also quotes findings from a 2002 poll commissioned by *Education Week* to the effect that "the public not only trusts school boards, it also believes that school boards are the single most important institution in determining the quality of public schools—more important than parents, governors, state assemblies, or the U.S. president."

14. U.S. Bureau of the Census: see http://factfinder.census.gov/jsp/saff/SAFFInfo .jsp?_pageId=tp5_education.

15. Because the power to zone is the power to exclude, the land use authority of local governments is one discriminatory tool worth mentioning. Many municipalities employ restrictive land use regulations (e.g., low-density zoning, limits on new residential permits), costly infrastructure requirements, and difficult approval processes that make it difficult to build affordable homes (Robinson and Grant-Thomas 2004, 38). The scarcity of affordable housing effectively locks many blacks and Latinos out of high-opportunity suburban neighborhoods (Ihlanfeldt 2004; Pendall 2000). Local authority to regulate land use and zoning is not constitutionally mandated, but instead derives from the Supreme Court's 1926 decision in *Euclid v. Ambler* and the fact that almost all states have granted home rule to localities ("Democracy or Distrust?" 1998). Richard Thompson Ford notes that exclusionary zoning has a "self-perpetuating quality": by excluding a class of people from the community, "a locality constructs a political space in which it is unlikely that an

electoral challenge to the [exclusionary] ordinance will ever succeed ... in many cases, the only significant vote that will be taken in the exclusionary ordinance is the first vote" (Ford 1994, 1871).

16. The two election exceptions were 1992 and 1996, both featuring a major third-party candidate and won by Bill Clinton. Data for 1972–1996 election results by race are available at the New York Times website Portrait of the Electorate, at http://www.nytimes.com/library/politics/elect-port-religion.html.

17. The authors do go on to note that "on some votes more salient for them, African Americans are actually marginally better represented than whites" (Griffin and Newman 2004, 28).

18. In the 2000 Census, 15 percent of the U.S. population identified themselves as having German ancestry; 11 percent, Irish ancestry; 9 percent, English ancestry; and 6 percent, Italian ancestry (Brittingham and de la Cruz 2004, 2).

19. See the Sentencing Project website at http://www.sentencingproject.org/IssueArea Home.aspx?IssueID=4.

20. See ibid., at http://www.sentencingproject.org/Admin/Documents/publications/fd_bs_fdlawsinus.pdf

21. For example, Shelby Steele argues that the popularity of anti-black conspiracy theories in black communities reveals nothing as much as the presence and power of the "enemy memory," itself a form of false consciousness, within individual African Americans and the community as a whole (Steele 1990).

22. Six in ten white respondents to a 2001 national survey by the *Washington Post*, the Kaiser Family Foundation, and Harvard University believed that blacks had *equal or better* access to health care than whites do (Kane 2001). Half thought blacks and whites had similar levels of education, and half thought blacks enjoyed comparable job status. Similarly, the findings of a recent study of white Americans' attitudes toward reparations for African Americans suggest that "white resistance to reparations for Black Americans stems from fundamental biases in estimating the true cost of being Black" (Mazzocco et al. 2006).

23. The white Alabaman man interviewed as part of the FrameWorks Institute's research on how people think and talk about race speaks for many: "How long ago was [slavery]? A hundred years? ... Black people are mayors, congressmen, doctors, lawyers. What have they got to complain about? They've got the same opportunities I have. I think their only handicap is if they think, you know, "I'm being crapped on because I'm Black" (Gilliam 2006, 8). Similarly, in opposing reparations for black slavery, conservative commentator David Horowitz asks: does the existence of a substantial black middle class "not suggest that economic adversity is the result of failures of individual character rather than the lingering after-effects of racial discrimination and a slave system that ceased to exist well over a century ago?" Horowitz's brief against reparations for African Americans, "Ten Reasons Why Reparations for Blacks Is a Bad Idea for Blacks—and Racist Too," is available at the Free Republic's website at http://www.freerepublic.com/forum/a3a54b37c6b16.htm.

24. For example, a few years ago the Jim Crow Study Group of the Rogers School of Law at the University of Arizona found that at least eight Southern states still had laws designed to prevent public school integration or support segregated private schools. Attention also has been paid recently to the continuing existence of racial restrictive covenants in property deeds and the governing documents of homeowners associations across the country.

25. The line appears at the end of the documentary film *Race is a Four Letter Word*: see http://www.lumiere.net.nz/reader/item/1058.

References

Amy, Douglas, Frederick McBride, and Robert Richie. 2000. "New Means for Political Empowerment: Proportional Voting." *Poverty and Race* (November–December 2000). Available online at http://www.prrac.org/full_text.php?text_id=138&item_id=1789&newsletter_id=53&header=Search%20Results.

Anderson, Rebecca, Betsy Leondar-Wright, Meizhu Lui, Barbara Robles, and Rose Brewer. 2006. *The Color of Wealth: The Story behind the U.S. Racial Wealth Divide.* New York: New Press.

Behrens, Angela, Christopher Uggens, and Jeff Manza. 2003. "Ballot Manipulation and the 'Menace of Negro Domination': Racial Threat and Felon Disenfranchisement in the United States, 1850–2002." *American Journal of Sociology* 109, no. 3: 559–605.

Bond Huie, Stephanie A., Patrick M. Krueger, Richard G. Rogers, and Robert A. Hummer. 2003. "Wealth, Race, and Mortality." *Social Science Quarterly* 84, no. 3: 667–684.

Bonilla-Silva, E. 2003. *Racism without Racists: Color-Blind Racism and the Persistence of Racial Inequality in the United States.* Lanham, Md.: Rowman and Littlefield.

Brittingham, Angela, and G. Patricia de la Cruz. 2004. *Ancestry: 2000.* U.S. Bureau of the Census. Washington, D.C.: Government Printing Office.

Brown, Michael K., Martin Carnoy, Elliott Currie, Troy Duster, and David B. Oppenheimer. 2005. *Whitewashing Race: The Myth of a Color-Blind Society.* Berkeley: University of California Press.

Cashin, Sheryll. 2004. *The Failures of Integration: How Race and Class Are Undermining the American Dream.* New York: PublicAffairs Books.

Charles, Camille Z. 2003. "The Dynamics of Racial Residential Segregation." *Annual Review of Sociology* 29: 167–207.

Children's Defense Fund. 2005. *The State of America's Children.* Available online at http://www.childrensdefense.org/site/DocServer/Greenbook_2005.pdf?docID=1741.

The Condition of Education 2007. 2007. U.S. Department of Education, National Center for Education Statistics (NCES 2007-064). Washington, D.C.: U.S. Government Printing Office. Available online at http://www.nces.ed.gov/pubs2007/2007064.pdf.

The Condition of Education 2006. 2006. U.S. Department of Education, National Center for Education Statistics (NCES 2006-071). Washington, D.C.: U.S. Government Printing Office.

Clotfelter, Charles, Helen F. Ladd, Jacob Vigdor, and Justin Wheeler. 2007. "High Poverty Schools and the Distribution of Teachers and Principals." *North Carolina Law Review* 85: 1345–1379.

Conley, Dalton. 1999. *Being Black, Living in the Red: Race, Wealth, and Social Policy in America,* Berkeley: University of California Press.

Darling-Hammond, Linda. 2004. "Inequality and the Right to Learn: Access to Qualified Teachers in California's Public Schools." *Teachers College Record* 106, no. 10 (October): 1936–1966. "Democracy or Distrust? Restoring Home Rule for the District of Columbia in the Post-Control Board Era." 1998. *Harvard Law Review* 111, no. 7: 2045–2062.

Dinkes, R., E. F. Cataldi, G. Kena, and K. Baum. 2006. "Indicators of School Crime and Safety: 2006," NCES 2007–003/NCJ 214262, U.S. Departments of Education and Justice. Washington, D.C.: U.S. Government Printing Office.

DeNavas-Walt, Carmen, Bernadette D. Proctor, and Cheryl Hill Lee. 2005. *Income, Poverty, and Health Insurance: Coverage in the United States, 2004.* U.S. Bureau of the Census, Current Population Reports, P60-229. Washington, D.C.: U.S. Government Printing Office.

Digest of Education Statistics 2005. 2006. U.S. Department of Education, National Center for Education Statistics. Washington, D.C.: U.S. Government Printing Office.

Education Trust. 2006. *Funding Gaps 2006.* Available online at http://www2.edtrust.org/NR/rdonlyres/CDEF9403-5A75-437E-93FF-EBF1174181FB/0/FundingGap2006.pdf.

Fass, Sarah, and Nancy K. Cauthen. 2006. *Who Are America's Poor Children? The Official Story.* National Center for Children in Poverty. Available online at http://www.nccp.org/publications/pub_684.html.

Ford, Richard Thompson. 1994. "The Boundaries of Race: Political Geography in Legal Analysis." *Harvard Law Review* 107, no. 8: 1841–1922.

Gilliam, Frank D. 2006. "The Architecture of a New Racial Discourse." FrameWorks Institute. Available online at http://www.frameworksinstitute.org/clients/gilliam_memo1106.pdf.

Gilens Martin. 2005. "Inequality and Democratic Responsiveness." *Public Opinion Quarterly* 69: 78–96.

Griffin, John, and Brian Newman. 2004. "Race and Political Inequality in America: How Much and Why?" Prepared for the 2004 Annual Meeting of the Midwest Political Science Association, Chicago, April 15–18. Available online at http://americandemocracy.nd.edu/working_papers/files/race_and_political_inequality.pdf

Harper-Ho, Virginia. 2000. "Noncitizen Voting Rights: The History, the Law and Current Prospects for Change." *Law and Inequality* 18, no. 2: 271–322.

Hayduk, Ronald. 2004. "Democracy for All: Restoring Immigrant Voting Rights in the U.S." *New Political Science* 26, no. 4: 499–523.

Hollinger, David A. 2003. "Amalgamation and Hypodescent: The Question of Ethnoracial Mixture in the History of the United States." *American Historical Review* 108(5): 1363–1390.

Howell, William G., ed. 2005. *School Boards and the Future of Education Politics.* Washington, D.C.: Brookings Institution Press.

Hunter, Molly A. 2005. "Requiring States to Offer a Quality Education to All Students." *Human Rights Magazine,* Fall. Available online at http://www.abanet.org/irr/hr/Fall05/requiring%20states.html.

Hutchings, Vincent L., and Nicholas A. Valentino. 2004. "The Centrality of Race in American Politics." *American Review of Political Science* 7: 383–408.

Ihlanfeldt, Keith R. 2004. "Exclusionary Land-Use Regulations within Suburban Communities: A Review of the Evidence and Policy Prescriptions." *Urban Studies* 41, no. 2: 261–283.

Ignatiev, Noel. 1995. *How the Irish Became White: Irish-Americans and African-Americans in 19th Century Philadelphia.* New York: Verso.

Jacobson, Matthew Frye. 1998. *Whiteness of a Different Color: European Immigrants and the Alchemy of Race.* Cambridge, Mass.: Harvard University Press.

Kane, Eugene. 2001. "In 2001 America, Whites Can't Believe Blacks Treated Unfairly." *Milwaukee Journal Sentinel,* July 15, 3B.

Katznelson, Ira. 2005. *When Affirmative Action Was White: An Untold History of Racial Inequality in Twentieth-Century America.* New York: W. W. Norton.

Kim, Claire Jean. 2000. "Clinton's Race Initiative: Recasting the American Dilemma." *Polity* 33, no. 2: 175–197.

Kinder, Donald R., and Lynn M. Sanders. 1996. *Divided by Color: Racial Politics and Democratic Ideals.* Chicago: University of Chicago Press.

Kochhar, Rakesh. 2004. "The Wealth of Hispanic Households: 1996 to 2002." Pew Hispanic Center. Available online at http://pewhispanic.org/files/reports/34.pdf.

Loury, Glenn, 2002. *The Anatomy of Racial Inequality.* Cambridge, Mass.: Harvard University Press.

Massey, Douglas S. 2000. "Residential Segregation and Neighborhood Conditions in U.S. Metropolitan Areas." Pp. 391–434 in *America Becoming: Racial Trends and Their Consequences*, vol. 1, ed. Neil Smelser, William Julius Wilson, and Faith Mitchell. Washington, D.C.: National Academy Press.

Massey, Douglas S., and Nancy A. Denton. 1993. *American Apartheid: Segregation and the Making of the Underclass.* Cambridge, Mass.: Harvard University Press

Mauer, Mark. 2004. "Felon Disenfranchisement: A Policy Whose Time Has Passed?" *Human Rights* 31, no. 1: 16–17.

Mayer, Daniel P., John E. Mullens, and Mary T. Moore. 2000. "Monitoring School Quality: An Indicators Report." National Center for Education Statistics. U.S. Department of Education, NCES 2001–030.

Mazzocco, Philip J., Timothy Brock, Gregory Brock, Kristina Olson, and Mahzarin Banaji. 2006. "The Cost of Being Black: White Americans' Perceptions and the Question of Reparations." *Du Bois Review* 3: 261–297.

McKenzie, Evan. 1994. *Privatopia: Homeowner Associations and the Rise of Residential Private Governments.* New Haven, Conn.: Yale University Press

Mickelson, Roslyn. 2003. "When Are Racial Disparities in Education the Result of Racial Discrimination? A Social Science Perspective." *Teachers College Record* 10(6): 1052–1086.

Oliver, Melvin L., and Thomas M. Shapiro. 1995. *Black Wealth/White Wealth: A New Perspective on Racial Inequality.* New York: Routledge.

Ong, Paul, and R. Varisa Pataporn. 2006. "Asian Americans and Wealth: The Role of Housing and Non-housing Assets." Paper prepared for Closing the Wealth Gap Research Forum Assets Learning Conference. Available online at http://www.frbsf.org/community/research/assets/AsianAmericanWealth.pdf.

Orfield, Gary, and Chungmei Lee. 2005. *Why Segregation Matters: Poverty and Educational Inequality.* Cambridge, Mass.: Civil Rights Project at Harvard University. Available online at http://www.civilrightsproject.ucla.edu/research/deseg/Why_Segreg_Matters.pdf.

Orfield, Gary, and Nancy McArdle. 2006. "The Vicious Cycle: Segregated Housing, Schools and Intergenerational Inequality." Joint Center for Housing Studies, Harvard University, Cambridge, Mass. Available online at http://www.jchs.harvard.edu/publications/communitydevelopment/w06-4_orfield.pdf.

Orzechowski, Shawna, and Peter Sepielli. 2003. "Net Worth and Asset Ownership of Households: 1998 and 2000." U.S. Bureau of the Census, Washington, D.C. Available online at http://www.census.gov/prod/2003pubs/p70-88.pdf.

Passel, Jeffrey. 2004. "Election 2004: The Latino and Asian Vote." Urban Institute Immigration Studies Program. Available online at http://www.urban.org/UploadedPDF/900723.pdf.

Pendall, Rolf. 2000. "Local Land Use Regulation and the Chain of Exclusion." *Journal of the American Planning Association* 66, no. 2: 125–142.

powell, john a. 2000. "Addressing Regional Dilemmas for Minority Communities." Pp. 218–246 in *Reflections on Regionalism*, ed. Bruce Katz. Washington, D.C.: Brookings Institution Press.

Robinson, Lisa, and Andrew Grant-Thomas. 2004. "Race, Place, and Home: A Civil Rights and Metropolitan Opportunity Agenda." Civil Rights Project at Harvard University, Cambridge, Mass. Available online at http://www.civilrightsproject.harvard.edu/research/metro/Race_Place_Home.pdf.

Roediger, David. 1991. *The Wages of Whiteness: Race and the Making of the American Working Class.* London: Verso.

Roithmayr, Daria. 2004. "Locked in Segregation." *Virginia Journal of Social Policy and the Law* 12, no. 957.

Rubenstein, Ross, Amy Ellen Schwartz, and Leanne Stiefel. 2006. "Rethinking the Intradistrict Distribution of School Inputs to Disadvantaged Children." Unpublished paper prepared for the Rethinking Rodriguez: Education as a Fundamental Right Conference. Boalt Hall School of Law, University of California, Berkeley, April. Available online at http://www.law.berkeley.edu/centers/ewi/research/k12equity/rubenstein-schwartz -stiefel_paper.pdf.

Schuman, Howard, Charlotte Steeh, Lawrence Bobo, and Maria Krysan. 1997. *Racial Attitudes in America: Trends and Interpretations,* rev. ed. Cambridge, Mass.: Harvard University Press.

Sen, Amartya. 1999. *Development as Freedom.* London: Oxford University Press.

Shapiro, Thomas M. 2004. *The Hidden Cost of Being African American: How Wealth Perpetuates Inequality.* New York: Oxford University Press.

Snipp, C. Matthew. 2003. "Racial Measurement in the American Census: Past Practices and Implications for the Future." *Annual Review of Sociology* 29: 563–588.

Statistical Abstract of the United States: 2006. 2005. U.S. Bureau of the Census, Washington, D.C.

Steele, Shelby. 1990. *The Content of Our Character.* New York: St. Martin's Press.

Swain, Carol M. 2002. *New White Nationalism in America: Its Challenge to Integration.* London: Cambridge University Press.

Thomas B. Fordham Institute. 2006. *Fund the Child: Tackling Inequity and Antiquity in School Finance.* June. Available online at http://www.100percentsolution.org/fundthe child/FundtheChild062706.pdf.

Tulsa Race Riot. 2001. "A Report by the Oklahoma Commission to Study the Tulsa Race Riot of 1921." Available online at http://www.okhistory.org/trrc/freport.pdf.

Uggen, Christopher, and Jeff Manza. 2002. "Democratic Contraction? The Political Consequences of Felon Disenfranchisement in the United States." *American Sociological Review* 67: 777–803.

U.S. Bureau of the Census. 2006. *Public Education Finances 2004.* Annual Survey of Local Government Finances. Available online at http://www2.census.gov/govs/school/ 04f33pub.pdf.

———. 2007. "Census Bureau Reports on Residential Vacancies and Homeownership." U.S. Department of Commerce News, April 27 release. Available online at http://www .census.gov/hhes/www/housing/hvs/qtr107/q107press.pdf.

Walters, Pamela Barnhouse. 2001. "Educational Access and the State: Historical Continuities and Discontinuities in Racial Inequality in American Education." *Sociology of Education* 74: 35–49.

———. 2007. "Explaining the Durable Racial Divide in American Education: Policy Development and Opportunity Hoarding from *Brown* to Vouchers." Unpublished paper presented at the Social Dimensions of Inequality Conference, Russell Sage Foundation and Carnegie Corporation, University of California, Los Angeles, January.

Wolfe, Barbara, and Robert Haveman. 2001. "Accounting for the Social and Non-Market Benefits of Education." In *The Contribution of Human and Social Capital to Sustained Economic Growth and Well-Being,* ed. J. Helliwell. Organization for Economic Cooperation and Development/Human Resources Development Canada. Vancouver: University of British Columbia Press.

1

Color Lines in a Multiracial Nation

An Institutional Demographic Overview of the
United States in the Twenty-First Century

NANCY MCARDLE

T he racial profile of the United States has changed dramatically over
just three and a half decades, within the lifetime of even the youngest
baby boomer. In 2005 one in three residents was a racial or ethnic
minority, up from one in six in 1970. Hispanics are now the largest minority
group and are projected to be a quarter of the total population by midcentury, when no single major racial or ethnic group will claim the majority.
Further, the younger age structure of the minority population means that
this racial transition will occur considerably sooner among the young. The
old black–white paradigm—never entirely adequate—is now completely
deficient, and diversity within race/ethnic groups, fueled by continued foreign immigration from a host of countries, complicates the picture even
further. The once rigid color line, demarcating both the separation and
inequality between races, has become blurred. Moreover, stark regional differences mean that these racial dynamics are playing out differently across
the nation.

Because the history of slavery, Jim Crow, and discrimination against
blacks has defined America's fundamental racial struggle, the color line must
first be addressed in the context of African Americans. Just as it was highlighted by the 1968 Kerner Commission report which warned of "two societies, one black, one white—separate and unequal," the ongoing inequality of
blacks was once again brought to the forefront in the aftermath of Hurricane
Katrina, when the flood waters laid bare the plight of those relegated to lower
ground and without the resources to flee. The nation has made much progress

since the civil rights era of the 1950s and 1960s, yet stubborn problems remain, particularly for certain black subgroups. The emergence of the black middle class, higher levels of homeownership, income, and educational attainment over the long run, and less racial animosity testify to this progress. Yet even middle-class and professional blacks have been unable to use these assets to move into neighborhoods which include the same resources available to similarly situated whites. Residential segregation, while easing in some locations, is still at very high levels in those metropolitan areas where most blacks live, isolating them in communities with poorer educational and employment opportunities and greater health risks. The gap between black and white unemployment has remained essentially unchanged over four decades, while black poverty and income levels remain among the worst among major racial and ethnic groups, exacerbated by the high share of black single-parent and single-earner households. Young black men face particular difficulties, posting high dropout rates, disconnection from the workforce, and incarceration rates that often lead to disenfranchisement and inability to obtain employment. In a tragic cycle, men who leave prison often return to their previous neighborhoods with few good options and considerable temptation to return to criminal activity.

Despite continued inequality across a wide range of measures, many whites believe that blacks have essentially achieved parity and that "race neutral" policies are needed to ensure a "level playing field." Or that, as a nation, we have tried to address these inequalities to the best of our ability, and those remaining are a matter of individual responsibility or neutral market forces. Indeed, court decisions which affirm this view have been responsible for rolling back much of the progress in school desegregation that was achieved in the South. Blacks and whites hold fundamentally different views regarding the availability of equal employment, educational, and housing opportunities and the importance of racial discrimination in limiting these opportunities. Given the conservative policy climate and the composition of the U.S. Supreme Court, the likelihood of major policy initiatives to address these inequalities is small, making it even more important for researchers to reveal these disparities so starkly and engagingly that people will accept a common understanding and more effectively look for solutions.

Like African Americans, Native Americans have endured a long history of subjugation and oppression, so their very survival as a people is a victory. Yet, with high rates of interracial marriage and with population growth due, in part, to people's increased self-identification of Indian heritage, the very definition of the Indian "race" is somewhat murky. Further, because the Indian population is relatively small—less than the number of Chinese Americans in the United States—and is divided among five hundred tribes, many surveys do not provide separate estimates for Indians, but aggregate them with "others." We do know that they have among the lowest economic and educational status of any racial group and are disproportionately dependent on public assistance. While Indians have higher levels of homeownership than many minority groups, they are more likely to live in inadequate and crowded housing. They also suffer high levels of infant mortality, alcoholism, and diabetes. Approximately 40 percent live on reservations, and those living on or near Indian lands tend to have worse outcomes than Indians overall. Because of their relatively small numbers, complicated sovereignty issues, and a lack of data, the Native American situation is sometimes easy to overlook. But, as they progress further toward self-determination and economic advancement, we cannot forget the descendants of America's first inhabitants and the struggles that they still face.

Latinos, particularly Latino immigrants, are the face of the next major civil rights struggle in the United States. In many ways, Latino socioeconomic, demographic and health outcomes are better than African Americans', and they generally face lower levels of segregation and discrimination. Yet, because their population is surging during a politically conservative era, their opportunity to take part fully in the American dream is unsure. Geographic concentration of immigrants, most of whom are Latinos, has raised concern about stresses on schools, hospitals and other social services. Major legislation which would designate illegal immigrants as felons, criminalize anyone who provides assistance to the undocumented, and attempt to deport all 11.5 million to 12 million undocumented immigrants has garnered considerable support. With a terrorist attack inside the United States or a downswing in economy, demands for such action could become even more intense.

The socioeconomic status of Latinos varies considerably, in part according to their country of origin, length of time in the United States, and English ability. A number of factors work in their favor, including relatively high employment rates, multiple earner households, two-parent families, and generally positive health outcomes, despite a disproportionate lack of health insurance. And, the longer they remain in the United States, the more they progress up the economic ladder. Though they experience considerable discrimination, they are sometimes favored by employers over African Americans. Still, as the economy increasingly rewards higher education and a continued influx of low-skilled immigrants puts downward pressure on wages, Latinos will continue to fall behind unless they can upgrade their skills. Currently their lower educational attainment has led to the lowest earnings levels and occupational status of all major groups. With many Latino children attending poorly performing schools that are highly segregated by race, income, and language ability and a high share dropping out of school, much more needs to be done to assist Latinos gain a foothold above the lowest rungs of the economic ladder.

Education has been instrumental in securing the success of many Asian populations in the United States. With higher levels of educational attainment, school test scores, college persistence rates, income, occupational status, two-parent families, and health status than whites overall, Asians are also the least residentially segregated from whites. In fact, relative to whites with similar income profiles, Asians actually live in more affluent neighborhoods. Still, Asians are even more heterogeneous than Latinos in terms of culture, language, and country of origin, and vary considerably across the socioeconomic spectrum as well. While all groups contain examples of individuals overcoming great odds, some Asian subgroups, such as Cambodians and Hmong, are among the most impoverished in the nation. In celebrating the success of the Asian experience overall, we must not use too broad a brush and neglect the needs and stories of those who continue to struggle. And, during a period of retrenchment around immigration policy, it is also instructive to recall that the same Asian nationalities that are now sometimes termed "model minorities" were despised, excluded, and interned within just the last one hundred fifty years of our nation's history.

This chapter provides, in much greater detail, a view of our major institutions through the lens of race as we move into the twenty-first century. Beginning with a description of the racial composition of the population, both now and in the projected future, it proceeds to examine disparities and interactions among major racial groups in our most important institutions: the home, place of worship, neighborhood, school, workplace, and political arena. It documents significant progress in some areas as well as stagnation and decline in others. The rungs of the racial hierarchy are increasingly jumbled, though a wide gulf still separates whites and Asians from blacks, Hispanics, and American Indians. Lastly it highlights important research questions that will help guide our way as we face the challenges of a changing nation.

The Elusive Concept of Race: Practical and Theoretical Concerns

Any broad discussion of racial characteristics and trends immediately confronts both practical and theoretical difficulties. Data have been collected unevenly in terms of racial groups and time periods across a wide range of subject areas. Thus, we are forced to make the best use of the data we have, acknowledging that, because of small sample sizes, changes in definitions, or simply lack of any collected data, the picture may be somewhat less than comprehensive.

A more fundamental problem concerns the very meaning of race. The delineations most commonly used in law, public policy, and social discourse in the United States are largely the result of governmental decisions and have little meaning in many parts of the world. Historically the concept has been murky and changeable. At one point, immigration officials classified Italians, Irish, and some Southeastern Europeans as separate "races." In the 1930 Census, Mexicans were classified as a separate "race," unless they were determined to be obviously white by the census taker. After much protest, Mexicans were restored to the "white" race. Defining an individual's race has also evolved, from a period in which "one drop" of non-white blood was enough to make one "non-white," to a more common acceptance of multiracial identity. Currently, the Census Bureau and most researchers identify five individual races, as defined by the Office of Management and Budget: white; African American or black; Asian; Native Hawaiian and other Pacific Islanders; American Indian and Alaska Natives; plus a possible sixth option, "Other Race." In addition, beginning with the 2000 Census, respondents were allowed to self identify as more than one race, and 2.4 percent of the population did. While federal agencies must use and report data according to this classification scheme, it is clearly somewhat problematic. American Indian and Alaska Natives include well over five hundred tribes from throughout the nation. The Asian category is determined solely by geography and includes groups as different as Pakistani and Hmong, with scores of differing cultures, histories, and languages. The largest Asian groups include the Chinese, Filipinos, Indians, Vietnamese, Koreans, and Japanese.

Layered on top of these racial definitions is the concept of Hispanic or Latino ethnicity, which also includes a diverse set of groups, distinguished by a common ancestry, culture and language, though this commonality may be in the distant past. Because Hispanic ethnicity is a concept separate from race, there are classifications for Hispanic blacks and non-Hispanic blacks, Hispanic whites and non-Hispanic whites, etc., for all racial groups. Hispanics do not fit neatly into one racial category. In the 2000 Census, close to half of Hispanics self-identified as "white," while almost as large a share (42 percent) self-identified as "Other." Just 2 percent identified as "black" and 6 percent as "multiracial." Many Hispanics wrote on their census forms the words "Hispanic" or "Latino" in the race category. When given the opportunity to pick a particular Hispanic group, six in ten Hispanics identified as "Mexican"; one in ten "Puerto Rican;" 5 percent Central American; 4 percent Cuban; 4 percent South American; and 2 percent Dominican.

Added to these complexities of racial and ethnic identification is the argument over whether making racial classifications is, in fact, harmful and divisive to society. Some scholars argue that, because race is almost entirely a social construct, collecting and reporting information by race serves to highlight meaningless disparities and perpetuate fallacious images of "the other" in the eyes of our citizens. It is certainly true that race has virtually no physical basis. In 2005, scientists at Penn State announced that they had found the tiny genetic mutation that "explains the first appearance of white skin in humans tens of thousands of years ago," a mutation so small that "it involves the change of just one letter of DNA code out of the 3.1 billion letters in the human genome."[1] But it is also true that significant differences exist between races over a wide range of important socioeconomic indicators, many of which are not explainable by any other factor, and that racism continues as a force in U.S. society. Without data, we are essentially in the dark about the size of and trends in racial disparities and are, therefore, are sorely hindered in our ability to counter them. As one geneticist at the National Human Genome Institute commented, "You may tell people that race isn't real and doesn't matter, but they can't catch a cab. So unless we take that into account it makes us sound crazy."[2]

Thus, for the purposes of this paper, we will use the term "race" to mean either race or Hispanic origin and, unless specified otherwise, utilize the following mutually exclusive categories:

- Non-Hispanic whites, termed "whites"
- Non-Hispanic blacks or African Americans, termed "blacks"
- Hispanics or Latinos, who may be of any race
- Non-Hispanic Asians and Pacific Islanders, termed "Asians"
- Non-Hispanic American Indians and Alaska Natives, termed "Native Americans"

When drawn from census-based data from 2000 onward, racial groups will generally refer to those who classified themselves as the specified race "alone" as opposed to those who classified themselves as the specified race in combination with other races. When possible and particularly informative, information for Hispanic and Asian subgroups will also be presented.

Population Growth: The Changing Face of the Nation

While the composition of future population growth is not entirely predictable, certain dynamics already in place assure that racial and ethnic minorities will become an increasingly large share. The rapid growth of the Hispanic population, fueled by immigration, a young age structure and high fertility rates, is profoundly changing the face of the United States and will continue to do so for the foreseeable future. Large numbers of Hispanics have lived in the Southwest and certain cities for decades, if not centuries, but as recently as 1970 they still made up less than 5 percent of the total U.S. population. In recent decades, however, Hispanic growth has skyrocketed. Between 1990 and 2004, Hispanics grew by 85 percent, over sixteen times the rate of the non-Hispanic white population. Hispanics now total over 40 million, and one in seven U.S. residents is Hispanic.[3]

Foreign immigration has been a chief catalyst of Hispanic growth, both directly and indirectly. Following the Hart-Cellar Immigration Act of 1965, immigration to the United States surged, with the foreign-born population reaching almost 35 million in 2004 or 12 percent of the population (see Figure 1.1).[4] While the chief purpose of the Act was to eliminate national origin quotas that disproportionately favored northern Europeans, its emphasis on family reunification facilitated the entrance of many Hispanic immigrants, particularly Mexicans. Currently, almost half of all foreign-born residents living in the United States are Hispanic,[5] up from about one in six in 1970.[6]

Many Hispanics can trace their ancestry in this nation back for generations, but two in five are foreign-born, and one in five entered the United States during the 1990s alone. Puerto Ricans are U.S. citizens by birth and so are counted as part of the native-born population, even those born in Puerto Rico who have now relocated to the U.S. mainland. If these residents were included with the "foreign-born," the foreign-born share of Hispanics would be significantly higher.

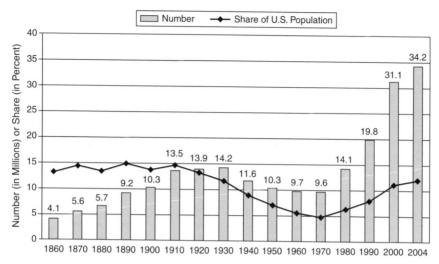

FIGURE 1.1 The foreign-born population in the United States, 1860–2004. (*Sources:* Campbell Gibson and Emily Lennon, *Historical Census Statistics on the Foreign-Born Population of the United States: 1850–1990,* Table 1, U.S. Bureau of the Census, Internet release, March 9, 1999 (1860–2004 data); U.S. Bureau of the Census, *The Foreign-Born Population: 2000,* C2KBR-34 (2000 data); U.S. Bureau of the Census, *Foreign-Born Population of the United States,* Current Population Survey, March 2004, Detailed Tables, PPL-176 (2004 data).)

Immigration also contributes to Hispanic population growth indirectly, by increasing the number of young women of childbearing age who have high fertility rates. The median age of Hispanics in the United States is just twenty-six, compared to thirty-nine for non-Hispanic whites. Almost two in five Hispanics is under age twenty-one.[7] The birthrate for Hispanics in 2004 was 40 percent higher than for black and Asian women and 60 percent higher than for other racial groups. As with many characteristics, fertility varies substantially within Hispanic subgroups. Among Mexicans, there were 106 births per thousand women of childbearing age in 2003 versus 62 births per thousand Puerto Rican or Cuban women.[8] A young age structure paired with high birthrates translated into Hispanic births outpacing deaths by a ratio of over eight to one between 2000 and 2004, and natural increase (births minus deaths) slightly outstripping immigration as the primary driver of Hispanic population growth (see Table 1.1).[9]

True estimates of the Hispanic population are complicated by the relatively large share who are undocumented. Most of the data in this chapter come from the decennial census and various surveys that do not distinguish between the documented and undocumented. Yet undocumented residents may be reluctant to participate in such surveys and therefore be underrepresented. According to recent estimates by immigration experts using a variety of techniques, there

TABLE 1.1 COMPONENTS OF POPULATION CHANGE BY RACE, 2000–2004 (in thousands)

	Total Population Change	Natural Increase			Net International Migration	Share of Growth Due to:	
		Births	Deaths	Net		Natural Increase	International Migration
Total	12,231	17,198	10,297	6,901	5,330	56.4	43.6
Non-Hispanic White	2,264	9,629	8,366	1,263	1,001	55.8	44.2
Hispanic	6,016	3,726	454	3,272	2,744	54.4	45.6
Black	1,797	2,624	1,237	1,387	410	77.2	22.8
Asian	1,780	725	159	566	1,214	31.8	68.2
American Indian	44	28	5	23	20	52.3	45.5
Multiracial	541	538	62	476	64	88.0	11.8

Note: Racial groups except for whites include Hispanic members of those groups. "Asian" includes Pacific Islanders. "American Indian" includes Alaskan Natives.

Source: U.S. Bureau of the Census, "Table 5: Cumulative Estimates of the Components of Population Change by Race and Hispanic or Latino Origin for the United States," April 1, 2000, to July 1, 2004, NC-EST2004-05, June 9, 2005.

were 11.5 million to 12 million unauthorized immigrants residing in the United States as of 2006, representing almost one of every three foreign-born residents. Mexicans accounted for 56 percent of the undocumented and other Latin American countries about 22 percent.[10] Thus the undocumented are overwhelmingly Hispanic.

According to Census Bureau projections, which take into account births, deaths, and foreign immigration, Hispanics will become even more powerful engines of population growth in the future. Over the next two decades, they will be responsible for close to half of the total U.S. growth and will make up 18 percent of the population by 2020 and close to a quarter by 2050 (see Figure 1.2).[11] Their presence will be even greater among young age groups. By 2020, Hispanics will make up 24 percent of residents under age 18, 30 percent by 2050.[12]

Immigration will continue to play a vital role, one that is likely underestimated in official Census Bureau estimates. As detailed by the Harvard Joint Center for Housing Studies, "For at least two decades, the Census Bureau has consistently underestimated the number of foreign-born individuals living in the [United States] and used improbably low assumptions about future immigration to project population growth. History suggests, however, that high-side estimates of immigration prove more realistic. This nation continues to have a great demand for labor and a strong appeal to people around the world who are willing to take great risks—including entering the country illegally—to make a life here. Nonetheless, the Census Bureau's current population projections assume that immigration will run at about 850,000 arrivals a year, even though current estimates put that number closer to 1.2 [million]–1.3 million."[13]

On the other hand, political realities may inhibit the degree to which past immigration patterns persist. Legislation to construct a lengthy wall along the Mexican border, increase penalties on employers who hire the undocumented, make illegal presence in the United States a felony, and criminalize those people

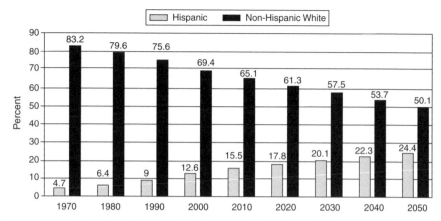

FIGURE 1.2   Hispanic and non-Hispanic white share of the population, 1970–2050. From 2000 forward, "white" refers to those who identified their race as "white alone." (*Sources:* Campbell Gibson and Kay Jung. *Historical Census Statistics on Population Totals by Race, 1790 to 1990, and by Hispanic Origin, 1970 to 1990, for the United States, Regions, Divisions, and States,* Working Paper Series no. 56, U.S. Bureau of the Census, September 2002; *U.S. Interim Projections by Age, Race, and Hispanic Origin,* Internet release, March 18, 2004.)

who provide any sort of aid to the undocumented have gained some traction in Congress. Another terrorist attack on U.S. soil or a significant economic downturn could lead to major immigration limitations in the future.

Changes to immigration law have most dramatically affected the Asian population in the United States, whether through provisions emphasizing family reunification, preferences for workers in occupations with labor shortages, or allowances for refugees, many of who were displaced during the Vietnam War. As recently as the 2000–2004 period, foreign immigration accounted for over two thirds of Asian population growth. Two thirds of all Asians in the United States are foreign-born, and about one in three entered this country during the 1990s. Roughly a quarter of all immigrants in the United States are Asian, up from about one in ten in 1970. Nativity status does vary considerably across Asian subgroups, however. Approximately two in five Japanese are foreign-born, compared to about four in five Koreans. These differences are shown in Table 1.2. This chart presents a wide range of socioeconomic characteristics from the 2000 Census for major racial subgroups. We will refer back to it throughout the chapter to make comparisons and point out particularly striking variations.

While immigration is an especially strong driver of population growth for Asians, natural increase is also important. Fertility among Asians is second only to Hispanics and is 40 percent higher than for non-Hispanic whites. Thus, Asians and Pacific Islanders are projected to increase their share of the population from 3.6 percent in 2000 to 5.4 percent in 2020 and 8 percent in 2050.

TABLE 1.2   VARIATION IN SOCIOECONOMIC CHARACTERISTICS BY RACE AND RACIAL SUBGROUP, 2000

	Population (in thousands)	Median Age	Average Household Size	Share of Families Headed by Single Mother	Share Not Speaking English at Home	Share Foreign-Born	Share of Age 25+ with Bachelor's Degree	Median Household Income	Per Capita Income	Poverty Rate	Home-ownership Rate
Total	281,421	35.4	2.6	10.2	18.9	11.1	24.4	41,994	21,587	12.4	66.2
Non-Hispanic											
White	194,553	38.6	2.4	6.9	9.5	3.5	27.0	45,367	24,819	8.1	72.4
Black	33,948	30.5	2.7	28.2	9.4	5.7	14.3	29,445	14,489	24.8	46.6
American Indian	2,069	30.3	3.0	18.3	29.4	1.2	11.9	30,293	13,152	25.7	57.5
Asian	10,123	33.1	3.1	5.4	83.2	69.3	44.2	51,967	21,893	12.6	53.3
Chinese	2,433	35.5	2.9	4.2	87.3	70.9	48.1	51,444	23,756	13.5	58.4
Filipino	1,850	35.5	3.4	7.8	82.0	67.7	43.8	60,570	21,267	6.3	60.0
Indian	1,679	29.3	3.1	2.5	84.9	75.4	63.9	63,669	27,514	9.8	46.9
Vietnamese	1,123	30.5	3.7	7.2	95.5	76.1	19.4	45,085	15,655	16.0	53.2
Korean	1,076	32.7	2.8	6.1	87.8	77.7	43.8	40,037	18,805	14.8	40.1
Japanese	797	42.6	2.3	3.9	51.8	39.5	41.9	52,060	30,075	9.7	60.8
Cambodian	172	23.8	4.4	16.8	97.0	65.8	9.9	36,155	10,366	29.3	43.6
Hispanic	35,306	26.0	3.6	14.5	85.2	40.2	10.4	33,676	12,111	22.6	45.7
Mexican	20,641	24.4	3.9	11.8	85.2	41.5	7.5	33,644	10,918	23.5	48.4
Puerto Rican	3,406	27.7	3.0	24.9	85.9	1.4	12.5	30,644	13,518	25.8	34.4
Cuban	1,242	40.3	2.8	7.5	90.6	68.5	21.2	36,671	20,451	14.6	57.6
Dominican	765	29.6	3.6	27.9	96.7	68.2	10.9	29,099	11,773	27.5	20.2
Central American	1,687	29.0	3.9	14.1	94.9	75.8	9.5	35,517	13,012	19.9	31.7
South American	1,354	33.0	3.2	11.4	93.0	76.6	25.2	41,132	17,645	15.0	41.2

Notes: "Asian" category does not include Pacific Islanders. Income data as of 1999. "Single mother" defined as female head of household with no husband present and with own children under eighteen at home. Data in this table are for the purpose of making comparisons between racial groups and may vary from data presented in text because of different variable definition, different year of survey, or sampling differences.

Sources: Population totals from U.S. Bureau of the Census, 2000 Decennial Census, Summary File 2; other data from Summary File 4.

The adoption of a multirace classification for the first time in the 2000 Census had a particularly large effect on estimates of Asian population growth. Nationally, 2.4 percent of the population identified themselves as being two or more races in 2000, while 16.7 percent of Asians or Pacific Islanders did.[14] Thus, depending on whether one uses a 2000 population figure that reflects those who identified themselves as "Asian alone" or as "Asian in combination with other races," the Asian/Pacific Islander population grew over the 1990s by either 46 percent or 76 percent. Most of the statistics cited in this chapter will refer to "Asian alone," but the current high level of multiracial identification coupled with significant intermarriage, discussed later, portends another layer of complexity in the future discussion of race.

Black Americans, until recently the largest racial minority group, have seen their share of the nation's population increase only marginally over the past several decades, rising from 11 percent of the population in 1970 to just 12 percent in 2004. Natural increase has been the primary driver of growth, contributing over three fourths of black increase between 2000 and 2004. In contrast, foreign immigration plays a smaller role for blacks than it does for any other major racial group. Immigration of Afro-Caribbeans and Africans has boosted the black population, and these groups have grown substantially faster than native-born blacks. According to the Mumford Center at the University at Albany, State University of New York, these two groups made up just 4 percent of the black population in 1990 but were responsible for 17 percent of the black population growth over the 1990s. Still, the foreign-born make up just 6 percent of all U.S. blacks.[15]

The Census Bureau projects that the black population will continue its relatively slow growth and make up 13.5 percent of the population in 2020 and 14.6 percent in 2050. The black share of the child population is projected to remain relatively unchanged at 15–16 percent. Unlike other minority groups with much higher rates of intermarriage, the share of blacks who report themselves as being multiracial is relatively low at 5 percent.

American Indian and Alaska Natives are by far the smallest of the major racial groups and one of the hardest populations to describe. In 2000, two out of five Indians described themselves as multiracial, meaning that 1990s population growth ranged from 26 percent to just over 100 percent, depending on whether one uses the 2000 figure for "American Indian and Alaska Natives alone" or "in combination with other races." Even the low growth estimate outstrips that which one would predict based on natural increase and immigration. For the past several decades, the Indian population has grown as more and more people self-identify themselves as Indian.

Non-Hispanic whites will continue to constitute the majority of the U.S. population until shortly after midcentury, but their low fertility, older age structure and relatively slow level of immigration will inevitably lead to their declining share of the population. In 2004, four of six U.S. residents were non-Hispanic white, down from five of six in 1970. Over the 1990s, the white population grew by just 5 percent, the slowest of any major racial group. The shift in the racial

TABLE 1.3 MISPERCEPTIONS ABOUT RACIAL COMPOSITION OF THE U.S. POPULATION, 1995

	White Responses	Black Responses	Asian Responses	Hispanic Responses	Actual 1995 Percentages
What percentage of the U.S. population is:					
White?	49.9	45.5	54.8	46.7	73.6
Black?	23.8	25.9	20.5	22.7	12.0
Hispanic?	14.7	16.3	14.6	20.7	10.3
Asian?	10.8	12.2	8.3	10.8	3.4

Note: Response percentages are averages of the estimates made by those polled. Hispanics may be of any race. Percentages do not total 100 because other races are not shown.

Source: Richard Morin, "A Distorted Image of Minorities: Poll Suggests That What Whites Think They See May Affect Beliefs," Washington Post, October 8, 1995, reporting data from the Washington Post–Kaiser Family Foundation–Harvard University Survey. Actual 1995 percentages are from the U.S. Bureau of the Census.

composition can be seen by examining the white share of different age groups. Whites make up four out of five people age sixty and older but just three of five people under age twenty.

Because less than one in twenty whites is an immigrant and only about one in eighty-five is a recent immigrant, it is startling to learn that foreign immigration currently contributes over 40 percent of white population growth. Even low levels of immigration are meaningful in comparison to the other main component of population growth—natural increase, which is depressed by the high ratio of white deaths to births. Consider the following illustration: the number of births to whites is about three times the number of births to Hispanics. But the number of white deaths is more than 18 times the number of Hispanic deaths. These dynamics lead to a numerical natural increase in the much larger white population that is less than 40 percent of the numerical increase in the Hispanic population. With the lowest birthrate and oldest age structure among major groups, non-Hispanic whites are guaranteed to constitute a smaller share of the future population. The Census Bureau estimates that they will make up 61 percent in 2020 and 50 percent in 2050. For the child population, whites will make up 53 percent in 2020 and 43 percent in 2050.

Interestingly, while the United States is not projected to become a "majority-minority" nation until the middle of the century, most Americans felt that we had reached that point over a decade ago, when the United States was actually just over a quarter minority.[16] Whites, blacks, and Hispanics all believed that the United States was at least half black, Hispanic, or Asian in a 1995 poll, when the true share was just 26 percent (see Table 1.3).[17] Blacks and Hispanics both believed that their group constituted twice the share of the U.S. population that they actually did. The cognitive reasons for these misperceptions are a provocative area of analysis, but part of the answer probably lies in the fact that, in the regions and neighborhoods where most of these minorities reside, they are greatly over-represented compared to national averages.

A Patchwork Nation: Regional Diversity and Change

National figures illustrate the ongoing racial transformation of the United States but obscure the wide variation regionally and within metropolitan areas. Many areas of the nation, indeed entire states and metro areas, are already "majority-minority," while others remain virtually all white. Because of this heterogeneity, the dynamics described throughout this chapter have different impacts in different regions, and approaches to dealing with racial inequities cannot be "one size fits all."

Hispanics are most concentrated in the fast-growing West and South where they make up a quarter and an eighth of the population, respectively. Over four in ten residents of New Mexico and three in ten residents of California and Texas are Hispanic.[18] Hispanic growth has been characterized by both "concentration and dispersal."[19] More than half of Hispanics live in California and Texas alone, and over three quarters live in the top seven states.[20] But, as they continue to add numbers to traditional locations, Hispanics are also moving to new areas. Over the 1990s, the Hispanic population doubled in twenty-two states, with the Southeast experiencing particularly fast growth. In Florida, Oregon, Washington, Nevada, Georgia, North Carolina, Virginia, and Massachusetts, Hispanics grew by over 200 percent and by over 200,000 people.[21]

While immigration from abroad has bolstered all regions, Hispanic domestic migration within the United States has mostly benefited the South. Domestic migration is movement within the United States, as opposed to movement from abroad. Florida experienced the highest net domestic in-migration of Hispanics, followed by Nevada, Arizona, and Georgia. The Northeast and West actually saw net domestic out-migration over the 1995–2000 period.[22]

The South has also benefited from continued strong domestic in-migration of blacks. Between 1995 and 2000, twice as many blacks moved into the South as moved out, while all other regions lost black domestic migrants. Georgia gained the most blacks, garnering twice the net in-migration as the next most attractive state, North Carolina, followed by Florida and Texas. By 2000, 55 percent of blacks lived in the South, and blacks made up about a fifth of the South, compared to about an eighth of the nation overall.

Like Asians, American Indians are heavily concentrated in the West, with close to half residing in that region and another 30 percent living in the South. Moreover, over a third (35 percent) of Indians live in an American Indian/Alaska Native/Hawaiian Homeland.

Whites are most evenly distributed across the four regions. Close to half of whites still live in the Northeast and Midwest, but these regions lost over 800,000 and 500,000 net white domestic migrants respectively between 1995 and 2000. The South continues to gain most whites, attracting 870,000 migrants, with over half going to Florida. Significant gains also occurred in Arizona and North Carolina. Among metropolitan areas, whites favor "suburban-like" metros such as Phoenix, Las Vegas, Atlanta, and Denver, in the West and South.

Asians exhibit the most concentration in their regional settlement patterns, with half residing in the West, which continues to experience by far the heaviest foreign immigration. Over a third of Asians (36 percent) live in California alone. Domestic migration had relatively little impact on Asian regional patterns, although the South, particularly Nevada, Texas, and Georgia did attract in-migrants, while the Northeast lost Asians.

In addition to regional shifts, the United States also continues to become more metropolitan, with over 80 percent of the population now residing in met-ropolitan areas. The overwhelming majority of Asians (95 percent) and blacks (87 percent) are metro dwellers, compared with just 78 percent of whites.[23] For-eign immigration has helped to stabilize many big cities and consequently increased the minority share of city populations. Now, fourteen of the largest twenty cities are majority-minority.[24] Many of these would have lost population over the 1990s had it not been for foreign immigration. Further, the large metro areas that include Los Angeles, San Francisco, Houston, and Miami are also now majority-minority. Latino and Asian immigration has particularly boosted large metro areas. While 35 percent of all U.S. residents live in the largest metro areas (those with over 5 million people), 45 percent of Latinos and almost 60 percent of Asians reside in those large metros.

Minorities have also made inroads into the suburbs and constituted 25 per-cent of suburban populations in 2000, up from 18 percent in 1990.[25] Among 102 large metro areas studied by demographer William Frey, minorities made up the bulk of suburban population growth. Within those metros, 39 percent of blacks, 50 percent of Hispanics, 55 percent of Asians, and 73 percent of whites now live in the suburbs.[26]

Ripples in the Pond: Achievement, Challenges, and Interaction across Institutions

The institutions in which people live out their lives, strive for success and hap-piness, and interact with others can be seen as a series of concentric circles, moving outward from the home to the neighborhood, school, workplace and civic/political arena. These next sections will explore the major differences between racial groups in each of these sectors, the particular challenges they face, and the degree to which they interact with other groups.

It Begins at Home

Household Composition

Differences in life opportunities start young, and the marital status of a child's parents and the composition of the family of origin have profound influences on children's well-being throughout their lives. Research has shown that "chil-dren born to unmarried mothers are more likely to grow up in a single-parent household, experience instability in living arrangements, live in poverty, and have socio-emotional problems. As these children reach adolescence, they are more likely to have low educational attainment, engage in sex at younger ages, and have a premarital birth. As young adults, children born outside of marriage are more likely to be idle (neither in school nor employed), have lower occupational status and income, and have more troubled marriages and divorces than those born to married parents."[27] Children raised in foster care experience particular challenges. Black children have long started life under the most difficult family circumstances, yet there are increasing signs of hope as black teen and out-of-wedlock birthrates decline. At the same time, the growing Hispanic population is exhibiting decidedly more negative trends.

Only about a third of black children live with two married parents compared to over three quarters of whites, and almost one in ten do not live with either parent.[28] Black children are more likely than others to be raised by grandparents and are also extremely over-represented in foster care. Although they make up only one in six of all minor children, over one in three children living in foster care is black.[29]

While divorce is the prime contributor to the number of white children in single-parent families, a larger factor for blacks is the high proportion of children born out of wedlock. Over two thirds of black births are to unmarried women, compared to a quarter of white births.[30] After climbing between 1980 and 1995, the share of black births out of wedlock has held steady through 2004. This development is associated with the dramatic decline in the black teenage birthrate that fell by almost 50 percent between 1990 and 2004 to stand at 63 births per 1,000 black females age fifteen to nineteen. Although this rate is still over twice that of whites, it does represent a narrowing of the gap (see Figure 1.3).[31]

Hispanic children are more likely to be raised in married couple homes, with two thirds being raised by two married parents, but several demographic trends are sobering. The share of births out of wedlock has increased notably from 30 percent in 1985 to 46 percent in 2004. Further, birthrates to Hispanic teens have declined more slowly than for other groups. Thus, the Hispanic rate of 83 births per 1,000 females age fifteen to nineteen is now the highest of any group and three times the rate for non-Hispanic whites.

Asian households most closely mirror the stereotypical U.S. family. Married couples with children are common, far exceeding the U.S. average, and 83 percent of Asian children live with two married parents, the highest share of any racial group. Single-parent households are least common. Just one sixth of births to Asian/Pacific Islander women occur outside of marriage, considerably less than the quarter of births to non-Hispanic whites.

Household composition may be most important as it relates to childrearing, but racial differences in composition and size have other impacts as well. In an increasingly suburban nation in which the "soccer mom" is the most visible and sought-after political demographic, it is surprising to learn that married couples with minor children at home make up only a quarter of all households. The most

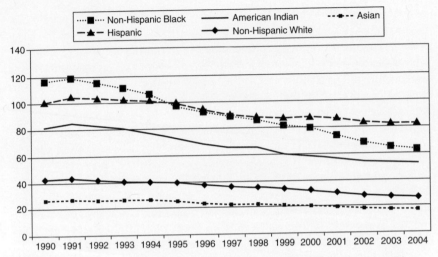

FIGURE 1.3 Trends in teen birthrates by race/ethnicity, 1990–2004 (births per 1,000 females age fifteen to nineteen). "Asian" includes Pacific Islanders; "American Indian" includes Alaskan Natives. (*Sources:* Child Trends Data Bank, available online at http://www .childtrendsdatabank.org/indicators/13TeenBirth.cfm. The data are compiled from National Vital Statistics Reports, various years, National Center for Health Statistics, Hyattsville, Md.)

common household types are empty-nesters (married couples without minor children at home) and people living alone, each representing over a quarter of households (see Figure 1.4).[32]

Hispanics are much more likely than the national average to live in multiple-person households and households with children, a fact reflected in their much larger average household sizes. In 2000, the average Hispanic household size was 3.6 persons, a full one person greater than the national average.[33] Hispanic households frequently contain extended family such as cousins, aunts, and uncles. These larger households, often related to chain immigration, have helped reduce Hispanic housing costs but have also led to overcrowding and, in some cases, harassment and prosecution for perceived or real violations of zoning ordinances.

Asians also have larger household sizes than the national average, but exhibit substantial diversity across subgroups. The average Japanese household has 2.3 persons while the average Cambodian household is almost twice as large, with 4.4 persons.[34]

Intermarriage
Racial change has influenced not only the size and composition of the American family, but also the racial diversity and interaction within families as intermarriage has become more common. Less than forty years ago, anti-miscegenation laws were still constitutional at the federal level. Though it was rendered invalid by the Supreme Court's ruling, Alabama's provision against miscegenation was

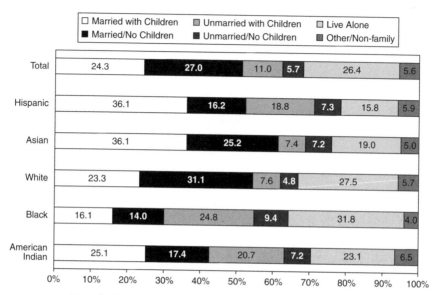

FIGURE 1.4 Household composition by race, 2004. Race groups are non-Hispanic. "Asian" includes Pacific Islanders; "American Indian" includes Alaskan Natives. (*Source:* U.S. Bureau of the Census, Current Population Survey, March 2004.)

not repealed until 2000, and even then, 40 percent of voters voted to keep the ban. Yet, 5 percent of marriages are now interracial and 3 percent are between Hispanics and non-Hispanics, up from 1 percent each in 1970."[35]

Whites are the least likely to intermarry, with just 3 percent of white couples involved in interracial marriages in 2000. Yet this rate is a marked increase from the .4 percent in 1970. Even though they are least likely to intermarry, the larger size of the overall white population means that the greatest number of interracial marriages is between a white and a minority spouse.

Latinos commonly intermarry, with about a quarter of marriages being to a non-Hispanic. Puerto Ricans are most likely to intermarry (21 percent), a phenomenon that is likely related to their U.S. citizenship and the ease with which they, as compared to non-citizen Hispanics, can marry. Two million children are now growing up in households headed by a mixed Hispanic–non-Hispanic couple, up threefold from 1970.

Asians are also likely to intermarry, with about one in seven married to a non-Asian. Interestingly this share has declined somewhat since 1970, perhaps as greater immigration has increased the size of the Asian marriageable pool. Asian women are over twice as likely to be in interracial marriages as are Asian men.

American Indians have the highest intermarriage rates, with almost 60 percent intermarried. This figure represents a decline from 1990, as many who previously would have identified themselves as "Indian" instead chose the "multiracial" category after it became available in the 2000 Census.[36]

Blacks marry outside their race much less frequently than do other minorities. In 2000, about one in fourteen blacks had a spouse of another race. Still, this rate was seven times that recorded in 1970. In contrast to Asians, black men are "more than twice as likely as black women to intermarry, a differential that has widened in recent years."[37]

Black–white intermarriage and relationships have been particular flashpoints over our nation's history. While black interracial marriages are still not common, the share of blacks who approve of dating whites is very high. About 82 percent of blacks approve of black men dating white women or black women dating white men. The rates of white approval for dating blacks are lower and, interestingly, the share of whites approving of white men dating black women (72 percent) exceeds that share approving of black men dating white women (65 percent).[38]

A number of factors suggest that interracial marriage will continue to rise. First, among Asians and Hispanics, the second and third generations are more likely to intermarry than are the first, and these later generations will surely grow in both absolute size and share of the population. For example, the Pew Hispanic Research Center estimates that second generation Hispanics will increase from 28 percent of all Hispanics in 2000 to 36 percent in 2020.[39] Second, younger and better-educated people are more likely to intermarry than are older and less-educated Americans. A recent Gallup poll shows that the share of people approving of interracial dating between blacks and whites is dramatically higher among the young. Ninety-five percent of those age eighteen to twenty-nine approve, compared to just 45–46 percent of those age sixty-five and older.[40]

However, interracial romantic relationships that include blacks still seem to bear a special stigma. In polls of teenagers, "While no more than 11 percent of teens thought that white/Hispanic and White/Asian couples would be ostracized by their respective race groups, about a quarter said that White/Black couples would be." Further, "Among couples who had dated interracially, at least 90 percent of white, Hispanic, and Asian teens said that their parents acquiesced but only 59% of black students said that their parents were comfortable."[41]

Still Worshiping Apart

Before turning from an examination of families to neighborhoods, we pause to discuss an institution that uniquely overlaps both sectors, the place of worship.[42] Communities of worship, tied together by commands to love each other and welcome the stranger have the potential to be centers of interracial healing and solidarity. But history, culture, worship styles, denominational differences, and residential patterns, to name a few factors, still conspire, as Martin Luther King Jr. said, to make "eleven o'clock Sunday morning . . . the most segregated hour." While some churches espouse multiculturalism and consciously attempt to diversify their congregations through a variety of outreach strategies, others question whether integrated worship is either necessary or prudent. The vision of an interracial beloved community is at times at odds with the desire to maintain cultural and liturgical differences that have developed over time and which give people strong feelings of comfort and familiarity.

Blacks were originally segregated into separate churches during slavery and later through Jim Crow laws and discrimination. Statistics differ, but most largely agree that blacks and whites still generally worship separately. In a 2000 New York Times poll, 90 percent of whites said that they attend churches with few or no blacks, and 73 percent of blacks say they attend churches with few or no whites.[43] A 2000 study by the Congregations Project found that just 8 percent of churches are truly multiracial.[44]

Because the capacity to have an integrated congregation depends on the diversity of local residents or those willing to travel a distance to worship, it is unsurprising that the most integrated churches are in the more diverse West and in larger cities. Among Protestants, Pentecostal churches tend to be the most integrated.

Catholic churches are substantially more integrated; with large and growing Hispanic populations mixing with established white ones. Because Catholic parishes are traditionally defined by geographic boundaries, as metropolitan areas have become increasingly Hispanic, so have many parishes. However, simply belonging to the same parish does not assure integration. Many churches have essentially established different parishes within the parish, with separate masses in Spanish and Latino priests serving Hispanic parishioners. Like many of the ethnic parishes that existed around the turn of the twentieth century, these congregations provide important connections with Latino culture and religious traditions as well as places of support and information for immigrants. Further, as in Latin America, more Hispanics are now joining evangelical churches that cater specifically to them. Similarly, Asian Christians, particularly Vietnamese and Koreans, have also often established their own congregations in the United States.

Few data exist on racial composition in non–Christian churches. Given the overlap between ethnic background and religion, Jewish synagogues remain overwhelmingly white. Islam may be the most the most diverse of the larger religious bodies. In a survey of U.S. mainstream Islam mosques, blacks were found to be dominant in 27 percent, Southeast Asians in 28 percent, and Arab Americans in 15 percent, with the remainder being more pluralistic.[45]

Neighborhoods: The Fulcrum of Opportunity

Of the many dimensions of interracial separation in the United States, residential location and segregation is the most pivotal fulcrum of denied opportunity because of its strong association with schooling, access to employment, neighborhood services and amenities, a healthy physical environment, and other factors. Segregation has most commonly been measured in terms of the dissimilarity index. This index, ranging between 0 and 100, measures the degree to which members of two racial groups are evenly dispersed throughout a geographic area in relation to each other. A value of 0 represents complete integration in which the racial composition of each neighborhood—defined usually as a census tract—exactly matches the racial composition of the overall area of interest—whether it be the nation, a metro area, a city, or another geographic area. So, for example, if a metro area is half black and half white, every census tract would also be half black and half white to achieve a dissimilarity score of 0. A score of 100 represents total apartheid, in which the races are completely separated into different geographic areas. "A value of 60 (or above) is considered very high. It means that 60 percent (or more) of the members of one group would need to move to a different tract in order for the two groups to be equally distributed. Values of 40 or 50 are usually considered a moderate level of segregation, and values of 30 or below are considered to be fairly low."[46] This section will mostly focus on two-way segregation, between whites and a specified minority group, but will end with a brief discussion of segregation measures between three or more racial groups, an increasingly important indicator in analyzing multiracial communities.

Blacks continue to be the group most segregated from whites, yet slow but steady progress has been made.[47] Black segregation declined over the 1990s (though at a slower rate of improvement than over the 1980s) and, though still high, is at its lowest level since the 1920s. As of 2000, the dissimilarity index between blacks and whites was 65, an improvement of 9 points since 1980. Looked at another way, 65 percent of blacks or of whites would have to move to another census tract in order for there to be complete integration. Importantly, residential segregation of children is even higher than it is for adults, as white families with children more commonly move to the outer suburbs, and many white urban dwellers do not have children. Segregation is lowest in areas with small black populations and in the West, where blacks are outnumbered by Latinos and Asians. In metropolitan areas that were less than 5 percent black in 2000, the dissimilarity index was only 45, down 12 percentage points since 1980. In contrast, in those older and larger cities of the Northeast and Midwest where most blacks live, segregation declined very slowly and is still at very high levels. Forty years after Martin Luther King Jr. moved his family into a Chicago slum to protest housing conditions and advocate for open housing, 80 percent or more of blacks or of whites in Detroit, Milwaukee, New York, Chicago, and Newark would have to move to achieve integration. Not only are areas with smaller black populations more integrated, they also have a higher probability of being stably integrated over time. In her research of the characteristics of stably integrated neighborhoods, Ingrid Ellen found positively related factors to be: metros with smaller black populations, lower segregation levels, a lack of history of intense racial competition for housing, greater distance from areas center of minority concentration, more rental housing, and a secure set of neighborhood amenities which could be linked to large stabilizing institutions such as universities.[48]

Segregation is so pernicious partly because it is highly related to the socioeconomic status of the neighborhood in which people live, even independent of their own household characteristics. For example, blacks are more likely to live in poorer neighborhoods than whites, even after controlling for their own income levels.[49] In 2000 the average black lived in an area with a median household income that was $16,152 less than the area where the average white resided, and that disparity had increased over the 1990s. Even when comparing households with incomes over $60,000, the gaps remained essentially the same. Looking at the opposite end of the income spectrum, 45 percent of poor black children lived in severely distressed neighborhoods in 2000, characterized by high poverty, high level of dropouts, high shares of single parent families, and high shares of young men disconnected from the workforce, compared to only 5 percent of poor white children.[50]

Just as income differences cannot explain away segregation, neither can preferences. When asked, 78 percent of blacks reported a desire to live in racially mixed communities, 14 percent to live in mostly black communities, and 4 percent in mostly non-black communities.[51] A recent study by Adelman found that, in Atlanta, Boston, Los Angeles, and Detroit, even when middle-class blacks prefer to live in integrated neighborhoods, on average they live in neighborhoods that are about 60 percent black and 30 percent white. In contrast, middle-class whites who say that they prefer to live in integrated neighborhoods reside in neighborhoods that are 10 percent black and 85 percent white.[52]

Trends in housing discrimination partially underlie both the weakening of segregation for blacks and its remaining importance. The Department of Housing and Urban Development's 2000 Housing Discrimination Study used matched pairs of testers to investigate discrimination in both the sales and rental market. In the rental market, the incidence of white-favored treatment compared to blacks declined from 26 percent in 1989 to 22 percent in 2000. In the sales market, the incidence of white-favored treatment declined from 29 percent in 1989 to 17 percent in 2000, although the geographic steering of blacks to certain neighborhoods increased.[53] With whites favored in about a fifth of cases, the enforcement of fair housing laws is still clearly important, but the general trend of lessening discrimination against blacks is encouraging. Even with this progress, however, it may take considerable time for blacks to overcome the fear and perception of being unwelcome in certain neighborhoods that has accumulated over generations.

Hispanics are less segregated residentially from whites than are blacks, but they are experiencing stubborn and even rising segregation levels as their populations increase. The overall dissimilarity index for Hispanics remained steady between 1980 and 2000 at about 58. But this aggregate trend is somewhat deceiving. Hispanic segregation is highest in those metro areas in which they constitute a larger share of the population. However, on net, Hispanics are moving into areas that contain smaller Hispanic populations and have lower existing segregation levels. By moving into these areas and settling in segregated ways, they push up segregation levels in those areas. So, in census tracts that were less than 5 percent Hispanic in 1980, the segregation index rose from 35 to 40 between 1980 and 2000.

The Mumford Center further analyzed Hispanic segregation according to self-identified race (white, black, or other) and found telling differences. Hispanic blacks are segregated from whites to virtually the same high degree as are non-Hispanic blacks. In contrast, Hispanic whites (who are disproportionately Cuban) are much less segregated from other whites and, in fact, are more integrated with non-Hispanic whites than they are with non-Hispanic blacks. Hispanics who describe their race as "other" have segregation patterns that are intermediate. When it comes to segregation, race matters, regardless of Hispanic ethnicity.[54]

Similar to the black experience, though to a lesser extent, Hispanics live in poorer neighborhoods than do whites, even after controlling for their own household incomes. This disparity increased over the 1990s. Among households with incomes over $60,000, Hispanics saw the income gap between their neighborhoods and that of similar whites increase from $8,967 to $11,544. Focusing on disparities among the poor, Hispanic children are four times as likely to live in severely distressed neighborhoods than are poor white children.

Hispanics also favor racially mixed neighborhoods, though they are more likely than blacks to prefer neighborhoods that include high shares of their own group, possibly reflecting the desire of immigrants to live among those with familiar language and customs. When asked to choose their most preferred neighborhood type, 61 percent of Hispanics chose "mostly mixed," 19 percent chose "mostly Hispanic," and 11 percent mostly non-Hispanic.[55]

In tests of housing discrimination in the rental market, there was no significant decline in adverse treatment of Hispanics over the 1990s. Whites were favored 26 percent of the time in tests versus Hispanics. However, the incidence of white-favored treatment in the home-buying market did decline significantly, from 27 percent in 1989 to 20 percent in 2000. This discrepancy in the experience of Hispanic renters and homebuyers is one that we will see repeated across a number of other measures. The experience of native-born, English speaking, whiter, home-buying Hispanics is distinctly different from that of many recent immigrants who tend to be Spanish-speaking renters.

Asian residential segregation from whites is in the moderate range (42), lower than other minority groups, and has remained relatively unchanged since 1980. To some extent, Asian segregation has followed the same general pattern as Hispanics, with the highest levels of segregation in those metros with higher Asian concentration, and slightly increasing segregation rates in those areas with small but growing Asian populations.

Unlike blacks and Hispanics, Asians on average tend to live in neighborhoods with higher incomes than whites of similar economic status. This advantage is particularly strong in the South. In the Northeast, however, this advantage disappears, and Asians live in neighborhoods with lower incomes than comparable whites.

Researchers have most often analyzed segregation between just two racial groups at a time, usually between whites and one minority group. However, as the historic black–white dichotomy becomes less relevant with the growth of more multiracial communities, new analysis and techniques have been developed to measure segregation between three or more groups. One such study using these metrics came to the intriguing conclusion that "diversity tends to have little overall effect on segregation or on the segregation of any particular group with the notable exception of African Americans. Greater diversity is associated with lower Black segregation. This result is consistent with previous findings that Black segregation tends to be lower in multiethnic areas. It is also consistent with the hypothesis that Hispanics and Asian and Pacific Islanders may serve as 'buffer' groups between initially White and Black neighborhoods, resulting in less segregation between Blacks and others. . . . Basically, having multiple minority groups may moderate the single minority vs. White majority thinking that dominated in the past."[56]

Educational Equity and Opportunity: Where the Future Is Formed

In a nation where residential location almost completely determines the school one attends, and where many public schools are primarily financed through local property taxes, the connections between residential segregation, school segregation, and school quality are tightly interwoven. Because blacks and Hispanics, even those with relatively high incomes, tend to live in areas with fewer resources than those areas inhabited by similar whites and Asians, the schools attended by black and Latino children tend to have less resources, less qualified teachers and fewer opportunities. A 2005 report by the Education Trust found that, in thirty of forty-nine states studied, high minority school districts receive less money for each child than low minority districts. Across the nation, $614 less of state and local funds is spent per pupil in districts educating the most students of color compared with those educating the fewest students of color. This gap grows to $964 less per student when taking into account the higher cost necessary to educate students in high poverty districts.[57] Further, because Federal Title I funds are allocated, in part, upon the average per pupil spending in each state, high-spending states receive more funds per poor child than low-spending states, exacerbating existing inequalities.[58]

The difficulties of providing effective, high quality education in schools where large shares of the children are dealing with the multi-faceted challenges of living in poverty are well established. Certainly, some concentrated-poverty schools have attained exceptional results, but, overall, the challenges of retaining good teachers and successfully educating a student population in which significant numbers of children are transitory, face health problems, have undereducated and often single parents, and encounter other barriers to learning are severe. In fact, low-poverty schools are twenty-two times more likely to be "high performing," as measured by consistent test score growth and performance over time than are high-poverty schools. And low-poverty, low-minority schools are eighty-nine times more likely to be consistently "high performers" than are high-poverty, high-minority schools.[59] With the economic returns to education continuing to grow, inequality in educational opportunity has strong ramifications for the rest of a student's life and for the well-being of our nation as a whole.

School Segregation

Test scores and the achievement gap between racial groups have dominated recent educational policy and discussion, as have, to some degree, the arguments around equitable and adequate funding of schools. Yet the implications of increasing racial segregation in schools have merited little attention, despite the relationship between racial and income segregation and the mounting evidence of the benefits of multiracial classrooms.

More than fifty years after the landmark *Brown vs. Board of Education* decision, which declared that "segregation is inherently unequal," the trend is toward re-segregation of black students. This development is particularly marked in the South where for three decades court decisions and civil rights laws had produced some of the most integrated schools in the nation. As described by the Civil Rights Project at Harvard University, "During the period when executive agencies and the courts actively enforced desegregation (1964–1970), the percent of black students in white schools increased more than 14-fold in six years. Over the next eighteen years, to the high point in 1988, the increase in the share of black students in majority-white schools was about 33 percent. However, after the Supreme Court's 1991 *Dowell v. Oklahoma City* decision which 'authorized a return to neighborhood schools even if it would create segregation' many desegregation efforts were abandoned. Since 1988, the share of black students in such schools fell from 44 percent to 30 percent, substantially below the level achieved by 1970."[60] As noted earlier, residential segregation between whites and blacks has actually been decreasing, so the increase in school segregation is more likely a result of changes in law which have affected school assignment plans. While some school districts had originally desegregated under court order, others developed voluntary plans, such as ones that would allow parents a choice about to send their children to school, but constrain that choice if it would intensify school segregation beyond a certain limit. In 2007, the U.S. Supreme Court, in a narrow 5–4 decision, struck down voluntary school integration plans in Seattle, Washington, and in Jefferson County, Kentucky, ruling that they were unconstitutional and not "narrowly tailored" to achieve a compelling state interest.[61] While the decision was a serious blow to desegregation efforts, the opinion of Justice Anthony Kennedy left open the possibility that race could be considered as a factor in some instances, for example in the drawing of school attendance zones with an eye toward the racial composition of residents who fall within those zones. Many school districts with voluntary desegregation plans are now looking to assess the constitutionality of their plans and considering modifications such as taking student socioeconomic characteristics and residential location into account when making assignments, either instead of or in addition to race.

TABLE 1.4   EXPOSURE TO OTHER RACES IN SCHOOLS, 2002–2003

Percent Race in Each School, %	Racial Composition of School Attended by Average					Racial Composition of All Schools
	White Student	Black Student	Latino Student	Asian Student	American Indian Student	
White	78	30	28	45	44	59
Black	9	54	12	12	7	17
Latino	8	13	54	20	11	18
Asian	3	3	5	22	2	4
Amer. Indian	1	1	1	1	36	1
Total	100	100	100	100	100	100

Source: Gary Orfield and Chungmei Lee, Why Segregation Matters: Poverty and Educational Inequality, Civil Rights Project, Harvard University, Cambridge, Mass., January 2005.

The extent to which public school students are educated separately can be illustrated by the "exposure index," which shows the racial composition of the school attended by the average member of a specified racial group. For example, an exposure index of 35 for blacks relative to whites would mean that the average black student attends a school that is 35 percent white. This statistic is most helpful when compared to the racial composition of the larger area of interest. Knowing that the average black student attends a school that is 35 percent white means one thing if the enrollment for all schools is 35 percent white and another if the enrollment for all schools is 85 percent white.

As of 2002–2003,[62] public schools were just 17 percent black, a percentage that had grown only slightly over the previous decade. However, the average black child attended a school that was 54 percent black. In contrast, while whites made up 59 percent of all students, the average black child attended a school that was just 30 percent white.

Schools were 18 percent Hispanic, up sharply from 12 percent in 1991–1992. However, the average Hispanic student attended a school that was 54 percent Hispanic and 28 percent white. Native American students are also quite segregated. While they made up only 1 percent of public school students, their schools were, on average, over a third American Indian. This segregation is partly due to enrollment of about 50,000 students in Bureau of Indian Affairs schools on reservations, but the vast majority of Indian students attend regular public schools (see Table 1.4).

Asian students are considerably less segregated from whites and attend the most racially diverse schools of any group. Still, while they made up just 4 percent of all public school students in 2002–2003 (up slightly from 3.6 percent in 1991–2002), the average Asian student attended a school that was 22 percent Asian, five times the national average.

White students are least exposed to other racial groups. Whites made up 59 percent of public schools in 2002–2003, down from 67 percent in 1991–1992, but the average white student attended a school that was 78 percent white.

Forty-one percent of white students go to schools that are 90 percent or more white. In a nation that is becoming increasingly multiracial, many whites students will have virtually no experience in working with and relating to others of differing racial backgrounds.

Private schools and public charter schools are actually more racially segregated than are public schools. The segregation of charter schools is of particular concern because they are funded by public monies. Although charters often have the authority to draw their enrollment from a wider geographic area than do other public schools and hence to enhance diversity, many of their students come from just one or two racial groups. Few have pursued outreach strategies that would make classroom diversity one of the benefits of choice.

One of the misconceptions about integration is that it is demeaning to minorities because it implies that just sitting next to whites in schools will improve minority education. While there is increasing evidence that being educated in multiracial schools has benefits for all students, the clearest harm of segregation is its link with poverty. According to the Civil Rights Project, "Concentrated poverty turns out to be powerfully related to both school opportunities and achievement levels. Children in these schools tend to be less healthy, to have weaker preschool experiences, to have only one parent, to move frequently and have unstable educational experiences, to attend classes taught by less experienced or unqualified teachers, to have friends and classmates with lower levels of achievement, to be in schools with fewer demanding pre-collegiate courses and more remedial courses, and to have higher teacher turnover. Many of these schools are also deteriorated and lack key resources. The strong correlation between race and poverty show that a great many black and Latino students attend these schools of concentrated poverty.

Blacks and Latinos attend public schools that have about twice the share of poor students as those schools attended by average whites and Asians. In 2002–2003, the average white student attended a school in which 23 percent of the students were poor (defined as being eligible for free or reduced lunch), and the average Asian student attended a school that was 27 percent poor. In sharp contrast, the average black and Latino student attended schools where half of the students (49 percent and 48 percent) were poor. Viewed another way, while blacks and Latinos together made up 35 percent of the public student population, they made up 63 percent of students attending high-poverty schools (those 50–100 percent poor) and 80 percent of extreme poverty schools (those 90–100 percent poor).[63]

Another important dimension of segregation is between English language speakers and English language learners, particularly Latinos. In 2000–2001, when public schools were 16 percent Latino, the average English language learner attended a school that was 61 percent Latino.[64] Concentrating students with limited English ability, who often live in homes where Spanish is spoken at home, in schools which are segregated by race, language, and most likely poverty, cannot be the best learning environment and the one most likely to improve their English skills.

Within-School Segregation

While segregation *between* schools has received relatively little attention in recent years, segregation *within* schools, which is harder to measure, has received even less. This form of segregation takes place in a number of ways, primarily through the practice of tracking, but also through the disproportionate number of minority students who are identified as having a disability and educated in separate and more restrictive environments.

According to educational researcher Roslyn Arlin Mickelson, "Blacks, Latinos, and Native Americans disproportionately are found in lower tracks where curricula and instructional practices are weaker. Not only are blacks and other ethnic minorities (other than Asians) more likely than whites to be assigned to lower tracks, but research indicates that blacks and whites with similar ability learn in different tracks, especially in racially desegregated school systems or systems where blacks are a numerical minority. The relative absence of black students in higher-level courses and their disproportionate enrollment in lower-level ones is an underemphasized component of the race gap in achievement."[65] The lack of black students in advanced placement (AP) classes is particularly acute. Despite tripling in number over the last decade, the share of blacks in AP classes is just 5.5 percent, a third of their percentage of all high school students.[66] In many states, high-minority schools offer far fewer AP classes than do predominantly white schools. Because AP classes contribute more weight to grade point average and are factored more heavily in college admissions processes, the lack of opportunity to take AP disadvantages minority students. And, because AP credit can count toward college work, it can reduce the costs of college as well.

Moreover, according to the Civil Rights Project,

> Minority students, specifically black and Native American students, are significantly more likely than white students to be identified as having a disability. For example, in most states, African American children are identified at one and a half to four times the rate of white children in the disability categories of mental retardation and emotional disturbance. In the national data, Latino and Asian American children are under identified in cognitive disability categories compared to whites, raising questions about whether the special education needs of these children are being met. However, school and district data showing instances of Latino overrepresentation suggest that there are both over and under representation concerns for these minority groups.

Once identified, minority students are more frequently removed from the general education program and educated in a more restrictive environment. For instance, African American and Latino students are about twice as likely as white students to be educated in a restrictive, substantially separate educational setting. Given that students with special needs benefit most when they are educated in the least restrictive environment to the maximum extent appropriate, the data on educational settings raise serious questions about the quality of special education provided to Latino, black, and other minority students compared to whites.[67]

The Achievement Gap: Beyond the Numbers

The implementation of the No Child Left Behind Act (2002) has thrown a spotlight on the racial achievement gap by making schools accountable for the educational progress of individual racial and ethnic groups. These gaps are most commonly measured by test scores that are used to determine whether schools are making "adequate yearly progress," with the ultimate goal that all children should rank as "proficient" in math and reading by 2014. However, each state can choose which test it will use to measure progress, and these can differ markedly between states. Thus, overall progress in student achievement is better measured with the National Assessment of Educational Progress (NAEP), commonly known as the Nation's Report Card. The discussion below particularly focuses on the NAEP Long Term Trend assessments that measure reading and math proficiency for nine- and seventeen-year-olds.[68]

Over the long term, the reading scores of black children have increased significantly and the gaps with whites have narrowed. However, most of this progress occurred in the 1970s and 1980s. Younger black children have once again made progress in quite recent years. For nine-year-olds, the gap in reading closed from 44 points in 1971 to 32 points in 1980 and then from 35 points in 1999 to 26 points in 2004. In math there has been steadier progress, with the gap narrowing from 35 points in 1973 to 23 points in 2004.

Among young Hispanic students there were similarly impressive results. In both reading and math, scores for nine-year-olds rose to their highest levels in 2004 and gaps with whites closed to their lowest levels on record. Hispanic scores average five to six points higher than blacks in both reading and math.

Recent progress has been much less encouraging for older students, however. For seventeen-year-old black students, the reading gap with whites narrowed dramatically from 53 points in 1971 to 20 points in 1988 before growing again to 29 points in 2004. For math scores, there was a significant narrowing of the gap from forty points in 1973 to twenty-one in 1990, before widening to thirty-one in 1999 and closing slightly to twenty-eight by 2004. Older Hispanic students also saw declining scores and increasing gaps with whites in both math and reading between 1999 and 2004.

The Long Term Trend assessments of the NAEP do not report data for Asians and American Indians.[69] Instead, a comparison of recent years from the regular NAEP standard assessment gives some idea of how these groups perform. This assessment measures students in grades 4 and 8 instead of at ages nine and seventeen. Asians in both grades have seen increasing scores in reading and now equal the scores of whites. Asian scores have also increased in math and exceed whites' scores by six points. American Indian scores in both reading and math are essentially the same as Hispanics' and lead blacks by a few points, yet they trail white scores by twenty to thirty points.

Rising educational attainment is to be celebrated, yet the high stakes of high stakes testing are raising concerns that students who do not score well on achievement tests will be more likely to drop out of school or be pushed out and not graduate with their class. Because of the substantial consequences to a school if it does not make adequate yearly progress among all its subgroups, those students more likely to fail the required tests may be held back a grade. Grade retention is one of the chief determinants of dropping out. Other critics suspect that some students who may not score well are essentially pushed out, by administratively moving them out of regular classrooms to GED or similar programs (or strongly encouraging them to move) or through over-enforcement of disciplinary measures.[70]

Already there are large discrepancies in the percentages of students of different races who graduate from high school on time with their class. Researchers from the Urban Institute have estimated that, nationally, based on sizes of classes in successive school years, only half of black students who enter ninth grade will graduate with a regular diploma in twelfth grade four years later, compared to 75 percent of white students. In New York and Wisconsin, the "graduating on time" gap between white and black students is 40 percentage points. This dynamic is even stronger for males. Only about 43 percent of black males graduate on time with a regular diploma. Similarly, just 53 percent of Hispanics received their diploma four years later, and only 48 percent of Hispanic males.[71]

Dropping out has strong negative implications for employment and lifetime earnings and is also connected with crime and imprisonment, especially for black men. Among African American men born between 1965 and 1969, 22 percent had prison records by 1999, compared to 3 percent of white men. But among high school dropouts, over half of African American men born in that age cohort had a prison record by 1999, compared with 13 percent of white male dropouts. Black men in this cohort were twice as likely to have been in prison by age thirty-four (22 percent) as they were to have attained a bachelors' degree (13 percent). In contrast, the share of white men having been incarcerated (3 percent) was a just a tenth of the share with a bachelor's degree.[72]

Attitudes about Education and Iintegration:
Different Race; Different View

Given the separation of blacks and whites in neighborhoods and schools and the very few whites who attend high-minority schools, it is not surprising that blacks and whites hold profoundly different views about the state of educational opportunity. While almost two thirds of whites believe that there are equal educational opportunities for white and black children in the United States, only about a third of blacks believe this.[73]

In a truly shocking statistic, the share of blacks saying that black children have as good a chance as white children to get a good education declined to just half in 2003, below its previous low point in 1962 (53 percent) and well below its high point of 64 percent in 1995.[74]

Blacks and whites also differ in their beliefs about the most important ways to increase educational opportunities for black children. Whites ranked "more family responsibility" first (11 percent), followed by "have the same standards/ equal opportunity (10 percent). Blacks rated as first "have the same standards/ equal opportunity" (12 percent), tied with "better teachers (12 percent). "More family responsibility" ranked only in fifth place, with 5 percent of blacks saying it would be the most important way to increase opportunity.[75]

Ironically, as segregation increases, a majority of the population continues to state that racially integrated schools are "better for kids." Sixty percent of whites, 54 percent of blacks, and 44 of Hispanics say integrated schools are "better for kids" while less than 10 percent of each group says integration is "worse for kids." Among Hispanics, the native-born more commonly believe in integration's merits. Fifty-one percent of native-born Hispanics believe integration is better for kids, compared to 38 percent of foreign-born Hispanics.[76]

Higher Education: No Longer a Luxury

Obtaining a high school diploma is only the first necessary step in an economy that increasingly rewards higher education. In 1999, full-time workers with a bachelor's degree made 1.8 times the income of those with only a high school diploma, up from 1.5 times in 1975. Over an entire work life, the additional income of having a bachelor's degree rather than a diploma would total almost $1 million. The additional earning power of having an advanced degree has increased even more.[77]

Consistent with their population growth, minorities have also increased their share of college enrollment. Over the 1991–2001 period, the number of whites enrolled actually declined by 5 percent. Over the same period, Hispanic enrollment grew by 75 percent, Asian by 54 percent, African American by 37 percent, and Indian by 35 percent.[78] However it is important to look beyond the number enrolled, which is partially driven just by the changing racial composition of the young adult population, to examine the share of each racial group that is attending college.

Among high school graduates age eighteen to twenty-four, both whites and blacks increased their college participation rates over the 1990s before stagnating after 1999. Blacks, particularly black women, made some progress in closing the gap with whites over the 1990–2002 period, as their college participation rates rose from 33 percent to 40 percent. By 2000–2002, the black participation rate was 5.6 percentage points below whites versus an 8.4 percentage point gap in the early 1990s. However, participation rates for black males have not consistently risen above their 1990 level. The Hispanic picture is much less sanguine, with the college participation rate remaining unchanged over the past decade and the large gap with whites growing. Once again, females did better than males. By 2000–2002, the college participation gap with whites was 11.5 percentage points, an increase over the 7.5 percentage point gap seen in 1990–2002.[79]

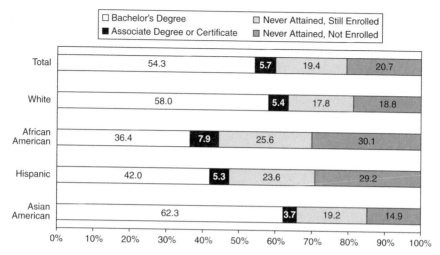

FIGURE 1.5   Degree attainment rates among degree-seeking postsecondary students who enrolled in 1995–1996, after five years, by race/ethnicity. (*Sources:* American Council on Education, "Twenty-first Annual Status Report on Minorities in Higher Education," February 2005. Original data are from U.S. Department of Education, National Center for Health Statistics, Beginning Postsecondary Students Longitudinal Study.)

Just as entering college is the next step through the educational pipeline beyond a high school diploma, remaining in college and obtaining a degree is the necessary further step beyond enrollment. Among white students who enrolled in college in 1995–1996, 58 percent had obtained a bachelors degree after 5 years (up from 52 percent of those first enrolled in 1989–1990). Nineteen percent of whites had not attained their degree and were no longer enrolled five years later, down from 25 percent during the earlier period (see Figure 1.5).[80]

Unfortunately college persistence rates for blacks and Hispanics are much more sobering. Five years after enrolling, just 36 percent of blacks had obtained a bachelor's degree (down from 42 percent of those who first enrolled in 1989–1990). Thirty percent of blacks had not attained their degree and were no longer enrolled five years later, up from 27 percent during the earlier period. After five years, 43 percent of Hispanics had obtained a bachelor's degree (down from 44 percent of those first enrolled in 1989–1990). Twenty-nine percent of Hispanics had not attained their degree and were no longer enrolled five years later, virtually unchanged from the earlier period.[81]

Asians had the best persistence rates, which remained fairly unchanged over the study period. After five years, 62 percent of Asians had obtained a bachelor's degree, while 15 percent had not attained their degree and were no longer enrolled.[82]

One reason behind the declining persistence rates for blacks and Hispanics is the skyrocketing costs of education. The costs of attending a private college rose to an average of $29,026 per year in 2005, $12,127 for four-year public universities. The average debt for graduating seniors who borrow funds for college is just under $20,000.[83] Meanwhile, grants, which are most beneficial to low-income students, have declined as a share of federal financial aid as loans have increased. Tax credits and deductions, that tend to disproportionately benefit those in higher tax brackets, are also of growing importance. Pell grants, a major source of assistance to low income students, have changed little over time in terms of average inflation-adjusted amount per recipient, even as college costs have well outpaced inflation.

The shift by certain states toward merit-based, as opposed to needs-based, scholarships disproportionately helps higher income Asians and whites. Examining programs in Florida and Michigan, education researchers Heller and Marin found that, in 1998, the Florida Bright Futures scholarship rate was 43 percent for Asian/Pacific Islanders and 35 percent for whites. In contrast, the scholarship rate for African Americans was less than 9 percent and for Hispanics was about 18 percent. The Michigan Education Assessment Program scholarship rate was 52 percent for Asian/Pacific Islanders and 34 percent for whites, compared with less than 8 percent for African Americans and 25 percent for Hispanics.[84]

Looking more broadly, the Lumina Foundation found that between 1995 and 2000, scholarship aid to families making $40,000 or less increased by 22 percent, while aid to families with income over $100,000 grew by 125 percent.[85] Because black and Latino scholars are more likely to be low income, these disparities most negatively impact them. Financial considerations affect not only whether a student can attend and stay in college, but also the types of institutions they attend. In 2002, for example, 51 percent of Hispanics attended community colleges versus 41 percent of whites, at least in part because of lower cost and the ability to live at home.[86]

Two landmark Supreme Court decisions in 2003 established guidelines for affirmative action in college admissions. The court found that diversity was a "compelling governmental interest" and that colleges could consider race and ethnicity in admissions to some extent. In *Grutter v. Bollinger*, it found that the admissions policy of the University of Michigan Law School was lawfully designed to achieve the compelling interest of diversity. But in *Gratz v. Bollinger*, it found that the university's undergraduate admissions policy was not "narrowly tailored" enough to be lawful.[87]

The majority opinion in *Grutter* found that diversity in higher education has "substantial" benefits, citing evidence from the university and *amici curiae* (including from military and business representatives) that showed that diversity breaks down stereotypes, invigorates classroom discussion, and helps prepare students to work in a diverse economy. Justice Sandra Day O'Connor emphasized that although a person's race does not predict his or her viewpoint, it is "likely to affect an individual's views." Keeping higher education opportunity open to all races, she wrote, enables "effective participation by members of all racial and

TABLE 1.5   IF TWO EQUALLY QUALIFIED STUDENTS WERE ACCEPTED
TO COLLEGE, WHO WOULD BE ADMITTED?

	White Student, %	Black Student, %	Same Chance, %
Response by:			
Non-Hispanic White	21	24	50
Black	64	4	29
Hispanic	46	9	41

Source: Gallup Organization, poll, June 6–25, 2005. The historical poll results on race relations
were accessed online through Gallup Brain (http://institution.gallup.com) on November 12, 2005.

ethnic groups in the civic life of our Nation" and permits universities to "cultivate
a set of leaders with legitimacy in the eyes of the citizenry."[88]

Selective universities that have used affirmative action in the past are now
trying to hone their admissions processes to consider race but not run afoul of
the prohibitions against mechanistic use as condemned in *Gratz*.

Recent research by Princeton University researchers has found that eliminating affirmative action in elite universities and ignoring race would result in a
sharp decline in black admissions with little gains for whites. Without affirmative
action they found that the "acceptance rate for African American candidates
would fall nearly two-thirds, from 33.7% to 12.2%." The long-term impact may
even be worse if admitting such small numbers of blacks reduced applications
and yield for minority applicants in future years. The acceptance rate for whites
would rise only by only .5 percentage points. Asian students would fill four out
of five places not taken by African Americans and Hispanics, with the Asian
acceptance rate rising from 18 percent to more than 23 percent.[89]

As discussed earlier, blacks and whites have distinctly differing views on
whether equal educational opportunities exist for black and white children in
the United States. They differ similarly in their opinions about equal opportunity in college admissions. When asked, "If 2 equally qualified students were
accepted to college, who would be admitted?" only one in five whites said the
white student would be admitted, while over three in five blacks said that
the white student would be admitted. A quarter of whites said that the black
student would be admitted; less than one in twenty blacks agreed. Half of whites
said the students would have the same chance of admission, versus about three
in ten blacks. Hispanic responses fell halfway between the black and white opinions (see Table 1.5).[90]

From Civil Rights to Economic Advancement

For many civil rights leaders, the struggle for legal rights during the 1960s has
long since evolved into a struggle for economic opportunity, equity, and advancement. Educational differences are partly responsible for the lower economic

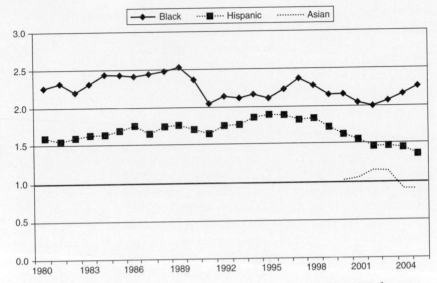

FIGURE 1.6 Ratio of minority unemployment rates to white rate, 1980–2005, for population sixteen years and over ethnicity. (*Source:* U.S. Department of Labor, Bureau of Labor Statistics, Current Population Survey, multiple years, data extracted January 13, 2006.)

status of blacks and Latinos and the relatively higher status of Asians. This status is reflected in unemployment levels, types of occupation, earnings, and household incomes.

Employment and Occupation

Obtaining and holding a job is the first rung on the economic ladder and the centerpiece of the 1996 Welfare Reform Act that provided strong incentives to transition from welfare to work. Welfare reform and the very strong economic growth of the 1990s led to substantial employment gains for all groups. Unemployment rates for blacks now hover around ten percent, just half the rate experienced in the early 1980s. The gap between black and white unemployment rates has also declined from the very high levels of the 1980s and early 1990s, when black unemployment was almost two and a half times that of whites. Yet, looking over the last four decades, despite various fluctuations, essentially no lasting progress has been made in reducing the unemployment gap. Blacks continue to be unemployed at over twice the rates of whites (see Figure 1.6).[91]

Disconnection from the workforce especially plagues young black men who are even less connected to jobs than were young blacks thirty years ago. Andrew Sum of Northeastern University found that the employment rate for blacks age twenty to twenty-four over the 2000–2003 period averaged just 57 percent, down from 80 percent in the late 1960s. He further found that a full quarter of African American men aged twenty to sixty-four were not employed at any time during the year during 2002, a rate twice as high as whites and Hispanic males.[92]

The unemployment situation for blacks and particularly for males after the 2001 recession is particularly worrisome. Generally, entering a recession, black unemployment worsens to a greater extent than does white unemployment, but it improves to a greater extent coming out. However, an examination of changes in unemployment during the 13 months of recovery after both the 1990s and 2001 recessions by the Economic Policy Institute found a startling difference. During the early part of the 1990s recovery, the unemployment rate for blacks fell by .6 points. But during the first thirteen months span of the most recent recovery, black unemployment *increased* by .8 points—for black men by 1.4 points, and for black women by .3 points.[93] This worsening of black unemployment during an economic recovery suggests an ominous break from the past and the need for further exploration into its causes.

High black unemployment is partially due to the spatial mismatch between the segregated, urban, and inner suburban neighborhoods where many blacks live and the location of job growth in the outer suburbs. Metropolitan areas with the highest levels of residential segregation also have the highest level of black job mismatch. In 2000, blacks were still the most physically isolated group from jobs, but over the 1990s this mismatch fell by 13 percent. Most of this improvement was due to the movement of blacks into communities closer to jobs rather than the creation of new jobs in or near established black communities.[94]

In 2005, Mexican President Vicente Fox ignited a firestorm by commenting that Mexican immigrants to the United States take jobs "that not even blacks want to do."[95] The extent to which immigrant labor takes jobs from other workers, especially minority workers, and depresses wages is still not clear. But it is clear that job opportunities are a prime draw of Latinos to the U.S. Latinos now make up 13 percent of the nation's labor force and are expected to make up half of the growth through 2020.[96] While Latino unemployment rates exceed those of whites (7 percent versus 4.8 percent in 2004), there exists quite a bit of subgroup variability. In 2004 the unemployment rate was 8.3 percent for Mexicans, and just 4 percent for Cubans.[97] Further, foreign-born Hispanics have lower unemployment rates than do native-born Hispanics (6 percent versus 8 percent).[98]

Unemployment is rare among Asians and even lower than white unemployment. In 2004, over nineteen of twenty Asians in the labor force were employed, with little difference between Asian women and men.

Occupation is often the mediating link between education and earnings. For example, the median earnings of full-time cashiers in 1999, just 7.6 percent of who were college graduates, was $17,048.[99] In contrast, the median earnings of full-time computer software engineers, 76.6 percent of who were college graduates, was $64,031. While a full discussion of the occupational differences between racial groups is beyond the scope of this paper, we will highlight some of the stark contrasts.

Both black men and women are considerably under-represented in management and professional jobs, which tend to be among the highest paying, though black women fare somewhat significantly better than black men (see Table 1.6).[100]

TABLE 1.6 OCCUPATION BY RACE/ETHNICITY, 2000 (percent in each occupational category)

	Non-Hispanic				Asian							Hispanic			
	Total	White	Black	American Indian	Total	Indian	Chinese	Filipino	Japanese	Korean	Vietnamese	Total	Mexican	Puerto Rican	Cuban
Male:															
Management, professional, and related	31.4	34.7	20.0	20.9	47.1	63.5	55.1	34.2	54.2	43.5	28.8	14.6	11.5	19.9	29.4
Service	12.1	10.1	19.4	16.6	12.4	5.5	14.9	16.6	11.0	9.7	14.9	19.0	19.4	19.7	13.1
Sales and office	17.9	18.2	18.3	13.7	19.0	17.6	15.8	23.6	18.6	26.5	14.9	14.8	12.8	20.0	21.0
Farming, fishing, and forestry	1.1	.8	.6	1.9	.4	.2	.1	.6	.6	.2	.8	3.6	5.1	.6	.5
Construction, extraction, and maintenance	17.1	17.3	13.3	23.9	6.4	3.1	4.6	8.8	7.8	7.4	10.0	21.9	23.9	15.0	16.8
Production, transportation, and material moving	20.5	19.0	28.4	23.0	14.8	10.1	9.4	16.2	7.8	12.8	30.6	26.1	27.5	24.7	19.1
	100.0	100.0	100.0	100.0	100.0	100.0	100.0	100.0	100.0	100.0	100.0	100.0	100.0	100.0	100.0
Female:															
Management, professional, and related	36.2	38.7	29.7	30.0	41.7	53.7	49.0	41.3	46.8	34.1	24.8	22.9	20.5	28.8	34.5
Service	18.0	16.1	24.2	24.0	16.1	9.5	12.7	18.2	12.8	19.8	24.5	25.6	26.1	19.9	16.2
Sales and office	36.7	37.7	34.8	35.2	29.6	28.1	26.3	31.8	35.8	33.8	23.0	34.8	34.0	40.1	39.7
Farming, fishing, and forestry	.3	.2	.1	.4	.2	.2	.1	.4	.3	.2	.2	1.4	2.3	.2	.2
Construction, extraction, and maintenance	.7	.7	.8	1.4	.5	.3	.4	.4	.4	.5	.9	.9	.9	.7	.7
Production, transportation, and material moving	8.0	6.6	10.4	9.1	11.9	8.1	11.5	7.8	3.9	11.6	26.6	14.3	16.2	10.3	8.8
	100.0	100.0	100.0	100.0	100.0	100.0	100.0	100.0	100.0	100.0	100.0	100.0	100.0	100.0	100.0

Source: Author's tabulations of the U.S. Bureau of the Census, 2000 Decennial Census, Summary File 4.

Conversely, blacks are over-represented in lower-paying service jobs and black men in transportation and material-moving occupations.

Hispanics are even less represented in management and professional jobs than are blacks, though once again, women fare better than men. The share of Hispanics in management and professional jobs actually decreased over the 1990s, leading to an increasing separation from whites by industry. Most recently arrived Hispanic cohorts have lower occupational status than previously arrived cohorts, even among those with the same levels of education and experience. Within Hispanic subgroups as well, there is considerable variation, with Cubans in management/professional jobs at about the national average rate, and Mexicans, especially Mexican men, the most under-represented. Hispanic men are more commonly found in service occupations, particularly building and grounds cleaning, food preparation and serving.[101] They are also over-represented in construction and production jobs, and in farming/fishing/forestry in which they are five times as likely to be employed than the average U.S. worker. Hispanic women are over-represented in the service sector, agriculture, and in production. Mexican women work in production occupations at twice the national average.

Strong housing markets until quite recently, increasing opportunities in hotel work, and mechanization of farm work have all led to a shift in the industries in which Mexican immigrants work.[102] Newer immigrants are twice as likely to work in the construction and hospitality industries and half as likely to work in agriculture than those who immigrated fifteen or more years ago.

Consistent with their advanced education, Asians have the highest shares of managers and professionals, especially among men. Forty-seven percent of Asian men hold these positions, a rate 50 percent above the national level. Among Asian subgroups, Indians are managers or professionals at twice the national average. Eleven percent of Asian men and 22 percent of Indian men are in the computer and mathematical occupations, compared to 3 percent of all men. For most groups, except for Japanese, Asians are over-represented in the professional specialties as opposed to in management. While there is considerable variation in occupation, even the Vietnamese, who hold management and professional jobs least commonly among major Asian subgroups, were represented in these occupations at just under the national level (29 percent of Vietnamese versus 31 percent of all workers).

Asian women and Vietnamese men are also over-represented in production jobs. In contrast, Asians are less commonly found in the service sector (except for Filipinos and Vietnamese), in construction, and, for women, in sales and office occupations.

Much of the research on segregation in the workplace has focused on whether blacks and whites work in the same occupations. Only recently have there been studies examining whether different races labor in the same physical workplaces. Tomaskovic-Devey and others found that a fairly substantial improvement in workplace integration occurred after the Civil Rights Act of 1964, though it varied by sector, but that the progress stalled after 1980. Moreover, progress in Latino integration in the workplace "is weak and not strongly tied to the temporal pattern of civil rights legislation." Last, they found that racial desegregation is more pronounced when the federal government aggressively advocates equal employment opportunity laws, a priority not in strong evidence under recent administrations.[103]

One of the most integrated sectors of society, both in terms of the workplace and residential settings, is the military. As we approach the sixtieth anniversary of President Harry Truman's executive order that called for "equality of treatment for all persons in the armed services, without regard to race, color, religion or national origin," it is instructive to examine the status of minorities in the armed services and the factors leading to greater integration in that sector.[104]

The black share of military personnel skyrocketed after the end of the Vietnam War, particularly in the Army, where black participation is greatest, as blacks "perceived the military to be a more racially fair employer than the civilian labor force." However, since the late 1980s, the black share of the Army and Marines has declined and the Air Force has shown slight increases. Only in the Navy has the share continued to steadily climb. Still, as of 2002, blacks were very over-represented in the military, making up one out of five enlisted males and one out of three enlisted females, compared to approximately one in eight civilians aged 18 to 44. Within the services, blacks are more likely than other racial groups to be in functional support and administrative specialties. "Blacks are underrepresented in officer ranks compared to their share of enlisted personnel, but their share has increased to 9 percent in 2002—similar to share of civilian college graduates."[105]

Hispanics are underrepresented in the military compared to their proportion of the younger civilian population, but unlike blacks, their shares are increasing quickly, particularly in the Marines where they made up just 5 percent of the corps in 1985 but almost 15 percent in 2002. Like blacks, Hispanics are underrepresented among officers, but unlike blacks, they are more concentrated in combat specialties rather than administrative or supply occupations.

Because of the importance of integration in the military and the need for leaders who can work well in a multiracial setting, an *amicus* brief in the *Grutter v. Bollinger* University of Michigan admissions case was filed by twenty-nine former high-ranking officers and civilian leaders of the military.[106] The court quoted that brief in noting that "the military cannot achieve an officer corps that is *both* highly qualified *and* racially diverse unless the service academies and the ROTC used limited race-conscious recruiting and admissions policies."

In describing the causes behind the success of racial integration in the military, Moskos and Butler, two academicians who study military manpower issues, conclude:

- Racial discrimination cannot be tolerated within the leadership of any organization. . . . In the Army, racist behavior ends a soldier's career.

- Focus on black opportunity, not on prohibiting racist expression. . . . It would be foolhardy to consider absence of white racists as a precondition for black achievement.
- Install qualified black leaders as soon as possible. The quickest way to dispel stereotypes of black incapacity is to bring white people into contact with highly qualified African-American leaders.[107]

The military not only creates an integrated workplace but also contributes to some of the most diverse and integrated residential communities in the nation. The metropolitan areas of Lawton, Oklahoma; Jacksonville and Fayetteville, North Carolina; Colorado Springs, Colorado; and Killeen-Temple, Texas, top the list of the most racially diverse and integrated metros in the nation and all contain or border a military base.[108]

Discrimination and Affirmative Action

Education, experience, demographics, preferences, and spatial mismatch all contribute to differences in employment by race and ethnicity. Yet the perception remains, especially among blacks, that there are more insidious forces at work. When asked whether there are equal job opportunities for minorities in the United States, 59 percent of non-Hispanic whites agreed, compared to just 23 percent of blacks and 45 percent of Hispanics.[109]

The disparities persist when asked about affirmative action. Forty-four percent of whites favor affirmative action, compared to 72 percent of blacks and 62 percent of Hispanics. These results mirror the very different perceptions between racial groups about what affirmative action does. Sixty-five percent of blacks and 63 percent of Hispanics said that it "ensured access" while just 24 percent of blacks and 29 percent of Hispanics said that it gave "special preferences." In strong contrast, the majority of whites (54 percent) said that affirmative action gave special preferences, while just over a third (35 percent) said it ensures access.[110]

From Jobs to Money: Earnings and Income

As relatively low-skilled Hispanics continue to enter the workforce and education becomes even more important in determining wages, the earnings gap between Hispanics and whites has widened. By 2004, Hispanic female full-time workers made 72 percent of the earnings of white women, down from 85 percent in 1979. For men, the Hispanic ratio fell from 74 percent of white earnings to 66 percent. Earnings of black women fell from 92 percent of white women's in 1979 to 87 percent in 2004, while black men's ratio was relatively unchanged at 78 percent.[111]

Economist James P. Smith has endeavored to explain the wage gap between white, Hispanic and black men. He found that, after controlling for a small set of variables—schooling, age, English language ability, the wage gap for Hispanic men becomes small. Schooling and age may be enough to close the wage gap for Hispanics males. These factors are important for blacks as well, though the key educational determinant has shifted from high school graduation to college education. Nevertheless, for blacks much more so than Hispanics, even accounting for education and years on the job experience does not eliminate the earnings gap with white males.[112]

Long-term data on Asian wage trends are not available. However, consistent with their overall higher education and occupational status, Asian earnings currently exceed earnings of whites for both males and females. In 2004, full-time Asian women workers earned 5 percent more than whites and men 10 percent more.[113]

The high concentrations of blacks and especially Hispanics in low-skilled jobs and Asians and whites in higher-skilled jobs mean that the increasing structural divergence in the economy toward more greatly rewarding education and skills will have a disparate negative impact on Hispanics and blacks. Education and skills enhancement are necessary if blacks and Hispanics are going to move up the economic ladder.

Earnings data, while useful in measuring outcomes in the workplace and returns to education, are not as helpful in assessing a household's ability to buy a car, put a child through college, or provide financially for a family's everyday needs. Each of these purchases is most commonly done based on household income, in which the earnings of several household members may be combined, rather than just on an individual's earnings. Thus, in measuring the aggregate purchasing power and economic well being of a household, it is useful to examine the number of earners per household and the aggregate household income. With more workers per household, even workers with relatively low individual earnings can combine to increase overall household income. For largely this reason, Hispanics, despite having lower earnings than blacks, have higher household incomes. And Asians boost their household incomes even higher than individual earnings would suggest.

Asians and Hispanics have fairly similar earners-per-household profiles, with Hispanics having a slightly lower share of households with no earners at all (see Figure 1.7).[114] For each group, almost half of households have two or more earners. The share of Asians and Hispanics having no earners is much lower than for white and black households. Forty-three percent of whites have two or more earners per household, although over one in five has no earners at all, a phenomena partially attributable to the older age structure of the white population. Black households also have over a fifth of households with no earners but a much smaller share of two or more earner households. Only a third of black households contain two or more earners.

Average earnings combine with the number of earners per household to determine household income, magnifying inequality for blacks and modifying it for Hispanics. As of 2003–2004, Asians had the highest median household income, followed by whites, Hispanics, American Indians and then blacks (see

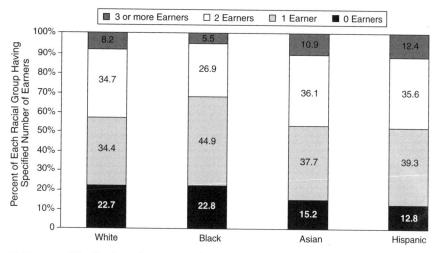

FIGURE 1.7   Distribution of earners per household by race, 2003. (*Source:* U.S. Bureau of the Census, "Historical Income Tables: Households, Table H-12: Household by Number of Earners by Median and Mean Income," last online revision, February 11, 2005.)

Table 1.7).[115] But medians and averages do not tell the complete story; it is necessary to look at other points along the income distribution. Focusing first on the bottom, poverty rates for blacks and Hispanics are about three times that of non-Hispanic whites. Nevertheless, each group saw dramatic improvement during the 1990s and reached their lowest poverty rates on record. Since, 2000 however, Hispanic poverty has moved up slightly, but black rates have climbed more significantly. Asians, despite considerably higher median incomes than whites, have historically also had higher poverty rates. They, too, experienced considerable progress over the 1990s and now have almost closed the gap with whites. Not surprisingly, variations exist among Asian subgroups. As of 1999, poverty rates ranged from 6 percent for Filipinos to 29 percent for Cambodians, many of whom entered the United States as refugees (see Table 1.2). American Indians experience very high poverty rates as well, essentially the same as blacks.

TABLE 1.7   HOUSEHOLD INCOME AND POVERTY, 2003–2004 (two-year average)

	Median Household Income	Poverty Rate, %
All Races	44,436	12.6
Non-Hispanic White	49,019	8.4
Black	30,288	24.6
American Indian	32,510	24.4
Asian	57,357	10.8
Hispanic	34,062	22.2

Source: U.S. Bureau of the Census, *Income, Poverty and Health Insurance Coverage in the United States: 2004*, P60-229, issued August 2005.

Over the long term, the black middle class has grown substantially. "The portion of black households making $75,000 to $99,999, for example, increased nearly fourfold between 1967 and 2003, rising to 7 percent of the black population. The portion of white households in that income range merely doubled, to 11.5 percent."[116] Yet many policy analysts and others are concerned that this progress is not intergenerational, not deeply rooted in assets, and therefore precarious.

Wealth: The Foundation of Prosperity

Over the last decade, much of the discussion about racial economic inequality has turned toward a discussion of differences in wealth, rather than income, and asset-based assistance plans such as individual development accounts have burgeoned. Wealth holdings provide a safety net in times of financial difficulty and also can provide capital to finance further education, start a business, make investments, improve one's home, or pass along to future generations. Wealth is distributed even more unequally among the races than is income.

As Tom Shapiro, one of the foremost researchers on wealth and race, writes about the gap between whites and blacks, "The racial wealth gap in 1988 was $60,980, meaning that the net worth of white households on average was this much larger than for African-Americans. By 2002 it had increased to $82,663. Isolating the period and dynamics of the past decade a little more closely, the racial wealth gap grew by $14,316 between 1996 and 2002. In the past decade, then, white wealth grew and then leveled off; black wealth grew and then declined. As a result, the overall racial wealth gap ratio persists at roughly a dime on the dollar, while the dollar amount of the racial wealth gap grew."[117]

Shapiro also uses the concept of the Asset Poverty Line to compare wealth among racial groups. "The fundamental idea is to determine an amount of assets a family needs to meet its basic needs over a specified period, under the extreme condition that no other sources of income are available. We decided to tie this figure to the official income-poverty standard. In 1999 the official U.S. government poverty line for a family of four stood at $1,392 a month. In order to live at that poverty line for three months, a family of four needs a private safety net of at least $4,175. Families with less than $4,175 in net financial assets in 1999, then, are 'asset-poor.'"[118]

Over half of black American families fell below the Asset Poverty Line in 1999. This represents a positive trend for black families, as it was 67 percent in 1984 and has declined steadily over fifteen years. This downward trend is encouraging, although an asset poverty rate of 54 percent is shamefully high and more than twice the rate of white families. In 1984 one in four white families fell below the Asset Poverty Line; this rate remained steady in 1989, rose in 1994 to 33 percent, and then fell back to 25 percent in 1999.[119]

Hispanics have somewhat higher levels of wealth than blacks but still less than a tenth that of whites.[120] Yet Hispanics face their own challenges. First, because many are young, relatively new entrants into the U.S. job market and work in certain types of industries, they are much less likely to have pensions of any kind.

Among men, only 28 percent of Hispanics, versus 44 percent of blacks and 52 percent of whites, had any kind of pension coverage as of 2000.[121] The ability of many Hispanic (and other immigrants) to accumulate wealth in the United States is also affected by remittances of monies back to their families in their countries of origin. The Inter American Development Bank estimates that $40 billion was remitted from people in the United States to Latin America and the Caribbean in 2005.[122] Many Hispanics also tend to operate outside the mainstream banking system. The Federal Deposit Insurance Corporation estimates that almost half haven't opened a basic account.[123] For a variety of reasons including convenience, comfort, lack of knowledge or occasionally price, many use systems of check cashing agencies, payday loans and other nontraditional financial services which can entail much larger fees than mainstream services and thus reduce savings.

Current inequalities in wealth by race have immense implications for future generations. While the amount of money that will pass between generations over the next half century or so is the matter of some debate (Boston College researchers estimate a conservative $25 trillion will pass to all heirs from the estates of those age eighteen and over as of 1998[124]), it is clear that whites will receive the vast majority of inheritances, thereby exacerbating existing inequalities.

The primary component of wealth for most American households is homeownership, and home equity is an even more important part of the wealth portfolio for minorities than it is for whites. In 2002 home equity was 63 percent of total net worth for blacks, 61 percent for Latinos, and 38.5 percent for whites.[125]

As minorities have moved from cities to suburbs, they have increasingly become homeowners. Historical discriminatory policies such as restrictive covenants and redlining blocked minorities from suburban areas where homeownership boomed after World War II and made it difficult for them to get mortgage financing to buy in the city neighborhoods where they lived. These de jure forms of discrimination have now been banned for decades, and new outreach programs, flexible and innovative mortgage products, and specific minority lending goals for government-sponsored secondary mortgage market actors, such as Fannie Mae and Freddie Mac, have all helped to narrow the homeownership gap between whites and minorities. Nevertheless, these gaps remain wide, mirroring and perpetuating the wealth inequalities developed over time.

The black homeownership rate rose from 42 percent in 1994 to 48 percent in 2006, yet blacks still own homes at just two thirds the rates of whites.[126] Some of this difference is due to age, household composition, and income differences, but, even after controlling for these variations, a gap remains.

While blacks have moved increasingly to homeownership, segregation and a reluctance of whites to move into predominantly black communities have limited home price appreciation in black communities. Shapiro has found that, over thirty years, houses in predominantly black neighborhoods appreciated $28,000 less than similar homes in white neighborhoods.[127]

Hispanic homeownership has been increasing as well and now exceeds that of blacks. Realtors and lenders have increasingly reached out to this growing market, hiring bilingual agents and adapting requirements to the special financial situations faced by immigrants, such as lack of traditional credit and employment history. Homeownership rates have risen for Hispanics overall, but aggregate numbers hide their true progress because the steady streams of new immigrants, who tend to be renters at first, depress homeownership rates. For example, 49.4 percent of all Hispanic households owned their homes in 2005, but the rate for Hispanic immigrants was 42.6 percent and the rate for recent immigrants significantly lower. Among Hispanic subgroups, 2000 homeownership rates ranged from a low of 20 percent for Dominicans, many of whom live in New York City where homeownership rates overall are very low, to 58 percent for Cubans (see Table 1.2).[128]

Asians, given higher incomes and education, and greater propensity to live in married couple households, have even higher ownership rates, 61 percent in 2006. Among Asians, however, there is also considerable diversity, ranging from 40 percent for Koreans to 61 percent for Japanese in 2000.[129]

The benefits of homeownership are accompanied by increased risk, as dramatically illustrated by recent home price declines and record-setting foreclosure rates. Financial downturns can lead not only to the loss of one's housing, as with rentership, but also to the loss of wealth in the form of home equity. Many organizations, previously primarily concerned with promoting ownership, have turned to attempting to rescue homeowners in danger of losing their homes because of unaffordable sub-prime or predatory loans that strip borrowers of their equity through high interest rates, hidden fees, and deceptive practices. The Center for Responsible Lending found that, in 2006, 2.2 million sub-prime loans made in recent years had already failed or would end up in foreclosure, costing homeowners up to $164 billion.[130] These losses will fall disproportionately on black and Latino owners. 52 percent of home loans made to African American borrowers and 41 percent made to Latinos in 2006 were sub-prime, compared to just 22 percent made to non-Hispanic white borrowers.[131] Clustering of sub-prime loans in minority communities means that consequences of resulting forecloses reverberate across whole neighborhoods, reducing property values, increasing crime and abandoned buildings and making it more difficult for other owners to refinance or sell their homes. While the expansion of credit opportunities to minority communities led to record homeownership rates, the sub-prime and foreclosure crisis put many of those gains in jeopardy.

"As Long as You've Got Your Health"

Many of the factors discussed thus far—housing, education, location of residence, and financial circumstances—combine with behavior and unexplained factors to influence what is arguably a person's most valuable asset: his or her physical health. Racial disparities in health persist, sometimes explainable and sometimes mysterious. Despite notable progress, blacks consistently exhibit the most pessimistic health statistics.

Life expectancy is one of the most basic vital statistics and one that took on an unexpected political angle in 2005 when the Bush administration argued that the current Social Security system disadvantaged blacks because their shorter life spans meant that they drew less than their fair share of benefits.[132] While blacks still lag whites in terms of life span by over five years, the gap has been closing over time and now is at the smallest recorded. In 2003, white newborns had an average life expectancy of 78 years, compared with 72.8 years for black newborns. "Recent increases in life expectancy have been especially pronounced among black males, whose average life expectancy increased from 64.5 years in 1990 to 69.2 years in 2003 (preliminary estimate), following a decline in life expectancy in the late 1980s. Some of this increase reflects declines in homicide rates among black males during the mid- and late-1990s. Despite these increases, however, black children are still almost twice as likely as white children to die before reaching age 20."[133]

In addition to their shorter life spans, blacks compare poorly with other racial groups across a wide range of other health indicators:

- They are more likely to develop cancer and have the highest cancer death rate.
- They have a prostate cancer death rate twice as high as any other group.
- Although the rate of newly diagnosed breast cancer for black women is 13 percent lower than for white women, blacks have a higher mortality than any other group.
- Forty percent of black men and women have some form of heart disease compared to 30 percent of white men and 24 percent of white women. Blacks are also 29 percent more likely to die from heart disease.
- More than half of all black women age twenty to seventy-four are obese.
- Blacks are twice as likely as whites to have diabetes.
- Blacks are ten times more likely than whites to die of AIDS, which is the leading cause of death for black women age twenty-five to thirty-four and the third leading cause for black men that age.[134]

Blacks are also less likely to have the financial capability to deal with health problems. Not only do they have lower household incomes and assets, but they are also 80 percent more likely to lack health insurance than whites.[135] Recent studies have found that health crises are the primary cause of bankruptcy.[136]

Hispanics have a decidedly more positive health situation, with longer life expectancies, lower levels of infant mortality, and lower likelihood of dying of heart disease than non-Hispanic whites. They also are significantly less likely to smoke. However, Hispanics, particularly Mexicans, have higher levels of being overweight and obese, which is likely linked to being one and a half times more likely than whites to have diabetes (about a third of which is undiagnosed). Among Hispanics, Puerto Ricans are more likely to suffer from HIV/AIDS, asthma, and infant mortality. While Hispanics made up 14 percent of the U.S. population in

2002, they made up 20 percent of AIDS cases and were three times as likely to die of AIDS than their white counterparts.[137] A third of Hispanics lack health insurance, three times the rate of whites.[138] Lack of health insurance and reluctance of undocumented residents to seek health care may explain Hispanics' lower levels of screening for prostate cancer and higher levels of cervical cancer.

Although they have better general health, Hispanics face a particularly disturbing increase in workplace fatalities. Between 1992 and 2000, the workplace death rate for Hispanics soared by 53 percent while it dropped by 10 percent for non-Hispanics. The Hispanic rate has continued to climb since 2000.[139] The high proportions of Hispanics in dangerous jobs, particularly construction, as well as language barriers that may make training more difficult, and fear of complaining about unsafe conditions may all play a part in the deadly conditions some Hispanic workers face.

Despite infant mortality rates about 70 percent higher than whites', overall life expectancy for American Indians differs fairly little from that of whites. Women's life expectancies exceed those of whites by about two years while Indian men trail whites by about two years. Indians do have higher rates of stomach cancer and obesity and an incidence of diabetes that is more than twice that of whites. Obesity and diabetes may be linked to an above average incidence of alcoholism. Though numbers are small, Indians are also disproportionately affected by HIV/AIDS—being three times more likely to have AIDS than whites.[140] Last, Indians, particularly Indian women, are quite likely to smoke. In 2002, 41 percent of American Indians smoked, compared to 22 percent of non-Hispanic blacks, 24 percent of non-Hispanic whites, 17 percent of Hispanics, and 13 percent of Asians.[141] A full third of adult Indian women smoked, compared to just a fifth of all adults.[142] Next to Hispanics, Indians are the least likely of all groups to have health insurance.[143]

Asians, particularly Asian women, have life expectancies well in excess of other groups and lead non-Hispanic whites by about six years. In general Asians exhibit superior health profiles, though they do have some specific problems. Asians/Pacific Islanders have higher rates of stomach cancer than do whites, and cervical cancer rates are particularly high in Vietnamese women.[144] Given the attention paid to marketing of cigarettes in Asian countries, it is perhaps surprising that Asian Americans have the lowest smoking prevalence rates among all racial groups. This Asian advantage is due to less smoking among women, who smoke at rates less than a third those of non-Hispanic whites. Asians also have the lowest incidence of obesity, but are more prone to diabetes relative to those whites of similar weight,[145] possibly due to drastic change in diet that occurs among some Asian immigrants when they move to the United States. Asians are the minority group most likely to have health insurance, though they still trail whites (82 percent versus 89 percent in 2002–2004).[146]

The factors explaining racial health disparities are varied and complicated. One factor, however, is surely the segregated living patterns discussed earlier, which most greatly disadvantage blacks and to some extent Hispanics. Various studies have linked poor black and Hispanic communities to a variety of risk factors including exposure to higher potentially dangerous air toxins. A 2005 analysis of Environmental Protection Agency data by the Associated Press found that blacks are 79 percent more likely to live in neighborhoods where industrial pollution is suspected of posing the greatest dangers to health.[147] Segregated black and Hispanic neighborhoods have fewer supermarkets but more fast food vendors, environments that are less conducive to physical activity, more aggressive marketing of unhealthy products such as alcohol and tobacco, and lower quality housing that contributes to mold, asthma, lead paint poisoning, and roaches.

The negative health effects of stress have also been tied to living in disadvantaged neighborhoods and, more recently, to the experience of discrimination itself. There is increasing evidence that the stress of experiencing discrimination can be linked to heart disease in blacks.[148] Interestingly, it is perceptions of discrimination in ambiguous situations, rather than when the discrimination is obvious and intentional, that seem to lead to greater stress.

A Civic Voice: The Unfinished Struggle

The fight for voting rights was one of the most prominent struggles of the civil rights era, and its success ensured that poll taxes, literacy tests, and other overt manifestations of discrimination are things of the past. Indeed, as of mid-2008, Senator Barack Obama was the presumptive Democratic nominee for president, earning votes from many whites as well as blacks and helping to draw record voter turnout in many states. Still, forty years after the passage of the Voting Rights Act, the share of blacks of voting age who are registered to vote or who do vote is actually lower than it was in the mid 1960s, despite gains over the last two elections. The growth of Hispanic and Asian populations has not translated proportionately into political power because they are less likely to be of voting age, to be citizens, to register, or to vote than whites. The battle against Jim Crow was won, but new challenges remain to incorporate the nation's diverse peoples into political and civic life.

In the 2004 election, 56 percent of voting age blacks did vote, up 6 percentage points from 1996 but still less than the 59 percent who voted in 1964. Sixty-four percent of blacks were registered in 2004 versus 66 percent in 1968.[149] Because voting rates for whites also declined over the period, the black–white gap narrowed, but the white voting rate is still 10 percentage points higher.

The voting gap is partly due to blacks' lower education and income levels, both of which depress voting rates. Interestingly, though, studies during the 1990s show that blacks are more likely register but less likely to actually vote than are whites of similar economic status.[150]

Another factor that disproportionately disadvantages blacks is the disenfranchisement of felons and ex-felons. States have long limited voting rights for some criminals, but the dramatic increase in the prisoner population in recent years means that the absolute number of people disenfranchised has grown considerably. This issue received substantial attention during the close 2000 presidential election, when an estimated 600,000 ex-felons in Florida (more than a quarter of whom were black) were unable to vote.[151] Over the last decade, several states have liberalized their laws in order to expand voting rights to ex-felons. However, these efforts are sometimes perceived as having a political tinge. Because of the over-representation of blacks, and the much higher affiliation of blacks with the Democratic Party, extending the vote to more ex-felons is seen as a potential boon to the Democrats.

According to the Sentencing Project:

- Forty-eight states and the District of Columbia prohibit inmates from voting while incarcerated for a felony offense.
- Thirty-six states prohibit felons from voting while they are on parole, and thirty-one of these states exclude felony probationers as well.
- Three states (Florida, Kentucky, and Virginia) deny the right to vote to all ex-offenders who have completed their sentences. Nine others disenfranchise certain categories of ex-offenders or permit application for restoration of rights for specified offenses after a waiting period.
- Each state has developed its own process of restoring voting rights to ex-offenders, but most of these restoration processes are so cumbersome that few ex-offenders are able to take advantage of them.

According to the Sentencing Project, "13 percent of black men are disenfranchised, seven times the national average. _Given current rates of incarceration, three in ten of the next generation of black men can expect to be disenfranchised at some point in their lifetime. In states that disenfranchise ex-offenders, as many as 40 percent of black men may permanently lose their right to vote." Further, "About a third (1.7 million) of disenfranchised persons are ex-offenders who have completed their sentences."[152]

Latinos and Asians face additional challenges stemming largely from their citizenship status and, to some degree, language barriers. The number of Latino votes cast in 2004 was up 23 percent over 2000, more than twice the growth rate of whites. Still, even this rapid increase fell well behind Latino population growth. Because of the youth of the Latino population and the high share that are not citizens, "Only one out of every four Latinos added to the U.S. population is an added voter."[153]

Even among those eligible by age and citizenship, Latinos and Asians are much less likely to vote than are whites and blacks. Among eligible voters in the 2004 election, just 44 percent of Asians and 47 percent of Latinos voted, versus 67 percent of whites and 60 percent of blacks.[154] But as native-born members come to make up larger shares of these groups, and more move into voting ages, Asians and Hispanics will surely play a more prominent role in the future. Currently just about 40 percent of each group is eligible to vote, but this should increase to about 50 percent by 2025.[155]

Still, the power of Hispanics to wield political clout is not entirely limited by the number of Hispanic voters. The ability to mobilize large numbers of supporters in immigration reform demonstrations across the country has highlighted the ability of Hispanics to forcefully promote issues that affect them, partner with progressives and other immigrants in coalitions, and garner significant media attention. Large numbers and organizational ability further presage increasing political strength.

Minority representation among office holders is far below that of the general population, but relative to the dismal record of the past, there has been substantial progress. Of the nearly 2000 people who have served in the U.S. Senate between 1789 and 2005, only eighteen have been minority.[156] As of mid-2007, Congress as a whole included the largest number of people of color in its history. The U.S. Senate included three Hispanic, two Asian, and one black member. The House of Representatives included forty-two black members (including two delegates), twenty-seven Hispanic members (including one delegate,) seven Asian members, and one Native American.

Looking across all levels of elected government, the number of black officials has risen fairly steadily and dramatically from about 1,500 in 1970 to roughly 9,000 as of 2001. As the number of black office holders has climbed, there has also been a dramatic shift from men to women being elected, according to the Joint Center for Political and Economic Studies. In the early 1970s, there were 5.4 black men elected for every black woman. By the 1995–2001 period, there were 5.9 new women for every new man.[157] Much of this change came at city and school board levels and likely reflects the greater voting levels and education of black women as well as their lower incarceration rates.

For Hispanics, the number of elected officials also rose from about 3,100 in 1985 to 5,200 in 2000, before declining to 4,700 in 2004. This entire decline occurred at the education and school board level.[158]

Interestingly, one level where minorities have actually been over-represented relative to the population is the presidential Cabinet. President Clinton and President Bush each appointed Cabinets that included at least a third people of color during each of their two terms. President Bush also appointed the first two black secretaries of state and first Hispanic attorney-general.[159] Thus, at these most visible levels of government, racial diversity has now become common, and, indeed, expected.

While the Voting Rights Act eliminated most flagrant voting rights violations, there remain areas of concern. For example:

1. Voting procedures and mechanisms that, in practice, dilute the minority vote. "A study by the House Committee on Government Reform found that voters in low-income, high-minority congressional districts throughout the country were three times more likely to have their votes for president discarded [due to ballot spoilage in 2000] than those in more affluent, low-minority districts and were twenty times more likely to have their votes for

Congress go uncounted." Additional analysis by the Civil Rights Project found that black votes were consistently spoiled "even when comparing counties with identical income, education, and other factors."[160]

2. Poll monitoring by the Asian American Legal Defense and Education Fund in twenty-three cities in the 2004 election found that, although local election workers worked hard to comply with federal laws, limited English-proficient Asian Americans had much difficulty in voting due to lack of interpreters or translated materials, provisional ballots were not always offered or counted, poll workers made improper or excessive demands for identification, and poll workers were rude or hostile, to name just a few problems.[161]

3. Redrawing of electoral districts continues to potentially threaten minorities' voting power and rights. In 2004 in Massachusetts, for example, the courts "enjoined elections in 17 districts because the legislature's redistricting plan, in the court's words, "sacrificed racial fairness to the voters on the altar of incumbency protection."[162] Voting districts were ordered redrawn due to violations of the Voting Rights Act.

Clearly, while the pivotal victories of the past should not be discounted, people of color hold many more elected seats than in the past, and diversity is now commonplace in the presidential Cabinet, challenges remain on several fronts. Gaining the right to vote is great value in itself but has little practical effect if people choose not to use it. Given the monumental impact that government has on issues that concern all residents, whether it be schools, healthcare, defense policy, Social Security, or many others, we cannot be a true democracy while the voices of so many are unheard. Additional work must be done to ensure that all votes are fairly counted and that all citizens have the opportunity and desire to vote.

Forward Together

This chapter has documented the changing racial composition of the population, historically and in the projected future, as well as patterns of disparities among major racial groups in the home, places of worship, neighborhoods, schools, workplaces, and the political arena. Clearly, issues of racial identity, opportunity, and interaction have become substantially more complex in just a few decades and promise to become even more so. Following are ten observations or sets of questions that emerge from the data and that can shed important light on the status of the color line in the future.

1. The demographic factors driving minority population growth in the United States are already largely in place, even without further significant levels of immigration. However, immigration can certainly accelerate this trend. At the time of this writing we are once again struggling with the political, economic, and moral arguments that surround immigration law and policy. We

are a nation of immigrants and concede that much of our nation's strength and progress come from our willingness to accept newcomers with new energy and ideas. Yet we are frightened by the foreigner who reminds us of the September 11 tragedy and the possibility of new terrorism. We know that many industries depend on immigrants—indeed, even undocumented immigrant labor—and appreciate the lower prices we pay but are concerned that immigrants take work from others, particularly other low-income or minority workers who need a leg up. Can we form a unified national consensus that looks rationally at the costs and benefits of immigration and leads to a coherent and enforceable policy?

2. The varying age structures of the white and minority populations will lead to different racial profiles of the young and the old, just as the large baby boom generation is becoming elderly. The child and working age populations will become increasingly minority, while whites will be a large share of retirees. Over the last four decades we have seen a dramatic juxtaposition in the poverty rates between the young and old. The poverty rate for the elderly has declined from significantly above the child rate to well below, as Social Security and other programs have benefited the old. What implications will the differing racial age profiles have for our willingness to confront and fund issues that especially affect particular age groups? To what extent is the social contract between Americans still valid as we move more toward an "ownership society?"

3. Given patterns of intermarriage and multirace identification, what will be the significance of race in the future? Opinion polls clearly show that it matters much less to the young than to the old. Will intermarriage and multiracial children become the primary means of integration? Will this trend extend to blacks who intermarry less frequently? Will interracial spouses and their multiracial children become so commonplace that the race of a person such as Tiger Woods, a self-described "cablinasian," will not even be worth a mention?

4. Will the traditionally strong Hispanic family structure hold, or will the escalating share of children born out of wedlock and high teen birthrate lead inexorably to negative social and economic consequences? Similarly, as they assimilate, will many of Hispanics' and Asians' protective health attributes be lost? What can be done to strengthen and protect these positive traits and behaviors?

5. The South, once the epicenter of racial strife, will increasingly be the crucible in which new racial dynamics will play out. Bolstered by continuing foreign immigration, the South is also the only region to attract domestic migrants of all races, some in very large numbers. As new neighborhoods are formed, many in cities that are considerably more "suburban-like" in feel and structure than Northern cities, new patterns will emerge, likely encompassing several racial groups. Will the growth of neighborhoods that contain substantial numbers of three or more racial groups provide buffers that will ease

historical segregation patterns between blacks and whites? And will this diversity lead to communities that will be attractive to all races and bring stability both to populations and housing values? To what extent will these neighborhoods be stably integrated? How will the abandonment of school desegregation plans in the South affect residential patterns?

6. Is the rising segregation of Hispanics merely transitory and related to immigrant preferences to live in communities that remind them of home and provide cultural support? Will it lessen over time, or will Hispanic barrios solidify into segregated areas as intransigent as the segregated black neighborhoods of the Northeast and Midwest?

7. Education is clearly the key to the economic success of all groups and particularly to minorities who do not have accumulated family wealth as a safety net. Will the system of accountability and sanctions under No Child Left Behind truly boost the educational levels of all and reduce the achievement gap? Can quality education be delivered in increasingly segregated schools? How will recent and future court rulings impact racial diversity in education?

8. The old black–white dichotomy in race relations is no longer adequate, and there exists considerable diversity within the Hispanic and Asian populations. Still, across many dimensions, whites and Asians consistently fare better than do blacks, Hispanics, and American Indians. Will the divide between these sets of groups persist? Moreover, many of the factors that put Hispanics at a lower socioeconomic position than blacks, such as English ability, citizenship status, education, and age, are ones that can be overcome with time or over generations. Indeed, some studies show that controlling for a small number of such variables virtually eliminates the gaps in indicators of well-being between Hispanics and whites, but does not eliminate the gaps between blacks and whites. The growth of the black middle class is a very positive sign. Nevertheless, while politically delicate, continued research is needed to identify the reasons why many blacks continue to lag other groups in unexplained ways.

9. The status of American Indians is also particularly troubling and harder to measure. The small size of this population (they are a tenth the size of the Mexican American population and less than the number of Chinese Americans) means that they are sometimes not represented in surveys of socioeconomic well-being. Yet we know from decennial census data that they have very high levels of poverty and very low levels of educational attainment, income, and health insurance coverage. Issues of tribal sovereignty further complicate the picture. Despite these difficulties, their unique history makes it important that their needs not be lost in the impassioned debate concerning larger racial and ethnic groups.

10. Whites and blacks hold profoundly different views about the reality of racial inequality across a wide field of topics, including educational and employment opportunities. Are peoples' views so distorted by their individual expe-

riences and prejudices that they cannot accommodate factual evidence? Or are there ways for researchers to illustrate truths so starkly and engagingly that people will accept a common understanding and more effectively turn to look for solutions?

There is no doubt that we have come a long way toward at least blurring the color line over the last half century. The problems documented here are not nearly as pernicious as those faced by the civil rights activists of the 1950s and 1960s. Yet the color line does remain, even as its intensity and position changes. We should not rest until it is completely erased.

Notes

1. Rick Weiss, "Scientists Find DNA Change That Explains White Skin," *Washington Post,* December 16, 2005, A1.

2. Ibid.

3. Campbell Gibson and Kay Jung, "Historical Census Statistics on Population Totals by Race, 1790 to 1990, and by Hispanic Origin, 1970 to 1990, for the United States, Regions, Divisions, and States," Working Paper Series no. 56, U.S. Bureau of the Census, September 2002; U.S. Bureau of the Census, "Annual Estimates of the Population by Sex, Race and Hispanic or Latino Origin for the United States: April 1, 2000, to July 1, 2004," NC-EST2004-03, released June 9, 2005.

4. U.S. Bureau of the Census, "Characteristics of the Population by U.S. Citizenship Status, Table 1.1: Population by Sex, Age, and U.S. Citizenship Status: 2004," Internet release, February 22, 2005.

5. Data on the foreign-born share of the population for 2005 are calculated from U.S. Bureau of the Census, Current Population Survey, 2005, Annual Social and Economic Supplement.

6. U.S. Bureau of the Census, "We the American Foreign Born," WE-7, September 1993.

7. Calculations are from the 2000 Decennial Census, Summary File 4.

8. Joyce A. Martin et al., "Births: Final Data for 2003," National Vital Statistics Reports, vol. 54. no. 2, U.S. Department of Health and Human Services, September 8, 2005.

9. Data on components of population change data for all races are from U.S. Bureau of the Census, Population Division, "Table 5: Cumulative Estimates of the Components of Population Change by Race and Hispanic or Latino Origin for the United States: April 1, 2000, to July 1, 2004," NC-EST2004-0.

10. Jeffrey S. Passel, "The Size and Characteristics of the Unauthorized Migrant Population in the U.S. Estimates Based on the March 2005 Current Population Survey," Pew Hispanic Center, Washington, D.C., March 7, 2006.

11. Pew Hispanic Center, "Hispanics: A People in Motion: Trends 2005," Washington, D.C., 2005.

12. Data on population projections for all races from U.S. Bureau of the Census, "U.S. Interim Projections by Age, Sex, Race, and Hispanic Origin," Internet release, March 18, 2004.

13. Joint Center for Housing Studies of Harvard University, *The State of the Nation's Housing: 2005* (Cambridge, Mass.: Harvard University, 2005).

14. U.S. Bureau of the Census, "The Two or More Races Population: 2000," Census 2000 brief, C2KBR/01-6, November 2001.

15. John R. Logan and Deane Glenn, "Black Diversity in Metropolitan America," Lewis Mumford Center for Comparative Urban and Regional Research, University of Albany, Albany, N.Y., August 15, 2003.

16. Richard Morin, "A Distorted Image of Minorities: Poll Suggests That What Whites Think May Affect Their Beliefs," *Washington Post,* October 8, 1994, A1 (reporting data from Washington Post–Kaiser Family Foundation–Harvard University Survey).

17. U.S. Bureau of the Census, "Resident Population Estimates of the United States by Sex, Race, and Hispanic Origin: April 1, 1990, to July 1, 1999, with Short-Term Projection to November 1, 2000," Internet release, January 2, 2001.

18. Analysis of 2000 Decennial Census, Summary File 1.

19. Pew Hispanic Center, "Hispanics."

20. Joshua Bonilla, "Executive Summary: A Demographic Profile of Hispanics in the U.S.," Population Resource Center, Washington, D.C., October 2001.

21. "Hispanics."

22. Data on migration by region and race are from Jason P. Schacter, "Migration by Race and Hispanic Origin: 1995–2000," Census 2000 Special Reports, CENSR-13, U.S. Bureau of the Census, October, 2003.

23. U.S. Bureau of the Census, "Table 22: Population by Metropolitan and Nonmetropolitan Residence, Sex, Race, and Hispanic Origin: March 2002," Internet release, May 28, 2003.

24. Analysis of 2000 Decennial Census, Summary File 1.

25. John R. Logan, "The New Ethnic Enclaves in America's Suburbs," Lewis Mumford Center for Comparative Urban and Regional Research, University at Albany, Albany, N.Y., 2001.

26. William H. Frey, "Melting Pot Suburbs: A Census 2000 Study of Suburban Diversity," Census 2000 Series, Brookings Institution, Washington, D.C., June 2001.

27. Data on share of children born to unwed mothers by race are from Child Trends Data Bank, "Percentage of Births to Unmarried Women."

28. Data on the share of children living with zero, one, or two parents are from Child Trends Data Bank, "Family Structure."

29. Data on the share of children in foster care are from idem, "Foster Care."

30. Data on the share of women born to unwed mothers by race are from idem., "Percentage of Births to Unmarried Women."

31. Data on the trends in teen births by race are from idem, "Teen Births,"

32. Analysis of the 2005 Current Population Survey, Annual Social and Economic Supplement.

33. Analysis of the 2000 Decennial Census, Summary File 1.

34. Analysis of the 2005 Current Population Survey, Annual Social and Economic Supplement.

35. Statistics on intermarriage in this section are from Sharon M. Lee, "New Marriages, New Families: U.S. Racial and Hispanic Intermarriage," *Population Bulletin,* Population Reference Bureau, June 2005. For this intermarriage discussion, race and Hispanic origin are considered separate categories.

36. Lee, "New Marriages."

37. Ibid.

38. Gallup Organization, "Historical Poll Results on Race Relations."

39. Pew Hispanic Center, "Hispanics."

40. Jeffrey M. Jones, "Race, Ideology and Support for Affirmative Action," Gallup Organization.

41. Allison Stein Wellner, "U.S. Attitudes toward Interracial Dating Are Liberalizing," Population Reference Bureau, Washington, D.C., June 2005.

42. Much of the discussion in this section is derived from: Robert K. Vischer, "Racial Segregation in American Churches and Its Implications for School Vouchers," *Florida Law Review* 53 (2001): 204–215; Kevin D. Dougherty, "How Monochromatic Is Church Membership? Racial–Ethnic Diversity in Religious Community" *Sociology of Religion* 64 (2003): 65–85.

43. As cited in "Divided by Faith?" *Christianity Today*, October 2, 2000, 34.

44. M. O. Emerson and C. Smith, *Divided by Faith: Evangelical Religion and the Problem of Race in America* (New York: Oxford University Press, 2000).

45. Ihsan Bagby, Paul M. Perl, and Bryan T. Froehle, "The Mosque in America: A National Portrait," Council on American–Islamic Relations, Washington, D.C., 2001.

46. Lewis Mumford Center for Comparative Urban and Regional Research, "Ethnic Diversity Grows, Neighborhood Integration Lags Behind," University at Albany, Albany, N.Y., revised December 18, 2001.

47. For trends in dissimilarity between 1980 and 2000, see ibid.

48. Ingrid Gould Ellen, *Sharing America's Neighborhoods: The Prospects for Stable Racial Integration* (Cambridge, Mass.: Harvard University Press, 2000).

49. Data on the income levels of neighborhoods where the average members of typical races reside from the Lewis Mumford Center for Comparative Urban and Regional Research, "Separate and Unequal: The Neighborhood Gap for Blacks and Hispanics in Metropolitan America," University at Albany, Albany, N.Y., October 13, 2002.

50. William O'Hare and Mark Mather, "The Growing Number of Kids in Severely Distressed Neighborhoods: Evidence from the 2000 Census," Annie E. Casey Foundation, Baltimore, and Population Reference Bureau, Washington, D.C., revised October 2003.

51. Josephine Mazzuca, "For Most Americans, Friendship Is Colorblind," Gallup Organization.

52. Robert M. Adelman, "The Roles of Race, Class, and Residential Preferences in the Neighborhood Racial Composition of Middle-Class Blacks and Whites," *Social Science Quarterly* 86, no. 1 (March 2005): 209–228.

53. U.S. Department of Housing and Community Development, "Discrimination in Metropolitan Housing Markets: National Results from Phase 1, Phase 2, and Phase 3 of the Housing Discrimination Study (HDS), 2000.

54. John R. Logan, "How Race Counts for Hispanic Americans," Lewis Mumford Center for Comparative Urban and Regional Research, University at Albany, Albany, N.Y., July 14, 2003.

55. Mazzuca, "Friendship Is Colorblind."

56. John Iceland, "Beyond Black and White: Residential Segregation in Multiethnic America" *Social Science Research* 33, no. 2 (June 2004): 248–71.

57. Education Trust, "The Funding Gap 2005: Low-Income and Minority Students Shortchanged by Most States," Winter 2005.

58. Idem, "Funding Gaps: 2006" (December, 2006).

59. Douglas N. Harris, "Ending the Blame Game on Educational Inequity: A Study of 'High Flying Schools' and NCLB," Education Policy Research Unit, Arizona State University, Tempe, March 2006.

60. Gary Orfield and Chungmei Lee, "Brown at 50: King's Dream or *Plessy's* Nightmare?" Civil Rights Project, Harvard University, Cambridge, Mass., January 2004.

61. *Parents Involved in Community Schools, Petitioner v. Seattle School District No. 1 et al.; Meredith v. Jefferson County Board of Education,* U.S. Supreme Court, no. 05-908, 2007.

62. Exposure indices for 2002–2003 are from Gary Orfield and Chungmei Lee, "Why Segregation Matters: Poverty and Educational Inequality," Civil Rights Project, Harvard University, Cambridge, Mass. January 2005; exposure indices for 1991–1992 are from idem, "Brown at 50."

63. Ibid.

64. Erica Frankenberg, Chungmei Lee, and Gary Orfield, "A Multiracial Society with Segregated Schools: Are We Losing the Dream?" Civil Rights Project, Harvard University, Cambridge, Mass., January 2003.

65. Roslyn Arlin Mickelson, "The Incomplete Desegregation of the Charlotte–Mecklenburg Schools and Its Consequences, 1971–2004," in *School Resegregation: Must the South Turn Back?* ed. John Charles Boger and Gary Orfield (Chapel Hill: University of North Carolina Press, 2005), 87–110.

66. Tamar Lewin, "The Two Faces of A.P.," *New York Times,* January 8, 2006, 24.

67. Civil Rights Project, Harvard University, "Racial Inequity in Special Education: Executive Summary for Federal Policy Makers," June 2002.

68. The long-term trend data are from National Assessment of Educational Progress (NAEP), "Long-Term Trend Database," National Center for Education Statistics, U.S. Department of Education, Washington, D.C.

69. The 2005 NAEP data for Asians and American Indians are from idem, "Assessment Results: Reading by Race/Ethnicity and Mathematics by Race/Ethnicity."

70. Alisa Hicklin, "Latino Dropouts and High Stakes Testing," Project for Equity, Representation, and Governance, Texas A&M University, College Station, September 2003.

71. Gary Orfield, Daniel Losen, Johanna Wald, and Christopher B. Swanson, "Losing Our Future: How Minority Youth Are Being Left behind by the Graduation Rate Crisis," Civil Rights Project, Harvard University, Urban Institute, Advocates for Children of New York, and Civil Society Institute, Cambridge, Mass., and Washington, D.C., revised March 11, 2004.

72. Bruce Western, Vincent Schiraldi, and Jason Ziedenberg, "Education and Incarceration," Justice Policy Institute, Washington, D.C., August 28, 2003.

73. Joseph Carroll, "Race and Education 20 Years after *Brown v. Board of Education,*" Gallup News Service, May 14, 2004.

74. Ibid.

75. Ibid.

76. Pew Hispanic Center/Kaiser Family Foundation, "National Survey of Latinos: Education," Summary and Chartpack, "Chart 30—Racial Integration," January 2004.

77. Jennifer Cheesman Day and Eric C. Newburger, "The Big Payoff: Educational Attainment and Synthetic Estimates of Work-Life Earnings," U.S. Bureau of the Census, P23-210, July 2002.

78. American Council on Education. Center for Advancement of Racial and Ethnic Equity for Policy Analysis. "Twenty-first Annual Status Report on Minorities in Higher Education," Washington, D.C., February 2005.

79. Ibid. , 5–6

80. Ibid., 17.

81. Ibid.

82. Ibid.

83. Sandy Baum and Kathleen Payea, "Trends in College Pricing: 2005," College Board, Washington, D.C., 2005.

84. Donald E. Heller and Christopher J. Rasmussen, "Merit Scholarships and College Access: Evidence from Florida and Michigan," in *Who Should We Help? The Negative Social Consequences of Merit Scholarships,* ed. Donald E. Heller and Patricia Marin (Cambridge, Mass.: Civil Rights Project, Harvard University, 2002).

85. Alvin P. Sanoff, "Restricted Access," *Lumina Foundation Focus* (Summer 2003).

86. Thomas Bailey, Davis Jenkins, and Timothy Leinbach, "What We Know about Community College Low-Income and Minority Student Outcomes: Descriptive Statistics from National Surveys," Community College Research Center, Teachers College, Columbia University, New York, January 2005.

87. *Gratz et al. v. Bollinger et al.,* U.S. Supreme Court, no. 02-516, 2002.

88. *Grutter v. Bollinger et al.* U.S. Supreme Court, no. 02-241, 2002.

89. Thomas J. Espenshade, and Chang Y. Chung, "The Opportunity Cost of Admission Preferences at Elite Universities," *Social Science Quarterly* 86, no. 2 (2005): 293–305.

90. Gallup Organization, "Historical Poll Results on Race Relations."

91. U.S. Department of Labor, Bureau of Labor Statistics, "Historical Unemployment Rates by Race."

92. Andrew Sum et al. "Trends in Black Male Joblessness and Year-Round Idleness: An Employment Crisis Ignored," Center for Labor Market Studies, Northeastern University, June 2004.

93. Economic Policy Institute, "African Americans in the Current Recovery," Economic Snapshots, April 6, 2005.

94. Steven Raphael and Michael Stoll, "Modest Progress: The Narrowing Spatial Mismatch between Blacks and Jobs in the 1990s," Living Census Series, Brookings Institution, Washington, D.C., December 2002.

95. Quoted in "Mexican Leader Criticized for Comment on Blacks," CNN, May 15, 2005, available online at http://www.cnn.com/2005/US/05/14/fox.jackson/index.html.

96. Pew Hispanic Center, "Hispanics: A People in Motion: Trends 2005" (Washington, D.C.: 2005).

97. U.S. Bureau of the Census, "The Hispanic Population in the U.S., Detailed Tables 2004, Table 9.2: Labor Force and Employment Status of the Civilian Population 16 Years and over by Sex and Hispanic Origin Type: 2004," last online revision, December 14, 2005.

98. U.S. Department of Labor, Bureau of Labor Statistics. "Table 1: Employment Status of the Foreign-born and Native-born Populations by Selected Characteristics, 2003–04 Annual Averages," May 12, 2005.

99. U.S. Bureau of the Census, "Table 2: Earnings by Detailed Occupation, 1999," last online revision, May 13, 2004.

100. Data on occupation by industry and sex are calculated from the 2000 Decennial Census, Summary File 4.

101. Maude Toussaint-Comeau, Thomas Smith, and Ludovic Comeau Jr., "Occupational Attainment and Mobility of Hispanics in a Changing Economy," Pew Hispanic Center, Washington, D.C., 2005.

102. Rakesh Kochhar, "Survey of Mexican Migrants, Part 3: The Economic Transition to America," Pew Hispanic Center, Washington, D.C., December 2005.

103. Donald Tomaskovic-Devey et al, "Documenting Desegregation: Estimates of U.S. Workplace Sex and Ethnic Segregation: 1966–2000," paper presented at the Annual Meeting of the American Sociological Association, San Francisco, 2004.

104. Data in this section on racial representation in the military are from David R. Segal and Mady Wechsler Segal, "America's Military Population." Population Bulletin, Population Reference Bureau, Washington, D.C., December 2004.

105. Ibid., 20.

106. *Grutter v. Bollinger et al.*, Amici Curia Brief in Support of Respondents by Lieutenant-General Julius W. Becton et al., U.S. Supreme Court, nos. 02-516, 02-241.

107. Charles C. Moskos and John Sibley Butler, *All That We Can Be: Black Leadership and Racial Integration the Army Way* (New York: Basic Books, 1997), 132–135.

108. Based on calculations of the 2000 Decennial Census, Summary, File 1.

109. Gallup Organization, "Historical Poll Results on Race Relations."

110. Ibid.

111. U.S. Department of Labor, Bureau of Labor Statistics, "Highlights of Women's Earnings in 2004," report no. 987, September 2005.

112. James P. Smith, "Race and Ethnicity in the Labor Market: Trends over the Short and Long Term," in *America Becoming: Racial Trends and Their Consequences*, vol. 2, ed. Neil J. Smelser, William Julius Wilson, and Faith Mitchell (Washington, D.C.: National Academy Press, 2001).

113. U.S. Department of Labor, Bureau of Labor Statistics, "Highlights of Women's Earnings in 2004."

114. U.S. Census Bureau, "Historical Income Tables: Households, Table H-12: Household by Number of Earners by Median and Mean Income," last online revision, February 11, 2005.

115. Idem, "Income, Poverty, and Health Insurance Coverage in the United States: 2004," P60-229, August 2005.

116. Alec Klein, "A Tenuous Hold on the Middle Class: African Americans on Shifting Ground," *Washington Post*, December 18, 2004, A1.

117. Thomas Shapiro and Melvin Oliver, "Closing the Racial Wealth Gap," Monthly Perspectives, Institute on Assets and Social Policy, Brandeis University, Waltham, Mass., September 2005, 1.

118. Thomas M. Shapiro, *The Hidden Cost of Being African-American* (New York: Oxford University Press, 2004), 37–38.

119. Ibid.

120. Rakesh Kochhar, "The Wealth of Hispanic Households: 1996 to 2002," Pew Hispanic Center, Washington, D.C., October 2004.

121. Ross Eisenbrey and William Spriggs, "Two Steps Back: African Americans and Latinos Will Lose Ground under Social Security 'Reform,'" Economic Policy Institute Issue Brief no. 212, July 14, 2005.

122. Inter-American Development Bank, Multilateral Investment Fund, "Remittances 2005: Transforming Labor Markets and Promoting Financial Democracy : Statistical Comparisons," Buenos Aires, November 2005.

123. Garance Burke, "Financial Education for Hispanics Urged," Associated Press, December 16, 2005.

124. John Havens and Paul Schervish. "Why the $41 Trillion Wealth Transfer Estimate Is Still Valid: A Review of Challenges and Questions," *Journal of Gift Planning* (January 2003).

125. Kochhar, "Wealth of Hispanic Households."

126. U.S. Bureau of the Census, "Housing Vacancies and Homeownership," Annual Statistics 2006. Blacks include Hispanic members.

127. Shapiro, "Hidden Cost."

128. Analysis of the 2000 Decennial Census, Summary File 4.

129. Ibid.

130. Center for Responsible Lending, "Losing Ground: Foreclosures in the Subprime Market and their Cost to Homeowners," December 2006.

131. Idem, "A Snapshot of the Subprime Market," November 28, 2007. The analysis of the 2006 Home Mortgage Disclosure Act data was reported by the Federal Financial Institutions Examination Council.

132. Associated Press, "NAACP: Bush 'Playing Race Card' with Social Security," *USA Today*, April 11, 2005.

133. Donna L Hoyert, Hsiang-Ching Kung, and Betty L. Smith, "Deaths: Preliminary Data for 2003," *National Vital Statistics Reports*, vol. 53, no. 15, table 6; Child Trends Data Bank, "Life Expectancy."

134. U.S. Department of Health and Human Services, "Minority Health Disparities at a Glance," HHS fact sheet, July 12, 2004.

135. U.S. Department of Commerce, "Income, Poverty, and Health Insurance Coverage in the United States: 2004," P60-229, August 2005.

136. David U. Himmelstein, Elizabeth Warren, Debora Thorne, and Steffie Woolhandler, "MarketWatch: Illness and Injury as Contributors to Bankruptcy," *Health Affairs*, February 2005.

137. U.S. Department of Health and Human Services, "Minority Health Disparities at a Glance."

138. U.S. Department of Commerce, "Income, Poverty, and Health Insurance Coverage in the United States."

139. Jim Hopkins, "Deaths of Hispanic Workers Soar 53 Percent," *USA Today*. March 24, 2002.

140. U.S. Department of Commerce, "Income, Poverty, and Health Insurance Coverage in the United States."

141. American Lung Association, "Trends in Tobacco Use," Epidemiology and Statistics Unit, New York, November 2004.

142. U.S. Department of Health and Human Services, "Minority Health Disparities at a Glance."

143. U.S. Department of Commerce, "Income, Poverty, and Health Insurance Coverage in the United States."

144. U.S. Department of Health and Human Services, "Minority Health Disparities at a Glance."

145. Marguarite McNeely and Edward J. Boyko, "Type 2 Diabetes Prevalence in Asian Americans," *Diabetes Care* 27, no. 1 (2004): 66–69.

146. U.S. Department of Commerce, "Income, Poverty, and Health Insurance Coverage in the United States."

147. David Pace, "More Blacks Live with Pollution," Associated Press, December 13, 2005.

148. Rob Stein, "Study Links Discrimination, Blacks' Health," *Washington Post*, May 1, 2005, A17.

149. U.S. Bureau of the Census, "Historical Time Series Tables: A-1 Reported Voting and Registration by Race, Hispanic Origin, Sex, and Age Groups: November 1964 to 2004," Voting and Registration, last revised June 16, 2005. For voting rights data, "whites" are non-Hispanic whites after 1976 and all whites before; blacks and Asians include Hispanic members for all years.

150. Katherine Tate and Kim DeFronzo, "Unequal Participation in American Politics and Its Implications for Children and Family Policies," University of California, Irvine, May 11, 2000.

151. Kari Huus, "Laws Barring Felons from Voting Hit Blacks Hard," MSNBC, October 4, 2005.

152. "Felony Disenfranchisement Laws in the United States," Sentencing Project, Washington, D.C., November 2005.

153. Roberto Suro, "Latino Power? It Will Take Time for the Population Boom to Translate," *Washington Post,* June 26, 2005, B1.

154. U.S. Bureau of the Census, "Voting and Registration in the Election of November 2004," online tables, last revised May 25, 2005.

155. Jeffrey Passel, "Election 2004: The Latino and Asian Vote," Urban Institute, Immigration Studies Program, Washington, D.C., July 27, 2004).

156. Kathy Kiely, "Parties Putting Minority Candidates on A-List," *USA Today,* December 26, 2005, 4A.

157. Joint Center for Political and Economic Studies, "Black Elected Officials: A Statistical Summary 2001," Washington, D.C., December 2003.

158. National Association of Latino Elected and Appointed Officials, "National Roster of Hispanic Elected Officials, Annual," Washington, D.C., 2005.

159. Susan Page, "Bush Opening Doors with a Diverse Cabinet," *USA Today,* December 9, 2004.

160. Civil Rights Project, Harvard University, "Democracy Spoiled: National, State, and County Disparities through Uncounted Ballots," July 2002.

161. Asian American Legal Defense and Education Fund, "Asian American Access to Democracy in the 2004 Elections," August 2005.

162. *Black Political Task Force v. Galvin.* U.S. District Court for the District of Massachusetts, Civil Action no. 02-11190, February 24, 2004.

Bibliography

Acevedo-Garcia, Dolores. "Housing, Neighborhoods, Segregation and Health: The Role of Fair Housing in Reducing Health Disparities." Unpublished ms., Harvard School of Public Health, Boston.

Adelman, Robert M. "The Roles of Race, Class, and Residential Preferences in the Neighborhood Racial Composition of Middle-Class Blacks and Whites." *Social Science Quarterly* 86, no. 1 (March 2005): 209–228.

Amer, Mildred L. "Membership of the 109th Congress: A Profile." Congressional Research Service, Library of Congress, Washington, D.C., October 25, 2005.

American Council on Education, Center for Advancement of Racial and Ethnic Equity for Policy Analysis. "Twenty-first Annual Status Report on Minorities in Higher Education." Washington, D.C., February 2005.

American Lung Association. "Trends in Tobacco Use." Epidemiology and Statistics Unit, New York, November 2004. Available online at http://www.lungusa.org/atf/cf/%7B7A 8D42C2-FCCA-4604-8ADE-7F5D5E762256%7D/SMK1.pdf.

Andrews, Edmund L. "Blacks Hit Hardest by Costlier Mortgages." *New York Times,* September 14, 2005.

Asian American Legal Defense and Education Fund. "Asian American Access to Democracy in the 2004 Elections." August 2005. Available online at http://www.aaldef.org/images/2005-08-18_ElectionReport.pdf.

Associated Press. "NAACP: Bush 'Playing Race Card' with Social Security." *USA Today,* April 11, 2005. Available online at http://www.usatoday.com/news/washington/2005-04-11-naacp-bush_x.htm.

Bagby, Ihsan, Paul M. Perl, and Bryan T. Froehle. *The Mosque in America: A National Portrait.* Washington, D.C.: Council on American–Islamic Relations, 2001. Available online at http://www.cair-net.org/mosquereport/Masjid_Study_Project_2000_Report.pdf.

Bailey, Thomas, Davis Jenkins, and Timothy Leinbach. "What We Know about Community College Low-Income and Minority Student Outcomes: Descriptive Statistics from National Surveys." Community College Research Center, Teachers College, Columbia University, New York, January 2005.

Baum, Sandy, and Kathleen Payea. "Trends in College Pricing: 2005," College Board, Washington, D.C., 2005. Available online at http://www.collegeboard.com/prod_downloads/press/cost05/trends_college_pricing_05.pdf.

Bean, Frank D., Jennifer Lee, Jeanne Batalova, and Mark Leach. "Immigration and Fading Color Lines in America." Russell Sage Foundation, New York, and Population Reference Bureau, Washington, D.C., July 2004.

"Black Elected Officials: A Statistical Summary 2001." Joint Center for Political and Economic Studies, Washington, D.C., December 2003.

Black Political Task Force v. Galvin. U.S. District Court for the District of Massachusetts. Civil Action no. 02-11190, February 24, 2004.

Bocian, Debbie Gruenstein, and Richard Zhai. "Borrowers in High Minority Areas More Likely to Receive Prepayment Penalties on Subprime Loans." Center for Responsible Lending, Durham, N.C., January 2005. Available online at http://www.responsible lending.org/pdfs/rr004-PPP_Minority_Neighborhoods-0105.pdf.

Bonilla, Joshua. "Executive Summary: A Demographic Profile of Hispanics in the U.S." Population Resource Center, Washington, D.C., October 2001. Available online at http://www.prcdc.org/summaries/hispanics/hispanics.html.

Burke, Garance. "Financial Education for Hispanics Urged." Associated Press, December 16, 2005.

Carroll, Joseph. "Race and Education 20 Years after *Brown v. Board of Education.*" Gallup News Service, May 14, 2004.

Center for Responsible Lending. "Losing Ground: Foreclosures in the Subprime Market and Their Cost to Homeowners," Durham, N.C., December 2006.

———. "A Snapshot of the Subprime Market." Analysis of 2006 Home Mortgage Disclosure Act data reported by the Federal Financial Institutions Examination Council, Durham, N.C., November 28, 2007.

Child Trends Data Bank. "Birth and Fertility Rates." Available online at http://www .childtrendsdatabank.org/indicators/79BirthRates.cfm.

———. "Educational Attainment." Available online at http://www.childtrendsdatabank .org/indicators/6EducationalAttainment.cfm.

———. "Family Structure." Available online at http://www.childtrendsdatabank.org/ indicators/59FamilyStructure.cfm.

———. "Foster Care." http://www.childtrendsdatabank.org/indicators/12FosterCare.cfm.

———. "Life Expectancy." Available online at http://www.childtrendsdatabank.org/ indicators/78LifeExpectancy.cfm.

———. "Parental Education." Available online at http://www.childtrendsdatabank.org/ indicators/67ParentalEducation.cfm.

———. "Percentage of Births to Unmarried Women." Available online at http://www.child trendsdatabank.org/indicators/75UnmarriedBirths.cfm.

———. "Teen Births." Available online at http://www.childtrendsdatabank.org/indicators/ 13TeenBirth.cfm.

———. "Young Adults in Jail or Prison." Available online at http://www.childtrendsdata bank.org/indicators/89YoungAdultsJailPrison.cfm.

Civil Rights Project, Harvard University. "Democracy Spoiled: National, State, and County Disparities Through Uncounted Ballots," July 2002. Available online at http://www .civilrightsproject.ucla.edu/research/electoral_reform/residual_ballot.php.

———. "Racial Inequity in Special Education: Executive Summary for Federal Policy Makers," June 2002. Available online at http://www.civilrightsproject.harvard.edu/research/specialed/IDEA_paper02.php.

Day, Jennifer Cheesman, and Eric. C. Newburger. "The Big Payoff: Educational Attainment and Synthetic Estimates of Work-Life Earnings." P23-210, U.S. Bureau of the Census, July 2002.

Denton, Nancy A., and Stewart E. Tolney, eds. *American Diversity: A Demographic Challenge for the Twenty-first Century.* Albany: State University of New York Press, 2002.

"Divided by Faith?" *Christianity Today,* vol. 44, no. 11, October 2, 2000, 34. Available online at http://www.christianitytoday.com/ct/2000/011/1.34.html.

Dougherty, Kevin D. "How Monochromatic Is Church Membership? Racial–Ethnic Diversity in Religious Community." *Sociology of Religion* 64 (2003): 65–85.

Dye, Jane Lawler. "Fertility of American Women: June 2004." U.S. Bureau of the Census, P20-555, December 2005.

Eaddy, W. Randy, Carolyn A. Sawyer, Kzuhiro Shimizu, Ray McIlwain, W. Swain Wood, Debbie Segal, and Kilpatrick Stockton. "Residential Segregation, Poverty, and Racism: Obstacles to America's Great Society." Lawyers' Committee for Civil Rights under Law, Washington, D.C., June 2003.

Economic Policy Institute. "African Americans in the Current Recovery." Economic Snapshots, April 6, 2005. Available online at http://www.epinet.org/content.cfm/webfeatures_snapshots_20050406.

Education Trust. "The Funding Gap 2005: Low-Income and Minority Students Shortchanged by Most States," Winter 2005. Available online at http://www2.edtrust.org/NR/rdonlyres/31D276EF-72E1-458A-8C71-E3D262A4C91E/0/FundingGap2005.pdf.

———. "Funding Gaps: 2006," December 2006. Available online at http://www2.edtrust.org/NR/rdonlyres/CDEF9403-5A75-437E-93FF-EBF1174181FB/0/FundingGap2006.pdf.

Eisenbrey, Ross, and William Spriggs. "Two Steps Back: African Americans and Latinos Will Lose Ground under Social Security 'Reform.'" Economic Policy Institute Issue Brief no. 212, July 14, 2005.

Ellen, Ingrid Gould. *Sharing America's Neighborhoods: The Prospects for Stable Racial Integration.* Cambridge, Mass.: Harvard University Press, 2000.

Emerson, M. O., and C. Smith. *Divided by Faith: Evangelical Religion and the Problem of Race in America.* New York: Oxford University Press, 2000.

Espenshade, Thomas J., and Chang Y. Chung. "The Opportunity Cost of Admission Preferences at Elite Universities." *Social Science Quarterly* 86, no. 2 (2005): 293–305.

Fasenfest, David, Jason Booza, and Kurt Metzger. "Living Together: A New Look at Racial and Ethnic Integration in Metropolitan Neighborhoods, 1990–2000." Living Census Series, Brookings Institution, Washington, D.C., April 2004.

"Felony Disenfranchisement Laws in the United States." Sentencing Project, Washington, D.C., November 2005. Available online at http://www.sentencingproject.org/pdfs/1046.pdf.

Frankenberg, Erica, Chungmei Lee, and Gary Orfield. "A Multiracial Society with Segregated Schools: Are We Losing the Dream?" Civil Rights Project, Harvard University, Cambridge, Mass., January 2003.

Frey, William H. "Census 2000 Reveals New Native-Born and Foreign-Born Shifts across U.S." Research Report no. 02-520, Population Studies Center, University of Michigan, Ann Arbor, August 2002.

———. "Charticle." *Milken Institute Review* (2003): 7–10.

————. "Melting Pot Suburbs: A Census 2000 Study of Suburban Diversity." Census 2000 Series, Brookings Institution, Washington, D.C., June 2001.

————. "Metro Magnets for Minorities and Whites: Melting Pots, the New Sunbelt, and the Heartland." Population Studies Center, University of Michigan, Ann Arbor, February 2002.

Frey, William H., and Dowell Myers. "Racial Segregation in U.S. Metropolitan Areas and Cities, 1990–2000: Patterns, Trends, and Explanations." University of Michigan Population Studies Center Research Report no. 05-573, Ann Arbor, April 2005.

Gibson, Campbell, and Kay Jung. "Historical Census Statistics on Population Totals by Race, 1790 to 1990, and by Hispanic Origin, 1970 to 1990, for the United States, Regions, Divisions, and States." Working Paper Series no. 56, U.S. Bureau of the Census, September 2002.

Glaeser, Edward, and Jacob L. Vigdor. "Racial Segregation in the 2000 Census: Promising News." Survey Series, Brookings Institution, Washington, D.C., April 2001.

Gratz et al. v. Bollinger et al. U.S. Supreme Court. No. 02-516, 2002. Available online at http://www.supremecourtus.gov/opinions/02pdf/02-516.pdf.

Grutter v. Bollinger et al. U.S. Supreme Court. No. 02-241, 2002. Available online at http://www.supremecourtus.gov/opinions/02pdf/02-241.pdf.

Grutter v. Bollinger et al. Amici Curia Brief in Support of Respondents by Lieutenant-General Julius W. Becton et al. U.S. Supreme Court. Nos. 02-516 and 02-241. Available online at http://www.umich.edu/%7Eurel/admissions/legal/gru_amicus-ussc/um/MilitaryL-both.pdf.

Hamilton, Brady E., Stephanie J. Ventura, Joyce A. Martin, and Paul D. Sutton. "Preliminary Births for 2004," Tables 1–2. National Center for Health Statistics, Hyattsville, Md., 2005. Available online at http://www.cdc.gov/nchs/products/pubs/pubd/hestats/prelim_births/prelim_births04.htm.

Harris, Douglas N. "Ending the Blame Game on Educational Inequity: A Study of 'High Flying Schools' and NCLB." Education Policy Research Unit, Arizona State University, Tempe, March 2006. Available online at http://www.asu.edu/educ/epsl/EPRU/documents/EPSL-0603-120-EPRU.pdf.

Harrison, Paige M., and Allen J. Beck. "Prison and Jail Inmates at Midyear 2004." Bureau of Prison Statistics Bulletin, U.S. Department of Justice, April 2005.

Havens, John, and Paul Schervish. "Why the $41 Trillion Wealth Transfer Estimate Is Still Valid: A Review of Challenges and Questions." *Journal of Gift Planning* (2003): 11–15, 47–50.

Heller, Donald E., and Christopher J. Rasmussen. "Merit Scholarships and College Access: Evidence from Florida and Michigan." Pp. 25–40 in *Who Should We Help? The Negative Social Consequences of Merit Scholarships,* ed. Donald E. Heller and Patricia Marin. Cambridge, Mass.: Civil Rights Project, Harvard University, 2002.

Hellerstein, Judith, and David Neumark. "Workplace Segregation in the United States: Race, Ethnicity and Skill." National Bureau of Economic Research Working Paper no. 11599, September 2005.

Hicklin, Alisa. "Latino Dropouts and High Stakes Testing." Project for Equity, Representation, and Governance, Texas A&M University, College Station, September 2003.

Himmelstein, David U., Elizabeth Warren, Debora Thorne, and Steffie Woolhandler. "MarketWatch: Illness and Injury as Contributors to Bankruptcy." *Health Affairs,* February 2005. Available online at http://content.healthaffairs.org/cgi/content/full/hlthaff.w5.63/DC1.

"Historical Poll Results on Race Relations." Gallup Organization. Gallup Brain, November 12, 2005.

Hopkins, Jim. "Deaths of Hispanic Workers Soar 53 Percent." *USA Today,* March 24, 2002.

Hoyert, Donna L., Hsiang-Ching Kung, and Betty L. Smith. "Deaths: Preliminary Data for 2003." National Vital Statistics Reports, vol. 53, no. 15, table 6. Available online at http://www.cdc.gov/nchs/data/nvsr/nvsr53/nvsr53_15.pdf.

Huus, Kari. "Laws Barring Felons from Voting Hit Blacks Hard." MSNBC, October 4, 2005. Available online at http://msnbc.msn.com/id/9008232.

Iceland, John. "Beyond Black and White: Residential Segregation in Multiethnic America." Social Science Research 33, no. 2 (June 2004): 248–271.

Iceland, John, Daniel H. Weinberg, and Erika Steinmetz. "Racial and Ethnic Residential Segregation in the United States: 1980–2000." U.S. Bureau of the Census, CENSR-3, August 2002.

Inter-American Development Bank, Multilateral Investment Fund. "Remittances 2005: Transforming Labor Markets and Promoting Financial Democracy: Statistical Comparisons." Buenos Aires, November 2005.

"Interracial Teen Dating." USA Today/Gallup poll, October 13–20, 1997.

Jamieson, Amie, Hyon B. Shin, and Jennifer Day. "Voting and Registration in the Election of November 2000." U.S. Bureau of the Census, P20-542, February 2002.

Joint Center for Housing Studies. The State of the Nation's Housing: 2005. Cambridge, Mass.: Harvard University, 2005.

Jones, Jeffrey M. "Most Americans Approve of Interracial Dating." Gallup Organization. Gallup Brain. October 7, 2005.

———. "Race, Ideology and Support for Affirmative Action." Gallup Organization. Gallup Brain, August 23, 2005.

Kiely, Kathy. "Parties Putting Minority Candidates on A-List." USA Today, December 26, 2005, 4A.

Klein, Alec. "A Tenuous Hold on the Middle Class: African Americans on Shifting Ground." Washington Post, December 18, 2004, A1.

Kochhar, Rakesh. "Latino Labor Report, 2004: More Jobs for New Immigrants but at Lower Wages." Pew Hispanic Center, Washington, D.C., May 2005.

———. "Survey of Mexican Migrants, Part 3: The Economic Transition to America." Pew Hispanic Center, Washington, D.C., December 2005.

———. "The Wealth of Hispanic Households: 1996 to 2002." Pew Hispanic Center, Washington, D.C., October 2004.

Lee, Sharon M. "New Marriages, New Families: U.S. Racial and Hispanic Intermarriage." Population Bulletin, Population Reference Bureau, Washington, D.C., June 2005.

Leonder-Wright, Betsy, Meishu Lui, Gloribell Mota, Dedrick Muhammad, and Mara Voukydis. "State of the Dream 2005: Disowned in the Ownership Society." United for a Fair Economy, Boston, January 10, 2005. Available online at http://faireconomy.org/press/2005/StateoftheDream2005.pdf.

Lewin, Tamar. "The Two Faces of A.P." New York Times, January 8, 2006. Available online at http://www.nytimes.com/2006/01/08/education/edlife/apee.html?pagewanted=1.

Lewis Mumford Center for Comparative Urban and Regional Research. "Ethnic Diversity Grows, Neighborhood Integration Lags Behind." University at Albany, Albany, N.Y., revised December 18, 2001. Available online at http://mumford.albany.edu/census/WholePop/WPreport/page1.html.

———. "Separate and Unequal: The Neighborhood Gap for Blacks and Hispanics in Metropolitan America." University at Albany, Albany, N.Y., October 13, 2002. Available online at http://mumford.albany.edu/census/SepUneq/SUReport/SURepPage1.htm.

Logan, John R. "America's Newcomers." Lewis Mumford Center for Comparative Urban and Regional Research, University at Albany, Albany, N.Y., 2003. http://mumford.albany.edu/census/NewComersReport/NewComer01.htm.

———. "From Many Shores: Asians in Census 2000." Lewis Mumford Center for Comparative Urban and Regional Research, University at Albany, Albany, N.Y., October 6, 2001.

———. "How Race Counts for Hispanic Americans." Lewis Mumford Center for Comparative Urban and Regional Research, University at Albany, Albany, N.Y., July 14, 2003.

———. "The New Ethnic Enclaves in America's Suburbs." Lewis Mumford Center for Comparative Urban and Regional Research, University at Albany, Albany, N.Y., 2001. Available online at http://mumford.albany.edu/census/suburban/SuburbanReport/page1.html.

Logan, John R., and Glenn Deane. "Black Diversity in Metropolitan America." Lewis Mumford Center for Comparative Urban and Regional Research, University at Albany, Albany, N.Y., August 15, 2003.

Martin, Joyce A., Brady E. Hamilton, Paul D. Sutton, Stephanie J. Ventura, Fay Menacker, and Martha L. Munson. "Births: Final Data for 2003." National Vital Statistics Reports, vol. 54, no. 2, U.S. Department of Health and Human Services, September 8, 2005.

Mazzuca, Josephine. "For Most Americans, Friendship Is Colorblind." Gallup Organization. Gallup Brain, July 13, 2004..

McNeely, Marguarite, and Edward J. Boyko. "Type 2 Diabetes Prevalence in Asian Americans." Diabetes Care 27, no. 1 (2004): 66–69.

Metropolitan Center for Urban Education. "With All Deliberate Speed: Achievement, Citizenship and Diversity in American Education." Steinhardt School of Education, New York University, 2005. Available online at http://education.nyu.edu/metrocenter/brownplus/reports.pdf.

Mickelson, Roslyn Arlin. "The Incomplete Desegregation of the Charlotte–Mecklenburg Schools and Its Consequences, 1971-2004." Pp. 97–110 in School Resegregation: Must the South Turn Back? ed. John Charles Boger and Gary Orfield. Chapel Hill: University of North Carolina Press, 2005.

Morin, Richard. "A Distorted Image of Minorities: Poll Suggests That What Whites Think May Affect Their Beliefs." Washington Post, October 8, 1994, A1.

Moskos, Charles C., and John Sibley Butler. All That We Can Be: Black Leadership and Racial Integration the Army Way. New York: Basic Books, 1997.

"National Roster of Hispanic Elected Officials, Annual." National Association of Latino Elected and Appointed Officials, Washington, D.C., 2005.

National Voting Rights Institute. Electronic update, March 2004. Available online at http://www.nvri.org/updates/e-updates/update_march_2004.html.

O'Hare, William, and Mark Mather. "The Growing Number of Kids in Severely Distressed Neighborhoods: Evidence from the 2000 Census." Annie E. Casey Foundation, Baltimore, and Population Reference Bureau, Washington, D.C., revised October 2003.

Orfield, Gary, and Chungmei Lee. "Brown at 50: King's Dream or Plessy's Nightmare?" Civil Rights Project, Harvard University, Cambridge, Mass., January 2004.

———. "Why Segregation Matters: Poverty and Educational Inequality." Civil Rights Project, Harvard University, Cambridge, Mass., January 2005.

Orfield, Gary, Daniel Losen, Johanna Wald, and Christopher B. Swanson. "Losing Our Future: How Minority Youth Are Being Left behind by the Graduation Rate Crisis." Civil Rights Project, Harvard University, Urban Institute, Advocates for Children of New York, and Civil Society Institute, revised March 11, 2004.

Pace, David. "More Blacks Live with Pollution." Associated Press, December 13, 2005. Available online at http://abcnews.go.com/Health/wireStory?id=1402790&CMP=OTC-RSSFeeds0312.

Page, Susan. "Bush Opening Doors with a Diverse Cabinet." USA Today, December 9, 2004.

Parents Involved in Community Schools, Petitioner v. Seattle School District No. 1 et al.; Meredith v. Jefferson County Board of Education. U.S. Supreme Court, no. 05-908, 2007. Available online at http://www.supremecourtus.gov/opinions/06pdf/05-908.pdf

Passel, Jeffrey. "Election 2004: The Latino and Asian Vote." Urban Institute Immigration Studies Program, Washington, D.C., July 27, 2004. Available online at http://www.urban.org/UploadedPDF/900723.pdf.

———. "Estimates of the Size and Characteristics of the Undocumented Population." Pew Hispanic Center, Washington, D.C., March 21, 2005.

———. "The Size and Characteristics of the Unauthorized Migrant Population in the U.S. Estimates Based on the March 2005 Current Population Survey." Pew Hispanic Center, Washington, D.C., March 7, 2006.

Pew Hispanic Center. "Educational Attainment: Better than Meets the Eye, but Large Challenges Remain." Fact sheet, Washington, D.C., January 1, 2002.

———. "Hispanics: A People in Motion: Trends 2005." Washington, D.C., 2005.

Pew Hispanic Center/Kaiser Family Foundation. "National Survey of Latinos: Education." Summary and Chartpack, January 2004.

Pew Research Center for the People and the Press. "The 2004 Political Landscape: Evenly Divided and Increasingly Polarized." November 5, 2003. Available online at http://people-press.org/reports/display.php3?ReportID=196.

Raphael, Steven, and Michael Stoll. "Modest Progress: The Narrowing Spatial Mismatch Between Blacks and Jobs in the 1990s." Living Census Series, Brookings Institution, Washington, D.C., December 2002.

Reed, Cheryl L., and Monifa Thomas. "Blacks Hurt by Gap in Home Values." *Chicago Sun Times*, November 13, 2005, A20.

Robinson, Corre L., Tiffany Taylor, Donald Tomaskovic-Devey, Catherine Zimmer, and Matthew W. Irvine Jr. "Studying Race or Ethnic and Sex Segregation at the Establishment Level." *Work and Occupations* 32 (February 2005): 5–38.

Rusk, David. "The 'Segregation Tax': The Cost of Racial Segregation to Black Homeowners." Brookings Institution Survey Series, Washington, D.C., October 2001. Available online at http://www.brook.edu/es/urban/publications/rusk.pdf.

Saad, Lydia. "Do Sparks Fly When Blacks and Whites Are Neighbors?" Gallup Organization. Gallup Brain, July 26, 2005

Saenz, Rogelio. "Latinos and the Changing Face of America." Russell Sage Foundation and Population Reference Bureau, Washington, D.C., July 2004.

Sanoff, Alvin P. "Restricted Access." *Lumina Foundation Focus*, Summer 2003, 5–24.

Schacter, Jason P. "Migration by Race and Hispanic Origin: 1995–2000." Census 2000 Special Reports, U.S. Bureau of the Census, CENSR-13, October 2003.

Segal, David R., and Mady Wechsler Segal. "America's Military Population." Population Bulletin, Population Reference Bureau, December 2004.

Shapiro, Thomas M. *The Hidden Cost of Being African-American.* New York: Oxford University Press, 2004.

Shapiro, Thomas, and Melvin Oliver. "Closing the Racial Wealth Gap." Monthly Perspectives, Institute on Assets and Social Policy, Brandeis University, Waltham, Mass., September 2005.

Smelser, Neil J., William Julius Wilson, and Faith Mitchell, eds. *America Becoming: Racial Trends and Their Consequences,* vols. 1–2. Washington, D.C.: National Academy Press, 2001.

Smith, James P. "Race and Ethnicity in the Labor Market: Trends over the Short and Long Term." Pp. 52–97 in *America Becoming: Racial Trends and Their Consequences,* vol. 2, ed. Neil J. Smelser, William Julius Wilson, and Faith Mitchell. Washington, D.C.: National Academy Press, 2001.

Stainback, Kevin, Corre L. Robinson, and Donald Tomaskovic-Devey. "Race and Workplace Integration." *American Behavioral Scientist* 48 (May 2005): 1200–1228.

Stein, Rob. "Study Links Discrimination, Blacks' Health." *Washington Post,* May 1, 2005, A17.

Stoll, Michael. "African Americans and the Color Line." Russell Sage Foundation, New York, and Population Reference Bureau, Washington, D.C., July 2004.

Sum, Andrew, Ishwar Khatiwada, Frimpomaa Ampaw, Paulo Tobar, and Sheila Palma. "Trends in Black Male Joblessness and Year-Round Idleness: An Employment Crisis Ignored." Center for Labor Market Studies, Northeastern University, Boston, June 2004.

Stoops, Nicole. "Educational Attainment in the United States: 2003." U.S. Bureau of the Census, P20-550, June 2004. Available online at http://www.census.gov/prod/2004pubs/p20-550.pdf.

Suro, Roberto. "Latino Power? It Will Take Time for the Population Boom to Translate." *Washington Post,* June 26, 2005, B1.

Suro, Roberto, and Audrey Singer. "Latino Growth in Metropolitan America: Changing Patterns, New Locations." Survey Series, Census 2000, Brookings Institution, Washington, D.C., June 2002.

Tate, Katherine, and Kim DeFronzo. "Unequal Participation in American Politics and Its Implications for Children and Family Policies." University of California, Irvine, May 11, 2000.

Tomaskovic-Devey, Donald, Catherine Zimmer, Corre Robinson, Tiffany Taylor, Tricia McTague, Kevin Stainback, and Jamie Wolf. "Documenting Desegregation: Estimates of U.S. Workplace Sex and Ethnic Segregation: 1966–2000." Paper presented at the Annual Meeting of the American Sociological Association, San Francisco, 2004.

Toussaint-Comeau, Maude, Thomas Smith, and Ludovic Comeau Jr. "Occupational Attainment and Mobility of Hispanics in a Changing Economy." Pew Hispanic Center, Washington, D.C., 2005. Available online at http://pewhispanic.org/files/reports/59.1.pdf.

U.S. Bureau of the Census. "Annual Estimates of the Population by Sex, Race and Hispanic or Latino Origin for the United States: April 1, 2000, to July 1, 2004." NC-EST2004-03, released June 9, 2005, last online revision, February 11, 2005.

———. "The Asian and Pacific Islander Population in the United States: March 2002." Current Population Reports, P20-540, May 2003.

———. "The Black Population in the United States: March 2002." Current Population Reports, P20-541, April 2003.

———. "Characteristics of the Population by U.S. Citizenship Status. Table 1.1: Population by Sex, Age, and U.S. Citizenship Status: 2004." Internet release February 22, 2005. Available online at http://www.census.gov/population/www/socdemo/foreign/ppl-176.html#cit.

———. "Cumulative Estimates of the Components of Population Change by Race and Hispanic or Latino Origin for the United States: April 1, 2000 to July 1, 2004." Table 5. Population Division, NC-EST2004-0. Available online at http://www.census.gov/popest/archives/2000s/vintage_2004.

———. "Current Population Survey, 2005." Annual Social and Economic Supplement, Available online at http://www.census.gov/cps.

———. "The Hispanic Population in the United States: March 2002." Current Population Reports, P20-545, June 2003.

————. "The Hispanic Population in the U.S., Detailed Tables 2004, Table 9.2: Labor Force and Employment Status of the Civilian Population 16 Years and over by Sex and Hispanic Origin Type: 2004." Last online revision, December 14, 2005. Available online at http://www.census.gov/population/www/socdemo/hispanic/cps2004.html.

————. "Historical Income Tables: Households, Table H-12: Household by Number of Earners by Median and Mean Income." Last online revision, February 11, 2005. Available online at http://www.census.gov/hhes/income/histinc/inchhtoc.html.

————. "Historical Time Series Tables: A-1—Reported Voting and Registration by Race, Hispanic Origin, Sex, and Age Groups: November 1964 to 2004." Voting and Registration, last revised June 16, 2005. Available online at http://www.census.gov/population/www/socdemo/voting.html.

————. "Housing Vacancies and Homeownership." Annual Statistics, 2006.

————. "Income, Poverty, and Health Insurance Coverage in the United States: 2004." P60-229, August 2005.

————. "Resident Population Estimates of the United States by Sex, Race, and Hispanic Origin: April 1, 1990, to July 1, 1999, with Short-Term Projection to November 1, 2000." Internet release, January 2, 2001. Available online at http://www.census.gov/popest/archives/1990s/nat-srh.txt.

————. "Table 2: Earnings by Detailed Occupation, 1999." Last online revision, May 13, 2004. Available online at http://www.census.gov/hhes/income/earnings/call2usboth.html.

————. "Table 22: Population by Metropolitan and Nonmetropolitan Residence, Sex, Race, and Hispanic Origin: March 2002." Internet release, May 28, 2003. Available online at http://www.census.gov/population/socdemo/race/api/ppl-163/tab22.pdf.

————. "Table 22. Resident Population by Region." Statistical Abstract of the United States, 2004–2005.

————. "The Two or More Races Population: 2000." Census 2000 Brief, C2KBR/01-6, November 2001.

————. "U.S. Interim Projections by Age, Sex, Race, and Hispanic Origin." Internet release, March 18, 2004. Available online at http://www.census.gov/ipc/www/usinterimproj.

————. "Voting and Registration in the Election of November 2004." Online tables, last revised May 25, 2005. Available online at http://www.census.gov/population/www/socdemo/voting/cps2004.html.

————. "We the American Foreign Born." WE-7, September 1993.

U.S. Department of Education, National Center for Education Statistics, Higher Education General Information Survey (HEGIS), "Fall Enrollment in Colleges and Universities," surveys, 1976, 1980; 1990–2002 Integrated Postsecondary Education Data System (IPEDS), "Fall Enrollment Survey" (IPEDS-EF: 90-99), Spring 2001–Spring 2003.

————. "The Long-Term Trend." National Assessment of Educational Progress (NAEP), Nation's Report Card. Available online at http://nces.ed.gov/nationsreportcard/ltt/results2004.

————. "Assessment Results: Mathematics by Race/Ethnicity." NAEP, Nation's Report Card. Available online at http://nces.ed.gov/nationsreportcard/nrc/reading_math_2005/s0026.asp?printver=.

————. "2005 Assessment Results: Reading by Race/Ethnicity." NAEP, Nation's Report Card. Available online at http://nces.ed.gov/nationsreportcard/nrc/reading_math_2005/s0011.asp?printver=.

————. "Postsecondary Participation Rates by Sex and Race/Ethnicity: 1974–2003." Issue brief, March 2005.

U.S. Department of Health and Human Services (HHS). "Minority Health Disparities at a Glance." HHS fact sheet. July 12, 2004.

U.S. Department of Housing and Community Development. "Discrimination in Metropolitan Housing Markets: National Results from Phase 1, Phase 2, and Phase 3 of the Housing Discrimination Study (HDS), 2000." Available online at http://www.huduser.org/publications/hsgfin/hds.html.

U.S. Department of Labor, Bureau of Labor Statistics. "Highlights of Women's Earnings in 2004." Report no. 987, September, 2005.

———. "Historical Unemployment Rates by Race." Available online at http://www.bls.gov/cps.

———. "Table 1: Employment Status of the Foreign-born and Native-born Populations by Selected Characteristics, 2003–04 Annual Averages." May 12, 2005. Available online at http://www.bls.gov/news.release/forbrn.t01.htm.

Vischer, Robert K. "Racial Segregation in American Churches and Its Implications for School Vouchers." *Florida Law Review* 53 (2001): 204–215.

Weiss, Rick. "Scientists Find DNA Change That Explains White Skin." *Washington Post,* December 16, 2005, A1.

Wellner, Allison Stein. "U.S. Attitudes toward Interracial Dating Are Liberalizing." Population Reference Bureau, Washington, D.C., June 2005.

Western, Bruce, Vincent Schiraldi, and Jason Ziedenberg. "Education and Incarceration." Justice Policy Institute, Washington, D.C., August 28, 2003.

Winseman, Albert L. "Race and Religion: Divisions Steeped in History." Gallup Organization. Gallup Brain, August 10, 2004.

I

Foundations of Multiracial Inequality

2

Color Lines in the Mind

Implicit Prejudice, Discrimination,
and the Potential for Change

Nilanjana Dasgupta

I n 1959 John Howard Griffin, a White journalist, traveled through the
segregated South as a Black man. He darkened his skin with medication,
shaved his hair, and exchanged his privileged White life for the life of a
working class Black man (Griffin 1960). The book *Black Like Me* chronicles
his experiences as he crosses the color line. Griffin's experiences as a Black
man ran the gamut from legal segregation in public spaces, to "hate stares"
and intimidation that enforced rigid social customs about "appropriate"
interracial interactions, to polite but firm refusal of employment. This was a
society in which the color line separating Black from White was rigidly
upheld; where bigotry was blatant; and where few people publicly questioned
the legitimacy of a race-based hierarchy.

A lot has changed in fifty years. Grassroots social movements dedicated
to the civil rights of historically disadvantaged groups have produced far-
reaching changes in the laws and policies that govern civil society. These legal
changes have also shifted social norms and individual attitudes (Albert and
Albert 1984; Chong 1991; Gitlin 1987; Levy 1992; Williams 1987). The notion
that prejudice and discrimination against disadvantaged groups, most notably African Americans and other racial/ethnic minorities, is illegitimate and
unethical has become an increasingly mainstream philosophy. These changes
in American public opinion are clearly reflected in national surveys that
reveal racist attitudes have declined steadily over the past few decades
(Brigham 1972; Karlins et al. 1969; Kluegel and Smith 1986; Maykovich 1971,
1972; Schuman et al. 1997). In addition to the changed social mores, the color

line in American society today has become vastly more complex than the Black–White divide in the 1950s, as immigration and globalization have changed the racial/ethnic composition of the American population.

Despite optimistic trends in the direction of dismantled legal barriers, greater diversity, and egalitarian attitudes, other evidence reveals glaring structural inequalities that continue to exist in several areas of everyday life—healthcare, housing, education, employment, and the justice system (Daniels 2001; Leonhardt 2002; Portwood 1995; Raudenbush and Kasim 1998; Stohlberg, 2002). One reason for the discrepancy between evidence that *individuals' attitudes* have become more egalitarian and other evidence revealing *structural disparities* may be that, until recently, individuals' attitudes have been measured by relying solely on what people say—their self-reported (or conscious) thoughts and opinions. This heavy reliance on conscious attitude measurement has resulted in the underestimation of the pervasiveness of prejudice in two ways. First, because contemporary social norms frown upon overt expressions of prejudice, people may not be willing to report their attitudes honestly, especially if those attitudes violate social norms (Dovidio and Gaertner 1986; Jones and Sigall 1972). Second, when asked about their opinions about minority groups, people are likely to be vigilant and thoughtful in their responses, whereupon they may draw a sharp distinction between their personal attitudes and societal stereotypes ("Society at large is prejudiced against Group X, but I am not"). But when they are not vigilant, this sharp distinction may become blurry; their personal views and societal views may start to overlap and jointly influence people's implicit or unconscious judgments and behavior (Banaji 2001; Banaji and Greenwald 1994; Dasgupta 2004; Greenwald and Banaji 1995; Nisbett and Wilson 1977). These reasons prompted social psychologists to develop new theories of unconscious or implicit prejudice and stereotypes and new measurement tools that do not rely so heavily on people's willingness and ability to accurately report their thoughts and actions (Crosby et al. 1980; Gaertner and Dovidio 1977; Jones and Sigall 1972; see also Nisbett and Wilson 1977).

Attitudes and beliefs are considered to be *unconscious* or *implicit* when people express them without being fully aware of what they are saying and its implications or without having the ability to control and change their responses at will (Bargh 1994, 1997; Greenwald and Banaji 1995). One might ask—how can attitudes be measured without people's awareness and control? This is a reasonable question given that the most common way to measure attitudes is by asking people to reflect on their opinions and then report how they feel about a particular group or issue using questionnaires or interviews. There is a different way of conceptualizing attitudes: that is, at a basic level an attitude is simply a mental association between a group and a good or bad feeling. These mental associations vary in psychological strength. Some attitudes are strong and therefore "pop into mind" quickly and easily, whereas other attitudes are weak and take longer to come to mind. For example, if a person holds a strong negative attitude toward a group, when she or he sees a member of that group, the negative evaluation should come to mind quickly and automatically. By contrast, if a person holds a weak negative attitude toward a group, when she or he encounters a group member, the negative evaluation should come to mind much more slowly. In other words, *the speed with which good or bad evaluations come to mind* can serve as an indirect indicator of people's attitudes toward particular groups without researchers having to rely on people's self-reports of how they feel.

People may be implicitly biased in their thoughts and actions even if their explicit attitudes are unbiased. Because individuals are often unaware of their subtle bias and cannot easily correct such thoughts and actions, implicitly biased actions may occur repeatedly, accumulating over time and across individuals. As a result, the negative effects of biased actions may add up quickly to produce large structural disparities in employment, housing, healthcare delivery, treatment by the criminal justice system, etc. Because each instance of bias is subtle, seemingly innocuous, and clearly not explicit bigotry, at face value it appears as though the days of prejudice and discrimination are in the past. But one just has to scratch below the surface to discover that current inequalities on many socioeconomic and sociopolitical indicators may be traced back to many small actions favoring historically privileged groups (White Americans) over less privileged groups (African Americans, Latinos, Asian Americans, and immigrants).

Implicit attitudes are typically measured using computer-driven rapid response tasks that capture the speed with which good versus bad thoughts come to mind when people are shown individuals who belong to particular groups. In one such task, the Implicit Association Test (IAT), participants see faces of individuals (e.g., African Americans and White Americans) and words with good or bad meaning (e.g., joy versus death) flash briefly on a computer screen one at a time (Greenwald et al. 1998). As these pictures and words appear on the screen participants are instructed to group them rapidly by pressing one of two computer keys. In one part of the IAT they are instructed to group together Black faces and good words by pressing the same key and White faces and bad words by pressing a different key. In another part of the IAT, the groupings are reversed: now they are instructed to group Black faces and bad words using one key and White faces and good words using a different key. The basic premise of the IAT is that if participants unconsciously associate bad concepts more strongly with Black than White Americans, then the task in which they have to group together Black with bad and White with good ought to be subjectively easier and yield faster responses than the task in which they have to group together Black with good and White with bad. The difference in the speed of response to these two tasks in terms of reaction time provides a measure of implicit racial preference for Whites compared to Blacks.

Implicit Preference and Prejudice along Color Lines: Research Evidence and Practical Applications

Initial investigations of the nature of implicit prejudice and stereotypes focused entirely on the attitudes held by members of advantaged groups toward members of disadvantaged groups. The primary prediction of this early research was that individuals who belong to socially advantaged groups would favor their own group at the expense of other (less advantaged) groups in terms of evaluations, judgments, and behavior. This prediction is consistent with social identity theory, which argues that when people strongly identify with their ingroup and when their self-esteem is linked to the perceived worthiness of their ingroup, they will tend to favor their ingroup and sometimes derogate other outgroups (Abrams and Hogg 1988, 1990; Bourhis 1994; Bourhis et al. 1997; Oakes and Turner 1980; Rubin and Hewstone 1998; Tajfel 1981; Tajfel and Turner 1986; Turner et al. 1987).

By now almost a hundred studies have documented individuals' tendency to rapidly associate positive characteristics with ingroups more than outgroups (i.e., ingroup favoritism) as well as the tendency to associate negative characteristics with outgroups more than ingroups (i.e., outgroup derogation). For example, White Americans, on average, implicitly prefer their own group over African Americans. That is, they are faster at associating good concepts (joy, peace) with Whites compared to Blacks; likewise they are faster at associating bad concepts (death, vomit) with Blacks compared to Whites (Dasgupta and Greenwald 2001; Dasgupta et al. 2000; Devine 1989; Dovidio et al. 2002; Fazio et al. 1995; Greenwald et al. 1998; Kawakami et al. 1998; McConnell and Leibold 2001; Nosek et al. 2002; Rudman et al. 2001; von Hippel et al. 1997; Wittenbrink et al. 1997, 2001).

The pervasiveness of implicit bias along color lines is not limited to pure negative evaluations (disliking); it also emerges in the form of group-specific stereotypes. For example, race-based stereotypes link Black men with hostility, danger, and crime; people learn these stereotypes passively through exposure to mass media, peer opinions, etc. Once learned, these stereotypes automatically influence their judgments of Black men in crime-relevant situations. For example, people are more likely to misidentify objects seen for a split second in the presence of Black men as deadly weapons rather than innocuous tools; however, they are more likely to misidentify the same objects seen in the presence of White men as innocuous tools rather than deadly weapons (Correll et al. 2002; Greenwald et al. 2003; Payne 2001). The biasing influence of implicit racial stereotypes on weapon misidentification occurs even when people have the conscious goal to avoid using racial stereotypes to make their judgments, and it occurs regardless of participants' own race (both White and Black Americans show the same effect; Correll et al. 2002; Payne et al. 2002).

These simple laboratory experiments about race-based errors in weapon identification have a clear and disturbing parallel in the real world. Such errors distort people's rapid judgments about who is armed and dangerous and can lead to fatal mistakes such as the fatal shooting of Amadou Diallo, a West African man, in 1999. Four New York City police officers searching for a rape suspect knocked on Amadou Diallo's door to question him. When he came to the door he reached inside his jacket, at which point the officers shot at him forty-one times, hitting him with nineteen bullets. The object Diallo was reaching for turned out to be his wallet. What led to this tragic incident? Were these police officers overly racist or is it possible that their split second decision about what Diallo was pulling out of his pocket was unconsciously triggered by stereotypes linking Black men with crime? The answer to these questions are critical because it determines whether the best way to eliminate such costly human errors involves changing police officers' conscious racial attitudes by instituting sensitivity training or by changing their unconscious associations about race and crime.

These questions have motivated recent research in social psychology. Some preliminary data suggest that race bias in decisions to shoot may be reduced when individuals have more contact with African Americans which is likely to weaken racial stereotypes (Correll et al. 2002), and when they gain extensive practice at making accurate decisions in simulated situations where the race of the suspect is unrelated to the presence of a weapon (Plant and Peruche 2005; Plant et al. 2005). However, other related studies demonstrate that although police officers with extensive training in law enforcement show less implicit race bias in decisions to "shoot" in crime-related simulations compared to civilians from the same community, such bias is not completely erased even in the case of trained police officers (Correll et al., 2005). Thus, the conditions required to completely eliminate error-riddled decisions to shoot remains an open issue for now and is being pursued by several researchers.

Although one might tacitly assume that all individuals who are categorized into a particular racial minority group are equally likely to be targets of implicit stereotyping, recent research reveals that is not the case. Individuals who have more Afrocentric facial features (darker skin color, broader nose, and fuller lips) are more likely to be targets of implicit bias than others who have more Eurocentric facial features (lighter skin color, narrow nose and lips) (Blair, Judd, and Fallman 2004; Blair et al. 2002; Livingston and Brewer 2002). Interestingly, both Black and White individuals with Afrocentric facial features (regardless of their racial group) are unconsciously judged in terms of Black stereotypes compared to other Black and White individuals with Eurocentric facial features (Blair et al. 2002). Feature-based stereotyping occurs even when people are instructed to avoid stereotyping, which suggests that stereotypic beliefs influence first impressions of others without perceivers' awareness and cannot be easily corrected by activating conscious intentions to avoid prejudice.

What might be the consequence of race-based stereotypes of physical appearance in the real world? A recent archival study suggests that such stereotypes may have implicitly influenced sentencing decisions for defendants convicted of felonies (Blair, Judd, and Chapleau 2004). An analysis of a random sample of inmate records in the state of Florida revealed that, although Black and White inmates who had equivalent criminal histories received roughly equivalent sentences, inmates with more Afrocentric features (regardless of their race) received harsher sentences than those with less Afrocentric features even though the felonies they committed were equivalent in seriousness as judged by Florida's ten-point felony rating system. Like the laboratory findings described above, these archival findings based on real world convictions suggest that racial stereotyping based on the facial features of offenders is a form of bias that is largely overlooked.

Variations in skin color and Afrocentric features among Black Americans also influence individuals' socioeconomic and professional outcomes in life. Sociological research has found that light complexioned African Americans command higher status jobs and higher incomes than their darker complexioned counterparts, even after family background variables are controlled (Hill 2000; Keith and Herring 1991). For example, using a national sample of Black women and men from the National Survey of Black Americans (1979–1980), Keith and Herring (1991) found even after taking into account demographic and family variables such as parental education, parental socioeconomic status, urban/rural differences, age, marital status, etc., African Americans with darker complexions had fewer years of formal education; they were less likely to be employed in high-level professional positions; and they had lower personal and family income than their lighter complexioned peers. Using different methodology, Hill (2000) found conceptually similar results. One explanation for the association between dark complexion and decreased socioeconomic success is that Afrocentric physical appearance may automatically activate negative racial stereotypes about lesser competence in the mind of perceivers which in turn may lead to disparate treatment. This argument is consistent with evidence that darker complexioned African Americans typically report more instances of discrimination than their lighter complexioned peers (Klonoff and Landrine 2000). Analogous to Blair and colleagues' controlled laboratory studies, in many cases, perceivers may be unaware that the presence or absence of Afrocentric physical appearance (rather than race per se) influenced their impressions of Black individuals.

Because of the long history of Black oppression in the United States, not surprisingly most of the research on implicit bias has focused on Whites' implicit bias against Blacks and its implications in the real world. However, as the demographics of the United States became increasingly varied in the twentieth century due to immigration from Latin America and Asia, research ventured into new territory by examining Americans' implicit attitudes toward Latinos, Asians, and immigrants. This research shows that implicit bias is not limited to Whites' attitudes toward Blacks. Rather, White Americans also implicitly favor their own group over Latinos and Asians (Ashburn-Nardo et al. 2001; Devos and Banaji 2005; Ottaway et al. 2001; Rudman et al. 1999; Son Hing et al. 2002; Uhlmann et al. 2002). Specifically, Whites exhibit implicit bias against Latin American facial features and dark skin and show preference for European facial features and light skin. Such preference for "Europeanness" extends beyond esthetic preferences. Specifically, Latinos of European appearance enjoy far better socioeconomic outcomes in the United States than Latinos of native appearance. This socioeconomic difference in the experience of Latinos as a function of skin color was vividly documented in an article in the *New York Times* which described the experience of Cuban immigrants in the United States using as examples two friends of similar socioeconomic background who moved to the United States at the same time. The person whose appearance was mulatto and others like him experienced greater economic difficulty post-immigration than his friend whose appearance was European and others like him. Such differences in socioeconomic standing are often evident years after immigration (Ojito 2000).

Whites' implicit attitudes toward Asian Americans reveal a different sort of bias that may be labeled, in shorthand, as the perpetual foreigner status. Although a core value in American society explicitly endorsed by most Americans and the bedrock of Anglo-American jurisprudence is the right to equal treatment for all American citizens, such values have not necessarily been internalized at an implicit level. This is illustrated by people's strong propensity to equate American with White: when research participants are asked to think of who is American, Whites come to their mind more quickly and automatically than Asian Americans. Even when people are shown images of Asian American celebrities (e.g., Connie Chung, Michael Chang) compared to White European celebrities (e.g., Hugh Grant, Katarina Witt), Asian American celebrities are implicitly perceived to be more foreign and less American than their European counterparts (Devos and Banaji 2005). In other words, Asian Americans remain perpetual foreigners in the eyes of American society despite their American nationality. This perpetual foreigner status may explain why Asian Americans are sometimes treated with suspicion about their national allegiance in situations involving perceived threats to national security. Consider the case of countless Japanese Americans who were forced into internment camps during World War II because they were suspected of being potential spies for Japan or the recent case of Wen Ho Lee, a Chinese American scientist at the Los Alamos laboratory who was accused of spying for China but eventually acquitted because of lack of evidence. These examples of implicit anti-Asian bias reveal a different form of negative stereotyping than other types of racial bias described earlier.

The prevalence of implicit preference for groups in power and bias against powerless groups is not limited to the United States. Similar findings have also been obtained in Britain, Germany, and Australia where members of the majority group (White Britons, Germans, and Australians) tend to implicitly favor their ingroup over racial/ethnic minorities such as aborigines in Australia, Blacks in Britain, and Turks in Germany (Gawronski et al. 2003; Lepore and Brown 1997; Locke et al. 1994).

From Implicit Bias in the Mind to Outward Action

In the past two decades, most of the laboratory research on implicit prejudice and stereotypes has revolved around demonstrating that members of majority groups implicitly favor their own group over outgroups even though their explicit or self-reported attitudes often reveal greater support for equality. These findings raise the question: is it possible that implicit biases are merely private thoughts that remain confined to the mind? Or do they affect people's outward actions in ways that are demonstrably harmful? If implicit prejudice and stereotypes do affect behavior, then it is easier to make the argument that these attitudes are likely to perpetuate social inequities and hierarchies despite tolerant explicit attitudes.

By now at least thirty studies have demonstrated that implicit attitudes influence people's judgments, decisions, and actions in insidious ways. For example, one study found that people's implicit racial attitudes, as measured by a rapid computer task, predicted their later nonverbal behavior (or "body language") toward a Black person (Fazio et al. 1995). The more implicit race bias participants exhibited on the computer task, the less friendly was their body language toward a Black interaction partner: implicitly prejudiced participants smiled less, made less eye contact, and were less comfortable with the Black person compared to less prejudiced participants. Implicit prejudice also correlated with participants' opinions about a particular racially divisive incident in recent American history—that is, the degree to which they attributed responsibility for the 1990 Los Angeles riots that occurred after the Rodney King trial around issues of police brutality to the local African American community. The same participants' explicit racial attitudes, however, did not correlate with their nonverbal behavior or attributions of responsibility. Other related research has demonstrated that the more implicit racial prejudice participants harbor, the more uncomfortable and anxious they appear during interracial interactions as rated both by Black interaction partners and by third party observers (e.g., participants make more speech errors, terminate the conversation more quickly, etc.; Dovidio et al. 1997; McConnell and Leibold 2001).

Understanding the link between implicit prejudice and subtle behavior may shed light on why everyday interracial interactions sometimes go awry with Black and White individuals coming away with very different impressions about their interactions with each other (Dovidio et al. 2002). Dovidio and colleagues found that when Black and White individuals interacted with each other, their opinions about interaction quality were based on very different types of information— Black individuals were more influenced by the subtle cues being communicated by their White partners (i.e., their implicit racial attitudes and nonverbal behavior) whereas White individuals were more influenced by the overt cues they were communicating (i.e., their own explicit racial attitudes and verbal behavior).

Besides nonverbal behavior, implicit race bias in the mind also influences people's behavior in simulated job interviews when they are asked to play the role of employers who are preparing to interview potential job candidates of varying racial backgrounds. Sekaquaptewa and colleagues found that participants who implicitly favored White Americans over African Americans were more likely to ask racially stereotypic interview questions to Black compared to White job candidates during simulated job interviews (Sekaquaptewa et al. 2003). Moreover, implicitly biased racial attitudes also influence how people interpret another person's ambiguous behavior. Implicitly biased people are more likely to use stereotypes to resolve ambiguity and "fill in the blanks" while evaluating a Black person compared to less biased participants (Rudman and Lee 2003, experiment 2).

Collectively, these data suggest that implicit preferences and prejudices are not merely private thoughts that remain confined to the mind. Rather, they affect people's outward actions in ways that may perpetuate and aggravate structural inequalities in situations such as the workplace. If implicit bias in the minds of employers unintentionally emerges in their nonverbal behavior and in the types of stereotypic questions they ask of Black job candidates (Dovidio et al. 1997; Fazio et al. 1995; McConnell and Leibold 2001; Sekaquaptewa et al. 2003), and if those job candidates are finely attuned to such subtle cues (Dovidio et al. 2002), it is reasonable to predict that these job interviews are unlikely to yield job offers from employers or job acceptances from the Black candidates compared to interviews with White candidates. More generally, although the interracial interactions in employment settings may appear to be racially neutral in terms of what people verbalize overtly, there may be an undercurrent of racial bias that is less detectable in everyday situations but that can be clearly measured in controlled studies.

Summary

The first generation of research on implicit attitudes and beliefs has demonstrated that members of historically advantaged groups often unconsciously favor their ingroups over less advantaged outgroups. Moreover, such implicit preferences and prejudices creep into people's behavior. These findings tell a clear story that has been replicated many times. Although this single-minded research focus has been enormously productive in revealing the existence of unconscious bias despite the scarcity of willingly expressed bias, the story is clearly not complete without considering how members of disadvantaged groups perceive their own group. A close inspection of the research reviewed above already contains hints that individuals who belong to disadvantaged groups do not always implicitly favor their ingroup in a manner that is a mirror image of their advantaged counterparts.

Implicit Preference for Outgroups

Social identity theory and most other social psychological theories of intergroup relations posit that people have a strong tendency to favor their ingroup in terms of their attitudes, beliefs, and behavior (e.g., self-categorization theory, Turner et al. 1987; social dominance theory, Sidanius and Pratto 1999; realistic conflict theory, Sherif 1967). While this is often true, people also have other reactions to in- and outgroups particularly in the context of power and status differences between groups. For example, system justification theory argues that people's attitudes and behavior may sometimes reflect the tendency to legitimize existing social hierarchies even at the expense of personal and group interest (Jost and Banaji 1994; Jost et al. 2004). In other words, in the case of individuals who belong to advantaged or dominant groups, their tendency to implicitly favor their ingroup relative to competing outgroups may be jointly influenced by their desire to preserve current social hierarchies (system justifying motive) and the desire to protect their own self-esteem (ego-justifying motive). In the case of individuals who belong to disadvantaged or subordinate groups, the two motivations work in opposition—the desire to protect self-esteem ought to elicit ingroup favoritism, but the desire to maintain current social arrangements ought to elicit *outgroup favoritism*. Put differently, there may be two independent sources of implicit attitudes. The first source, consistent with social identity theory, relies on group membership. To the extent that people's group membership is a meaningful source of self-beliefs and self-esteem, it should promote implicit preference for the ingroup relative to out-groups. The second source, consistent with system justification theory, is the mainstream culture's imposition of greater or lesser value on particular groups. Thus, for members of disadvantaged social groups, implicit liking for their own ingroup may be attenuated by the negative cultural representation of their group, whereas for members of advantaged groups, implicit liking for their ingroup may be exacerbated by the positive cultural representation of their group.

Consistent with system justification theory, a number of studies have revealed outgroup favoritism (or sometimes, less ingroup favoritism) in the case of disadvantaged groups, especially when people's attitudes and beliefs are assessed using indirect measures rather than self-report measures. For instance, Livingston (2002) measured the extent to which African Americans believe that the mainstream American culture regards their ingroup negatively and examined the extent to which such beliefs correlated with Black participants' implicit and explicit racial attitudes. He found that the more negativity African Americans perceived in the mainstream culture's opinion of their ingroup, the *less* they liked their ingroup at an implicit level, but the *more* they liked their ingroup at an explicit level. In other words, when the mainstream culture's opinion of one's own group is negative, one can reject those negative stereotypes consciously; however, those stereotypes creep into and bias one's unconscious opinions about one's ingroup.

Taking a different approach, Nosek and colleagues (2002) measured a large sample of White and Black participants' implicit and explicit racial attitudes via the Internet ($N > 17,000$). In terms of implicit attitudes, they found that whereas White Americans exhibited strong implicit ingroup favoritism on average and little individual variability, African Americans exhibited no ingroup favoritism on average, but more individual variability. In terms of explicit racial attitudes however, African Americans as a group reported stronger ingroup favoritism than did White Americans (see also Jost et al. 2004). Similar findings were obtained by Spicer (2000) and Ashburn-Nardo and colleagues (2003); in fact, in some of these studies African Americans showed preference for Whites over Blacks implicitly but not explicitly. Along the same lines, as discussed earlier, Black and White participants are equally likely to harbor implicit stereotypes associating African Americans with criminality which is revealed in their tendency to mistakenly "shoot at" Black compared to White fictitious characters in a videogame simulating a police chase. In a nutshell, the research summarized above illustrates that negative societal stereotypes affect African Americans' unconscious attitudes toward their own racial group in a negative way. Even though they may reject these stereotypes at a conscious level they cannot always do so at an unconscious level.

Even when group distinction is based on ethnicity or, even more simply, skin color, people sometimes implicitly prefer lighter-complexioned *outgroup members* over darker complexioned *ingroup members*. Within one's own group, people often favor lighter-complexioned individuals over darker-complexioned individuals. For example, my colleagues and I examined Hispanic American and Chilean participants' implicit attitudes toward Latinos (their ethnic ingroup) versus Anglos (their ethnic outgroup) and found that at an implicit level, Chileans strongly preferred Anglos over Latinos whereas Hispanic Americans did not favor either group on average. More interestingly, both Hispanic Americans and Chileans strongly (and implicitly) favored lighter complexioned ingroup members (called "*blanco*" in Spanish) over darker complexioned ingroup members (called "*moreno*" in Spanish). Implicit preference for Blancos was evident both among self-identified Moreno as well as Blanco participants in both countries, suggesting that preference for light skin among Latinos is not confined to one particular country (Uhlmann et al. 2002).

The degree of outgroup favoritism manifested by individuals who belong to disadvantaged groups appears to be influenced by several related factors: (1) the greater the power disparity between individuals' ingroup and a comparison outgroup, the less they implicitly like their powerless ingroup and the more they implicitly prefer the outgroup (Rudman et al. 2002); (2) individuals who strongly believe that the mainstream culture's opinion of their ingroup is negative are more likely to implicitly internalize those beliefs (Livingston 2002); and (3) individuals who endorse politically conservative beliefs are less likely to favor their powerless ingroup and more likely to prefer the powerful outgroup (Jost et al. 2004). Each of these factors is likely to produce unconscious preference for powerful outgroups on the part of individuals belonging to less powerful groups.

Can Implicit Bias Be Changed?

The pervasiveness of unconscious bias begs the question: can these preferences and prejudices be changed? If so how? Most of the social science research on prejudice reduction has relied heavily on making people aware of their bias, motivating them to change their attitudes, and relying on their willingness to correct negative attitudes. These interventions may not work quite so easily when it comes to unconscious bias that is expressed when people are least aware and vigilant. So, how can we change implicit bias? This question has grabbed social psychologists' attention over the past few years. This new research suggests that three factors may be able to undermine implicit bias in attitudes and behavior: (1) increasing diversity in people's local or immediate environments; (2) enhancing their intrinsic motivation to be egalitarian; and (3) giving people practice at behaving in an unbiased manner.

Increasing the Diversity of Local Environments
Decreases Implicit Bias

My collaborators and I have been exploring the role of local environments in attenuating unconscious bias. We started with the assumption that implicit prejudice and stereotypes are learned associations acquired and reinforced by immersion in mainstream cultural contexts where people observe that members of different groups are unequally located in different types of social roles. Some groups occupy more privileged and admired roles in society whereas other groups occupy less privileged and disliked roles. African Americans and other racial minorities automatically activate negative attitudes because people have learned to associate race with negative roles (e.g., the homeless person, the criminal) rather than positive ones (e.g., the parent, the business leader). These negative associations are learned and reinforced because people are typically immersed in environments where they are more likely to see racial minority groups in marginalized social roles and Whites in admired and valued social roles. As a result, when people think of racial minorities, negative associations pop into mind more quickly and easily than positive associations.

In our research, we asked one broad question: What would happen if we changed the local environment and immersed people in situations that afford more exposure to outgroup members in admired and valued social roles? Local environments may be changed by increasing people's exposure to admired members of disadvantaged groups through the mass media or through personal contact with outgroup members (e.g., friends, co-workers, acquaintances, etc.). To address this question, in one study, we created a situation in the laboratory where some participants were exposed to pictures and biographies of famous and admired African Americans (e.g., Martin Luther King Jr., Denzel Washington, Tiger Woods), whereas others were exposed to similar information about famous and admired White Americans (e.g., John F. Kennedy, Tom Hanks, Peter Jennings), and still others were shown information unrelated to race. We then measured participants' implicit racial attitudes both immediately after the media exposure and again 24 hours later (Dasgupta and Greenwald 2001). We found that participants who had been immersed in an experimental situation where they had repeatedly seen admired African Americans exhibited significantly less implicit race bias compared to others who were in a situation where they had repeatedly seen admired White Americans or non-racial stimuli. The observed reduction in implicit race bias endured even twenty-four hours later. Follow-up research using different types of stigmatized groups (gay men and lesbians) has replicated this basic finding and has also revealed that besides media exposure, personal contact with outgroup members plays an important role in attenuating implicit prejudice. People who had prior personal contact with outgroup members in the form of friends, co-workers, etc., showed substantially less implicit prejudice than others who had little prior contact with outgroup members (Dasgupta and Rivera in press; see also Dasgupta and Asgari 2004).

The power of the situation in undermining implicit racial bias has also been demonstrated in other studies that have revealed conceptually similar findings. For example, people exhibit less implicit race bias when a Black experimenter is present in the laboratory situation than when a White experimenter is present (Lowery et al. 2001). Similarly, people exhibit less implicit race bias when they see Black individuals in a positive social situation (e.g., family gathering, church) than a negative situation (e.g., street corner, gang war). Wittenbrink and colleagues (2001) found that participants who saw a brief video of a Black family gathering showed less implicit bias against African Americans than others who saw a brief video of a gang war where gang members were Black. Likewise, participants who saw Black individuals against the backdrop of a church showed less implicit anti-Black bias than others who saw the same individuals against the backdrop of a graffiti-covered street corner.

Applying these data to the real world, this evidence suggests that if we are serious about erasing implicit prejudice, we should consider changing local environments within institutions such as schools, colleges, businesses, and other workplaces to make them ethnically diverse, with a visible representation of minority groups that are typically invisible in mainstream society. Second, the data suggest that individuals from these groups must be particularly visible in socially valued leadership roles such as teachers, professors, managers, business leaders, medical professionals, and so on, instead of being relegated to devalued roles, which is often the case. Third, creating diverse local environments also has the benefit of enhancing opportunities for person-to-person contact between Whites and ethnic minorities under circumstances in which minority group members are clearly in influential roles rather than subservient roles. Fourth, another environment that can have a powerful effect if it highlights diversity is the mass media because it is often the primary vehicle by which the public learns about who is valued and who is not. Even today, at the dawn of the twenty-first century, we are more likely to see famous and influential public figures who are White (e.g., business leaders, politicians, celebrities, philanthropists, public intellectuals, etc.) in the news than others who are Black, Latino, Native American, or Asian. Similarly, in television shows, advertisements, and films, we are more likely to see lead characters and roles being played by White than non-White actors. Explicit decisions on the part of media executives to give more air time to racial and ethnic minorities in news media, advertisements, TV shows, and films, is likely to go a long way toward increasing the visibility of these groups and creating unconscious associations linking such groups with positive images.

Such changes in the mass media and in social institutions are most likely to happen with a combination of education (i.e., increasing awareness among individuals who control these institutions) together with incentives. If a small number of decision makers diversify the social institutions they control, their actions have the potential to produce large-scale change by affecting the thoughts and actions of all the people who live and work in those institutions.

Increasing Conscious Motivation and Control over Prejudiced Responses Decreases Implicit Bias

Although in general implicit prejudice is not easily derailed by conscious motivation, research suggests that some types of motivation (especially internally driven motivation to be non-prejudiced) can attenuate implicit racial prejudice. In other words, people who are motivated to be non-prejudiced because egalitarian values are important to their sense of self exhibit far less implicit race bias than others who are motivated by the desire to conform to social norms (Devine et al. 2002). Conceptually similar findings have been demonstrated in other studies. For example, people who are consciously committed to egalitarian attitudes do not express implicit negative stereotypes about African Americans compared to others who are less committed to egalitarian attitudes (Lepore and Brown 1997). Similarly, people who are vigilant and who train themselves to suppress negative stereotypes when they pop into mind can, over time, erase implicit bias from their thoughts (Kawakami et al. 2000).

Even when stereotypes and prejudices are automatically activated in the mind, whether or not they will bias individuals' outward behavior depends on how motivated they are to correct their biased actions, and how much control they have over the specific action in question. Just as implicit attitudes have been found to be remarkably malleable (e.g., Dasgupta and Greenwald 2001; Wittenbrink et al. 2001; for a review, see Blair 2002), so, too, behaviors are also quite malleable depending on the extent to which motivation and control are at play. For example, consider people's nonverbal "body language" such as smiling, eye contact, spatial distance, overall friendliness, and so on. Typically, people are relatively unaware of such nonverbal actions and thus don't try to control or correct them. However, this typical response masks a great deal of individual variability in people's vigilance over their own body language as well as that of others. Some people are more aware of nonverbal behaviors and more practiced at controlling and correcting them in real time while others are less adept at behavior correction. In our research we have found that conscious motivation to be egalitarian and practice at controlling one's nonverbal cues prevent implicit prejudice in the mind from leaking into action (Dasgupta and Rivera 2006). Those who are motivated to be egalitarian or who are practiced at controlling their nonverbal behavior do not exhibit behavioral bias. However, others who are less motivated to be egalitarian or less practiced at controlling their nonverbal actions exude negativity in their body language if they harbor biased thoughts.

In a similar manner, people may be able to prevent implicit bias in the mind from influencing their judgments of others if they possess the requisite motivation and control over their responses. Fazio and colleagues have found that White participants' motivation to control prejudice significantly affected whether or not their implicit attitudes affected their judgments of Black individuals (Dunton and Fazio 1997; Olson and Fazio 2004). Specifically, among participants who were not motivated to avoid bias, greater implicit prejudice in the mind produced less positive judgments about Black undergraduate students. However, among others who were highly motivated to avoid bias, greater implicit prejudice produced more positive judgments of Black students (Dunton and Fazio 1997). In other words, highly motivated participants overcorrected their judgment to prevent bias in their judgments (see also Olson and Fazio 2004).

Applying these data to the everyday settings, this evidence suggests that teaching egalitarian values explicitly can serve as a potential remedy for implicit bias. Although implicit prejudice is typically expressed mindlessly without awareness, people have the capacity to make themselves mindful about their thoughts and actions if they are sufficiently concerned about social equality and sufficiently vigilant about monitoring and correcting their thoughts and actions. If mindfulness and egalitarian values are internalized by individuals from an early age through parents, peers, and teachers, these values are likely to attenuate implicit bias. Moreover, egalitarian values are also learned indirectly when people (both children and adults) are immersed in ethnically diverse environments such as schools, colleges, and universities, which is often the first time that they interact with peers from other ethnic groups.

Conclusion

In the twenty years since the first studies on implicit prejudice and stereotypes we have come to know a few things with certainty. First, societal structure powerfully shapes people's cognitive structure without their conscious awareness. That is, societal inequalities are unknowingly learned and subsequently revealed in individuals' unconscious thoughts and actions even though those individuals may not consciously endorse racist attitudes. Implicit liking for Whites and bias against racial minorities are passively learned if people are immersed in environments where they observe that the individuals who possess and control the distribution of socioeconomic resources are predominantly White and individuals who possess the fewest resources are predominantly Black, Latino, Native American, and Asian. Such observations elicit admiration for Whites and disapproval for minorities, which in turn creates mental associations linking White-and-good and minority-and-bad. These mental associations are revealed in subtle thoughts and actions when people are not mindful. Because implicit bias operates without awareness, biased thoughts and actions occur repeatedly over time without correction in hiring decisions, healthcare delivery, business transactions, delivery of justice, and so on, in ways that favor White Americans over other groups. Here is a simple example: implicit preference for Whites may create greater camaraderie and an easy interaction between a White employer and a White job candidate during a job interview compared to a more awkward or stiff interaction between the same employer and a Black job candidate. Assuming that both candidates are equally qualified for the job, the employer may offer the job to the White candidate using as a tie breaker her overall good feeling from the interview with the White applicant as an indicator of his superior social skills. Given that good social skills are likely to be important for most jobs, such a decision seems reasonable at face value. However, the employer is likely to be unaware that her good feeling stems from implicit White-good associations rather than something about the White candidate himself. If left uncorrected, such actions are likely to occur repeatedly to create racial disparities between who gets offered good jobs (Whites) and who remains unemployed or under-employed (racial minorities).

A second issue highlighted by the research on implicit and explicit bias is the distinction between casually held egalitarian attitudes that people sometimes express because of their desire to conform to current social norms (e.g., political correctness) versus deeply held egalitarian attitudes that they express because of their personal standards and values about equality. People who report egalitarian attitudes because of political correctness are likely to exhibit implicit bias in their thoughts and actions despite their conscious disavowal of prejudice. However, others who report egalitarian attitudes because of their intrinsic personal standards are less likely to exhibit implicit bias because of greater mindfulness and behavior correction. It is latter form of egalitarianism that is important to convey to children and adults alike. This can be accomplished effectively by creating diverse environments in schools, colleges, and workplaces that provide opportunities for lasting interpersonal contact and friendships across racial boundaries. The casually held form of egalitarianism is ephemeral and unlikely to elicit unbiased behavior when social norms are unclear.

Finally, the research shows that implicit bias functions like an equal opportunity virus that infects both Whites and racial minorities. Specifically, at an unconscious level, members of racial minorities sometimes show implicit bias against their own group whereas White Americans show implicit preference for their own group. This is not surprising: if implicit bias is learned silently by immersion in mainstream culture where most people in influential and admired roles are White, it makes sense that both Whites and non-Whites who inhabit that culture will absorb the same biases and preferences. In contrast, both Whites and non-Whites who inhabit more diversified environments where they see African Americans, Asian Americans, Latinos, and other groups in visibly influential roles are less likely to show implicit bias. In other words, simply belonging to a minority group does not make individuals immune to implicit bias. Rather, it is often the choices people make (e.g., environments they choose to enter or avoid, friends they choose, and media they read and watch) that ultimately determine their implicit attitudes about race.

References

Abrams, D., and M. A. Hogg, 1988. "Comments on the Motivational Status of Self-esteem in Social Identity and Intergroup Discrimination." *European Journal of Social Psychology* 18: 317–334.

——. 1990. *Social Identity Theory: Constructive and Critical Advances.* New York: Springer-Verlag.

Albert, J. C., and S. E. Albert, eds. 1984. *The Sixties Papers.* New York: Praeger.

Ashburn-Nardo, L., C. I. Voils, and M. J. Monteith. 2001. "Implicit Associations as the Seeds of Intergroup Bias: How Easily Do They Take Root? *Journal of Personality and Social Psychology* 81: 789–799.

Ashburn-Nardo, L., M. L. Knowles, and M. J. Monteith. 2003. "Black Americans' Implicit Racial Associations and Their Implications for Intergroup Judgment." *Social Cognition* 21: 61–87.

Banaji, M. R. 2001. "Implicit Attitudes Can Be Measured." Pp. 117–150 in *The Nature of Remembering: Essays in Honor of Robert G. Crowder*, ed. H. L. Roediger III and J. S. Nairne. Washington, D.C.: American Psychological Association.

Banaji, M. R., and A. G. Greenwald. 1994. "Implicit Stereotyping and Prejudice." Pp. 55–76 in *The Psychology of Prejudice: The Ontario Symposium*, vol. 7, ed. M. P. Zanna and J. M. Olson. Mahwah, N.J.: Erlbaum.

Bargh, J. A. 1994. "The Four Horsemen of Automaticity: Awareness, Intention, Efficiency, and Control in Social Cognition." Pp. 1–40 in *The Handbook of Social Cognition: Basic Processes*, vol. 2, ed. R. S. Wyer Jr. and T. K. Srull. Hillsdale, N.J.: Erlbaum.

———. 1997. "The Automaticity of Everyday Life." Pp. 1–61 in *The Automaticity of Everyday Life: Advances in Social Cognition*, vol. 10, ed. R. S. Wyer Jr. Mahwah, N.J.: Erlbaum.

Blair, I. V. 2002. "The Malleability of Automatic Stereotypes and Prejudice." *Personality and Social Psychology Review* 6: 242–261.

Blair, I. V., C. A. Judd, and K. M. Chapleau. 2004. "The Influence of Afrocentric Facial Features in Criminal Sentencing." *Psychological Science* 15: 674–679.

Blair, I. V., C. A. Judd, and J. L. Fallman. 2004. "The Automaticity of Race and Afrocentric Facial Features in Social Judgments." *Journal of Personality and Social Psychology* 87: 763–778.

Blair, I. V., C. A. Judd, and M. S. Sadler. 2002. "The Role of Afrocentric Features in Person Perception: Judging by Features and Categories." *Journal of Personality and Social Psychology* 83: 5–25.

Bourhis, R. Y. 1994. "Power, Gender, and Intergroup Discrimination: Some Minimal Group Experiments." Pp. 171–208 in *The Psychology of Prejudice: The Ontario Symposium*, vol. 7, ed. M. P. Zanna and J. M. Olson. Mahwah, N.J.: Erlbaum.

Bourhis, R. Y., J. C. Turner, and A. Gagnon. 1997. "Interdependence, Social Identity and Discrimination." Pp. 273–295 in *The Social Psychology of Stereotyping and Group Life*, ed. R. Spears, P. J. Oakes, N. Ellemers, and S. A. Haslam. Oxford: Blackwell.

Brigham, J. C. 1972. "Racial Stereotypes: Measurement Variables and the Stereotype–Attitude Relationship." *Journal of Applied Social Psychology* 2: 63–76.

Chong, D. 1991. *Collective Action and the Civil Rights Movement*. Chicago: University of Chicago Press.

Correll, J., B. Park, C. A. Judd, and B. Wittenbrink. 2002. "The Police Officer's Dilemma: Using Ethnicity to Disambiguate Potentially Threatening Individuals." *Journal of Personality and Social Psychology* 83: 1314–1329.

Correll, J., B. Park, C. A. Judd, B. Wittenbrink, M. S. Sadler, and T. Keesee. 2005. "Across the Thin Blue Line: Police Officers and Racial Bias in the Decision to Shoot." Paper presented at the annual meeting of the Society for Experimental Social Psychology, San Diego, Calif., October 8.

Crosby, F., S. Bromley, and L. Saxe. 1980. "Recent Unobtrusive Studies of Black and White Discrimination and Prejudice: A Literature Review." *Psychological Bulletin* 87: 546–563.

Daniels, L. A. 2001. *State of Black America 2000*. New York: National Urban League.

Dasgupta, N. 2004. "Implicit Ingroup Favoritism, Outgroup Favoritism, and Their Behavioral Manifestations." *Social Justice Research* 17: 143–169.

Dasgupta, N., and S. Asgari. 2004. "Seeing Is Believing: Exposure to Counterstereotypic Women Leaders and Its Effect on Automatic Gender Stereotyping." *Journal of Experimental Social Psychology* 40: 642–658.

Dasgupta, N., and A. G. Greenwald. 2001. "On the Malleability of Automatic Attitudes: Combating Automatic Prejudice with Images of Admired and Disliked Individuals." *Journal of Personality and Social Psychology* 81: 800–814.

Dasgupta, N., D. E. McGhee, A. G. Greenwald, and M. R. Banaji. 2000. "Automatic Preference for White Americans: Eliminating the Familiarity Explanation." *Journal of Experimental Social Psychology* 36: 316–328.

Dasgupta, N., and L. M. Rivera. 2006. "From Automatic Anti-Gay Prejudice to Behavior: The Moderating Role of Conscious Beliefs about Gender and Behavioral Control." *Journal of Personality and Social Psychology* 91: 268–280.

————. In press. "When Social Context Matters: The Influence of Long-Term Contact and Short-Term Exposure to Admired Outgroup Members on Implicit Attitudes and Behavioral Intentions." *Social Cognition.*

Devine, P. G. 1989. "Stereotypes and Prejudice: Their Automatic and Controlled Components." *Journal of Personality and Social Psychology* 56: 680–690.

Devine, P. G., E. A. Plant, D. M. Amodio, E. Harmon-Jones, and S. Vance. 2002. "The Regulation of Explicit and Implicit Race Bias: The Role of Motivations to Respond without Prejudice." *Journal of Personality and Social Psychology* 82: 835–848.

Devos, T., and M. R. Banaji. 2005. "American = White?" *Journal of Personality and Social Psychology* 88: 447–466.

Dovidio, J. F., and S. L. Gaertner. 1986. *Prejudice, Discrimination, and Racism.* San Diego, Calif.: Academic Press.

Dovidio, J. F., K. Kawakami, and S. L. Gaertner. 2002. "Implicit and Explicit Prejudice and Interracial Interaction." *Journal of Personality and Social Psychology* 82: 62–68.

Dovidio, J. F., K. Kawakami, C. Johnson, B. Johnson, and A. Howard. 1997. "The Nature of Prejudice: Automatic and Controlled Processes." *Journal of Experimental Social Psychology* 33: 510–540.

Dunton, B. C., and R. H. Fazio. 1997. "An Individual Difference Measure of Motivation to Control Prejudiced Reactions." *Personality and Social Psychology Bulletin* 23: 316–326.

Fazio, R. H., J. R. Jackson, B. C. Dunton, and C. J. Williams. 1995. "Variability in Automatic Activation as an Unobtrusive Measure of Racial Attitudes: A Bona Fide Pipeline?" *Journal of Personality and Social Psychology* 69: 1013–1027.

Gaertner, S. L., and J. F. Dovidio. 1977. "The Subtlety of White Racism, Arousal, and Helping Behavior." *Journal of Personality and Social Psychology* 35: 691–707.

Gawronski, B., D. Geschke, and R. Banse. 2003. "Implicit Bias in Impression Formation: Associations Influence the Construal of Individuating Information." *European Journal of Social Psychology* 33: 573–589.

Gitlin, T. 1987. *The Sixties: Years of Hope, Days of Rage.* New York: Bantam.

Greenwald, A. G., and M. R. Banaji. 1995. "Implicit Social Cognition: Attitudes, Self-esteem, and Stereotypes." *Psychological Review* 102: 4–27.

Greenwald, A. G., D. E. McGhee, and J. L. K. Schwartz. 1998. "Measuring Individual Differences in Implicit Cognition: The Implicit Association Test." *Journal of Personality and Social Psychology* 74: 1464–1480.

Greenwald, A. G., M. A. Oakes, and H. G. Hoffman. 2003. "Targets of Discrimination: Effects of Race on Responses to Weapons Holders." *Journal of Experimental Social Psychology* 39: 399–405.

Griffin, J. H. 1960. *Black Like Me.* New York: Signet.

Hill, M. E. 2000. "Color Differences in the Socioeconomic Status of African American Men: Results of a Longitudinal Study." *Social Forces* 78: 1437–1460

Jones, E. E., and H. Sigall. 1972. "The Bogus Pipeline: A New Paradigm for Measuring Effect and Attitude." *Psychological Bulletin* 76: 349–364.

Jost, J. T., and M. R. Banaji. 1994. "The Role of Stereotyping in System-Justification and the Production of False Consciousness." *British Journal of Social Psychology* 33: 1–27.

Jost, J. T., M. R. Banaji, and B. A. Nosek. 2004. "A Decade of System Justification Theory: Accumulated Evidence of Conscious and Unconscious Bolstering of the Status Quo." *Political Psychology* 25: 881–920.

Karlins, M., T. L. Coffman, and G. Walters. 1969. "On the Fading of Social Stereotypes: Studies in Three Generations of College Students." *Journal of Personality and Social Psychology* 13: 1–16.

Kawakami, K., K. L. Dion, and J. F. Dovidio. 1998. "Implicit Stereotyping and Prejudice and the Primed Stroop Task." *Swiss Journal of Psychology* 58: 241–250.

Kawakami, K., J. F. Dovidio, J. Moll, S. Hermsen, and A. Russin. 2000. "Just Say No (to Stereotyping): Effects of Training in the Negation of Stereotypic Associations on Stereotype Activation." *Journal of Personality and Social Psychology* 78: 871–888.

Keith, V., and C. Herring. 1991. "Skin Tone and Stratification in the Black Community." *American Journal of Sociology* 97: 760–778.

Kleugel, J. R., and E. R. Smith. 1986. *Beliefs about Inequality: Americans' Views of What Is and What Ought to Be.* Hawthorne, N.Y.: Aldine de Gruyter.

Klonoff, E. A., and H. Landrine. 2000. "Is Skin Color a Marker for Racial Discrimination? Explaining the Skin Color-Hypertension Relationship." *Journal of Behavioral Medicine* 23: 329–338.

Leonhardt, D. 2002. "Wide Racial Disparities Found in Costs of Mortgages." *New York Times,* May 1, business sec., 1–3.

Lepore, L., and R. Brown. 1997. "Category and Stereotype Activation: Is Prejudice Inevitable?" *Journal of Personality and Social Psychology* 72: 275–287.

Levy, P. B. 1992. *Let Freedom Ring: A Documentary History of the Modern Civil Rights Movement.* New York: Praeger.

Livingston, R. W. 2002. "The Role of Perceived Negativity in the Moderation of African Americans' Implicit and Explicit Racial Attitudes." *Journal of Experimental Social Psychology* 38: 405–413.

Livingston, R. W., and M. B. Brewer. 2002. "What Are We Really Priming? Cue-based versus Category-based Processing of Facial Stimuli." *Journal of Personality and Social Psychology* 82: 5–18.

Locke, V., C. Macleod, and I. Walker. 1994. "Automatic and Controlled Activation of Stereotypes: Individual Differences Associated with Prejudice." *British Journal of Social Psychology* 33: 29–46.

Lowery, B. S., C. D. Hardin, and S. Sinclair. 2001. "Social Influence Effects on Automatic Racial Prejudice." *Journal of Personality and Social Psychology* 81: 842–855.

Maykovich, M. K. 1971. "Changes in Racial Stereotypes among College Students." *Human Relations* 24: 371–386.

———. 1972. "Changes in Racial Stereotypes among College Students." *British Journal of Social Psychiatry and Community Health* 6: 126–133.

McConnell, A. R., and J. M. Leibold. 2001. "Relations among the Implicit Association Test, Discriminatory Behavior, and Explicit Measures of Racial Attitudes." *Journal of Experimental Social Psychology* 37: 435–442.

Nisbett, R. E., and T. D. Wilson. 1977. "Telling More Than We Can Know: Verbal Reports on Mental Processes." *Psychological Review* 84: 231–259.

Nosek, B. A., M. R. Banaji, and A. G. Greenwald. 2002. "Harvesting Implicit Group Attitudes and Beliefs from a Demonstration Web Site." *Group Dynamics* 6: 101–115.

Oakes, P. J., and J. C. Turner. 1980. "Social Categorization and Intergroup Behaviour: Does Minimal Intergroup Discrimination Make Social Identity More Positive?" *European Journal of Social Psychology* 10: 295–301.

Ojito, M. 2000. "Best of Friends, Worlds Apart." *New York Times*, June 5, 1.

Olson, M. A., and R. H. Fazio. 2004. "Trait Inferences as a Function of Automatically Activated Racial Attitudes and Motivation to Control Prejudiced Reactions." *Basic and Applied Social Psychology* 26: 1–11.

Ottaway, S. A., D. C. Hayden, and M. A. Oakes. 2001. "Implicit Attitudes and Racism: Effects of Word Familiarity and Frequency on the Implicit Association Test." *Social Cognition* 19: 97–144.

Payne, B. K. 2001. "Prejudice and Perception: The Role of Automatic and Controlled Processes in Misperceiving a Weapon." *Journal of Personality and Social Psychology* 81: 181–192.

Payne, B. K., A. J. Lambert, and L. L. Jacoby. 2002. "Best Laid Plans: Effects of Goals on Accessibility Bias and Cognitive Control in Race-based Misperceptions of Weapons." *Journal of Experimental Social Psychology* 38: 384–396.

Plant, E. A., and B. M. Peruche. 2005. "The Consequences of Race for Police Officers' Responses to Criminal Suspects." *Psychological Science* 16: 180–183.

Plant, E. A., B. M. Peruche, and D. A. Butz. 2005. "Eliminating Automatic Racial Bias: Making Race Non-diagnostic for Responses to Criminal Suspects." *Journal of Experimental Social Psychology* 41: 141–156.

Portwood, S. G. 1995. "Employment Discrimination in the Public Sector Based on Sexual Orientation: Conflicts between Research Evidence and the Law." *Law and Psychology Review* 19: 113–152.

Raudenbush, S. W., and R. M. Kasim. 1998. "Cognitive Skill and Economic Inequality: Findings from the National Adult Literacy Survey." *Harvard Educational Review* 68: 33–79.

Rubin, M., and M. Hewstone. 1998. "Social Identity Theory's Self-esteem Hypothesis: A Review and Some Suggestions for Clarification." *Personality and Social Psychology Review* 2: 40–62.

Rudman, L. A., R. D. Ashmore, and M. L. Gary. 2001. "'Unlearning' Automatic Biases: The Malleability of Implicit Stereotypes and Prejudice." *Journal of Personality and Social Psychology* 81: 856–868.

Rudman, L. A., J. Feinberg, and K. Fairchild. 2002. "Minority Members' Implicit Attitudes: Automatic Ingroup Bias as a Function of Group Status." *Social Cognition* 20: 294–320.

Rudman, L. A., A. G. Greenwald, and D. S. Mellott. 1999. "Measuring the Automatic Components of Prejudice: Flexibility and Generality of the Implicit Association Test." *Social Cognition* 17: 437–465.

Rudman, L. A., and M. R. Lee. 2003. "Implicit and Explicit Consequences of Exposure to Violent and Misogynous Rap Music." *Group Processes and Intergroup Relations* 5: 133–150.

Schuman, H., C. Steeh, and L. Bobo. 1997. *Racial Attitudes in America: Trends and Interpretations*, 2nd ed. Cambridge, Mass.: Harvard University Press.

Sekaquaptewa, D., P. Espinoza, M. Thompson, P. Vargas, and W. von Hippel. 2003. "Stereotypic Explanatory Bias: Implicit Stereotyping as a Predictor of Discrimination." *Journal of Experimental Social Psychology* 39: 75–82.

Sherif, M. 1967. *Group Conflict and Cooperation*. London: Routledge and Kegan Paul.

Sidanius, J., and F. Pratto. 1999. *Social Dominance: An Intergroup Theory of Social Hierarchy and Oppression*. New York: Cambridge University Press.

Son Hing, L. S., W. Li, and M. P. Zanna. 2002. "Inducing Hypocrisy to Reduce Prejudicial Responses among Aversive Racists." *Journal of Experimental Social Psychology* 38: 71–78.

Spicer, C. V. 2000. "The Effect of Self-stereotyping and Stereotype Threat on Intellectual Performance." Unpublished Ph.D. diss., University of Kentucky, Lexington.

Stohlberg, S. G. 2002. "Minorities Get Inferior Care, Even if Insured, Study Finds." *New York Times,* March 21, 1.

Tajfel, H. 1981. *Human Groups and Social Categories.* Cambridge: Cambridge University Press.

Tajfel, H., and J. C. Turner. 1986. "The Social Identity Theory of Intergroup Behavior." Pp. 7–24 in *The Psychology of Intergroup Relations,* ed. S. Worchel and W. G. Austin. Chicago: Nelson-Hall.

Turner, J. C., M. A. Hoggs, P. J. Oakes, S. D. Reicher, and M. S. Wetherell. 1987. *Rediscovering the Social Group: A Self-categorization Theory.* Oxford: Blackwell.

Uhlmann, E., N. Dasgupta, A. Elgueta, A. G. Greenwald, and J. Swanson. 2002. "Subgroup Prejudice Based on Skin Color among Hispanics in the United States and Latin America." *Social Cognition* 20: 198–225.

von Hippel, W., D. Sekaquaptewa, and P. Vargas. 1997. "The Linguistic Intergroup Bias as an Implicit Indicator of Prejudice." *Journal of Experimental Social Psychology* 33: 490–509.

Williams, J. 1987. *Eyes on the Prize: America's Civil Rights Years, 1954–1965.* New York: Penguin.

Wittenbrink, B., C. M. Judd, and B. Park. 1997. "Evidence for Racial Prejudice at the Implicit Level and Its Relationship with Questionnaire Measures." *Journal of Personality and Social Psychology* 72: 262–274.

———. 2001. "Spontaneous Prejudice in Context: Variability in Automatically Activated Attitudes." *Journal of Personality and Social Psychology* 81: 815–827.

3

Structural Racism and Color Lines in the United States

ANDREW GRANT-THOMAS AND JOHN A. POWELL

E ven as the notion of "structural racism" gains currency inside and outside academia,[1] the term too often mystifies rather than clarifies. We
read that "structural racism" triggered the backlash in 1992 known as
the Los Angeles Riots ("Education Needed to Cut Mortality" 1992); impedes
community organizing in Buffalo, New York (Habuda 2003); and accounts
for the high incidence of lead poisoning among minority communities in
Rhode Island (Lord 2001). Exactly what structural racism is and how it promotes these outcomes is left unsaid, except for the implication that in our
ostensibly post–Archie Bunker world we must look beyond interpersonal
racism for the deep sources of inequality.[2]

Even relatively helpful treatments of structural racism usually describe
it, or offer disjointed examples of its expression, rather than explain how it
works. For example, Susan Williams relates structural racism to the (unelab-
orated) ways that social institutions "are designed to best fit and most reward
people who are members of the majority culture" or "have education, good
health, and all the other benefits of affluence, which are highly correlated
with race" (Williams n.d.). Henry Louis Taylor and Sam Cole define structural racism as a system, characterized by "its ability to hide, camouflage,
disguise, and conceal its true nature," that distributes material resources
unequally by race (Taylor and Cole 2001, 5). Fred Pincus understands structural *discrimination* (a "less pejorative term" than "racism," he writes) to comprise institutional policies and behaviors intended to be race-neutral that
nonetheless have harmful effects on racial minority groups (Pincus 1996, 187,

190).[3] These and similar analyses provide useful insights, but none offers a systematic account of how structural racism works to promote racial inequality. Nor do they agree on what structural racism is. The lack of clarity around what we mean by structural racism hampers our ability to build on the real gains made by two generations of antiracism activism. With the end of Jim Crow laws and a clear decline in the most blatant forms of interpersonal racial discrimination, "critical race projects" often lack the analytical specificity needed to ground the ongoing struggle against racial injustices. As a result, antiracist efforts can prove ineffective, even counterproductive. The absence of a clear understanding of structural racism also supports the cynicism of people who regard as "whining" any analysis that departs from strict individualist interpretations of racial outcomes today (Hochschild 1995, 105–108; Steele 1990).

The structural perspective we present in this chapter emphasizes the powerful impact of inter-institutional dynamics, institutional resource inequities, and historical legacies on racial inequalities today. These factors alone do not *determine* racial and ethnic outcomes. In arenas from employment to housing to health care, interpersonal racial bias remains an active and powerful contributor to racial inequality. Economic booms and recessions, globalization, and technological and medical innovation certainly matter. Insofar as group "culture" is an adaptation to restrictive or expansive opportunity structures, cultural factors may also play a role.[4] On the other hand, the social structures we emphasize promote racially inequitable distributions of social, political, and economic goods and services even in the absence of avowed "racists," even absent self-sabotaging behavior by racial minorities, and notwithstanding the play of macroeconomic, cultural and other large-scale factors. We believe that any promising attempt to dismantle the underpinning of durable racial inequality must account for the structural dynamics we highlight here.

In the remainder of this chapter we elaborate this structural perspective. In the first section, we present and critique the "individual racism" and "institutional racism" frameworks in order to establish the need for a complementary account of racial dynamics in the United States today. We outline our structural racism framework in the second section, and in the third section we expand on two of the dimensions to which the framework draws attention: the dependence of social outcomes on the joint operation of key institutions, and the importance of disparities in the resources commanded by functionally similar institutions such as schools or health care facilities. We conclude by noting some important analytical and practical implications of our argument.

Traditional Approaches to Thinking about Racism

In terms of our understanding of race and racism, the last fifty years of activism and theorizing seem to have left us back where we started. Before "racism" first became part of the popular discourse in the 1960s, "the problem of racial injustice and inequality was generally understood . . . as a matter of prejudiced attitudes or bigotry on the one hand, and of discriminatory actions on the other" (Winant 1998, 757). Today, both popular and scholarly definitions of racism similarly refer most often to beliefs and belief systems (e.g., doctrines of racial supremacy), to feelings (e.g., racial animus, bigotry), or to behaviors (e.g., discrimination) based on race (Bonilla-Silva 1997; Winant 2000).[5] Four features of this common conception about the nature of racism deserve mention.

On one hand, because we associate feelings, beliefs and behaviors primarily with individuals, most media and other popular accounts imply that racism is first and foremost a matter of *individual* agency. According to this conception, racism is lodged in the hearts and minds of individuals and manifest in the words they speak, the actions they perform, and the thoughts they harbor. The *essentialist* tinge of this construction is clear: one either *is* or *is not* racist, all the time or never. Defenses of President George W. Bush against the charge of racism that refer to his friendships with African Americans, to his appointment of non-whites to his cabinet, or to the Latino members of his extended family, draw on this essentialist logic. If the president is demonstrably "not racist" at times—as indicated, ostensibly, by the diversity of his friendship, family and cabinet circles—then he must be "not racist" at all other times as well.

As a rule, people's words and actions also are interpreted as racist only if they are *intentionally* enacted to produce outcomes that injure some or benefit others. Everyone agrees that the Bush administration's weak response to Hurricane Katrina hurt thousands of African Americans, who were disproportionately vulnerable to the ravages of the storm. But many Americans, wedded to the notion that racism requires deliberate intent and believing the president to be a "good man" who could not possibly have intended the suffering they viewed on their televisions, doubtless sympathized with his heated insistence that he was not a racist.[6] Finally, for many, racism requires that the offending word or act be *race-targeted*. Businesses that charge poor people higher prices to compensate for the real or perceived greater risks of selling them goods and services are not generally understood to be acting in a racist manner, though the correspondence between racial identity and poverty status in the United States is well-known.

Most Americans insist that racism, thus understood, is rare today. When high-profile events such as James Byrd's violent death, or radio personality Don Imus's reference to the mostly-black Rutgers University women's basketball team as "nappy-headed ho's," raise questions about the scope and impact of contemporary racism,[7] media coverage and public commentary routinely conclude that these are violations committed by a handful of people on the lunatic fringe, rare exceptions to the "rule" of racial tolerance that governs behavior (especially the behavior of *whites*) in the United States. Of course, the annual average of 161,000 racial or ethnic hate crime incidents reported by victims on the National Crime Victimization Survey between July 2000 and December 2003 begin to suggest that acts of racial hostility are fairly common, particularly since the figure doubtless understates the true incidence (Harlow 2005, 2–3).

Although the individualist, essentialist, intentionalist, and race-targeted model of racism reflects our present common sense about the nature of racism, anti-racism efforts have long recognized the model's weaknesses as a general or inclusive account. The "institutional racism" framework, formalized in the late 1960s, reflects an understanding that racism need not be individualist, essentialist, or intentional to work its effects. In Jim Crow laws and anti-miscegenation statutes, most obviously, many observers saw that the law, the institutions it governed, and even the broader culture itself related differently to African Americans than to whites. Those institutional and cultural practices generated a dynamic only weakly dependent on the self-conscious racial attitudes of the people engaged in them, if that. This suggested that while racist individuals had to be monitored and possibly reformed, rehabilitating our key social, political and cultural institutions was even more critical to the achievement of racial justice.

Furthermore, if, per the institutional racism perspective, "prejudice [is] an almost unavoidable outcome of patterns of socialization which [are] 'bred in the bone,' affecting not only whites but also racial minorities themselves," then people and institutions could cause racial harms without intending to do so in any meaningful sense (Winant 1998, 758). And if people socialized into racist habits of mind and practice can work to undo racism or mitigate its effects, as was true during the civil rights movement and is true now, if the power of historically racist institutions like the federal government can also be wielded to combat racism, then racism cannot be understood as an essential feature of individuals or institutions.

Institutional racism can be prescribed by formal rules but depends, minimally, on organizational cultures that tolerate such behaviors (Pincus 1996). Racist institutional policies neither require nor preclude the participation of attitudinally racist individuals. Laws mandating racial segregation in public places under Jim Crow offer clear examples, as do instructions to staff at Denny's restaurants around the country to "ask black customers for payment in advance under certain conditions," and the Shoney's restaurants' informal policy of not hiring African Americans for customer-contact positions in majority-white communities (Pincus 1996, 189). In both cases, the institutional nature of the discrimination emerged only in the context of investigations attendant to lawsuits.

Matched-pair audit studies provide direct measures of institutional racism in the job market. Researchers at the Massachusetts Institute of Technology and the University of Chicago recently reported that résumés with "white-sounding" names (e.g., Emily and Neil) received 50 percent more employment callbacks than those with "black-sounding" names (e.g., Tamika, Rasheed). The size of the discrepancy, coupled with the fact that the "level of discrimination [was] remarkably uniform across a variety of occupations and job requirements," suggests, at very least, institutional complicity in the preference for whites (Bertrand and Mullainathan 2004, 16). Similarly, William Julius Wilson's work in Chicago revealed that many city businesses use recruitment practices meant to exclude inner-city black residents from job consideration. He cites one partner in a downtown firm that "puts 'ads in the Northwest side of the city' [a Polish neighborhood] because the 'work ethic is better' among the residents there" (Wilson 1996, 134). In Wilson's sample, city employers who placed ads in metropolitan papers had black workers doing one third of their entry-level jobs (Wilson 1996, 134). Those targeting non-black neighborhoods had only half that proportion of blacks in similar positions.

The institutional racism framework reflects a broader recognition of the forms through which racialized power is deployed, dispersed, and entrenched. However, while elucidating ways in which racism is often non-individualist, non-essentialist, and non-intentionalist, by focusing on intra-institutional dynamics this framework fails to account for the ways in which the *joint* operations of social institutions produce important outcomes. This is a crucial gap, for it is often the interaction between institutions, rather than the operation of each in isolation, that generates racial group disparities. The individual and institutional racism approaches highlight dynamics triggered immediately by race; however, racism and racial inequality often originate in treatment inspired by non-race factors (e.g., place, class status, religious belief, language) that interact with race in patterned ways. This secondary racism, a function of inter-institutional relations, forms the leading edge of structural racism.

The Structural Racism Framework

We review and critique the theoretical frameworks of individual racism and institutional racism to underline their incompleteness, not to suggest that they are irrelevant to understanding racial inequality today. Each framework presents different ways of understanding the contemporary production of racial inequality. Each identifies different causes and has different implications for strategic intervention. We present the structural racism framework as one that offers important additional insight into the nature of racism today and as a model for effective social praxis.

One's capacity to flourish, or "to lead a life one has reason to value," is contingent on access to opportunity (Sen 1999). Opportunities, as we define them here, are resources and services that contribute to stability, advancement, and general well-being. Access to opportunity is not equally available to all. In American society, opportunity is produced and regulated by institutions, institutional interactions, and individuals, jointly and differentially providing and denying access along lines of race, gender, class, and other markers of social difference.

From both the individual and institutional racism perspectives, racist treatment attaches directly to the victim's race; the difference lies in the degree to which each sees racism as institutionally constrained. Where the individual racism view focuses on race-targeted, discretionary treatment, institutional racism speaks to the race-targeted and procedural (i.e., rule-based) dimension of racism. As institutional racism shifts our focus from the motives and actions of individual people to practices and procedures *within* an institution, structural racism shifts attention from the singular, intra-institutional setting to *inter-institutional* arrangements and interactions. "Inter-institutional arrangements and interactions" are what we mean by "structures."[8] We turn away from the internal dynamics of institutions not because those dynamics are incidental to the production of racial inequality, but because we want to highlight the degree to which, and means by which, inter-institutional arrangements themselves shape very important results. To draw on international systems theorist Kenneth Waltz's observation about systems theories in general, the notion of structural racism recognizes that "some part of the explanation of behaviors and outcomes is found in the system's structure" (Waltz 1979, 73). Because Americans often take individual people to be the main vehicles of racism, we generally fail to appreciate the work done by racially inequitable structures. But, in fact, all complex societies feature institutional arrangements that help to create and distribute benefits, burdens, and interests in society. These structures are neither natural nor neutral (Unger 2000).[9] And just as we cannot account for or address the impact of institutional racism by only considering a given individual's actions or psychological state, we cannot adequately understand the work structures do simply by looking at the practices and procedures of a single institution. The bird-in-the-birdcage metaphor works well here (Young 2001). If we approach the problem of durable racial inequality one "bar" (one form of disadvantage) at a time, it is hard to appreciate the fullness of the bird's entrapment, much less formulate a suitable response to it. Explaining the bird's inability to take flight requires that we recognize the connectedness of multiple bars, each reinforcing the rigidity of the others. In confronting racism we must similarly account for multiple, intersecting, and often mutually reinforcing disadvantages and develop corresponding response strategies.

Let us consider a real example of structurally induced racial inequality. Grades earned by high school students in advanced placement (AP), honors, and other college-prep courses arguably are the single most influential factor in college admissions decisions—often more important than overall grade-point average, class rank, or test scores, and far more important than "diversity" considerations (Geiser and Santelices 2004; Santoli 2002). Applicants who have taken AP classes and done well on AP exams are more likely to get into their preferred schools, receive generous financial aid, and graduate on time or early because of the course exemptions they may receive (Furry and Hecsh 2001). Such admissions policies are meant to be race-neutral. However, in a society where white students are much more likely than black and Latino students to attend high schools that offer such courses, and offer more of them (Brown 2004; Furry and Hecsh 2001; Solorzano and Ornelas 2002, 2004), counting AP performance heavily in admissions decisions is unfair and promotes inequality.

Three distinct structural processes intersect to generate racially biased outcomes here. First, higher education admissions policies effectively often make college access partly reliant on students' prior access to AP classes in high school. Second, these admissions policies discount the fact that high school participation in the AP program is extremely uneven. For example, research on California in the late 1990s found that whereas 15 percent of the state's public schools offered no AP courses, 17 percent offered fifteen or more (Solorzano and Ornelas 2002). Third, race enters the equation by way of historical legacies of racial injustice, complemented by contemporary forms of interpersonal, intra-institutional and structural bias, that place many minority students in the schools least likely to offer AP programming. Solorzano and Ornelas (2002) found that the California public schools offering many AP classes were often located in affluent suburban areas with small Latino and African American populations; the reverse was true of schools with few AP classes.

In short, even a basic understanding of how consideration of AP courses and test scores promotes racial inequality in college admissions decisions requires an analysis of the interactions between three complex institutions: housing markets, K–12 education, and higher education. Peer more closely and the importance of school district boundaries, educational funding arrangements, labor markets, and residential zoning practices come rapidly into view. The relations between these and other institutional actors are structural relations. Their joint operation has an effect on inequality independent of the dynamics within each of them. Again, a structural analysis does not provide a full explanation of how weighing AP participation heavily in college admissions decisions promotes racialized outcomes in higher education. A fuller explanation would also adopt an institutional racism lens to look at tracking practices in middle schools and high schools that reduce the presence of black and Latino students in the most challenging classes, including AP classes, for example. But without a structural analysis we guarantee ourselves only a partial understanding likely to generate inadequate remedies.

To state the case in more general terms, the AP example highlights three important structural dimensions: first, the interdependence of social outcomes and opportunities within and across institutional domains (e.g., the relationship between where a child lives and where she goes to school); second, the degree to which functionally similar institutional actors have similar resources (e.g., the distribution of AP courses across high schools); and third, the material and normative set of "starting conditions," given by history, on which these structural factors operate (e.g., residential segregation by race and ethnicity, racial distributions of wealth).

A social system is structurally inequitable to the degree that it is configured to promote unequal outcomes. A society marked by highly interdependent opportunity structures and large inter-institutional resource disparities will likely be very unequal with respect to the outcomes governed by those institutions and structures. Whether that inequality assumes a *racial* cast will depend, in large part, on the racial conditions in place when the current structural configuration came into being. The dynamic established by initial conditions can be very durable indeed. In a society that features structural inequalities with respect to opportunities and institutional resources, initial racial inequality in motion will likely stay in motion. But, again, actual outcomes, including the depth of inequality, will depend substantially on non-structural factors, dynamics at the individual and intra-institutional levels not least among them. A thorough analysis of a given racial disparity will look to all three levels.

In the next section we further develop our arguments about the interdependence of institutionally mediated social opportunities and the importance of inter-institutional resource imbalances—the first and second structural dimensions outlined above. Given space limitations that prevent a longer treatment of all three dimensions, we refer the reader to the introductory chapter of this volume for a discussion of some key ways in which decisions made and patterns established long ago have racial reverberations in our ostensibly "color-blind" era.

Social Opportunity as a Function of Inter-Institutional Dynamics

The general proposition that social institutional actors such as schools, businesses, courts and legislatures play major roles in shaping individual and group well-being requires little defense. Institutional actors matter for at least three reasons: first, because of the social goods under their purview (schools and education, hospitals and medical care, faith-based organizations and spiritual guidance, and so on); second, because of the roles they play in mediating access to other institutions; and, third, because of the access they provide to social networks with varying kinds and amounts of social capital. Because we will not explicitly address the social networking function of institutions in the pages ahead, the importance of social networks is worth underlining here. For many, the main appeal of membership in organizations such as alumni associations, book groups, country clubs, intramural sports teams, online communities, and even Ivy League and other elite colleges and universities lies in the networks they house.

The intuition about the value of good social networks finds ample support in research in arenas such as employment and health. For example, both employers and job seekers make significant use of personal networks. Using data from the Multi-City Study of Urban Inequality, Elliot (1999) found that four in five survey respondents reported using personal contacts to find work. In a 2001 Society for Human Resource Management/Wall Street Journal poll, 78 percent of job seekers and 61 percent of human resource professionals rated networking the most effective of 20 search methods presented ("Personal Networking Is Key" 2001). Peter Marsden and Elizabeth Gorman's survey of network research cites six studies in which at least half of the respondents said they got their first or current jobs through networking. Moreover, one in three job changers, if not more, finds new work without active searching. As Marsden and Gorman (2001, 472) note, "Job changes made without searching tend to be mediated by social networks."

Institutional actors matter in multiple ways. The dispensation of goods and services is their most obvious function. But they also shape access to other institutions and substantially determine the cast of our social networks. So parents want their children to attend the middle and high schools that teach the skills and knowledge that will gain entry into, and success in, the finest colleges and universities. But it's not just what you know, it's also who you know, and "school, work, and voluntary organizational foci provide the great majority of ties that are not kin" (McPherson et al. 2001, 431). Appreciating the importance of institutions as distributors of social opportunity requires that we keep their several functions in mind.

Opportunity and the Joint Operation of Institutions

Social opportunities are substantially interdependent. In the United States, favorable or unfavorable outcomes in one domain (e.g., housing) tend to promote favorable or unfavorable opportunities and outcomes in others (e.g., education, employment). Better-educated people tend to earn more money; wealthier people tend to be healthier. More than this, advantages or disadvantages tend to accumulate across multiple domains such that, for example, on average healthy people not only enjoy greater wealth than people who are less healthy, but *also* are more highly educated *and* earn more income *and* live in nicer neighborhoods *and* work at more prestigious jobs. The propensity for better or worse outcomes to correlate and cluster across social domains underpins the notion of social hierarchy.

The same phenomenon holds across institutions within the same domain. A poor work history in one's young adult years will likely hamper one's ability to secure future employment, get promotions, and earn high wages. A student judged precocious in elementary and middle school is more likely to be placed in college-prep classes in high school, making her a more appealing college admissions candidate. Offers of admission with generous financial aid packages in turn will make it more likely that she attends college and graduates on time. We could add examples from housing, health, criminal justice and other arenas.

From the transmissibility of advantage or disadvantage within and across domains it follows that racist injury in one arena can generate pernicious ripple effects in structurally proximate and, ultimately, in structurally distant arenas. "Cumulative discrimination" is the name given to the "measurement of discriminatory effects over time and across domains" (Blank 2005, 99).[10] For example, housing discrimination constrains many black and Latino youth to attend high-poverty schools (Robinson and Grant-Thomas 2004). Children in these schools are much less likely than their affluent peers to attend college, and more likely to drop out of school or complete their education in a correctional facility (Wald and Losen 2003). All three outcomes reduce the labor market options these young adults are likely to have, with grave implications for their chances to secure health and retirement benefits (Feder et al. 2001). Although empirical research on the dynamics and impact of cumulative discrimination has only just begun, "the large and continuing racial disparities in the United States are at least consistent with the possibility that cumulative discrimination is important" (National Research Council 2004, 227).

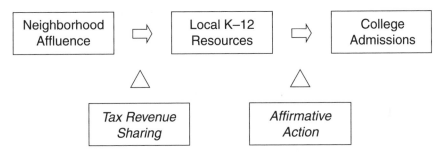

FIGURE 3.1   Tax revenue sharing and affirmative action as structural interventions.

The tendency of racially discriminatory outcomes to cascade across opportunity domains is a key feature of the current racial order in the United States. Insofar as discrimination dampens the success of minority efforts within and across domains, one corrective strategy is to identify and institute policies and practices that interrupt key in-domain or cross-domain linkages and thus dampen the effects of the initial harm. The appeal of universal health care is intelligible in these terms. Labor market discrimination is a big reason why racial and ethnic minorities are much more likely than whites to be jobless, do seasonal work, work part-time, or work in small businesses (Cherry 2001). Membership in any of these categories greatly reduces the likelihood of getting health insurance through an employer, which is how most insured Americans (61 percent in 2003) get coverage (DeNavas-Walt et al. 2003). The guarantee inscribed in a universal health care policy would sever the link between work status and health care coverage.

Tax-base sharing and affirmative action provide two more examples (Figure 3.1). Seventy-four percent of the students at the 146 most selective four-year colleges and universities in the United States come from the top socioeconomic quarter of American families, compared to only three percent of students who come from the bottom quarter (Carnevale and Rose 2004, 105–106). Children from affluent homes are twenty-five times more likely to attend the best colleges in part because they are much more likely to have attended the opportunity-rich public schools found in affluent neighborhoods and financed by local property taxes. Black, Latino and Indian children are only rarely found in those most privileged communities and schools. Regional tax revenue sharing attenuates the link between neighborhood affluence and school resources. Affirmative action policies moderate the link between high school resources and admission to selective colleges and universities.

If the functional interdependence of institutional actors and networks in generating social outcomes is the first, permissive face of structural racism, then *the fragmentation of decision-making authority across the institutions and networks that mediate those outcomes* is a critical corollary. As the discussion above suggests and every frustrated parent, teacher or principal (judge, doctor or social worker) knows, institutional outcomes are shaped, often dramatically, by inputs beyond the reach or control of particular institutional actors. So neighborhood dynamics, family resources, and government policies like "No Child Left Behind" do a great deal to shape educational outcomes (for better or worse), but schools exert little influence over any of them.

The fragmentation of decision-making authority has important implications for racial equity. First, absent efforts at coordination, even well-intentioned actors can produce misaligned and therefore discriminatory policies and practices. Many minority males in large urban school systems enter a "school-to-prison-to-dropout pipeline" created by education and juvenile justice systems working at cross-purposes (Balfanz et al. 2003). On one hand, resources that could support the neediest students and forestall their incarceration are used instead to enhance school security, raise test scores, and attend to administrative details. Reducing the number of incarcerated students is rarely a focus of school reform efforts (Balfanz et al. 2003, 81). On the other hand, contact with the juvenile justice system can doom struggling students to miss weeks or months of school; to receive inferior education while incarcerated; and, upon returning to public school, to try to catch up with coursework that may be unrelated to classes they took while detained. Few students who return to public schools manage to graduate (Balfanz et al. 2003).

Second, the fragmentation of authority can increase the number of battles that equity advocates must win to achieve their aims and introduces the possibility that victories in one arena will be undermined by developments in another. Throughout the postwar period the demise of formal Jim Crow in the South altered the policies and practices that regulated housing, public accommodation, voting, and schools, and assisted blacks in moving to urbanized areas and low-level industrial jobs. At the same time, the federal government was creating new programs and resources that encouraged whites and jobs to leave the central cities (powell and Graham 2002). As blacks poured into industrialized cities looking for opportunity and inclusion, opportunity was being relocated to emerging suburban white enclaves with new forms of legal protection. In city after city, blacks sued and won the right to desegregate schools only to watch whites and resources move to areas where new forms of segregation were emerging (powell and Graham 2002). These competing initiatives, embodied in the civil rights and suburbanization movements, continue to have a powerful impact on each other that equity advocates and the courts often overlook.

Third, the fragmentation of authority creates space for individual or institutional decision-makers to act on the basis of unscrupulous, possibly willfully racist motives. Historically, "state's rights" has been the cry of many concerned with protecting or promoting local white privilege against federal government interference. Today, many municipalities couple "restrictive land use regulations ... with costly infrastructure requirements and difficult approval processes that make affordable home building impractical, if not impossible" (Robinson and Grant-Thomas 2004, 38). The wish to manage growth and preserve open space may be a factor in some cases, but NIMBY (Not In My Back Yard) concerns—that an influx of low-income or minority neighbors would reduce neighborhood quality and property values—often are also in play.

The obvious response to the splintering of decision-making authority is better alignment between the policies and practices of relevant institutions that results in more racially just outcomes. One of three moves will bring about such an alignment: one institutional actor unilaterally changes its policies, two actors agree to coordinate their policies, or a central actor with overarching authority imposes an alignment. Recent decisions by elite universities such as Stanford, Harvard, and the University of Virginia to cover the educational expenses of the low-income students they admit fall into the first category.[11] Efforts around the country to implement articulation agreements between community colleges and four-year universities, or high school-college dual enrollment policies that ease students' transition to college, are examples of the second.[12] Although the federal government historically has often acted, or not acted, to promote racial and ethnic inequality, the use of federal power and authority to force institutional compliance with civil rights laws, especially at the state level, is an example of alignment imposed from above.

The operation of different institutional actors within and across domains such as education, employment, health and criminal justice jointly produce social opportunities and outcomes. We have suggested that this interdependence has profound implications for transmitting inequality across domains, and for remedying inequality. We turn now to a consideration of how the distribution of resources across similar institutions can shape group inequality.

Opportunity and Inter-Institutional Resource Disparities

Imagine a country in which public schools with the neediest students enjoyed per-pupil funding, facilities, and teacher-student ratios *at least* equal to those found in schools educating the most privileged. Suppose hospitals and clinics in poor or minority neighborhoods boasted personnel, infrastructure, and equipment *at least* as good as those in other areas. What if all municipalities provided adequate (or better) basic services, including public utilities, safety services, and playgrounds? Would such resource equivalence across functionally similar institutions guarantee equal opportunity outcomes for all? No. Several key questions would have to be answered affirmatively to earn that result. Do all people and groups enjoy comparable levels of access to those institutions? Having a world-class hospital down the street is of limited use to someone without health insurance or money to pay for services. Do people bring similar resources to their institutional engagements? Do they meet with comparable treatment within them? And so on.

That said, the fact that public institutions in the United States that serve the needy typically command far fewer resources, in absolute terms, than do those that serve the relatively privileged itself has critical implications for the distribution of opportunity in our society.

In the K–12 arena, for example, a recent study by the Education Trust found that in 2004, nationally, students in the poorest districts each received $825 less in state and local funds than did those in the wealthiest districts (Education Trust 2006). As the authors of the report note, given that poor students need more resources to match the achievements of more affluent students, the $825 gap actually understates the inequity gap. While recent litigation in several states and other school adequacy reforms has closed gaps in per pupil expenditure across districts, gaps across schools within districts remain substantial. An analysis of variations in spending across 89 elementary schools in the Columbus, Ohio, public schools, for example, revealed per student spending totals ranging from $3,045 to $8,165 (Condron and Roscigno 2003). Similarly, research on the State of California's ten largest districts found that, "for a student attending schools that serve predominantly low-income students, California spends $141,714 less on that student's teachers from kindergarten to her senior year, compared to a student who attends a wealthy school in these districts" (Education Trust–West 2005).

Of course, the crucial question isn't simply how much money is spent, but whether money is allocated to those resources that most effectively promote educational achievement, including challenging curricula, small class sizes, access to good after-school programs, and well-qualified, experienced teachers. The available data point to significant variation in the degree to which schools provide students with the resources that matter most. Among all high school students in 2000, for example, whereas 26 percent attended schools that provided no advanced courses in English, mathematics, science, or foreign language, 22 percent attended schools that offered at least four (U.S. Department of Education 2005, table 25-1). In 2003, student–teacher ratios in secondary schools ranged from 19 for schools with 1,500 or more students to 12.3 in schools with fewer than 300 students (U.S. Department of Education 2006, table 35-1). In 2001, with respect to each of seven types of after-school activity, non-poor students in kindergarten through eighth grade were between two (academic activities) and five (scouts) times more likely than poor students to participate (U.S. Department of Education, 2005: table 34-2). Clearly, along each of these important dimensions, among others, disparities in the distribution of educational resources that most shape student achievement remain substantial.

Physical infrastructure such as water and sewer service, roads and transit, and other critical public services, such as police and fire protection, offer more examples of institutionally mediated resources whose uneven provision shapes access to opportunity. Because public infrastructure and basic services are funded largely by local tax revenues, residents in poor municipalities are taxed at higher rates than those in more affluent areas to support these basic services—or receive lesser services and poorer infrastructure for the taxes they pay. Myron Orfield's review of fiscal capacity in the twenty-five largest metropolitan areas in 1998 revealed enormous inequalities across jurisdictions (Orfield 2002). For example, tax capacity per household in the Chicago region ranged from $204 in poor (5th percentile) municipalities to $2,422 in wealthy (95th percentile) ones, a 12:1 ratio

(Orfield 2002, 56). Across all twenty-five regions, that ratio ranged from 3.3 in Milwaukee to more than 31 in Cincinnati and Tampa. A wealthy community in Cincinnati or Tampa, thus defined, could apply thirty-one times the revenue per capita as the poorest to police and fire protection, street maintenance, sanitation and other basic services.

Federal funding decisions often exacerbate these place-based institutional resource disparities. Consider public transportation. Low income urban residents are especially dependent on public transportation, but only 20 percent of federal transportation funds support public transit, with state funding formulas usually dedicating still less proportionately (as little as 10 percent of all transportation spending; Sánchez et al. 2003). Outside of transit spending, roadway investments are also disproportionately targeted to suburban areas, leaving pothole-riddled streets in cities like Detroit, while millions are invested in new highways, roads and interchanges in the affluent suburbs.[13] The combination of low tax revenues, decaying infrastructures, and declining federal funding places many older, urban communities and their residents at significant risk.[14] The potentially disastrous consequences of that combination remain evident in New Orleans more than 18 months after the Katrina landfall. Low-income residents pay a substantial spatial premium for a wide range of goods and services provided by private institutions as well (Cashin 2004).

These disparities in education, infrastructure, services, and other resources have a distinctly racial cast. A focus on teacher quality, probably the most important single factor in shaping educational outcomes at the K–12 level, underlines the general point. Compared to their peers in low-minority schools, teachers in high-minority schools more often lack teaching experience or substantive credentials in the subjects they teach (Peske and Haycock 2006; Wirt et al. 2004). In Wisconsin, half of all teachers in high-minority schools (62 percent or more) have five or fewer years of experience; only one in five teachers assigned to very low-minority schools (less than 1.5 percent) does (Education Trust 2006). Using an index composed of five measures of teacher quality, all demonstrably related to student achievement, the Illinois Education Research Council found that four in five very high-minority schools (90 percent or more) place in the bottom quartile for teacher quality, versus only 10 percent of "minority-minority" schools who do (Presley et al. 2005).

Maps 3.1 and 3.2 show the distribution of quality teachers across the Austin and Baltimore regions. In Austin, the most experienced teachers are found outside of the city; less experienced teachers are concentrated in the region's large minority community east of I-35. In the Baltimore region, highly qualified teachers are much more likely to be concentrated in elementary schools outside of the City of Baltimore and the inner suburbs. The message is clear: schools with high concentrations of the neediest students lack a representative share, much less an equitable share, of our nation's most effective teachers.

The insight that *equally* distributed resources are not necessarily *equitably* distributed resources throws the racial cast of educational inequity into even

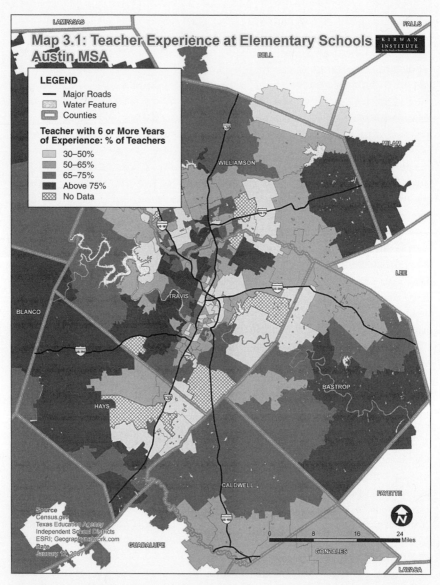

MAP 3.1 Teachers' experience at elementary schools in the Austin, Texas, Metropolitan Statistical Area. (*Source:* Census.gov, Texas Education Agency, Independent School Districts, ESRI; Geographynetwork.com. Prepared by the Kirwan Institute for the Study of Race and Ethnicity, January 12, 2007.)

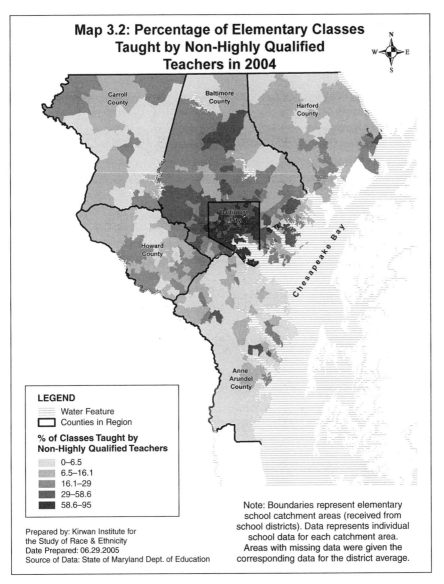

Map 3.2: Percentage of Elementary Classes Taught by Non-Highly Qualified Teachers in 2004

Carroll County

Baltimore County

Harford County

Chesapeake Bay

Baltimore City

Howard County

Anne Arundel County

LEGEND

≡ Water Feature
☐ Counties in Region

% of Classes Taught by Non-Highly Qualified Teachers

0–6.5
6.5–16.1
16.1–29
29–58.6
58.6–95

Note: Boundaries represent elementary school catchment areas (received from school districts). Data represents individual school data for each catchment area. Areas with missing data were given the corresponding data for the district average.

Prepared by: Kirwan Institute for the Study of Race & Ethnicity
Date Prepared: 06.29.2005
Source of Data: State of Maryland Dept. of Education

MAP 3.2   Percentage of elementary classes taught by non-highly qualified teachers in 2004. Boundaries represent elementary school catchment areas (received from school districts). Data represent individual schools for each catchment area. Areas with missing data were given the corresponding data for the district average. (*Source:* State of Maryland Department of Education. Prepared by the Kirwan Institute for the Study of Race and Ethnicity, June 29, 2005.)

greater relief. Detroit, Chicago, Newark, Cincinnati, and Cleveland, the five most racially segregated large metropolitan regions in the nation, have student poverty rates ranging from 64 percent (Cincinnati) to nearly 100 percent (Cleveland). As seen in Map 3.3, high-poverty (i.e., relatively high-need) schools in the Cleveland and Akron areas are found almost exclusively in African American neighborhoods, while low-poverty (i.e., low-need) schools are predominately white and suburban. These cases exemplify a national trend. In 2000, the average African American student attended a school with a poverty rate of 70 percent while the average white student attended a school with a 30 percent poverty rate (Logan 2002). Nevertheless, across the country in 2004, "$908 less per student [was] spent on students in the districts educating the most students of color, as compared to the districts educating the fewest students of color" (Education Trust 2006, 6). This figure represents state and local education spending; federal spending made up a mere 8.9 percent of public school revenues in 2004 (Education Trust 2006, 5).

Analyses by the Kirwan Institute for the Study of Race and Ethnicity in a number of major metropolitan areas have broadly assessed the correspondence between race and opportunity across a wide range of institutional contexts. Neighborhood conditions and indicators of resource availability and opportunity such as high-quality schools and job abundance can be quantified and mapped. These opportunity maps can then be compared to the distributions of racial groups across the regions. As seen in Table 3.1, in the major metropolitan regions on which Kirwan has conducted these analyses, large majorities of each region's African American and Latino populations reside in neighborhoods that are resource and opportunity-poor across a number of key institutional domains at once.[15] This kind of multi-institutional disadvantage reflects and fuels the structural disadvantage that underpins racial injustice in the United States today.

Conclusion

We need not insist that yesterday's mountain of prejudice is a mere molehill today to recognize that contemporary racial inequality depends on more than the self-conscious actions of racist individuals. We believe that interpersonal and institutional racisms remain potent contributors to the persistence of racial and ethnic inequities. But we also insist that any approach to remedying inequality that does not account for the role of inter-institutional arrangements and interactions and historical legacies (not discussed here) can at best enjoy only limited success.

A structural racism framework mandates that we study institutional processes, not in isolation, but with respect to other institutions with which they interact or share functions. Institutions and structures do not shape opportunities and outcomes in a social vacuum. The framework directs us to identify key leverage points through which we can enact positive change across multiple domains, and to be alert to the ripple effects likely to accompany any particular institutional initiative. Housing policy is one example of a critical leverage point, a structural fact that David Rusk, former mayor of Albuquerque, New Mexico,

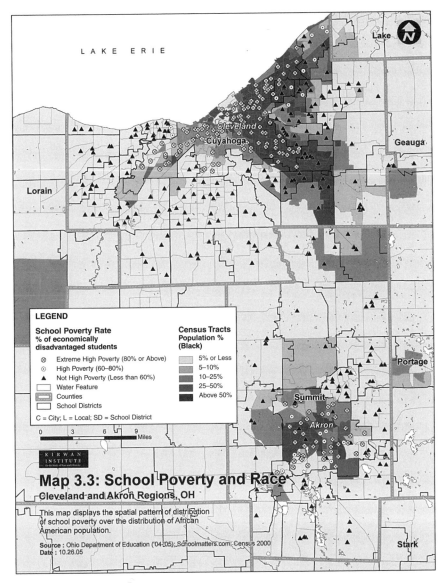

MAP 3.3 School poverty and race in Cuyahoga and Summit counties, Ohio. (*Source:* Ohio Department of Education (2004–2005); Schoolmatters.com; Census 2000. Prepared by the Kirwan Institute for the Study of Race and Ethnicity, October 26, 2005.)

TABLE 3.1   COMPARATIVE ANALYSIS: OPPORTUNITY MAPPING IN MULTIPLE CITIES
(population by race in very low or low opportunity areas)

	Total Population, %	Total Number
Cleveland Analysis: Twelve Indicator Based Analysis		
African Americans	79.9	147,666
Whites	20.3	180,955
Baltimore Analysis: Fourteen Indicator Based Analysis		
African Americans	72.4	501,058
Whites	18.3	289,717
Milwaukee Analysis: Five Indicator Based Analysis		
African Americans	84.4	127,974
Whites	15.7	207,859
African American Male Study, Seven Regions, Kids under Fourteen Only: Seventeen Indicator Based Analysis		
All Seven Regions		
African Americans	69	1,590,823
Whites	20	1,044,559
Atlanta		
Total Population (2000)	31	1,273,176
Black Males, 0–14	55	88,914
Black Females, 0–14	56	87,076
White Females, 0–14	12	31,574
White Males, 0–14	12	33,520
Chicago		
Total Population (2000)	31	2,536,552
Black Males, 0–14	76	163,168
Black Females, 0–14	76	158,527
White Females, 0–14	14	72,940
White Males, 0–14	14	76,526
Detroit		
Total Population (2000)	37	1,629,671
Black Males, 0–14	92	129,133
Black Females, 0–14	92	125,751
White Females, 0–14	18	54,411
White Males, 0–14	18	57,758
Houston		
Total Population (2000)	36	1,493,212
Black Males, 0–14	56	55,596
Black Females, 0–14	56	53,436
White Females, 0–14	25	69,377
White Males, 0–14	25	72,985
Los Angeles		
Total Population (2000)	38	3,661,427
Black Males, 0–14	62	73,067
Black Females, 0–14	62	71,577
White Females, 0–14	32	148,696
White Males, 0–14	32	154,933

TABLE 3.1 *Continued*

	Total Population, %	Total Number
African American Male Study, Seven Regions, Kids under Fourteen Only: Seventeen Indicator Based Analysis (*continued*)		
New York		
Total Population (2000)	39	3,651,529
Black Males, 0–14	68	189,096
Black Females, 0–14	68	194,914
White Females, 0–14	25	93,766
White Males, 0–14	25	98,748
Washington, D.C.		
Total Population (2000)	33	1,601,729
Black Males, 0–14	65	101,748
Black Females, 0–14	65	98,820
White Females, 0–14	14	38,708
White Males, 0–14	14	40,617

recognizes when he declares that "housing policy is school policy" (American Civil Liberties Union n.d.). A large research literature confirms that the bundle of goods and services to which one's community facilitates access, or does not, shapes opportunities and outcomes above and beyond the affect of personal or family characteristics. Housing policy is school policy, health policy, asset development policy, safety policy, employment policy, and more.

Although we have made frequent reference here to racial inequality and to racial gaps in institutional opportunity, we emphasize that white Americans, middle class Americans, and even those who try to isolate themselves from the problems associated with social "others" also stand to benefit from the use of a structural racism lens. As Lani Guinier and Gerald Torres (2003) remind us, people of color in the United States are like the miner's canary: their distress signals problems in our institutions and social structures that harm all racial groups, albeit to different degrees, and will harm even the relatively privileged among us absent remedial moves. Low-opportunity neighborhoods are home to far too many African Americans and Latinos, yes, but they are home to some whites and Asian Americans as well. Failing physical and social infrastructure ultimately undermines the economic competitiveness of entire metropolitan regions, not simply that of particular areas within them (Sohmer 2005). The Texas 10 Percent Plan, under which students graduating in the top 10 percent of their high school classes become eligible for admission to the state university of their choice, was a policy response to the gross under-representation of rural whites, as well as the under-representation of black and brown students, in the state's higher education system. The recognition of racism as structural, and our fates as linked across lines of race and class, is critical if we are to achieve the American aspiration of building a just, equitable and sustainable society for all.

Notes

1. A number of groups are dedicated to studying structural racism or have this framework at the center of their work. They include the Structural Racism Caucus, the Aspen Roundtable for Community Change, the Applied Research Center, the Center for Social Inclusion and the W. K. Kellogg Foundation. The Poverty and Race Research Action Council has also published a special newsletter on the topic (November–December 2006).

2. Carroll O'Connor played Archie Bunker on the 1970s television show *All in the Family*. As the TVLand website (http://www.tvland.com/shows/aitf) puts it, the show revolved around "blue-collar worker Archie Bunker and his family. Bigoted, opinionated and uneducated, Archie makes no bones about his racial and political views, which are borne out of every negative stereotype imaginable."

3. Some refer to "structural discrimination" or to "structural inequality," rather than to "structural racism." Others reject the use of the word "discrimination" as connoting an individualist and intentional approach. We flag this tension but do not think the exact phrase is critical to our efforts here (see Young 2001).

4. As Michael Brown and his collaborators note, the prevailing view of racial inequality in the United States is that inequality owes not to white racism, but to bad choices impelled by pathological group cultures (Brown et al. 2003). African Americans and, to some degree, Latinos, are generally regarded as the main purveyors of these "cultures of poverty" (D'Souza 1995; Gans 1996; Mead 1992).

5. For example, Dictionary.com defines racism as: (1) the belief that race accounts for differences in human character or ability and that a particular race is superior to others; (2) discrimination or prejudice based on race. Merriam-Webster online (http://www.merriam-webster.com/dictionary/racism) offers a similar definition: (1) a belief that race is the primary determinant of human traits and capacities and that racial differences produce an inherent superiority of a particular race; (2) racial prejudice or discrimination.

6. In an interview with NBC's Brian Williams, President Bush insisted, "You can call me anything you want, but do not call me a racist" (Shipp 2005).

7. In Jasper, Texas, in 1998, James Byrd, a black man, was tied to a pickup truck and dragged three miles to his death by three white men, all well-known white supremacists in the community: see Stewart 1999. More recently, in 2007, Don Imus casually made the aforementioned racialized and gendered comments in reference to a basketball team, leading to his firing from MSNBC (see Carter and Steinberg 2007).

8. There is no agreement among social scientists about what is meant by structures and yet there is substantial acknowledgement of the importance of structures in understanding society (Sewell 1992).

9. Consider work. It is a complex set of arrangements with status and compensation. That certain work is considered part of the "formal" work force, therefore paid and attached to status, while the work at home carries neither benefit, tends to benefit men and not women. This pattern is carried over into other institutions such as social security and unemployment benefits. One may notice that these arrangements often do not explicitly target men or women, nor are they under the control of any individual or even any given institutions. Because structures are patterned arrangements, there is no single incident or time that captures the meaning or importance of structures.

10. Blank (2005) elaborates on three ways that cumulative discrimination might occur:

> First, one may observe the cumulative impact of discrimination that arises from multiple interactions within a single social domain over time. An example would

be a study of whether and how discriminatory impacts might cumulate within the labor market from the initial hiring process, through multiple promotion, job change, and hiring experiences over an individual's worklife. Second, discrimination in one social domain may over time affect outcomes in another social domain. An example would be a study of the effects of discrimination in housing markets, traced through to its effect on educational access, and on future earnings. Third, discrimination may have cross-generational effects. An example would be a study of how educational discrimination in one generation may (through effects on wealth accumulation or lifetime earning opportunities) affect the educational and earning opportunities in the next generation." (Blank 2005, 99–100)

11. The policy change has likely had only modest impact. As Stanford's provost acknowledged, for example, the university already covers most costs for low-income students (Oresmus 2005).

12. The W. K. Kellogg Foundation's Engaging Latino Communities for Education project (ENLACE) is one example. ENLACE is "a multiyear initiative to strengthen the educational pipeline and increase opportunities for Latinos to enter and complete college." At the Chicago site, partners look to implement articulation agreements between community colleges and four-year universities. In Miami, high school and university partners have implemented dual enrollment policies that ease students' transition to college. In Santa Ana, parent–teacher–community dialogues (*pláticas*) allow parents and teachers to interact informally. For an overview, see http://www.wkkf.org/Programming/Overview.aspx?CID=16.

13. For more information regarding road inequities and fix-it-first strategies, see Surface Transportation Policy Project 2003; Thayer 2003.

14. In 2005, the American Society of Civil Engineers estimated that the cost to bring the nation's infrastructure up to a "good" condition was $1.6 trillion. Replacing wastewater treatment facilities alone is estimated to cost $390 billion over the next two decades. For more information, see http://www.asce.org/reportcard/2005/page.cfm?id=103.

15. The Kirwan Institute conducts opportunity mapping by comprehensively analyzing community characteristics in several key opportunity areas (school quality, neighborhood health and quality, economic access and public health). The institute has conducted this analysis in a dozen metropolitan regions: see www.kirwaninstitute.org.

References

American Civil Liberties Union. N.d. "The Case of *Thompson v. HUD*: A Briefing on Segregation and Public Housing in Baltimore." Available online at http://www.aclu-md .org/aTop%20Issues/Fair%20housing/ThompsonBriefing.pdf.

Balfanz, Robert, Kurt Spiridakis, Ruth Curran Neild, and Nettie Ledgers. 2003. "High Poverty Secondary Schools and the Juvenile Justice System: How Neither Helps the Other and How That Could Change." Pp. 71–90 in *Deconstructing the School-to-Prison Pipeline: New Directions for Youth Development,* ed. Johanna Wald and Daniel J. Losen. San Francisco: Jossey-Bass.

Bertrand, Marianne, and Sendhil Mullainathan. 2004. "Are Emily and Greg More Employable than Lakisha and Jamal? A Field Experiment on Labor Market Discrimination." *American Economic Review* 94, no. 4: 991–1013.

Blank, Rebecca. 2005. "Tracing the Economic Impact of Cumulative Discrimination." *American Economic Review* 95, no. 2: 99–103.

Bonilla-Silva, Eduardo. 1997. "Rethinking Racism: Toward a Structural Interpretation." *American Sociological Review* 62, no. 3: 465–480.

Brown, Michael, Martin Carnoy, Elliott Currie, and Troy Duster. 2003. *Whitewashing Race: The Myth of a Colorblind Society.* Berkeley: University of California Press.

Brown, Richard. 2004. *Changes in Advanced Placement Test Taking in California High Schools, 1998–2003. University of California All Campus Consortium on Research for Diversity. UC/ACCORD Papers.* Paper RR-002-0105. Available online at http://repositories.cdlib.org/ucaccord/papers/RR-002-0105

Carnevale, Anthony, and Stephen Rose. 2004. "Socioeconomic Status, Race/Ethnicity, and Selective College Admissions." Pp. 101–156 in *America's Untapped Resource: Low-Income Students in Higher Education,* ed. Richard Kahlenberg. Washington, D.C.: Century Foundation Press.

Carter, Bill, and Jacques Steinberg. 2007. "Off the Air: The Light Goes Out for Don Imus." *New York Times,* April 13, C2.

Cashin, Sheryll. 2004. *The Failures of Integration: How Race and Class Are Undermining the American Dream.* New York: PublicAffairs Books.

Cherry, Robert. 2001. *Who Gets the Good Jobs? Combating Race and Gender Disparities.* New Brunswick, N.J.: Rutgers University Press.

Condron, Dennis J., and Vincent J. Roscigno. 2003. "Disparities Within: Unequal Spending and Achievement in an Urban School District. *Sociology of Education* 76, no. 1: 18–36.

DeNavas-Walt, Carmen, Bernadette D. Proctor, and Robert J. Mills. 2003. *Income, Poverty, and Health Insurance Coverage in the United States.* U.S. Bureau of the Census, Current Population Reports, P60-226. Washington, D.C.: U.S. Government Printing Office.

D'Souza, Dinesh. 1995. *The End of Racism: Principles for a Multiracial Society.* New York: Free Press.

"Education Needed to Cut Mortality." 1992. *St. Louis Post-Dispatch,* May 12, 2B.

Education Trust. 2005. "The Funding Gap 2005: Low-Income and Minority Students Shortchanged by Most States." Special report. Available online at http://www2.edtrust.org/NR/rdonlyres/31D276EF-72E1-458A-8C71-E3D262A4C91E/0/FundingGap2005.pdf.

———. 2006. "Funding Gaps 2006." Available online at http://www2.edtrust.org/NR/rdonlyres/CDEF9403-5A75-437E-93FF-EBF1174181FB/0/FundingGap2006.pdf.

Education Trust–West. 2005. "California's Hidden Teacher Spending Gap: How State and District Budgeting Practices Shortchange Poor and Minority Students and Their Schools." Available online at http://www.hiddengap.org/resources/execsummary.pdf.

Elliott, James R. 1999. "Social Isolation and Labor Market Insulation: Network and Neighborhood Effects on Less-Educated Urban Workers." *Sociological Quarterly* 40: 199–216.

Feder, Judith, Larry Levitt, Ellen O'Brien, and Diane Rowland. 2001. "Covering the Low-Income Uninsured: The Case for Expanding Public Programs." *Health Affairs* 20, no. 1: 27–40.

Furry, William S., and Janet Hecsh. 2001. "Characteristics and Performance of Advanced Placement Classes in California." Report submitted to the Institute for Education Reform, California State University, Sacramento.

Gans, Herbert. 1996. *The War against the Poor: The Underclass and Antipoverty Policy.* New York: Basic Books.

Geiser, Saul, and Veronica Santelices. 2004. "The Role of Advanced Placement and Honors Courses in College Admissions." Paper CSHE-4-04, Center for Studies in Higher Education, University of California, Berkeley.

Guinier, Lani, and Gerald Torres. 2003. *The Miner's Canary: Enlisting Race, Resisting Power, Transforming Democracy.* Cambridge, Mass.: Harvard University Press.

Habuda, Janice L. 2003. "Panelists Press Drive for Cohesive Black Community." *Buffalo News,* November 18, B3.

Harlow, Carolyn Wolf. 2005. "Hate Crime Reported by Victims and Police." Bureau of Justice Statistics Special Report, U.S. Justice Department, Office of Justice Programs. Available online at http://www.ojp.usdoj.gov/bjs/pub/pdf/hcrvp.pdf.

Hochschild, Jennifer. 1995. *Facing Up to the American Dream: Race, Class, and the Soul of the Nation.* Princeton, N.J.: Princeton University Press.

Logan, John. 2002. *Choosing Segregation: Racial Imbalance in American Public Schools, 1990–2000.* Lewis Mumford Center for Comparative Urban and Regional Research. Available online at http://mumford.albany.edu/census/SchoolPop/SPReport/page1.html.

Lord, Peter B. 2001. "Another Generation Caught in a Sad Cycle." *Providence Journal-Bulletin,* May 13, 1E.

Marsden, Peter, and Elizabeth H. Gorman. 2001. "Social Networks, Job Changes, and Recruitment." Pp. 467–502 in *Sourcebook on Labor Markets: Evolving Structures and Processes,* ed. Ivar Berg and Arne L. Kalleberg. New York: Kluwer Academic/Plenum Publishers.

McPherson, Miller, Lynn Smith-Lovin, and James M. Cook. 2001. "Birds of a Feather: Homophily in Social Networks." *Annual Review of Sociology* 27: 415–444.

Mead, Lawrence. 1992. *The New Politics of Poverty.* New York: Basic Books.

National Research Council. 2004. *Measuring Racial Discrimination.* Washington, D.C.: National Academy Press.

Oremus, Will. 2005. "Tuition to be Waived for Low-Income Admits to Stanford." *Stanford Daily,* April 26.

Orfield, Myron. 2002. *American Metropolitics: The New Suburban Reality.* Washington, D.C.: Brookings Institution Press.

"Personal Networking Is Key in Finding a Job or Job Candidate, Says New Poll." 2001. PR Newswire. April 6. Available online at http://www.careerknowhow.com/persnetw.htm.

Peske, Heather, and Kati Haycock. 2006. *Teaching Equality: How Poor and Minority Students are Shortchanged on Teacher Quality.* Washington, D.C.: Education Trust.

Pincus, Fred. 1996. "Discrimination Comes in Many Forms." *American Behavioral Scientist* 40, no.2: 186–194.

powell, john, and Kathleen Graham. 2002. "Urban Fragmentation as a Barrier to Equal Opportunity." Pp. 79–97 in *Rights at Risk: Equality in an Age of Terrorism.* Washington, D.C.: Citizens' Commission on Civil Rights.

Presley, Jennifer, Bradford White, and Yugin Gong. 2005. *Examining the Distribution and Impact of Teacher Quality in Illinois.* Illinois Education Research Council. Available online at http://ierc.siue.edu/documents/Teacher%20Quality%20IERC%202005-2.pdf.

Robinson, Lisa, and Andrew Grant-Thomas. 2004. *Race, Place, and home: A Civil Rights and Metropolitan Opportunity Agenda.* Cambridge, Mass.: Civil Rights Project, Harvard University.

Sánchez, Thomas W., Rich Stolz, and Jacinta Ma. 2003. *Moving to Equity: Addressing Inequitable Effects of Transportation Policies on Minorities.* Cambridge, Mass.: Civil Rights Project, Harvard University. Available online at http://www.civilrightsproject.harvard.edu/research/transportation/MovingtoEquity.pdf .

Santoli, Susan P. 2002. "Is There an Advanced Placement Advantage? *American Secondary Education* 30, no. 3: 23.

Sen, Amartya Kumar. 1999. *Development as Freedom.* New York: Knopf.

Sewell, William. 1992. "A Theory of Structure: Duality, Agency, and Transformation." *American Journal of Sociology,* 98, no. 1: 1–29.

Shipp, E. R. 2005. "For Bush, Word 'Racist' Is Just a Distraction." *Augusta (Ga.) Chronicle,* December 21, A5.

Sohmer, Rebecca. 2005. "Mind the Gap: Disparities and Competitiveness in the Twin Cities." Brookings Institution. Available online at http://www.brookings.edu/metro/pubs/20051027_mindthegap.htm.

Solorzano, Daniel G., and Armida Ornelas. 2002. "A Critical Race Analysis of Advanced Placement Classes: A Case of Educational Inequality." *Journal of Latinos and Education* 1, no. 4: 215–226.

———. 2004. "A Critical Race Analysis of Latina/o and African American Advanced Placement Enrollment in Public High Schools." *High School Journal* 87, no. 3: 15–26.

Steele, Shelby. 1990. *The Content of Our Character: A New Vision of Race in America.* New York: St. Martin's Press.

Stewart, Richard. 1999. "Dragged into Infamy: Murder Case Forces Jasper to Revisit Horror of Slaying in June." *Houston Chronicle,* January 24, A1.

Surface Transportation Policy Project. 2003. "The State of Our Nation's Roads: Half of All Major Roads Are in Less than Good Condition." *Decoding Transportation Policy and Practice* 9. Available online at http://www.transact.org/library/decoder/roadcondition decoder.pdf.

Taylor, Henry Louis, Jr., and Sam Cole. 2001. "Structural Racism and Efforts to Radically Reconstruct the Inner-City Built Environment." Paper presented at the 43rd Annual Conference of the Association of Collegiate Schools of Planning, Cleveland, Ohio.

Thayer, Kelly. 2003. *Look Close: Flood of Money, Words Yield Scant Improvement in State Roads.* Michigan Land Use Institute. Available online at http://mlui.org/transportation/fullarticle.asp?fileid=16441.

Unger, Roberto Mangabeira. 2000. *Democracy Realized: The Progressive Alternative.* New York: Verso.

U.S. Department of Education, National Center for Education Statistics. 2005. *The Condition of Education 2005.* NCES 2005-094. Washington, D.C.: U.S. Government Printing Office. Available online at http://nces.ed.gov/programs/coe/2005/pdf/25_2005.pdf.

———. 2006. *The Condition of Education 2006.* NCES 2006-071. Washington, D.C.: U.S. Government Printing Office. Available online at http://nces.ed.gov/programs/coe/2006/pdf/34_2006.pdf.

Wald, Johanna, and Daniel Losen. 2003. "Defining and Redirecting a School-to-Prison Pipeline." *New Directions for Youth Development* 99: 9–15.

Waltz, Kenneth. 1979. *Theory of International Politics.* Reading, Mass.: Addison.

Williams, Susan. N.d. *Diversity and the Nature of Racism.* Available online at http://www.in.gov/judiciary/center/education/library/social/nature-of-racism.pdf.

Wilson, William Julius. 1996. *When Work Disappears: The World of the New Urban Poor.* New York: Knopf.

Winant, Howard. 1998. "Racism Today: Continuity and Change in the Post–Civil Rights Era." *Ethnic and Racial Studies* 21, no. 4: 755–766.

———. 2000. "Race and Race Theory." *Annual Review of Sociology* 26, no. 1: 169–185.

Wirt, J., S. Choy, P. Rooney, S. Provasnik, A. Sen, and R. Tobin. 2004. *The Condition of Education 2004.* NCES 2004-077. U.S. Department of Education, National Center for Education Statistics. Washington, D.C.: U.S. Government Printing Office.

Young, Iris Marion. 2001. "Equality of Whom? Social Groups and Judgments of Injustice." *Journal of Political Philosophy* 9, no. 1: 1–18.

II

Ambiguities of Racial and Ethnic Identity

4

"We Are Not Like Them"

Social Distancing and Realignment in the U.S. Latino Racial Hierarchy

CHRISTINA GÓMEZ

Many years ago I sat in a car waiting in the parking lot of a fast-food restaurant with friends. We were waiting for our dinner of *tacos, arroz,* and *orchata.* We were in the heart of the Mexican community on the south side of Chicago. It was the middle of summer, so men selling *paletas* were milling around ringing the bells on their carts. These ice cream-like bars in flavors of *mango, fresa,* and *tamarindo* were sold by immigrant Latino men who were dark and Indian-looking; they were men who reminded me of my own father, who had worked as an undocumented migrant farm worker picking fruit and vegetables. The smells and sounds were very familiar and comforting to me. This was home.

As we waited, somehow the conversation in the car moved to race. I made the comment that we, Latinos, had a "racial choice." Using my newly found graduate student voice and research that I was doing for my dissertation using census data, I explained that since the 1980 Census Latinos had the option to "choose" a race category, in addition to a Hispanic/Latino category. The choice was complicated by other variables such as what we might look like or what others thought of us, but it was clear that various choices were being made. One friend asked, "What do you mean, choose? We're white."

I was surprised by her response. Here she was, a socially conscientious Chicana, active in promoting racial and gender equality, claiming whiteness. She was college educated, now middle class, and living in the suburbs of Chicago in a predominantly white area. I responded that we actually have a "choice" and that many Latinos do not choose a white identity on the census, but rather they might select black, Indian, or other (some other race). This last category, I continued, is sometimes viewed as a type of Hispanic/Latino identifier, signifying a separate race category—a Latino racial category. "I am not white," I said adamantly, "or at least I am not white *like them.*"

My thoughts wandered over dinner, what exactly did I mean? Not white *like them?* Who was I referring to? Were they the *Americanos*—the people we often describe when we speak of white Americans—those tall, blond, blue-eyed men and women? The majority of Latinos are U.S.-born. In fact, according to the 2000 Census, approximately 60 percent of Latinos were American-born. I am American. I knew empirically that many Latinos self-identified as white, but somehow I had separated this group out.

Yet, here she was a Chicana like me and she identified as white. What did that make me? Was I white, too? And if I was white, did that make me less Chicana? Less Latina? Less sympathetic to the *causa?* Was it money and education that made her white, did *dinero blanquea* (money whiten)? I thought about this for a long time. What does "race" mean to the Latino community in the United States? And where do Latinos fit racially?

In this chapter I begin to explore the meaning of racial identity for Latinos in the United States and the social distancing that I believe is occurring. By 2050 this group, now the largest "minority," is expected to reach a staggering 102.6 million and constitute approximately 25 percent of the U.S. population. Yet, how to racially identify this collection of individuals has been unclear. Are they white/ *blanco?* Black/*negro*/*moreno?* Indian/*indio?* Or a multiracial group/*mestizo*/ *mulatto?* Or do they represent their own racial grouping? What are the political, social, and economic ramifications of the categories chosen? And, how is this group changing concepts of race in America?

I contend that Latinos are forcing a reconceptualization of race in the United States; Latinos are transgressing the boundaries of what we have understood racial identity to be while simultaneously expanding and contracting the confines of racial spaces. The physical presence of Latinos, with their varied racial phenotypes and designations, has loosened the noose of racial categorizations in the United States. Latinos have given new meaning to the tenet "*race is socially constructed,*" the mantra in every social science discipline. Their presence has reconfigured our understanding of race: Sammy Sosa may look black but he is Dominican; Christina Aguilera may look white but she is Ecuadorian; José Padilla (a.k.a. Abdullah al-Muhajir) may look Middle Eastern but he is Puerto Rican. They are all Latino. Race is socially constructed, not only at the societal level, but also at the individual level and Latinos exemplify this par excellence.

Clearly Latinos are not the only group that has transgressed racial and ethnic boundaries—Asian Indians, Cape Verdeans, as well as many other groups have also occupied ambiguous racial positions in the United States.[1] But because the populations of those groups have been much smaller and not as geographically dispersed, their impact has not been as notable. Since the 1980s, when Latinos first became an "official" category in the census, the United States has proclaimed the tremendous growth of the Latino population—the decade of the Hispanic has come and gone twice.

Yet at the same time, I fear that the racial realignment that Latinos are bringing about may harden racial designations of who is black and white and entrench race relations while escaping the difficult dialogue of race and racism that the United States needs to have. Because Latinos have had a racial option (of sorts), their choices shed light on how race is and has been navigated. In particular, social distancing from more marginalized groups becomes the way to survive and support white privilege, further bolstering a racial hegemonic system that has shaped both North America and South America.

¿Que Somos? Changing Categories for Latinos

It is clear a Latino explosion has been under way in the United States—look around and Latinos are everywhere. With such a significant presence in a country where race plays such a prominent role, it is amazing and significant that Latinos have managed to escape a clear racial classification. Although "officially" an ethnic group, according to the U.S. Census, Latinos/Hispanics are often considered a race category in surveys or forms,[2] distinguished from whites, blacks, Asians, and Native Americans. We often see categories such as white non-Hispanic and black non-Hispanic, often forgetting that these categories are not mutually exclusive. Historically, the group now known as Latinos derives from a variety of peoples (or race groups), including, but not exclusively, Natives of the Americas, Europeans, and Africans. Thus, placing Latinos within a single established race category or a Hispanic/Latino race category is inaccurate. In addition, Latinos come from a variety of countries that conceive of race or *raza* differently than the United States. Because of their different histories with colonialism, slavery, and independence, race has been constructed differently in Latin America than in the United States.

Race categories on government forms, as we are accustomed to in the United States, are basically non-existent in Latin America today; most censuses in Latin America do not ask a race question. However, personal descriptors or color categories in Latin America—such as *blanca*, *morena*, and *trigueña*—are often used to describe an individual and connote a racial ancestry. In the United States, race categories function as nouns, while in Latin America the categories are used as adjectives to describe an individual's phenotype, such as skin color, hair texture, or physical features. Furthermore, racial or color categories can be influenced by variables such as occupation, educational attainment, income, wealth, and social standing in the community. In Latin America, as in the United States, African and Indian ancestry can still carry negative connotations due to their own history of colonization and slavery; however, high socioeconomic standing can "lighten" an individual's category. For example, in Latin America, a poor dark-skinned individual might be called *negro* (black), yet the same individual, having earned a Ph.D., might be called *trigueño* (swarthy). Money can literally "whiten." Consequently, the understanding of "race" is different for most Latin Americans and more flexible but still problematic in that it is premised on a racist ideology. Latinos in the United States, both immigrants and native-born, are confronted by a different racial system that they must fit themselves into; there are inescapable racial categories that they must assign themselves to or be assigned. Yet the definitions of these categories are not well demarcated, and their many implications are profound and real.

Years ago when I first began this project, a family friend told me an interesting story about his arrival in the United States. Now in his seventies, Ramiro had come illegally from Mexico to Texas in the 1940s.[3] As he nervously waited to board a bus to California where friends had told him jobs were plentiful, he had to choose between the "colored" and "white" sections of the bus terminal to wait in. Although he only had limited English skills, he concluded that he should wait in the section for coloreds, since he believed he was not white. Ramiro had an olive complexion; tight, curly black hair; dark eyes; and a prominent nose. As a police officer walked toward him, Ramiro feared he would be asked for documentation of his residency status. He was illegal and assumed he was going to be caught and deported. To his surprise, the officer told him he was in the wrong section; he was not colored and should move to the white area. Ramiro said nothing and quickly moved. Ramiro had not yet figured out this new system. Back home he wasn't exactly considered white (*blanco*), since he was poor and uneducated and his physical features showed his mixed ancestry. Now in this new country he was unclear how to classify himself. When I asked him how he would classify himself today, he responded, "*Bueno, soy blanco* (Well, I am white)." "*¿Porqué?*" I asked. "*Bueno,*" he replied, "*no somos negros, así que tenemos que ser blancos* (Well, we are not black, so that must mean we are white)."

But he had not considered himself white fifty years ago.

Checking the Boxes

Over the decades, the U.S. Census has used a variety of identifiers for the Latino/ Hispanic population, including country of birth, Spanish surname, and Spanish language usage. What is surprising is that this population has not been considered a race group along with other groups such as white, black, American Indian, Japanese, Chinese, and a host of others. Only once in the history of the U.S. Census has a Latino national group been listed as a race group: Mexicans in the 1930 Census were listed along with other race groups but omitted thereafter. Generally, enumerators coded individuals of Latin American descent as white, unless they appeared to have African or Indian ancestry. It wasn't until the 1960 Census that individuals self-identified their own race category, with the head of household usually indicating the race category of other family members.

The 1980 Census was the first to include the Hispanic/Spanish question nationally,[4] in addition to the race question. The 1990 Census and 2000 Census also allowed this choice. Yet for many Latinos, this separation of race and ethnicity is confusing. Latinos often identify *only* by their national-origin descent, without dividing their identity into ethnic and racial categories, as is done in the United States. Racial categories or color categories (phenotype qualities) may be implicit, while in the United States, the distinction needs to be made. For example, an individual may only identify as Mexican or Panamanian but not as Indian *and* Mexican or black *and* Panamanian. However, any Latino who is in the United States for any length of time understands the different meanings and consequences that race and ethnic categories can have. Thus, choosing a particular race category is loaded with other social implications, both personal and public.

According to the 1980 census, 55.6 percent of Latinos classified themselves as white, 40 percent as other race, 2.7 percent as black, 1.1 percent as Asian and Pacific Islander, and .6 percent as American Indian and Aleut or Eskimo. Of those identifying as black, approximately 50,540 were Afro-Puerto Ricans; at least 18,000, Afro-Cubans; and smaller numbers, Afro-Panamanians and Afro-Mexicans. Given the non-binary Latin American modes of defining race, only a small proportion of Caribbean Spanish speakers with African ancestry identify as "black"—*negro, moreno,* or *prieto.* Hence, the 2.7 percent of Latinos who declared themselves black/*negro* or Afro-Latino on the 1980 Census probably falls far below the number that most native-born Americans would label black (Matory 1993). Researchers estimated that blacks constituted closer to 5 percent of Cuban immigrants prior to the Mariel boatlift in May 1980. During the boatlift, the percentage jumped to about 30 percent, which more closely reflects the percentage of blacks on the island. This migration, however, occurred after the 1980 Census.[5]

In 1990, the number of Latinos in the census who identified as white decreased to 51.7 percent, while the members of those who identified as black, Asian, American Indian, and other increased: 3.4 percent of Latinos identified as black; .7 percent as American Indian; 1.4 percent as Asian and Pacific Islander; and 42.7 percent as other. Between 1980 and 1990, the number of individuals (this includes Latinos and non-Latinos) who responded as "other" increased from 6.8 million to 9.8 million, a 45 percent increase; over 95 percent of those who responded as "other" were Latinos (U.S. Bureau of the Census 1992; Lee 1993, 83).

The choice of race and ethnic identity are not independent but are highly influenced by structural forces. Race in the United States has social and economic consequences; one's placement in the racial hierarchy has meaning and material consequences. This was made clear in the debates about whether to add a Latino/Hispanic box for the 2000 Census for the race question instead of having separate questions, as was done on the 1980 and 1990 censuses. This addition might decrease the number of Latinos who checked some other race. When tested by the Census Bureau in the mid-1990s, many Latinos objected to the inclusion of Latino as a race category.[6] The final decision was not to lump all Latinos together as a race category but to allow for differentiation. Instead, Latinos were allowed to choose their racial category or categories (since individuals were allowed to check more than one race category in 2000) along with Spanish/Hispanic/Latinos ethnicity choice.

Once again, the 2000 Census questionnaire separated race and the Spanish/Hispanic/Latino origin questions. The term "Latino" was added to the question, in addition to "Spanish/Hispanic." Question 7 read:

7. Is Person 1 Spanish/Hispanic/Latino? Mark the *"No"* box if *not* Spanish/Hispanic/Latino.

__ No, not Spanish/Hispanic/Latino   __ Yes, Puerto Rican
__ Yes, Mexican, Mexican Am., Chicano   __ Yes, Cuban
__ Yes, other Spanish/Hispanic/Latino—*Print group*

The race question followed the Spanish/Hispanic/Latino question and was broken into five main categories. For the first time in U.S. history, individuals were allowed to check one box or more. Question 8 read:

8. What is Person 1's race? Mark one or more races to indicate what this person considers himself/herself to be.

__ White
__ Black, African Am., or Negro
__ American Indian or Alaska Native—*Print name of enrolled or principal tribe.*

__ Asian Indian   __ Japanese   __ Native Hawaiian
__ Chinese   __ Korean   __ Guamanian or Chamorro
__ Filipino   __ Vietnamese   __ Samoan
__ Other Asian—*Print race*
__ Other Pacific Islander—*Print race*
__ Some other race—*Print race*

In 2000, the percentage of Latinos who identified as some other race was 42.2 percent; 47.9 percent identified as white racially; and only 2 percent identified as black (these are Latinos who chose only one race category). Because 6.3 percent of Latinos checked two or more races, it is difficult to compare the 1980 and 1990 censuses with the 2000 Census (Tafoya 2004). However, the majority of Latinos in the United States identify on the census as white or other racially. Only a small percentage identify as black, and even fewer as Indian or Asian. What is also true is that Latinos who identify as white are socioeconomically better off than Latinos who choose other or black. If race is a choice for Latinos, is it partly being driven by class?

My questions concerning how Latinos might understand their racial position in the United States originates from research done on ethnicity by sociologists Mary C. Waters and Herbert Gans on symbolic ethnicity and the formation of identity. Symbolic ethnicity is identification with an ethnicity that is present or called upon. It is an identification made by choice that brings pleasure or personal benefits, where there is no cost associated with being identified with the ethnic group. While it is important, ethnic membership need not influence the individual's life unless he or she wants it to (Waters 1990, 7). I initially wondered whether Latinos ever have this option or whether they tend to be viewed only as a racialized minority group. Were some Latinos experiencing an ethnic option? Becoming Mexican or Puerto Rican when called upon? Like other immigrant groups that have experienced a transformation from constrained to optional ethnicity (Alba 1990; Gans 1990), some Latinos might view themselves not necessarily as "minority people," but as a people, with whiteness being understood, with an ethnic identity—a Latino identity. Like some white ethnics, they might turn on their Latino-ness when convenient. On Cinco de Mayo, perhaps?

In her second book, *Black Identities: West Indian Immigrant Dreams and American Realities,* Mary C. Waters (1999) examines how West Indian immigrants to the United States and their children form identities. Although there is a common misconception that non-white immigrants must choose between race and ethnicity, Waters found otherwise:

> I viewed the immigrants as having to choose between a racial and an ethnic identity. This assumption arose out of a very American sense that black racial identity and the solidarity that it entails involve not having other identities. This is nonsense, of course. As I began talking with immigrants about their identities, I soon realized that identity was a much more fluid, malleable, and layered phenomenon that did not require people to choose between race and ethnicity. The immigrants were complex multiracial and multiethnic societies. Their "ethnic" as well as their "racial" identities reflect the history of those societies and the political and social meanings attached to those identities in American society. (Waters 1990, 6)

Like Latinos, West Indians have various options to choose from, but Latinos have even greater choices due to their more varied phenotype. West Indians were generally still considered "just black" by outsiders, and many second generation West Indians opt for or are forced into a black identity that emphasizes to a lesser extent their ethnic West Indian heritage. For most West Indians in the United States, their racial identity choice is constrained and in some cases trumps their ethnicity. Latinos are a more complicated case study. It is not just a choice of race *or* ethnicity but between race *and* ethnicity. Latinos have the option of choosing a racial identity (white, black, Indian, other/Latino) in addition to their ethnic heritage (Mexican, Puerto Rican, Cuban, Dominican, etc.).

But as we reevaluate our racial histories and move into the twenty-first century, we cannot forget that there has always been a constant negotiation of racial categories; since the inception of this country, racial categories have been mutable and malleable, although not explicitly. There is no reason to believe this negotiation of race has changed, especially given the influx of new immigrant groups since the 1960s that do not conform neatly as either black or white. However, what has changed is the rapid growth and density of a group that crosses racial boundaries. Since the 1960s the numbers of Latinos have exploded and have had a tremendous impact across the United States. Latinos are inhabiting, and transforming, the demographics of not only major cities like Los Angeles, New York, and Chicago, but also smaller cities like Manchester, New Hampshire; Little Rock, Arkansas; Nashville, Tennessee; and Raleigh, North Carolina. "Americans," especially white Americans, literally see Latinos in their daily lives, and what they are seeing does not clearly fall into a black–white racial system.

Consequently, Latinos have changed the rules of the race game. Their sheer physical presence, a racial ideology that allows for choice and change, and their multifarious physical characteristics have opened new doors of possibilities in the negotiations of racial identity. The problem of the twenty-first century is the problem not of the color line, but of the renegotiation of the color line, with Latinos tugging at either end.

Racial Options?

Latinos in the United States make "race choices" using their understanding of race and ethnicity from Latin America that encompasses a strong class component and allows for movement. In Latin America, as elsewhere, an individual's class position affects life chances; however, class can also reposition an individual's racial identifiers and, consequently, confer different privileges. Education, income, wealth, and social status can cause an individual to be viewed differently—both literally and figuratively.

Although class in Latin America affects racial identity, in the United States the inverse has been true: race affects class and life chances. Racial identification generally does not change because of the class position an individual holds in the United States; an individual's income, wealth, or occupation does not change his or her racial category. African American doctors, lawyers, and laborers are all considered black in the United States, and all might have difficulties hailing a taxicab in New York City. In quantitative studies that model how racial categories correlate with income, occupation, or wealth, introducing a non-white racial category in the equation usually has a negative effect. In other words, being a member of a non-white racial group will lower an individual's income, prospects for a job, or opportunity for promotion.

In economic human capital models, race generally functions as an independent variable influencing dependent variables such as income or educational attainment. In the United States we know that an individual's race affects life chances; like the variable sex, it is located on the right-hand side of the equation. Race is viewed as a fixed category that affects economic variables, and in the United States this has indeed proved to be the case. But in Latin America, race can also function as a dependent variable. Variables such as income, education, or occupation might influence the dependent variable—race. For Latinos, race is malleable; race is not fixed; and race interacts with other variables, in a multidirectional manner, allowing for change.

Although this "race choice" appears on its surface to be assimilationist and echoes the choices made by various ethnic groups that have come to the United States as racially ambiguous, I argue that it comes from a legacy of colonialism, slavery, and a racial ideology that values whiteness both in Latin America and in the United States. Because race in Latin America does not have the immutableness that it has in the United States, race choice for Latinos in the United States is a viable possibility. Money, education, occupation, phenotype, and social affiliations can shift a Latino's racial description.

Knowing that the racial ideology of the United States is one that still divides its population generally into a black–white racial paradigm,[7] and that both the United States and Latin America value whiteness over blackness and brownness, Latinos classify themselves as white racially as they move up the economic ladder. However, the category "white" has a different meaning for Latinos and encompasses more than just a racial classification. It symbolizes a position in society that includes a *mejoramiento,* or "betterment of conditions." This improvement might be an actual entrance into the middle class or just an improvement relative to one's origins.

First generation Latinos who enter the United States in search of economic advancement might view their situation with a "dual-frame of reference." Researchers Carola and Marcelo Suárez-Orozco (1995, 53) describe this as a process in which immigrants compare and contrast their current lot in the host society with their previous lives.[8] Recent immigrants see their current situation as better than where they came from, even though their current situation is not necessarily very good. In other words, what they can provide for themselves and their children is substantially better than what was possible in their home country—education, food, shelter, and material possessions seem attainable. *Somos pobres, pero no tan pobres como antes* (We are poor, but not as poor as before). This relative movement up the economic ladder affects identity as well: if being poor, uneducated, and marginalized is associated with Indianness and blackness, then doing economically better, providing an education for their children, and assimilating into society (or appearing to) is associated with whiteness. Latino identity is not lost; but there is a distancing from classifying themselves as non-white racially.[9] Certainly, the options are curtailed by their embodied phenotype, but the "one-drop" rule doesn't necessarily hold firm as it generally has for African Americans.[10] Consequently, Latinos do not view themselves in the same racial space as blacks; they may not even view themselves as their compatriots back home who are in a worse off position. The "other" begins to otherize, engulfing the racial and racist ideology of its antecedents and new host country. For the children of immigrants, those born and raised in the United States, the experience might be different; second and third generations might not have a dual frame of reference. They cannot make a comparison between their situation in the United

States and their native country. Consequently, if they have not managed to succeed economically, educationally, or socially in mainstream/white society they might identify more with marginalized groups and identify as non-white.

This idea of race choice is not radical or new; race in the United States has always incorporated this quality, and certainly other countries allow for this practice. I believe that we in the United States are gradually moving toward greater racial choice—certainly not for everyone, but for some this has already become a real possibility. Because of the large influx of Latin Americans as well as the increase of other groups such as multi- and bi-racials, some individuals now "choose" to belong to a race category.[11] This is not to say that race doesn't matter—race matters. But how Americans come to make a race choice and how others are making it for them includes a host of factors that are imbedded in how race has been constructed in the United States. And while some individuals may have a race choice, others will have one forced upon them. In other words, the very same variables that allow some individuals to move into another racial category will also constrain others.

While in the United States the idea of having a race choice appears odd or perhaps even impossible, we have to remember that *race is socially constructed*. It changes, it is reactive, and it is created within a context. As 42 million Latinos of varying phenotypes enter a society, their cultures, which include their ideas, values, and norms, enter with them. Salsa outsells ketchup, taco shells are sold in every grocery store, and Spanish-speaking politicians (Latinos and non-Latinos) are appearing all over. So, too, is the idea that race may not be what it appears, both literally and figuratively. This small but significant twist of racial ideology has already begun to reshape how we think about and construct notions of racial identity.

Notes

1. See, as examples, Ngai 1999; Halter 1993; Haney Lopez 1998.

2. I will use the terms "Latino" and "Hispanic" interchangeably to refer to individuals of Spanish-speaking Latin American origin. Many essays have been written on the usage of the terms "Latino" and "Hispanic": see, e.g., Giménez 1992; Hayes-Bautista and Chapa 1987. Pan-ethnic terms like "Latino" or "Hispanic" not only have political significance but are also dependent on age cohort and geography. When referring to the research of others authors, I will use the term that they have chosen.

3. The name has been changed for confidentiality.

4. The 1970 Census had a sub-sampling of Hispanics, only a 5 percent national sample was taken and only given in the Southwest. Since 1980, the U.S. Census has used various terms to describe individuals of Latin American descent. In 1980, the term used was "Spanish/Hispanic"; in 1990, "Spanish/Hispanic"; and in 2000, "Spanish/Hispanic/Latino."

5. Portes and Bach, as cited in Denton and Massey 1989, 794.

6. See Rodriguez 1992.

7. See, e.g., the discussion in Wu (2002) on how Asians have been left out of the discussion of race. He argues that acknowledging other non-black racial minorities may help in addressing racism against African Americans and other groups.

8. See Suárez-Orozco and Suárez Orozco 1995, 53.

9. The act of distancing oneself from a group so as not to be mistaken for or suffer the blame for the presumed transgressions or characteristics of that group has been an ongoing practice adopted by ethnic/race groups in the United States. In the late nineteenth century, Japanese immigrants differentiated themselves from Chinese immigrants because they feared that Americans would not distinguish them from one another. Because of Chinese exclusion, the Japanese made sure to distinguish themselves by wearing American clothes and eating American food: see Espiritu 1992, 21; Hayano 1981, 161; Ichioka 1988, 185. Bengalis in the early 1900s distanced themselves from blacks racially and tried to position themselves as white in order not to suffer the same discrimination: see Islam 1998. Waters (1990) shows that West Indians have highlighted their ethnic status to distance themselves from poor American blacks and stress their cultural values. This practice exists because of the power of race and racial identity. To be of a certain race/ethnic group—or, more to the point, not being considered white—could potentially lead to a high penalty. Throughout U.S. history, whiteness has trumped any other category, thus, if an individual could pass for white, or at least not be considered part of the denigrated group then that option might lessen discrimination or maybe even impart benefits.

10. For further discussion, see Davis 2001; Dominguez 1994.

11. See, e.g., Rockquemore and Brunsma 2002.

References

Alba, Richard. 1990. *Ethnic Identity: The Transformation of White America.* New Haven, Conn.: Yale University Press.

Davis, F. James. 2001. *Who Is Black? One Nation's Definition.* University Park: Pennsylvania State University Press.

Dominguez, Virginia R. 1994. *White by Definition: Social Classification in Creole Louisianan.* New Brunswick, N.J.: Rutgers University Press.

Denton, Nancy, and Douglas Massey. 1989. "Racial Identity among Caribbean Hispanics: The Effect of Double Minority Status on Residential Segregation." *American Sociological Review* 54, no. 5: 790–808.

Espiritu, Yen Le. 1992. *Asian American Panethnicity: Bridging Institutions and Identities.* Philadelphia: Temple University Press.

Gans, Herbert. 1990. "Symbolic Ethnicity." *Ethnic and Racial Studies* 2: 1–20.

Giménez, Martha E. 1992. "U.S. Ethnic Politics: Implications for Latin Americans." *Latin American Perspectives* 75: 7–17.

Halter, Marilyn. 1993. *Between Race and Ethnicity: Cape Verdean-American Immigrants, 1860–1965.* Urbana: University of Illinois Press.

Haney Lopez, Ian F. 1998. *White by Law: The Legal Construction of Race.* New York: New York University Press.

Hayano, David M. 1981. "Ethnic Identification and Disidentification: Japanese-American Views of Chinese-Americans." *Ethnic Groups* 3, no. 2: 157–171.

Hayes-Bautista, David E., and Jorge Chapa. 1987. "Latino Terminology: Conceptual Bases for Standardized Terminology." *American Journal of Public Health* 77: 61–68.

Ichioka, Yuji. 1988. *The Issei: The World of the First Generation Japanese Americans, 1885–1924.* New York: Free Press.

Islam, Naheed. 1998. "Knocking at the Back Door of Whiteness: Bangladeshi Immigrants and Contestation over Racial Categories." Paper presented at the Eastern Sociological Meetings, Philadelphia.

Lee, Sharon M. 1993. "Racial Classification in the U.S. Census: 1890–1990." *Ethnic and Racial Studies*, 16, no. 1: 75–94.

Matory, James L. 1993. "The Other African Americans." Lecture prepared for the Talcott Parsons Conference on Construction of Ethnicity, Harvard University, Cambridge, Mass.

Ngai, Mae M. 1999. "The Architecture of Race in American Immigration Law: A Reexamination of the Immigration Act of 1924." *Journal of American History* 1, no. 86: 67–92.

Rodriguez, Clara E. 1992. "Race, Culture, and Latino 'Otherness' in the 1980 Census." *Social Science Quarterly* 73, no. 4: 930–936.

Rockquemore, Kerry A., and David L. Brunsma. 2002. *Beyond Black: Biracial Identity in: Migration, Family Life and Achievement Motivation among Latino Adolescents*. Palo Alto, Calif.: Stanford University Press.

Tafoya, Sonya. 2004. "Shades of Belonging." Report. Pew Hispanic Center, Washington, D.C.

U.S. Bureau of the Census. 1992. *Current Population Reports. P23-182, Exploring Alternative Race-Ethnic Comparison Groups in Current Population Surveys*. Washington, D.C.: U.S. Government Printing Office.

Waters, Mary C. 1990. *Ethnic Options: Choosing Identities in America*. Berkeley: University of California Press.

———. 1999. *Black Identities: West Indian Immigrant Dreams and American Realities*. Cambridge, Mass.: Harvard University Press.

Wu, Frank. 2002. *Yellow: Race in America beyond Black and White*. New York: Basic Books.

5

The Paradox of the Puerto Rican Race

The Interplay of Racism and Nationalism under U.S. Colonialism

Anayra O. Santory-Jorge, Luis A. Avilés,
Juan Carlos Martínez-Cruzado, and Doris Ramírez

> *Nowadays, a . . . mistake is made: race is confused with nation and a sovereignty analogous to that of really existing peoples is attributed to ethnographic or, rather linguistic groups. . . . I want now to try and make these difficult questions somewhat more precise. . . . It is a delicate thing that I propose to do here, somewhat akin to vivisection; I am going to treat the living much as one ordinarily treats the dead.*
>
> —Ernest Renan, "What Is a Nation?"

Stating the Paradox

The aim of this chapter is to offer an interpretation of the seemingly contradictory results of the combined information of the 2000 U.S. Census data for Puerto Rico and the results of the 2003 University of Puerto Rico, Mayagüez Campus, Racial Classification Study (UPRM Study). On the 2000 U.S. Census, 80.5 percent of Puerto Ricans classified themselves as White, while 15.4 percent considered themselves either Black, African American, American Indian, Alaska Native, Asian, or some other race. Three years later, as part of the UPRM Study, only 45.9 percent chose to classify themselves as White, while 30.6 percent declined the use of the binary code (Black and White) for racial self-classification. Moreover, in the same study 78.5 percent of the population asserted the existence of a complete encompassing Puerto Rican race, with almost identical results among those who classified themselves as White, Black or those who rejected the binary code (80 percent, 83 percent, and 81 percent, respectively).

We have named the contrast between these results "the paradox of the Puerto Rican Race," a term also used by Duany (2003). We contend that the perception of paradoxical results is based on a perspective that takes racial ascriptions to be a descriptive language game with relatively stable referents and not, as we believe, a strategic language game deployed in a broader scenario of political and social conflict. To explain away the paradox and propose an alternative reading and a better interpretation of the "color lines" in the Puerto Rican context we emphasize: (1) the relational and strategic aspects of ethnic/racial ascriptions;[1] (2) the broader political context in which those ascriptions are deployed; and (3) their ability to express non-racial aspirations and conflicts.

Alive through Conflict: Identities as Strategies

Substantialists' views of social objects such as nations, social classes, or ethnic groups have given way to relational understandings of these entities (Bourdieu 1998 [1994]; Laclau 2000). Relational approaches emphasize the place that social objects might occupy in the social and symbolic spaces they share with other objects (Bourdieu 1998 [1994]). Those places are demarcated by social relations and stratifications and by discourses that confer meanings to objects. This view of social objects precludes a historical approach in which either referents or meanings remain constant, and insist on the need to

> avoid turning into necessary and intrinsic properties of some group . . . which belong to this group at a given moment in time because of its position in a determinate social space and in a determinate state of the supply of possible goods and practices. Thus, at every moment of each society, one has to deal with a set of social positions which is bound by a relation of homology to a set of activities . . . or of goods . . . that are themselves characterized relationally. (Bourdieu 1998 [1994], 4)

In the nineteenth and twentieth centuries, objects were the common grounds between the metaphysics of everyday language and the natural and social sciences; currently, space and location has become a more unifying theme. The world of the social scientist used to be full with objects, in some recent theoretical approaches it is better depicted by an array of Cartesian charts.

This relational view of social entities renders identities into fragile and fluid phenomena, contextualized in the political arena, an unavoidable dimension of every society. In conflict and competition scenarios common to all societies, it becomes clear that social identities' relational nature implies a negative quality: they are defined by what they are not. Identities are demarcated and kept alive through the constant opposition of those who constitute their outer limits, the constitutive exterior of each group (Laclau 2000; Laclau and Mouffe 2004).[2] That which is not "us" acquires a dual and paradoxical function: it demarcates "our" identity by threatening constantly "our" claim to be "us." In Laclau and Mouffe's view, antagonism—as Foucault's notion of power—shapes us up when it does not tear us down altogether.

Embedded in the arena of conflict, identities become fragile, fluid, and strategic in various ways. Within the American institutional framework, embracing certain identities, such as "White" or "minority," might improve one's chances for social mobility (Lassalle and Pérez 1997). Affirming certain identities could also prevent further hardships by, for example, establishing differences with lower groups in the racial hierarchy (Grosfoguel 1999; Ramos-Zayas 2003). Identities not only constitute a survival strategy for individuals and groups, but frequently their ascriptions constitute a favorite legitimizing tactic for establishing and maintaining social hierarchies. In the case of Puerto Rico, it is well documented that an early racialization of the islanders was a crucial element in the ideological campaign to justify colonialism (Duany 2002; Rivera Ramos 2001; Weiner 2001). In the United States, the ascription of ethnic/racial identities can also be a strategy for explaining social and economic inequalities. Racialization processes have shielded the pervasive American dream from critiques during periods of economic hardship, implying that social problems—or for that matter "underdevelopment"—have a racial rather than an economic and political origin. Grosfoguel says:

> In the USA a central myth is the "American dream." The USA is supposed to be the land of opportunities for immigrants from all over the world, where the harder you work, the more successful you become. One implication of this myth is that if an "ethnic" group fails, it is because they have not worked hard enough and that therefore there has to be something wrong with them. (Grosfoguel 1999, 242)

Class-based critiques, which provide a solid structural analysis of both economic cycles and colonial oppression, have been deflected by American society's acceptance of the ideology of individual opportunities, consensus, and the open society (Aronowitz 1997). Rather than removing obstacles to greater social and political equality, the United States has preferred "piecemeal reforms" that identify certain ethnic groups as victims or self-victimizers in need of some forms of state interventions. In this way, "Ethnic identities became markers of state-sponsored opportunity," and the American dream has been able, although shakily, to keep rallying consensus (Aronowitz 1997, 8).

The deployment of identities as political strategies vis-à-vis the state and private capital has contributed to muddling the distinctions between class and racial/ethnic categories in the United States. Class issues—or, better, issues that can be further clarified through the language of economic classes—are traditionally expressed and "solved" through ethnic or racial discourses. According to Ortner (1998), ethnic/racial identities always contain class identification elements. For example, "Black" or "Puerto Rican" usually implies poverty, while "Jewish" or "White" is associated with middle or upper middle class. Based on these veiled but common semantic implications, Ortner states that "there is no class in America that is not always racialized and ethnicized," therefore race and ethnicity have actually become in the United States "crypto-class positions" (Ortner 1998, 13).

It should be noted that identity discourses also can become at times political strategies that challenge precisely the desirability and soundness of the American dream. The experience of being racialized into the margins of mainstream society—where individual efforts and personal virtues do not seem to lead to a notable improvement in the quality of life—has been a fertile ground for alternative narratives that debunk the cheery optimism of conventional wisdom and values. For example, nationalist discourses in Puerto Rican communities in the United States, particularly those in Chicago, discontinued the "blaming the victim" mainstream discourse by offering a historical counter-narrative that linked poverty and marginalization in Puerto Rican communities in the mainland with United States colonialism in the Island (Ramos-Zayas 2003). The fact that Puerto Rican communities have some of the worst socioeconomic conditions in the United States cannot be explained without "a colonial regime that expropriated the land and incorporated the people as cheap labour in sugar plantations first and in manufacturing later in Puerto Rico and the USA" (Grosfoguel 1999, 244). Afrocentric narratives—like the Nation of Islam or the principles of Nguza Saba—have also challenged mainstream understandings of Blacks' racial marginalization and have offered an alternative set of values for community building, promoting, for example, collective rather than individual success.

Ironically, there is evidence that when members of marginalized groups are able to reframe their social situations according to alternative narratives, their chances for social mobility and "success" improve. Those discourses marked by disaffection with American ideology could improve integration to American society. Ramos-Zayas says:

> The performance of a Puerto Rican nationalism in Chicago and its strategies of political mobilization, ideological subversion, and grassroots historicizing raised critical consciousness among neighborhood adults and youth by promoting historical awareness and documenting their condition as racialized, colonial subjects. While one would think that such a critical stance would engender despair and resentment toward the dominant culture, the opposite appears to be true: this . . . encouraged the poor and working classes to destigmatize Puerto-Ricanness and, in some instances, facilitate the very upward mobility that was too often beyond the grasp of Puerto Rican's living in Chicago's Humboldt Park. (Ramos-Zayas 2003, 9)

A similar conclusion is reported in Hochschild's book *Facing Up to the American Dream: Race, Class and the Soul of the Nation*. After reviewing evidence on the comparative effects of the Nation of Islam, the Catholic school system, and the American military on poor Blacks, Hochschild concludes that "these institutions all emphasize discipline and are unusually successful in enabling poor Blacks actually to achieve the American dream," which suggests that despite its radicalism, "militant Black consciousness is as likely to reinforce as to oppose the dream's recipe for success" (Hochschild 1995, 315).

Before moving on to our discussion of the 2000 Census–UPRM Study results, we would like to consider one last set of questions concerning identities as political strategies: are all racial/ethnic identities bound to be co-opted by the existing institutional framework in which they are deployed? Does the interpretation of racial/ethnic identities as strategies confer an illegitimate status to the larger ideological context that renders them intelligible? Could there be a radical identity politics, one whose demands could not be fulfilled within the existing social ordering? This is a far-reaching discussion that exceeds our immediate interests but one, as will be shown, that has some bearing on the interpretation of our data. We respond to these questions based on Laclau and Mouffe's conceptions of power and hegemony.

In a beautiful passage reminiscent of Nietzsche, Laclau defines power as "the fingerprint of contingency":

> To repress something implies the capacity to repress, which implies power; but it presupposes also the need to repress, which implies a limitation of power. This means that power is nothing but the fingerprint of contingency, the point at which objectivity shows the radical alienation that defines it. Objectivity—the being of objects—is nothing but, in a sense, the sedimentation of power, a power that had its fingerprints erased. (Laclau 2000, 76)

Laclau and Mouffe interpret the exercise of hegemony as an ambiguous sign. On the one hand, it is a demonstration of power; on the other, it is a chronicle of political contentions and historical contingencies. At the ideological level, hegemony consists in the act of articulating an array of signs and distinctions into an all-encompassing view, which promotes and safeguards certain interests. These signs and distinctions do not have any particular meaning if considered by themselves since all meanings are relational. Therefore, identities per se cannot challenge any hegemonic view because in order to have some meaning they must be articulated within a larger narrative that antagonizes common understandings. Only alternative narratives can challenge mainstream ones and only narratives could assign meanings to identities.

Being a member of an ethnic/racial group and of a certain class acquires a "fixed" meaning only within a particular ideological articulation. The success of the American dream (or of any other ideology, for that matter) does not consist in its capacity for shielding itself from the corrosive demands of a subordinated racial or class group whose identity stands apart, defiant, and alternative. Hegemony is achieved by: (1) promoting particular understandings of the meaning of membership in those subordinate groups; and (2) by satisfying certain demands in such a way that those fixed understandings are not overthrown. Identity politics, in order to be radical, have to free the bearings that keep ethnic/racial meanings fixed within a particular dominant narrative and re-signify the resulting floating elements (Laclau 2000).

When identities—racial or otherwise—appear to us as objective attributes, it is because power has tricked us into forgetting the radical contingency of their existence. At some point in the past, either recent or distant, meanings attributed to certain identities, which appear today unchallenged, were a mere competing possibility. The "fingerprints" that have been erased through the combination of ideological and repressive measures make the social order apparently "objective." Unfortunately, identity politics has to do more than just proposing an alternative re-signification. It has to survive the antagonism implied by this process of re-signification; it has to escape being obliterated. Sometimes the obliteration of alternative readings is averted, because every dominant interpretation relies on meanings with shaky foundations. Those who manage to impose this ideological understanding of the social world cannot preclude future interpretations of the same signs. In addition, they cannot guarantee a static context of interpretation. Meanings are always in flight and so are social circumstances. Even repression, the full use of force, becomes in itself an ambiguous sign: it is a show of might and fright. As Laclau (2000) points out, repression signals the limits of power.

Our interpretation of the empirical findings about the racial self-ascriptions of Puerto Rican islanders will follow the premises discussed above. First, we will take the racial/ethnic ascriptions expressed in these studies to be relational identities chosen within a social and symbolic space shared by all others. Second, we will interpret racial/ethnic ascriptions as deployed strategies for expressing diverse aspirations and conflicts in different contexts. Third, we will ponder whether the racial/ethnic identities sketched by the respondents express conflicts and aspirations in racial garb.

Being White

In Puerto Rico, questions concerning the racial classification of individuals were introduced for the first time since 1950 through the questionnaire of the 2000 U.S. Census.[3] Before each decennial census, an Ad Hoc Committee was appointed with the goal of analyzing and making recommendations to the president of the Puerto Rico Planning Board regarding the questionnaire to be used in the upcoming census. Since the 1960 U.S. Census, the Ad Hoc Committee has always recommended the elimination of race-related questions from the questionnaires. For the 2000 U.S. Census, experts' criteria do not seem to have won over short-sighted political considerations, and the president of the Puerto Rico Planning Board disregarded the recommendations of the Ad Hoc Committee. It seems that the ruling, pro-statehood political party, Partido Nuevo Progresista, deemed beneficial to its annexationist purposes the use of the standard mainland questionnaire in which most racial/ethnic categories were alien to the majority of the population in the island (Goudreau 2000).

TABLE 5.1   RACIAL CLASSIFICATION IN PUERTO RICO: RESULTS OF THE
2000 U.S. CENSUS, MAYAGÜEZ CAMPUS, RACIAL CLASIFICATION STUDY

Subject (Under "one race")	%	Number
White	80.5	3,064,862
Black or African American	8.0	302,933
American Indian and Alaska Native	.4	13,336
Asian	.2	7,960
Native Hawaiian and other Pacific Islander	0	1,093
Some other race	6.8	260,011
Total	95.9	3,650,195

Source: U.S. Bureau of the Census, Profile of General Demographic Characteristics: 2000, DP-1.

At first, the results were shocking. Shortly after, they became a favorite object of mockery and jokes. While 75.1 percent of the respondents in the United States identified themselves as "Whites" (under "one race"), in Puerto Rico, the corresponding figure was 80.5 percent. The Puerto Rican population was claiming to be Whiter than that of the United States (Table 5.1).

A well-known cultural critic commented on the Census results on TV by saying that he

> could imagine that for the next decennial census, if the trend persists, Puerto Rico will become the only country in the world with a 100 percent White population. Delegations of countries such as Sweden, Denmark, Iceland, and Finland will come to the Island to witness the existence, in the midst of the Caribbean Sea, of such a White island, where anyone who is born without blue eyes or blond hair will be immediately sent to the Island of Vieques, that in time will become a racial reconfiguration camp. (Ríos Ávila 2003, 63)

In Puerto Rico, in contrast to the Hispanic—and, specifically, Puerto Rican—population of the United States, most people utilized the binary classification of "White" and "Black or African American" for racial identification in the 2000 U.S. Census. These results are even more surprising when taking into consideration two factors: (1) the importance of *mestizaje* in the founding myths of the nation; and (2) the fact that the racial semantic universe is rich enough to describe the diversity of color shades and phenotypes between Black and White (Duany 2002). The need of the Puerto Rican population on the island to classify themselves as "other race" seemed to have been less pressing than that of the U.S. Puerto Rican population in the mainland during other census and surveys. Marking the "other race" category has customarily been interpreted as a sign of rejection of the official U.S. racial categories, as well as a statement that cultural (Hispanic or Latino) or national (Puerto Rican) identities take precedence over racial identification (Rodríguez 2000).

TABLE 5.2   RACIAL CLASSIFICATION IN PUERTO RICO: RESULTS OF THE UNIVERSITY OF
PUERTO RICO, MAYAGÜEZ CAMPUS, RACIAL CLASSIFICATION STUDY

Question	White, % (N)	Black, % (N)	Don't Know, Can't Classify, Refused to Answer, % (N)
Can you classify yourself as White or Black, if you can, how would you classify yourself?	45.9 (189)	23.5 (97)	30.6 (126)

Source: UPRM Racial Classification Study, 2003.

Shortly after the 2000 U.S. Census, taking advantage of the availability of an Island-wide representative sample of the population, an interdisciplinary research team from the University of Puerto Rico, Mayagüez Campus, designed a survey—the UPRM Racial Classification Study—with the following objectives in mind: (1) to clarify processes of racial self-identification among Puerto Ricans islanders; (2) to identify factors that influence racial self-identification among Puerto Ricans, including both personal characteristics (education, social class, migratory experience, etc.) and methodological issues (which institution conducts the survey, different wording of questions, etc.); (3) to gauge the population's awareness of racial discrimination; and (4) to obtain information on the social desirability of including racial identifications in routinely collected governmental data. The research team had the expectation that the information gathered could shed light on the puzzling results obtained through the 2000 Census and that it would update collective understandings about the elusive ways in which the Island's population identifies its "colors" and how it traces the "lines." (A methodological discussion of the survey sample appears in the appendix.)

The UPRM Study offers data that challenge the results of the 2000 U.S. Census regarding the Whiteness of Puerto Ricans. The questionnaire includes an item that purposely departed from the census questionnaire's wording and that resulted in dramatic changes in the reported racial composition of the Island's population (Table 5.2). Given the choice to decline the binary selection of "White" and "Black," 45.9 percent of the population chose White, while 23.5 percent chose Black. An illuminating result is that 30.6 percent of the respondents refused or could not use the binary racial code.

In explaining the differences between the 2000 U.S. Census and the UPRM Study, the first thing to be considered is the set of options available to the respondents in each questionnaire. Given the widespread foundational myths concerning race on the island, the only reasonable alternatives available in the 2000 U.S. Census questionnaire were "White," "Black" or "other." In the UPRM Study, when racial self-identification was asked as an open-ended question, diversity reigned. Respondents identified themselves as Puerto Rican or Boricua (37 percent, $N = 170$); a mix of races, such as "mezcla," "trigueño," "javao," "mestizo," etc.[4] (16.5 percent, $N = 76$); White or Caucasian (18.5 percent, $N = 85$); African, or Black, or "prieto," or "de color" (10.6 percent, $N = 49$); Indian or "indígena" (5.4 percent,

$N = 25$); and Spaniards (2.6 percent, $N = 12$), among others. When instructed to select among "White" or "Black"—the two most chosen categories in the 2000 U.S. Census—almost one third of the respondents refused or could not apply one of these two choices. The differences in the selection of "White" as racial classification could be explained by the following rule of thumb: when in doubt about racial ascription, Puerto Ricans identify themselves as White. Also important is the methodological difference in data collection procedures between the two surveys. While the UPRM Study consisted of face-to-face interviews, the 2000 U.S. Census was a self-administered questionnaire completed by the head of the household. These outcomes reflect how different methods at times yield different results, even if conducted with the same population.

Why do Puerto Ricans, when compelled to choose between familiar yet unwieldy alternatives, choose "White" as their racial classification? *Blanqueamiento,* or the cultural and social desirability of Whiteness, in a mixed racial context is a powerful and obvious reason. In Puerto Rico, as well as in many Latin American countries, the dominant racial discourse insists on *mestizaje,* the racially mixed origins of the whole population (Duany 2002; Goudreau 2000; Torres 1998). The founding myths of the nation—most strikingly represented by the logo of the Institute of Puerto Rican Culture and taught to every child since elementary school—describe contemporary Puerto Ricans as the result of the fusion of three distinct "races": Spanish settlers (depicted as White), Taíno Indians, and African slaves. The cultural contributions made by these populations—racialized as sharply distinct groups—have been represented on highly uneven terms. These populations have been successfully racialized as homogenous groups, with different degrees of collective racial or ethnic conscience in the Puerto Rican imaginary, which makes it difficult to realize that racial groups are "inventions." Criollos were born in Spanish America, but their parents came from different (and at times antagonistic) ethnic groups in the very incipient Spain: Catalonians, Galicians, Majorcans, Canary Islanders, Corsicans, or Basques. Black slaves were even more heterogeneous. They could have been *bozales* (born in Africa: Carabalís, Gelófes, Mandingas, or Ibos), or they could have been born in the Americas. Indians were mainly Taínos, as mitochondrial DNA studies suggest (Martínez-Cruzado et al. 2001), but Amerindian slaves were also brought from the Bahamas, the Lesser Antilles, South America, Central America, and Mexico.

The Spanish contribution is hailed as the most significant, which is attributed to the importance of the language spoken by the population. Indians are represented as contributors of native food and lexicon. Taíno Indians were considered a distant and romantic referent with a very short presence in the history of modern Puerto Rico, until recent studies found that the maternal contribution of these Native Americans to the Puerto Rican gene pool is significant (Martínez-Cruzado et al. 2001). However, Indians have a significant and perhaps unwarranted grip on the contemporary popular imagination. Elements of Taíno culture are expressed through popular music, festivals, crafts, and—most recently—movies (Dávila 1997). Taínos are the only one of the three "races" in the founding myth of the

Puerto Rican nation with persons who portray themselves as direct descendants of the Taíno nation and that attempt to recover their imagined way of life.

Some scholars (Duany 2002; Torres 1998) have interpreted Taíno importance in the contemporary racial imaginary as a way of disregarding the more evident cultural contributions of Blacks. It might be a small but telling sign that while many descendants of criollos still flaunt their diverse Spanish origins and while Taíno ancestry is reimagined and celebrated, African roots are relatively unknown. While Spanish settlers were considered bearers of cultural contributions, Blacks—whether *bozales* (born in Africa) or natives from the Americas—were considered objects whose main identity corresponded to their property relations to the White men. Blacks were *esclavos* (slaves), *libertos* (freedmen), *coartados* (paying their way to freedom), or *cimarrones* (maroon).[5] Phenotypical—not cultural—qualities, such as the skin colors of *achocolatado, retinto, moreno, mulatto,* or *colorao,* were secondary distinctions. This constitutes an important explanation for why we still currently use more than a dozen names for darker skin tones but no African genealogies or distinct cultural reappropriations. With the remarkable exception of the African influence in the national music (Flores and Valentín-Escobar 2004) and national cuisine (Duprey de Sterling 2004), the African contribution to Puerto Rican culture is consistently downplayed.

Blanqueamiento might be a significant reason for many Puerto Ricans choosing "White" in the 2000 U.S. Census. Its counterpart, the low percentage of people (8 percent) who chose "Black" in that census—an amount that tripled in the UPRM Study (23.5 percent, $N = 97$)—was denounced by many as an instance of criptomelanism, the incapacity to recognize "one's real racial identity" (Ávila 2005). For example, Diaz Hernández, former director of the Institute of Puerto Rican Culture, asserted that "there are some genetic characteristics right there, that refused to be accepted because there is still prejudice against the Black race, we don't want to be Black" (Caquías Cruz 2002). Similarly, according to Professor Luis Otero, "Puerto Ricans feel embarrassed by its Black people" (Rodríguez Cotto 2003), and according to psychologist De Jesús y Alvarado, "That data reflects what Puerto Ricans want to be and not what they are" (Pérez 2001).

However, criptomelanism, as an interpretation of the 2000 U.S. Census results, has been challenged on several levels (Goudreau 2000). First, criptomelanism presupposes a substantialist approach to race in which racial self-ascription consists on recognizing a certain fact about oneself and not in cultivating an imaginary belonging. Second, it underplays the strategic uses of racial ascriptions, considering them to be descriptive language games. Third, accusations of criptomelanism ignore the larger historical and political contexts in which racial identifications are proclaimed and interpreted. To identify oneself as "White" or as "Black," for example, requires the capacity to deal with the historical baggage and the cultural implications that are part of the interpretational context.

Racial self-ascriptions are not compelled by ancestries or phenotypical features. They are selections made in situ that serve multiple purposes beyond mere descriptions. The variable, arbitrary, and polysemic uses of racial language in Puerto Rico, what Goudreau calls "fugitive semantic[s]," refers to the situation in which

> the same person could be described as trigueña, negra, india, de color o blanquita (copper color, Black, indian, colored or white) by different people in different moments. Moreover, one person could use all these terms to refer to another one in the same conversation. The meaning of each category will depend on the social context in which it is used and on the relations among those talking. (Goudreau 2000, 54)

While *trigueña, india,* and *de color* might be euphemisms to avoid the use of Black, *negra* could be used either as an insult or as a term of endearment, and *blanquita* is a racial term that refers to an upper-class woman. Therefore, a copper-colored woman might be characterized as *negra, negrita,* and *blanquita* to different people. In a context where racial identities are fluid and racial terms lack a fixed referent, Goudreau proposes that a "fugitive semantic" of racial naming serves the purpose of establishing closeness or demarcating distance between the interlocutors and those being referred to. In support of Goudreau's thesis, Ramos-Zayas has found that "among U.S.-born and raised Latinos, los blancos served to create a bond among Latino interlocutors (regardless of phenotype) to refer to non-Latino Whites and draw distinctions between Latinos who may 'look White' or even 'act White', and people who are 'real Whites' (los americanos)" (Ramos-Zayas 2001, 346). In Puerto Rico to be called *blanquita(o)* is to be cast away from who is speaking. However, to call oneself *blanco* (White)—the color par excellence of *los americanos*—could be interpreted as a defying attempt to breach the distance between White and other racial identities.

The fact that it was the federal government asking Puerto Ricans to identify themselves racially could have biased their selection of racial self-ascription. Checking "White" in a federal questionnaire is a symbolic way of establishing an equal footing in a very unequal political situation. Ríos Ávila (2003) voiced a common suspicion by suggesting that the color that one sees in oneself depends on who is watching. This "observer effect" self-characterization is an important element for explaining the paradoxical results of the census. An analysis of this observer effect demands scrutiny of the observers, the institutions "that were watching," the U.S. federal government and the University of Puerto Rico.

The University of Puerto Rico is one of modern Puerto Rico's oldest institutions. Highly respected for its academic standards, recognized for enhancing social mobility among talented Puerto Rican youth, and shielded from most of the major scandals that have afflicted other public institutions, the University of Puerto Rico could be characterized as an amicable interlocutor for whom—individually—nothing is to be gained and there are no reasons to be feared.

Public perceptions of the federal government are far more nuanced and ambiguous. Even though Puerto Rico is the leading manufacturer of pharmaceuticals in the world, its underground economy is considered to be as robust as its drug exports. This combination of cutting edge production and economic marginality results in a complex society in which formal and informal, legal and illegal economic activities fuel strong rates of personal consumption. Nonetheless, according to federal standards, poverty is rampant. About 50 percent of the population live in poverty; about 25 percent live in extreme poverty and survive through informal support networks and on the scant funds for nutritional assistance provided by the federal government (Colón Reyes 2005).

Despite the acute dependency of a significant percentage of the population, the federal government is more than a distant patron. Halfway between a disciplinary critic and a gullible benefactor, the federal government is associated with a stricter realm of law and order which nonetheless fails to understand local idiosyncrasy. Daily newspapers and TV news programs constantly refer to tensions between the federal government and local groups. Some debates are general, while others are more specific. As gasoline prices spiked during the summer of 2006, public discussions hinged on the federal regulations that prohibit the purchase of cheaper Venezuelan gas, allegedly, because of its high sulfur levels. Truck drivers wanted to be exempted from paying federal insurance while the Puerto Rico Olympic Committee complained that the federal government denied visas to the Cuban baseball team. Local universities discovered and decried the Solomon laws that unfairly protect the demodé Reserve Officers Training Corps (ROTC) Programs. Human rights groups protest capital punishment (which is forbidden in the Puerto Rican Constitution, but permitted under federal law) at Federal Court trials. Sometimes points of contention give way to massive opposition to the U.S. federal government. Recent years have seen the campaign for the liberation of Puerto Rican political prisoners, the fight against the presence of the U.S. Marines in Vieques, and the protests against the FBI's raid of the house where Filiberto Ojeda Ríos, leader of the armed independence group Los Macheteros, was assassinated.

For many Puerto Ricans, U.S. federal institutions (*los federales*) are to be kept at a convenient, and apparently impossible, distance. They should never be too far away as to risk all the perceived benefits of their proximity; but neither should they come close enough to submit everything to scrutiny. If one is to avoid a "federal case" the federal government is to be kept at bay.[6]

The lines of contention with the federal government are enhanced by an acute awareness of racial discrimination in the United States. Of the 133 UPRM Study respondents that acknowledged being discriminated against, 54.1 percent ($N = 72$) located their experience of discrimination in the United States. Puerto Ricans, many of whom live in both the United States and on the Island, have been described by Duany (2002) as perpetually "on the move" between those two scenarios. This phenomenon has provided most Puerto Ricans with personal experiences with racialization practices, racial discrimination, and social conditions in the United States. Grosfoguel remarks that

> no matter how "blond or blue-eyed" a person may be nor whether s/he can "pass," the moment that person identifies her/himself as Puerto

Rican, s/he enters the labyrinth of racial Otherness. Puerto Ricans of all colours have become a racialised group in the imaginary of White Americans, marked by racist stereotypes such as laziness, violence, stupidity and dirtiness. (Grosfoguel 1999, 245)

Therefore, racialization practices and racial discrimination of Puerto Rican communities in the United States reflect the gap between Puerto Ricans and White Americans.

In conclusion, Puerto Ricans occupy a subordinate position within the social and symbolic space they share with the United States. Their selection of racial identity in the 2000 U.S. Census and in the UPRM Study has to be interpreted within the context of a history of racial discrimination, political inequality, and acute economic dependency. Moreover, it is essential to consider a broader scenario of constant antagonistic political struggles between unequal forces. Racial self-ascriptions, therefore, are better understood in this case as collective and individual strategies that deflect the known hardships of disadvantageous racialization practices and subordinate identities. Finally, this gesture is more than a strategic choice. It is a symbolic attempt to level the field of discussion with a powerful and potentially antagonistic interlocutor by asserting equality in racial terms.

Being Puerto Rican

In addition to asserting Whiteness in the 2000 U.S. Census, Puerto Ricans racially self-identify in other ways. In the UPRM Study, they described themselves as constituting the Puerto Rican race. Probing the lines of the national founding myth of the three races, the UPRM Study asked respondents about the outcome of *mestizaje*. Since this was one of the first racial questions in the questionnaire—and consequently, not influenced by previous ones—the researchers were surprised to find that 78.5 percent thought that a Puerto Rican race actually existed. That is, eight out of ten Puerto Ricans expressed their belief in the existence of a Puerto Rican race. The data illustrates that the belief in the existence of the Puerto Rican race is quite robust, cutting across different racial, educational, and migratory experience groups (Table 5.3). Despite the inverse relationship between the belief in the existence of the Puerto Rican race and level of education, two thirds of the most educated groups expressed their belief in the Puerto Rican race.

Nevertheless, the racial classification of respondents seems to have nothing to do, at least statistically, with the existence of the Puerto Rican race. The belief in the existence of the Puerto Rican race is quite consistent across categories for racial self-identification as White, Black, or "do not know–cannot use–or does not apply" (79.9 percent, 82.5 percent, and 81.0 percent, respectively).[7]

The idea of the existence of the Puerto Rican race could be the crystallization of a racial identity that was formed in part through the interactions with racially differentiated populations in the United States. Research has suggested that

TABLE 5.3 QUESTION: DO YOU BELIEVE THAT THE PUERTO RICAN RACE EXISTS?

	Yes, % (N)	No, % (N)	Do Not Know, % (N)
General Population	78.5 (387)	16.4 (81)	5.1 (25)
Racial Self-Identification Group			
Whites	79.9 (151)	14.8 (28)	5.3 (10)
Blacks	82.5 (80)	16.5 (16)	1 (1)
Do not know; does not apply	81.0 (102)	13.5 (17)	5.6 (7)
Education Group			
Did not finish high school	89.2 (132)	5.4 (8)	5.4 (8)
High school degree	78.8 (93)	14.4 (17)	6.8 (8)
Started college	74.7 (74)	20.2 (20)	5.1 (5)
College degree	66.4 (71)	31.8 (34)	1.9 (2)
Migratory Experience Group			
Have not lived in the United States	77.5 (200)	17.8 (46)	4.7 (12)
Have lived in the United States	79.6 (179)	14.7 (33)	5.8 (13)

Source: UPRM Racial Classification Study, 2003.

Puerto Ricans in the United States were increasingly racialized as the rest of the U.S. population became aware that Puerto Ricans were something other than just Black or White (Duany 2002; Grosfoguel 1999). Grosfoguel and Georas (1996) assert that, being unable to place Puerto Ricans in a fixed racial category given the variety of phenotypical features among Puerto Ricans, White Americans increasingly classified them into a racialized category. Puerto Ricans became a new racialized subject, different from Whites and Blacks, sharing with the latter a subordinate position to Whites. According to Grosfoguel (1999), the film *West Side Story* probably marked the cinematic turning point in the process of assigning Puerto Rican as a racial minority, no longer to be confused with Asians, African Americans, or Chicanos in the national imaginary of White America.

Interestingly, the belief in the existence of a Puerto Rican race is practically the same among those respondents who have lived in the United States and among those who have not (79.6 percent and 77.5 percent, respectively). The fact that the personal experience of migration to the United States is statistically irrelevant to the assertion of the existence of the Puerto Rican race suggests that the collective experience of migration (47.2 percent of the respondents have lived in the United States) based on family links, the circular migration patterns characteristic of Puerto Rican movement, and the images of Puerto Ricans in the U.S. media constitutes an important element in the construction of the racial imaginary of the islander (Duany 2002).

Which are the racial components of this Puerto Rican race? When the respondents were asked, "Do you think that Puerto Ricans are a mixture of races?" 91.1 percent ($N = 452$) of participants agreed with this assertion. This is a predictable response given the importance of *mestizaje* in national founding myths and in key discourse on national identity, from Antonio Pedreira's *Insularismo* (1934), through José Luis González's *El país de cuatro pisos* (1981), and Rubén Ríos-Ávila's more contemporary *La raza cómica del sujeto en Puerto Rico* (2002). Multiple categories emerged in response to a question about the composition of mixed races. The Puerto Rican "mixture," according to the contemporary Puerto Rican imaginary, includes groups such as: the Taínos, the Spaniards, and the Africans (63.5 percent, $N = 299$; 67.3 percent, $N = 304$; and 58.8 percent, $N = 266$ of the respondents, respectively, recognized these racial elements). Other racial elements include: "Americans" (presumably citizens of the continental United States: 14.4 percent, $N = 65$); a mix of many races (8.0 percent, $N = 36$), Dominicans (5.1 percent, $N = 23$), and (with less than 5 percent each) Cubans and other Caribbean nationals. These new elements suggest that *mestizaje* continues its historical trajectory, adding to the mixture anyone who arrives to our shores or that we happen to meet in our frequent journeys. The Puerto Rican race, within the popular imagination, is dynamic and continually reinvents itself by identifying and incorporating new elements that coincide with changes in the Puerto Rican nation. If Puerto Rico is "on the move" (Duany 2002), the Puerto Rican race is on track.

Ríos Ávila states that the Puerto Rican race is also a comic, not a cosmic, race: "a comic world would be precisely a world that resists being governed by the rules of coherence, a world open in the indicative present, headed toward the open incompleteness of today's transience, not the utopian future of permanence" (Ríos Ávila 2002, 157).[8] This idea of a dynamic *mestizaje*, with no particular project of racial purity or destination, seems to underlie conceived notions about the Puerto Rican race in the island.

One question remains to be answered: does the positing of the existence of the Puerto Rican race contradict the previously discussed strategy of "being White" when probed by the federal government? At the level of racial self-ascriptions, UPRM Study respondents suggest that there is no contradiction between being Puerto Rican and classifying oneself within or outside of binary alternatives. The Puerto Rican race ignores phenotypical differences—that might be conspicuous to others and to Puerto Ricans in other contexts—and uses the national patronymic to invent itself as a race. The assertion of the Puerto Rican race by Puerto Ricans invokes what has traditionally been "imagined" as national ties.

Nonetheless, we interpreted the overwhelming selection of the "White" category in the 2000 U.S. Census as a racial selection among very few familiar options and a strategy to level the field of discussion with a powerful and potentially antagonistic interlocutor. We think that to imagine—in a different context—Puerto Rican collective ties as racial boundaries does not contradict what we believe was the underlying intention of the respondents of the census. Puerto Ricans were not able to choose among "Puerto Rican" and "White" in the 2000 U.S. census, so the selection of one category does not pre-empt the selection of the other. Even if they had the choice, as long as the political context within which the question is asked is perceived as lopsided and the historical meanings attached to each category imply Puerto Ricans' subordination, expressing the aspiration of equality will take precedence. Again, the strategic expression of an aspiration does not invalidate the rest of one's beliefs about one's identity. Rather than downplaying national ties, Puerto Ricans express their the awareness of subordination and belief in the existence of collective ties. Although these ties were unrecognized by the Other as indicated by their absence from, self-conceptualization is not threatened. After all, imagining national ties as a racial identity entails that what was thought before as culture is now considered as blood. Nationality is placed in a safer place when it is dressed in racial garb. This is how Ramos-Zayas expresses her belief in nation-as-blood that she found so often in the Puerto Rican community in Chicago:

> In autobiographical writings and daily conversations, barrio residents regarded Puerto Rican "blood" as a natural substance, a shared biogenetic material that they often thought constituted a permanent, unalterable aspect of a person's identity. National identity is naturally and biologically given, as it is determined first and foremost by "blood" or "birth." (Ramos-Zayas 2003, 157)

In conclusion, we argue that while Puerto Ricans deploy racial ascriptions in a strategic way, given the broader political, historical, and ideological context in which those identifications are elicited, they overwhelmingly subscribe to collective ties as blood relations. Puerto Ricans do not heed Renan's advice and "confuse" nation with race. Nowadays we would say that they imagine one within the other. They think of themselves as a really existing people, and they frame this belief in an outdated essentialist conception of nationality that is reminiscent of nineteenth-century nationalist notions of the German *Volk* or the French *peuple*. However, unlike Europeans, they consciously foreclose any ideal of racial purity or historical closure. Puerto Ricans are a people in the making, as still in the making is the contested political space they will occupy, either within the United States or among the broader group of nations. We, as Renan, had also done something akin to vivisection, with the hopes that the living may be understood on their own terms and not through those of the long time dead.

A Word on Policy

Salient words of caution follow from our interpretation of Puerto Ricans' racial choices. We first pay attention to a basic shortcoming admitted by the U.S. Bureau of the Census. Census officials publicly acknowledged that the racial data obtained could be controversial, if not unreliable. This technical documentation asserts that:

The data on race were derived from answers to the question on race that was asked of all people. The concept of race, as used by the Census Bureau, reflects self-identification by people according to the race or races with which they most closely identify. These categories are socio-political constructs and should not be interpreted as being scientific or anthropological in nature. Furthermore, the race categories include both racial and national origins groups. (U.S. Bureau of the Census, 2005)

In this technical note, which applies not only to Puerto Rico but to the United States as well, Census officials try to detach themselves from the racial elements of the Census. Since all the information elicited by the census questionnaire was self-reported, there is no need to stress the limitation of self-reporting procedures for the race variable. This technical note basically defeats the purpose of official statistics to use current standards of methodological rigor in order to produce knowledge for public use that is reliable, impersonal and backed-up by the credibility of numbers. What is the purpose of producing quantifiable information through a census if the information produced cannot be trusted?

Second, we would like to stress that critical researchers of quantitative methods, statistics, and censuses have questioned the validity of a positivist approach to social statistics, arguing that the credibility of numbers is a social and moral problem (Porter 1995). Self-interested institutions and individuals—whether a state bureaucracy concerned with the management of the population, or of a minority group demanding official recognition and visibility—shape the way a census is planned, conducted, and its results interpreted (Nobles 2000). Critical race theories aim at explaining how social and cultural identities are created and sustained in the context of an unequal and divided society. Within this framework, the paradoxical results of the racial classification of Puerto Ricans are not just the results of the idiosyncrasies of an island-nation, but constitute a prominent example of the interaction of racial discourses with broader processes of social and political domination.

Therefore, we would like to insist that a critical appraisal of racial statistics must depart from the reification of race as a fixed, natural, and non-historical concept before the uses of racial self-ascriptions can be considered. Careful historical analysis of official census questionnaires and related documentation should bring awareness of the practical and symbolic implications of the included concepts of race and the alternatives and instructions provided. Researchers should be aware of the current meanings attached to racial categories and alternative narratives that might challenge such symbolic ordering. This level of awareness will allow a reading of statistics along several interpretative axes that transcend the mere recollection of self-explaining data. As we have seen, numbers could express much more than mere descriptions; if framed in richer contexts, they could communicate more elusive things as collective conflicts and aspirations.

We would also propose a seldom established correlation between democracy and racial classification. Knowing that the Puerto Rican case confirms that democracy is a key element for adequate recollection of public data, we would like to propose the following: the higher and broader the democratic participation is, the more trustworthy will be any classification scheme. Lack of democracy brings resentment and distrust that make futile the attempt to obtain "reliable" information: the purpose of a census. Moreover, the use of a classificatory scheme presupposes its popularity and validity among those being classified. If more democracy implies a higher degree of popular participation in processes of government, the categories used will be acknowledged and, most important, valued. In the case of the 2000 U.S. Census conducted in Puerto Rico, democracy was the great absence. All researchers should take heed.

Appendix: Methodological Issues

This research constitutes a follow-up study of a previous survey conducted that used mitochondrial DNA of Puerto Ricans to identify the ethnic ancestry of the population (Martínez-Cruzado et al. 2001). The first survey, conducted in 2000, was based on a multistage probability sample of the non-institutionalized adult population of Puerto Rico. A first stage of the sample was designed to obtain households from the eight larger municipalities—namely, San Juan, Ponce, Mayagüez, Guaynabo Carolina, Bayamón, Caguas, and Humacao—and households from a sample of other smaller municipalities, with a probability of being selected proportional to the size of the population in the municipality. Within the selected municipalities, a probability sample of clusters of households was selected. In the second stage one person in each selected household was interviewed, according to specific rules provided to the interviewers. The sampling for the first survey resulted in 1,067 selected households, of which 986 were inhabited. A total of 876 selected persons were contacted, and 800 of them agreed to participate in the study, which produced a response rate of 81.1 percent (800/986).

The follow-up survey, initiated in 2002, used the 800-person sample contacted in the first survey as the target population. A total of 551 persons were contacted, of whom 496 agreed to participate and answered the face-to-face interview, which produced a response rate of 62 percent (507/800). A response rate of 62 percent is unusually small for survey research in Puerto Rico, but not unreasonably low for a follow-up study. Factors that influenced the response rates included: deaths, migration, disease, and inability to answer a relatively long questionnaire by senior citizens up to 96 years old.

A low response rate affects the representative character of the sample when it produces substantial differences with the target population. The age, sex, and maternal ancestry (through mitochondrial DNA testing) of the sample and the target population are comparable. Therefore, the authors conclude that this is a representative sample of the Puerto Rican adult population.

Notes

1. We use the term "racial/ethnic identity" because in Puerto Rico it is common to recognize the expression "racial identity," while "ethnic identity" or "ethnicity" is not a common term. "National" or "cultural identities" are expressions typically used to imply cultural differences among nations or groups, while "racial" seems to imply a deeper-than-cultural level of relatedness, exemplary of blood ties or family relations.

2. What is a *constitutive exterior*? Laclau admits that he borrowed this concept from Derrida's work. This is how Laclau (2000, 35) defines it: "The way we consider antagonism produces a 'constitutive exterior.' This is an exterior that *blocks* the identity of the 'interior' (and, simultaneously, blocks the condition for its own constitution.) In the case of antagonisms, the rejection does not originate in the 'interior' of one's identity; it originates, in its most radical sense, *in the exterior*. In this way its pure nature as a fact can not be reduced to any other underlying rationality."

3. The censuses' racial categories have been one of the main instruments of racial classification during both the Spanish and the American governments. For example, the "1530 census reported only 1148 Indians in Puerto Rico, 675 slaves and 473 servants" (Brau 1971 [1904]), while in 1899, during the first American-sponsored census, "61.8 percent of [Puerto Ricans] classified as White, 31.9 percent as mixed, and 6.2 percent as black" (Sanger et al. 1900). Racial categories suffer changes throughout history; for example, after the 1805 census the racial category "Indian" was never used again (Pico 1988, quoted in Goudreau 2000).

4. Rodríguez (2000, 108) explains that these terms are ambiguous and have many meanings in each country of the Spanish-speaking Caribbean. "*Mezcla*" and "*mestizo*" refers to a racially mixed person; "*trigueño*" refers to non–white-skin-color person; being light "*trigueño*" or dark "*trigueño*" and "*javao*" refer to the light-skin-color person with some Black features.

5. "The 1777 census reported a total of only 70,210 inhabitants in Puerto Rico. These were classified into 31,951 Whites, 24,164 'pardos' (light-skinned mixes mostly of Indian and White ancestry), 4747 free blacks, 4249 black slaves, 3343 'mulato' . . . slaves, and 1756 pure Indians": Martínez-Cruzado et al. 2001.

6. Puerto Ricans commonly use the expression "*¡Esto es un caso federal!*" which means that the situation being described has become really embroiled.

7. The UPRM Study questionnaire asked if respondents believe in the existence of the Puerto Rican race; no further probing was conducted if the respondent considered himself or herself a member of that race. Since this study was conducted among a representative sample of the Puerto Rican population living in Puerto Rico, researchers interpreted the belief in the existence of the Puerto Rican race as tantamount to a self-classification into that Puerto Rican race. We considered it unlikely that someone who is previously identified as Puerto Rican (in order to participate in the study), who lives in Puerto Rico, and who expresses the belief in the existence of the Puerto Rican race would not include himself or herself as a member of that race.

8. In Latin America, there is a tradition of expressing cultural ties at both the national and the transnational level as "racial." To this day, the date selected to commemorate the arrival of Christopher Columbus in America—October 12—is also known as *el día de la raza* (the race day). Therefore, these racial expressions are thought to be metaphorical. Ríos Ávila (2002), for example, discusses the "cosmic race" notion of the Mexican author José Vasconcelos as a meta-racial space composed of all races.

References

Aronowitz, S. 1997. "Between Nationality and Class." *Harvard Educational Review* 672: 188–207.

Ávila, J. 2005. "Siete reglas de etiqueta para el borincano." *El Nuevo Día*, October 16, 18.

Bourdieu, P. 1998 (1994). *Practical Reason: On the Theory of Action.* Trans. R. Johnson. Palo Alto, Calif.: Stanford University Press.

Brau, S. 1971 (1904). *Historia de Puerto Rico,* repr. ed.. San Juan: Porta Coeli.

Caquías Cruz, S. 2002. "Destacan los razgos de la raza negra en los boricuas." *El Nuevo Día,* March 23, 52.

Colón Reyes, L. 2005. *Pobreza en Puerto Rico: Radiografía del Proyecto Americano.* San Juan: Nueva Luna.

Dávila, A. 1997. *Sponsored Identities: Cultural Politics in Puerto Rico.* Philadelphia: Temple University Press.

Duany, J. 2002. *The Puerto Rican Nation on the Move: Identities on the Island and in the United States.* Chapel Hill: University of North Carolina Press.

———. 2003. "Paradojas raciales de los puertorriqueños." *El Nuevo Día,* March 12, 113.

Duprey de Sterling, E. 2004. *Cocina artesanal puertorriqueña.* Rio Piedras: Editorial de la Universidad de Puerto Rico.

Flores, J., and W. Valentín-Escobar, eds. 2004. "Puerto Rican Music and Dance: RicanStructing Roots/Routes, Parts I and II." *Centro Journal* 26, nos. 1–2.

González, J. L. 1981. *El país de cuatro pisos.* Río Piedras: Ediciones Huracán.

Goudreau, I. P. 2000. "La semántica fugitiva: 'Raza', color y vida cotidiana en Puerto Rico." *Revista de Ciencias Sociales* (Nueva Época) 9: 52–71 .

Grosfoguel, R. 1999. "Puerto Ricans in the USA: A Comparative Approach." *Journal of Ethnic and Migration Studies* 252: 233–249.

Grosfoguel, R., and C. Georas. 1996. "'Coloniality of Power' and Racial Dynamics: Notes toward a Reinterpretation of Latino Caribbeans in New York City." *Identities* 71: 85–125.

Hochschild, J. L. 1995. *Facing Up to the American Dream: Race, Class, and the Soul of the Nation.* Princeton, N.J.: Princeton University Press.

Laclau, E. 2000. *Nuevas reflexiones sobre la revolución de nuestro tiempo.* Buenos Aires: Nueva Visión.

Laclau, E., and C. Mouffe. 2004. *Hegemonía y estrategia socialista: Hacia una radicalización de la democracia.* Ciudad de Mexico: Fondo de Cultura Económica.

Martínez-Cruzado, J. C., G. Toro-Labrador, V. Ho-Fung, M. A. Estevez-Montero, A. Lovaina-Manzanet, D. A. Padovani-Claudio, H. Sanchez-Cruz, P. Ortiz-Bermudez, and A. L. Sanchez-Crespo. 2001. "Mitochondrial DNA Analysis Reveals Substantial Native American Ancestry in Puerto Rico." *Human Biology* 734: 491–511.

Nobles, M. 2000. *Shades of Citizenship: Race and the Census in Modern Politics.* Palo Alto, Calif.: Stanford University Press.

Ortner, S. B. 1998. "Identities: The Hidden Life of Class." *Journal of Anthropological Research* 541: 1–17.

Pedreira, A. S. 1934. *Insularism.* San Juan: Biblioteca de Autores Puertorriqueños.

Pérez, J. J. 2001. "La raza: Reflejo de lo que se quiere ser y no se es." *El Nuevo Día,* August 21, 12.

Pico, F. 1988. *Historia general de Puerto Rico.* Rio Piedras: Ediciones Huracán..

Porter, T. 1995. *Trust in Numbers: The Pursuit of Objectivity in Science and Public Life.* Princeton, N.J.: Princeton University Press.

Ramos-Zayas, A. Y. 2001. "Racializing the 'Invisible' Race: Latino Constructions of 'White Culture' and Whiteness in Chicago." *Urban Anthropology* 304: 341–380.

———. 2003. *National Performances: The Politics of Class, Race, and Space in Puerto Rican Chicago.* Chicago: University of Chicago Press.

Renan, E. 1990 (1882). "What Is a Nation?" Pp. 8–22 in *Nation and Narration,* ed. H. K. Bhabha. New York: Routledge.

Ríos Ávila, R. 2002. *La raza cómica del sujeto en Puerto Rico.* San Juan: Editorial Callejón.

———. 2003. *Embocadura.* San Juan: Editorial Tal Cual..

Rivera Ramos, E. 2001. *The Legal Construction of Identity: The Judicial and Social Legacy of American Colonialism in Puerto Rico.* Washington, D.C.: American Psychological Association.

Rodríguez, C. E. 2000. *Changing Race: Latinos, the Census, and the History of Ethnicity in the United States.* New York: New York University Press.

Rodríguez Cotto, S. D. 2003. "Resaltados dos legados antirracistas." *El Nuevo Día,* January 21, 20.

Sanger, J. P., H. Gannett, and W. T. Willcox. 1900. *The 1899 Census Report of Puerto Rico.* Washington, D.C.: Commonwealth Printing Office.

Torres, A. 1998. "La gran familia puertorriqueña 'Ej Prieta de Beldá.'" Pp. 285–306 in *Blackness in Latin America and the Caribbean: Social Dynamics and Cultural Transformations,* vol. 2, ed. A. Torres and N. E. Whitten Jr. Bloomington: Indiana University Press.

U.S. Bureau of the Census. 2005. "Summary File 1, 2000 Census of Population and Housing, Technical Documentation." B-12. Available online at http://www.census.gov/prod/cen2000/doc/sf1.pdf.

Weiner, M. 2001. "Teutonic Constitutionalism: The Role of Ethno-Juridical Discourse in the Spanish–American War." In *Foreign in a Domestic Sense: Puerto Rico, American Expansion, and the Constitution,* ed. C. D. Burnett and B. Marshall. Durham, N.C.: Duke University Press.

6

Shared Fates in
Asian Transracial Adoption

*Korean Adoptee Experiences of Difference
in Their Families*

JIANNBIN LEE SHIAO AND MIA H. TUAN

Asian international adoption, the practice of permanently placing children born in Asian countries with American parents, has gained widespread prominence in recent years. Nearly half of all foreign-born children being adopted today by Americans are from Asia, with the majority coming from China and Korea (U.S. Department of State 2006). Since these adoptive parents are predominantly White, most international adoptions are therefore also transracial adoptions, those involving the placement of children who are of a different race than their parents. As the practice continues to grow and spread, it begs the question: What is the broader significance of Asian adoption for U.S. race relations?

To some observers, the rising prevalence of this phenomenon suggests that barriers between racial groups are eroding. From Wal-Mart, Ikea, and Kodak advertisements to popular media accounts ("Adoptees and Identity" 2005; "Close Encounters" 2004; "International Adoption" 2001), Asian adoptees and their White parents have become highly visible symbols of racial progress. That White Americans have opened their hearts and minds to adopt children of a different race and culture is seen as an important indicator as well as promoter of racial integration. Others challenge this optimistic interpretation by noting the continuing significance of racialized beliefs and practices informing these unique family formations and the fact that they almost always involve placements of children of color with White parents (Briggs 2003; Yngvesson 2000). Employing perspectives such as post-colonialism or cultural studies, scholars argue that the practice amounts to the commodification of children of color from developing or war-torn nations and point to the broader systems of global inequality that encourage the practice (Anagnost 2000; Dorow 2006b; Volkman 2003; Yngvesson 2002). Depending on perspective, then, Asian adoption is significant for what the practice has to say about the conditions conducive to interracial acceptance and the inverse, the dynamics of racial inequality and its reproduction.

Asian adoption is also significant for studying an emerging trend in contemporary race relations research: inter-minority hierarchy. Scholars have noted the hierarchies of preference, racial as well as nation-based, that inform who parents choose to adopt and why (Dorow 2006a; Fogg-Davis 2002; Kennedy 2003; Maldonado 2006; Shiao et al. 2004). In the case of international adoption, Dalen and Saetersdal (1987, 44) argue that geographic distance impacts how racial and cultural differences are evaluated by adoptive parents, with international adoptees of color generally seen more favorably than domestic adoptees of color. "The cultural background represents few threats to the family unit when it is distant enough. . . . However, the cultural background is more threatening with a geographically present minority group of your own, especially if such a group has a marginal and low-status affiliation to society." In the case of adoptable Black children, domestic or international, geographic distance only goes so far in raising their desirability in the eyes of most prospective White parents. Despite recent high profile adoptions of African children by popular culture icons such as Madonna and Angelina Jolie–Brad Pitt, African and African American children available for adoption are generally deemed less desirable or even beyond the pale of consideration (Bartholet 1991; Fogg-Davis 2002; Maldonado 2006). The juxtaposition of "desirable" Asian adoptees and "less desirable" African and African American adoptees raises provocative issues about racial hierarchy that add fuel to the ongoing debate over the relative importance of race in America.

Another way to study the broader significance of Asian adoption involves taking a more intimate look at how adoptive families relate to difference within the family. To what extent is adoption openly discussed? How is race handled within the family? Do White families who adopt Asian children tend toward a colorblind philosophy or do they acknowledge differences based on race? What about cultural differences? To what extent is cultural exploration encouraged? Through their daily choices regarding what to acknowledge, sidestep, or disregard, individual families make decisions that have a cumulative impact on how Americans "do" diversity. As a result, these interracial families have much to tell us about the differences that matter to Americans and the terms under which integration takes place.

This essay is driven by these questions of how difference is negotiated within Asian adoptive families, and we explore them through an examination of the pioneering experiences of Korean adoptees who grew up between the 1950s and 1970s. We first situate the phenomenon of Korean adoption historically in U.S. race relations. We then "bring race back in" to the literature on international adoptions by observing how racial difference between Korean adoptees and their

White parents and kin highlights their visibility as a nontraditional family and challenges their status as a "normal" family. Central to our discussion is the scholarship of H. David Kirk, whose pioneering theory of adoption as a "shared fate" (Kirk 1984 [1964]) provides a rich theoretical framework for understanding not only how adoptive families relate to adoptive difference but also racial and cultural differences. Using semi-structured interviews from a unique dataset, we examine how Korean–White adoptive families dealt with differences and map them to Kirk's categories of "rejection of difference" and "acknowledgement of difference." We then explore how families dealt with the difference of race and whether their management of racial difference followed from their management of adoptive difference. We conclude with a discussion of what the phenomenon of Asian adoption means for racial progress in post–civil rights America.

Korean Adoption in Racial and Historical Perspective

In 1955, Harry and Bertha Holt revolutionized adoption practices by adopting eight Korean children left orphaned by the Korean War. While they were not the first to adopt foreign-born children, the Holts' decision received major media attention and galvanized thousands of other, mostly White, American families to follow suit. The Holts' actions publicly legitimized international adoptions on humanitarian as well as religious grounds. In response to overwhelming inquiries from prospective parents eager to provide homes to children in need or who saw in the Korean situation an opportunity to fulfill their own desire to become parents, the Holts founded the first and one of the largest international adoption agencies, Holt International Children's Services, thus institutionalizing the practice of adopting from abroad.

Of particular importance to scholars of race and ethnicity is the historical timing of the rise and institutionalization of Korean adoption. Starting during the 1950s, adoptions from Korea and their creation of interracial families preceded both the liberalization of U.S. immigration policy and the elimination of anti-miscegenation laws. Prior to the 1965 Immigration and Reform Act, racist exclusion acts had regulated the size and character of the Asian American population for almost a century (Ancheta 1998; Glenn 2002). Prior to the 1967 Supreme Court decision of *Loving v. Virginia,* sixteen states still barred interracial marriage between a White individual and a non-White individual. Positioned right on top of the juncture made by the new immigration and historic racial and ethnic relations, Korean–White adoptive families directly challenged traditional rules for racial engagement and intimacy. Despite this, White Americans who adopted from Korea were largely praised for their actions by fellow community members as well as by the popular press.

Furthermore, these placements continued even during the height of controversy over placements of domestic children of color, particularly African Americans and Native Americans, with White families (Fanshel 1972; Grow and Shapiro

1974; Ladner 1977). A milder debate appeared equating the practice of international adoption with colonial exploitation (Freundlich 2000; Ngabonziza 1988), but a similar controversy singling out Korean or other Asian placements did not emerge largely because no group or community voice emerged to challenge the practice. In the case of African and Native American placements, opposition arose directly from those communities in response to charges that their most precious resource, their children were being "stolen" from them (Abdullah 1996; Chestang 1972; Fanshel 1972). In the case of Korean adoption, there was no comparably organized or vocal Korean American community at that time from whom to draw strong opposition. Moreover, unlike other minority communities, children were not taken directly from Korean American communities but from a country half a world away and in the aftermath of a devastating war and intense period of national reconstruction. As a result, the practice continued to expand under a relatively positive and uncontested discourse (Shiao et al. 2004).[1]

Today, nearly one out of every five children adopted in the United States is an international adoptee (Placek 1999). For children under the age of two, that figure doubles to nearly two out of every five adoptions. As the availability of healthy White infants has declined in response to rising infertility, available birth control, and greater acceptance of single parenthood (Kim 1995), more and more prospective parents have looked abroad to adopt healthy babies. In recent years, Eastern Europe and Latin America—most notably, Russia and Guatemala—have become major sources for adoptable children. However, neither region compares to Asia in terms of sheer numbers. Asian countries account for 55.8 percent of all international adoptions that have taken place since 1948, and Korea alone accounts for 34.8 percent of all children adopted from abroad (see Figure 6.1).

Currently, China dominates the adoption scene and has accounted for the majority of Asian adoptees coming annually to the United States since 2000. Still, the country is a relatively recent addition to the adoption world with significant numbers, arriving only since the mid-1990s (Dorow 2006b; Tessler et al. 1999). Korean adoption, in contrast, stretches back fifty years to the Korean War. As a result, there are more adoptees from Korea than any other country, with estimates that anywhere between 110,000 to 150,000 Korean adoptees currently reside in the United States ranging in age from infancy to their fifties. This age range is important to emphasize because, compared to contemporary Chinese adoptees, most of whom are still preadolescents, the majority of Korean adoptees grew up under very different circumstances. Many came of age when the Internet did not exist; adoptee associations and resources (books, heritage camps, motherland tours) were rare; and the promotion of multiculturalism within the family was atypical. Keeping in mind the historically specific periods during which the practice of Korean–White adoption came into existence and matured, the pioneering experiences of this population serve as an important theoretical building block and empirical benchmark for studying Asian–White adoption and the Asian American experience more broadly.

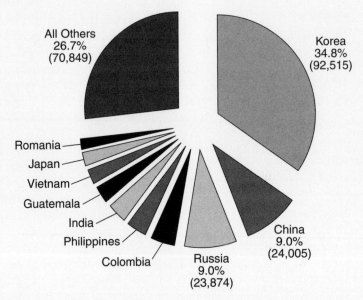

FIGURE 6.1 Cumulative international adoptions into the United States. The total number of children adopted from 1948 to 1987 is 137,437; the total number of orphan visas issued from 1989 to 2000 is 128,087. State Department data for "All Others" includes only the top twenty-plus source countries. (*Sources:* Howard Altstein and Rita Simon, *Intercountry Adoption: A Multinational Perspective* (New York: Praeger, 1991) (1948–1987); U.S. Department of State, "Immigrant Visas Issued to Orphans Coming to the United States: Top Countries of Origin," 2001, available online at http://travel.state.gov/orphan_numbers.html (fiscal year 1989–fiscal year 2000).)

Data and Methods

We employ data from our "Asian Immigrants in White Families" study, which includes interviews with a gender-stratified and random sample of fifty-nine adult Korean adoptees raised within White families.[2] Holt International Children Services provided access to placement records through procedures that protected the confidentiality of adoptees and their families. Using semi-structured interviews we prompted adoptees to reflect on their (1) early childhood; (2) postsecondary years; (3) current lifestyles and ethnic practices; and (4) personal identity. This technique combines a rough standardization of questions for each respondent with the opportunity for subjects to construct their answers out of their discursive fields albeit in conversation with the interviewer and the opportunity for researchers to provoke responses to the analytic categories of the relevant literatures.

The universe for the sample was the complete set of 3,255 Holt placements of Korean children to families living in California, Oregon, and Washington between the years 1950 and 1975. Forty-six percent of adoptees were one year old or younger at arrival; 25 percent, between one and two; and 29 percent, three years old or older. We restricted the range of placement years in order to interview subjects who were twenty-five years of age or older at the time of the interview in 2000 and could reflect with sufficient distance upon childhood and its salience for their adult lives. The final sample consisted of thirty-nine women and twenty men, approximately the same proportions as in the target population despite their equal stratification during recruitment.

Ironically, while our decision to only interview adoptees was in part a response to earlier criticisms about transracial adoption research and its over-reliance on parents' views (Hollingsworth 1997; Meier 1999), we now find ourselves open to the inverse criticism. Here we write about how adoptive families sort through differences without actually consulting parents. While we cannot assume that adoptees truly "know" their parents' motives, their subjective understanding reveals how difference was communicated to them and understood within the family.

Sorting through Adoptive Difference

The fields of social work and psychology have traditionally set the research agenda on Korean adoption, focusing on adoptees' social adjustment, family integration, and other developmental (physical, language, cognitive, self-esteem) issues (Baden 2002; Brooks and Barth 1999; Cederblad et al. 1999; Hollingsworth 1997; Kim 1978; Kim 1995; Lee 2003). Race and other forms of "difference" (i.e., cultural or linguistic) in these research designs have typically played the roles of potential barriers to successful outcomes (Simon 1994; Simon and Altstein 1987, 2000). By using the absence of difference as an indicator of how well adoptive families approximate biological families, the international adoption literature shows a preoccupation with difference as a threat to family cohesion and identity rather than as a social fact to which families might respond in varied ways with consequences more complex than simply success or failure by clinical standards. Instead of viewing transracial adoption solely through clinical assessments of pathology, we suggest exploring how families relate to their adoptive status and how race might complicate the steps they take to achieve normality in the eyes of others.

The first step toward examining the role of difference in Asian adoption is to analytically distinguish adoptive difference and racial difference. We find clues to such an approach in David Kirk's (1984 [1964]) pioneering book, *Shared Fate*, where he offers a comprehensive theory of how families created through adoption relate to being different from biological families. In Kirk's own words, the theory posits the following:

1. Childless couples entering upon adoption are confronted with a series of difficulties which we identified as role handicap.
2. This role handicap is reinforced by the attitudes of other people.
3. In the form of parental dilemmas, the role handicap is carried into the evolving family relationship.

4. To cope with their role handicap and feelings of alienation, the adopters take recourse to various supports for their roles. These coping mechanisms appear to be of two types: those which serve the adopters in denying that their situation is different from that of biological parents ("rejection-of-difference"), and those which serve the adopters in acknowledging that difference ("acknowledgement-of-difference"). (Kirk 1984 [1964], 98–99)

Developed during a time when adoption was stigmatized and shrouded in secrecy (Benet 1976), Kirk provided a theoretical framework for understanding how adoptive parents related to the circumstances that brought their family together. Out of this work came the categories "rejection of difference," for parents who deny any differences between adoptive and biological families, and "acknowledgement of difference," for parents who accept that differences exist; and the concept, "shared fate," for parents who acknowledge differences and openly share with their children in the uncertainties that arise from adoption.

While considered a classic among adoption researchers, Kirk's framework has been modified over the years in recognition that parenting strategies are not necessarily either–or but instead can fall along a continuum, change depending on context, or vary with the developmental stage of the adoptee or family (Kaye 1990). Some families may employ rejection of difference during early childhood as a way to cement intimate bonds of connection then shift to an acknowledgement of difference strategy as their children enter adolescence and face more questions regarding their family circumstances (Brodzinsky 1987).

Even with these modifications, questions remain regarding the contemporary utility of Kirk's work. Developed over forty years ago, some might argue that the theory is out of step with major changes that have occurred in the adoption world. Open adoptions, support for access to birth records, and the emergence of a vital adoption culture and identity (academic and popular press books, online and face-to-face communities, movies and documentaries) all signal a clear shift in opinion concerning how adoption is viewed and practiced (Carp 2000; Melosh 2002; Volkman 2003). Most significant, placement agencies now routinely counsel adoptive parents to not shy away from acknowledging the differences that come with adoption. In short, the tide has turned away from secrecy and stigma and toward openness and affirmation.

The same cannot be said for acknowledging differences based on race, however. Deep ambivalence remains in the adoption world and beyond regarding the wisdom of addressing racial differences and whether adoptive parents should encourage their children to develop a salient racial identity (Andujo 1988; Feigelman and Silverman 1983; Friedlander 1999; Kallgren and Caudill 1993). Families who adopt across racial lines still find themselves in the crosshairs of public debate regarding appropriate racial awareness, boundaries, and intimacy (Lee 2003). While some adoption agencies evaluate prospective parents regarding their readiness to adopt transracially and provide parenting classes and counseling on children's racial identity development, others make little or no effort in these areas (Kallgren and Caudill 1993). As a result, adoptive families are offered inconsistent and even contradictory advice regarding how to relate to familial differences created by race.

Rather than adoptive difference, then, we employ a modification of Kirk's framework to understand how families related to differences stemming from their children's race and to a less degree, cultural background. Did parents employ "rejection of difference" and deny any racial or cultural differences between themselves and their children? Did they employ "acknowledgement of difference" and assume that meaningful differences exist? Or, did parents draw upon a combination of distinct strategies for addressing adoptive, racial, and cultural differences?

Sorting through Adoptive and Racial Difference

We sorted adoptees based on responses to questions regarding how receptive their families were to acknowledging differences based on adoption, race, and culture and how their families actually dealt with concrete situations involving these three areas. More than half (53 percent, $N = 31$) grew up in families who employed rejection of difference and less than half (47 percent, $N = 28$) in families who employed acknowledgment of difference. We found that adoption, race, and culture were loosely coupled—families who acknowledged differences based on adoption were also more likely to acknowledge racial and cultural differences. Similarly, families that did not acknowledge adoptive differences usually did not acknowledge race, albeit they were more neutral to the issue of culture. Important variations did emerge, however. For instance, families were more receptive to acknowledging cultural differences than they were to acknowledging race. Moreover, we found enough variance among adoptees to warrant modification of Kirk's conception of shared fate. For Kirk, only parents who acknowledge differences are successful in creating a positive shared fate. Yet we found adoptees ($N = 8$) who claimed their parents employed rejection of difference as an overall strategy but still fostered a shared fate (see Table 6.1). Additionally, we found adoptees ($N = 13$) whose parents acknowledged differences but did not foster a shared fate as Kirk envisioned. Instead, adoptees were left to cope alone with trying situations. These were adoptees with parents who acknowledged differences based on adoption but drew the line at acknowledging racial differences. That is, they acknowledged their *adoptive* family status but not their *transracial* adoptive family status.

TABLE 6.1   FAMILY STRATEGY AND SENSE OF "SHARED FATE" ($N = 59$)

	Acknowledge Difference, % (N)	Reject Difference, % (N)
Shared fate	53.6 (15)	25.8 (8)
Cope alone	46.4 (13)	74.2 (23)
Total	100.0 (28)	100.0 (31)

Rejection of Difference

Families who rejected differences were unified by a desire to downplay the ways their children were different from the rest of the family. While the fact that their Asian children were adopted could not be denied given obvious physical differences, parents discouraged conversation about the circumstances that led to their adoption or why they chose to adopt from Korea. Instead, they encouraged their children to focus on their familial identities and to remember that they were first and foremost a "Morgan," a "Stevenson," or a "Stewart."

Forty-one-year-old Jennifer Welch, a top manager for an investment firm, shared how her mother became uncharacteristically upset when she expressed an interest in learning more about her Korean roots.

> JENNIFER: I read books about Korea. I do remember, it probably would have been in elementary school, and I think I revisited the topic once in junior high. My mom got very upset about it, having a deeper curiosity about my roots and her being, feeling very insecure about it. So, I didn't bring it up very often. I think only twice, actually.
>
> INTERVIEWER: Did you ever talk about that insecurity, or was that insecurity. . . .
>
> JENNIFER: She was really (pause) I think she was very afraid that I really (pause) I think she actually said something like, you know, "I'm just really afraid you'll like your other mom more." Um, you know, and "I don't want to lose you. You're my whole world." And so she would get embarrassed and cry really hard about the whole thing. So we didn't talk about it, you know, without (pause) we talked about it twice. And I remember I got curious for whatever reason sometime again in junior high. Um, she was more open to the idea then I think, um, but certainly didn't, you know (pause). That reaction stifled the requests in developing it further with her.

Jennifer's mother experienced her daughter's interest in Korea as a potential threat to their connection and her legitimacy as a parent. Without deliberately intending to do so, her mother's insecurity discouraged Jennifer from pursuing further cultural exploration as well as other subjects that drew attention to how she differed from her parents. About a third of adoptees from rejecter families ($N = 11$) specifically raised the issue of parental insecurity as key to their parents' discomfort in discussing issues that emphasized how they differed from their family. Adoptees sensed that their parents, particularly mothers, were threatened by their interest in learning more about birth parents, birth country, or in several cases Korean culture.

For Kirk, it is understandable why families might embrace rejection of difference as a strategy. The urge to smooth over any differences between parent and child can be great for parents with unresolved feelings about adoption (Friedlander 1999). However, adoptees are likely to have questions about the circumstances that brought them into their parents' lives. Why was I given up? Why did you decide to adopt me? What is Korea like, and in what ways am I like other Koreans? Moreover, as they venture further out into the world they are likely to encounter situations that trigger further feelings and questions. Why do some people dislike me because I am Asian? What do Koreans and other Asians think about people like me? By making taboo any discussion of the circumstances which led to the formation of their family, the consequences of being a racial minority, or what it means to be adopted, parents run the risk of eroding their children's ability to confide in them. The same topics that might create greater intimacy within the family if handled thoughtfully and with empathy can instead undermine its cohesion. As Kirk (1988, 20) puts it, "Rejection of difference in the short run soothes parental feelings of deprivation but in the long run has destructive consequences for the parent–child relationship."

In the case of transracial adoptive families, this admonition seems even more compelling given that adoptees wear one aspect of their differences on their faces and contend with intense questioning from the outside world about their background and family composition. Put simply, being "different" is part of their social reality.

Rejecter families were also unified by an adherence to a colorblind philosophy whereby racial differences were denied. Colorblindness refers here to the conscious decision to overlook or disregard the significance of race in both the private and public realms. According to adoptees, their Asian-ness was essentially "e-raced" or dismissed as a matter of significance. In describing her parents' attitude about race, forty-three-year-old Margaret Houston, the owner of a ceramic tile business, had this to say, "They never thought about the fact that I wasn't, that I wasn't White. It was just their way of getting a child and if that's the way they were going to have to do it, that was the way they were going to do it. It was no big deal."

To be sure, most White parents, as members of the racial majority, did not possess the knowledge, awareness, or skills to cope with the differences their children embodied and employed this strategy by default (Friedlander 1999). By ignoring race, parents hoped to avoid discussing and dealing with a topic that left them profoundly uncomfortable. As Linda King, a social worker in Seattle put it, "We weren't open about that." Grinning, she added, "Kind of like sex!" Surrounded by Whiteness their entire lives, many parents had little familiarity with other groups or cultures other than their own. Avoiding the topic and encouraging their children to ignore racially charged incidents just seemed the easier way to bypass issues that left them feeling incompetent and separate from their children.

Still, there was an important difference that divided rejecter families. While most rejecter families left adoptees to cope alone when confronted with trying situations, a smaller subset had more complex motives for employing this strategy and was more willing to aid their children when faced with challenges stemming from their adoption. We identified this group as rejecter families *with* a sense of shared fate, and they made up about a quarter of all rejecter families.

This group differed from other rejecter families in that they employed the strategy in part to help their children assimilate into their families and the White communities where they lived. According to twenty-seven-year-old Zachary White, a groundskeeper at a golf course, "I think they just tried to make me feel as much, you know, comfortable with being around here and being familiar, you know, kind of, I mean not really treating me like I was, you know, White, but trying to make me like I wasn't any different."

Rejecter families with a shared fate did not voluntarily bring up the subject of race/racism in America with their children for fear of needlessly planting seeds of worry and doubt over their sense of communal belonging. Instead they abided by a colorblind philosophy and raised their children to see themselves as individuals rather than members of a racial group. Nevertheless, they were ready to aid and comfort their children if any situation called for it, racial or otherwise. For example, twenty-seven-year-old Stephanie Mueller, a financial consultant from Portland, Oregon, claimed her parents downplayed her adoption and racial differences because they wanted her to feel completely secure as a family member. They did not want to draw attention to these aspects of her identity in case they might jeopardize her sense of attachment to the family. Still, Stephanie's parents did not leave her to cope alone with challenging situations. Their shared fate meant that they handled whatever life had to offer as a strong and cohesive unit.

While rejecter parents were uncomfortable dealing with differences based on adoption and race, we found that some were open and even mildly supportive if their children showed an interest in Korean culture. As we discuss elsewhere (Shiao et al. 2004, 11), parents tried "here and there" to encourage cultural exploration: "by bringing home a book from or about Korea, purchasing dolls or other artifacts, preparing or purchasing Korean foods like kimchi, attending a Korean or Asian-centered event (including Asian restaurants), or attending an adoptee-centered event." Because we did not speak directly with parents, we can only offer speculations on why discussions involving culture were perceived more favorably than race or adoption. Race, whether true or not, is often perceived by Whites as divisive, an issue that splits Americans (Bonilla-Silva 2003). Similarly, adoptive families avoided discussing race out of concern that it might divide their family. Culture, in contrast, is viewed more benignly by White Americans, especially since the concept is intertwined with notions of family and seen as something to be celebrated and shared between individuals (Gans 1979; Waters 1990). It is an easier leap for White Americans to celebrate cultural differences than to address the social and personal costs associated with being racially different (Anagnost 2000). Culture, in short, has the power to bring people together while discussions of race and adoption have the power to divide.

Acknowledgement of Difference

Ultimately for Kirk, the strategy best suited for the long term well-being of adoptive families is acknowledgement of difference. Families that are open about how their individual lives have become entwined, are empathic toward one another, and deal with issues that arise as cohesive units are the ones who have successfully fostered a shared fate. For Kirk, "such parental willingness to listen and to answer troublesome questions increases the child's trust in the parents and therefore the bonds between adopted child and the adoptive parents" (Kirk 1988, 15).

A little less than half of adoptees in our study ($N = 28$) came from families embracing acknowledgement of difference as a strategy, but again, variations emerged. The first group ($N = 15$) fits neatly within Kirk's vision. Parents encouraged their children to share their feelings about being adopted, good and bad, and were supportive if they expressed interest in visiting Korea, learning about their birth culture, or searching for birth parents. Especially for adoptees under thirty, their arrival date was referred to as their "anniversary" or "second birthday," was noted on the family calendar, and was treated as a time to celebrate by going out to dinner, reminisce, and in some cases, receive presents. Twenty-eight-year-old Brandon Luebke, a river rafting guide, recalled with pleasure the extra attention he received on his arrival anniversary: "We celebrated the, we had two birthdays. Like, we celebrated my birthday and our arrival date as well. So mine was April 15, and we always went out." Laughing, he amended his earlier declaration by adding, "Actually, I always celebrated mine on the sixteenth 'cause my dad was an accountant. April 15 was tax day!"

Parents in this group were also more willing to address the significance of race and racism in America. While only a handful independently brought up the topic as opposed to waiting for their children to raise the issue, they were willing to comfort their children and advocate on their behalf if necessary. Mona Brown, a corrections officer, was teased regularly during elementary school but recalled with satisfaction her mother's response.

INTERVIEWER: When you did come home from—when you were crying [from being teased], those kind of things, early on, how did your parents react—respond to that?

MONA: Um, my mom would just tell me the story of my adoption, that I was you know, a little different . . . and different good. . . . Oh, she said I could beat them up if I wanted to. That always works, you know? "If they tease you too much, you can hit 'em." Okay. Or I would tell them that, "You know, at least I was wanted," you know? 'Cause I was adopted. So I was chosen, you know? I'd always tell this one kid, "You weren't chosen. You just happened. You were a mistake." That would get him crying, so it worked. (Laughs)

These parents empathized with their children, discussed strategies for dealing with teasers, or intervened in school or elsewhere outside of the home.

The second group ($N = 13$), in contrast, departs significantly from Kirk's conception of acknowledgers and did not foster a shared fate within the family. According to adoptees, their parents took things to an extreme by overly focusing on their differences yet were unable or unwilling to provide aid or comfort when the need arose. Most disturbing to us were two adoptees who came from families with rigid hierarchies between the biological, adopted, and foster children. Both of their families had adopted and fostered an extraordinary number of children. Forty-one-year-old Samantha ("Sam") Cawthorne, an air traffic controller, discussed how after raising four biological children and remarrying, her mother decided to adopt four more children in addition to fostering many others:

> SAMANTHA: Well, what they did was they would call it, you know, the Number One family, you know like some family member's Number One, and you're from family Number Two. . . . We were always different families. We were never, we were always classified, when they were talking to other people. . . .
>
> Um, just the way they, you know, just the way they spoke about, you know my. . . . They would always say, my real kids. You know, my *real* children. . . . And it was always, the real, the real kids that are first family. My mother's first family.

While an extreme example this case aptly captures how the "acknowledgement of difference" strategy could be taken too far, a point also made by other adoption researchers (Brodzinsky 1987; Brodzinsky and Schechter 1990; Dalen 2005). Milder cases included parents who continually referred to adoptees as their "adopted Korean children" instead of simply as their children. While not trying to be hurtful, parental insensitivity to their children's situation left them feeling isolated from the rest of the family. Several adoptees also recounted volatile arguments when an angry and frustrated parent uttered the phrase, "You should be more grateful that we adopted you." While said in the heat of the moment such comments left their mark, in some cases permanently eroding trust and goodwill.

Adoptees in this second group were also left to cope alone when racism touched their lives. Even parents who enjoyed highlighting their children's "exotic" racial differences and the attention the family received for being different could not be counted on when those differences were experienced as liabilities by their children. While they basked in the compliments they typically received for being "generous," "kind," and "adventurous" for adopting foreign-born children, they were as dismissive about their children's experiences with racism as the majority of families who rejected differences.

Adoptees like forty-two-year-old Ross Green serve as a painful example. On one hand his mother repeatedly acknowledged that he was different because he was adopted:

INTERVIEWER: And how did they acknowledge your adoption while you were growing up?

ROSS: You know, I have a different perception of that. . . . To me, I always thought I was White. . . . And I was really upset when she told me, she used to tell me, well you know you're not really mine. And I would think, God, what a, you know, mean thing to say! (Laughter)

Yet when Ross sought reassurance during moments when he paid the price for being racially different, she doubted his credibility: "[Her] reaction was, um, 'That's not happening to you because it's not happening to Faith,' my sister. So they just denied it. . . . Yeah. If I told them, you know, a guy called me a chink, or you know, other racial name [she would reply] 'No they're not.' That was my mother." Ross was not alone in finding himself in the curious position of coming from a family that readily acknowledged its adoption status but refused to iden-tify or take responsibility for being a transracial adoptive family. Families like Ross's drew the line at recognizing the salience of racial difference and its impli-cations for the Asian children in their lives.

Conclusion and Implications

In this essay we have endeavored to show that Asian adoptees occupy a unique position in contemporary U.S. race relations. The question remains however, what does their unique position tell us about the state of race relations in general? Based on our extensive examination of the Korean adoptee experience, we would like to offer a few thoughts on this matter.

First, the mainstreaming of Asian adoption, particularly with the rise in China adoptions, signals an important shift in how White Americans conceive of family and who they are willing to embrace as family. More and more White Americans do not think twice about adopting an Asian child and see the practice as an uncontroversial means to creating a family. Each year an additional 10,000 Asian children are issued visas to join their adoptive families (U.S. Department of State 2006). Clearly, something big is happening. While obstacles may arise on the supply side as Asia tightens its selection criteria and seeks more domestic solutions to its overabundance of children, there is seemingly no end to the American demand side of the equation.

Second, our examination of the Korean adoptee experience indicates that, although the phenomenon of Asian adoption symbolizes a genuine form of interracial acceptance, it also accommodates prevailing patterns of White privi-lege. Ultimately, it is an option for parents to acknowledge or reject what race means in their children's lives.

And ultimately, it is parents who get to choose the terms under which racial integration takes place. The choice is theirs whether or not to aid their Asian children as they maneuver through a racially charged world. As our research shows, nearly two thirds of our adoptees ($N = 36$), those we categorized as "Cope

Alone," came from families that were not equipped to effectively handle the differences their Asian children embodied. At best, families were unprepared but willing to learn new skills and sensitivities as their children began to raise questions and face new challenges. At worst, families were resistant to changing their own views even to the point of dismissing their children's negative experiences. These were families that were unwilling to accept fuller responsibility for sharing their child's fate as a racial minority and adoptee.

Third, our research problematizes the concept of colorblindness and reveals its limits in practice. We found that what most parents did in the name of colorblindness did not eliminate race so much as it enabled them to believe that their own racial and social status could be transferred to their Asian children (Dalen 2005). Parents raised their children to be "normal," with little awareness that their definition of normal was White centered (Lipsitz 1998). And by normalizing Whiteness, parents essentially socialized their children to be White and to see the world from a White, rather than a race-free, perspective. Thus, far from being colorblind, many White parents, consciously or not, treated their Asian children as honorary Whites.

Twenty-seven-year-old homemaker Emily Stewart's story about her mother captures the curious and contradictory way this turn in thinking could play out. Although her mother adopted two Korean girls and preached to them the importance of racial tolerance as a general value, she forbade them from dating Blacks, Latinos, or even Asians. Not that there was really much chance of this ever happening, since Emily was raised in a small and predominantly Dutch community in Washington State. As she put it, "It was a closed-on-Sundays type of community . . . mostly just White, blond haired, blue-eyed Dutch kids." With her dark hair and strong Asian features, Emily was anything but the norm in her community. Here she describes a revealing conversation with her mother:

> EMILY: One weird thing about my mom is, she didn't want me dating any guys from other ethnic groups. She kind of treated me as if I was White. And I had some Asian friends that were . . . she didn't . . . she didn't want me dating them, she didn't want me dating, like, I was dating this Hispanic guy for a while and she didn't want me to date him because he wasn't White. And, like, "Well, what do you think I am?" you know?
>
> INTERVIEWER: What did she say?
>
> EMILY: . . . I'm not White and she said, "Well, that's different." You know, basically she meant, she meant probably culturally I think, but . . . I think even if I had dated, you know a White guy . . . I think she would have been OK with it. I think it was some weird version of racial stereotyping. . . . I don't know what it is.

Emily's mother went so far as to express disapproval for her to even date other Korean adoptees. "It was . . . it was an interracial thing. You know, 'I don't want you to date interracially.' So well, so you want me to date a White guy. But that's interracial, isn't it? ... [H]er comment just was that it was different it was just this feeling that she had about it ... the whole thing. ... It was so strange." Five adoptees, all women, were forbidden from dating men who were not White. All came from families who claimed to be colorblind yet received strong messages against dating men of color, particularly Black men. Understandably, such mixed messages were quite unsettling to adoptees. As Linda King put it, "It was confusing because I was, you know, raised with the idea that all races are supposedly equal and you are not supposed to see color and this kind of thing." In a twist to the historic policing of the sexual color line between Black men and White women, adoptees like Emily and Linda found themselves enfolded into what Evelyn Nakano Glenn (2002, 123) refers to as the mythology of pure White womanhood, and admonished to stay away from men who were not White.

To repeat, what some families did in the name of colorblindness was actually to teach their children to think and act like a White person. And in Emily's and Linda's cases, their socialization into Whiteness included rules about not dating anybody who was not also White.

Our research captures how the concept of colorblindness has been grossly misused by some in the wake of the civil rights era. A White adoptive parent can claim to be colorblind because he or she adopted a child of color, but that same parent can teach the child to avoid people who are not White. Such inconsistency, unfortunately, is both cause and symptom of what Omi and Winant (1994) characterize as the messy state of racial affairs today. Abundant research is available documenting the gap between the liberal principles that White Americans express regarding racial integration and the daily decisions they make in terms of where to live, who to befriend, what political legislation to support, and how to raise their children, which actually perpetuate racial separation. Unfortunately, our research into the Korean adoption phenomenon offers yet more evidence of the discrepancy between principle and practice.

Implications for Chinese Adoptees

And finally, it would be remiss of us to close without speaking to the clues our research findings offer for understanding contemporary Chinese adoption. While Korea may be the pioneer of Asian adoption, China is clearly its present and future. The number of Chinese children being placed with Americans continues to jump each year. Meanwhile, Korea has moved in the inverse direction after decades of dominating the international adoption scene.

One significant difference between the adoptees we studied and contemporary Chinese adoptees has to do with social climate. In contrast to the time periods when the majority of our adoptees came of age, the arrival of Chinese adoptees, still mostly in early childhood, has occurred during a historical period characterized by pro-diversity sentiments and an overall climate at worst queasy about diversity rather than opposed to it (Shiao 2005). As a result, we expect

Chinese adoptive families to relate to "difference" as less a threat and more as an opportunity compared to the Korean adoptive families we studied.

Indeed, Tessler and his associates (1999) find that China adoptive families, as a whole, show a stronger commitment to bicultural socialization and desire to embrace and celebrate cultural differences compared to earlier generations of Korean adoptive families. Furthermore, families adopting from China tend to identify biculturally as American and Chinese in recognition that the identity of the family, as a whole, shifts as a result of adopting across cultural lines. Embodying Kirk's concept of a "shared fate," the onus of responsibility is shared by the family and not just the adoptive child in acquiring a new identity. This stands in marked contrast to most of the families we studied who instead focused on changing their Korean children so they would fit into their White American families and communities.

What remains to be seen is whether adoptive parents of Chinese children will be any more likely to acknowledge the significance of racial differences and provide their children with necessary skills for what Fogg-Davis (2002) calls successful "racial navigation" in a race conscious society. Put another way, will families adopting from China embrace their transracial adoptive status as much as their international adoption status? As our research has shown, there is a clear line between celebrating cultural differences and addressing the social and personal costs associated with being racially different. In this regard, China adoptive families, still so early in their formation, have much to gain from the hard lessons learned from fifty years of Korean adoption.

Notes

1. Only in recent years have more critical voices emerged to raise concerns regarding the practice as the Asian American and former adoptee communities have grown in strength and voice (Anagnost 2000; Dorow 2006b; Hubinette 2003, 2006; Volkman 2003; Yngvesson 2000).

2. The one exception is a respondent whose adoptive father was White and adoptive mother was Korean.

References

Abdullah, Samella. 1996. "Transracial Adoption Is Not the Solution to America's Problems of Child Welfare." *Journal of Black Psychology* 22: 254–261.

"Adoptees and Identity." 2005. *Seattle Times,* January 23, 11.

Anagnost, Ann. 2000. "Scenes of Misrecognition: Maternal Citizenship in the Age of Transnational Adoption. *Positions* 8, no. 2: 389.

Ancheta, Angelo. 1998. *Race, Rights, and the Asian American Experience.* New Brunswick, N.J.: Rutgers University Press.

Andujo, Estela. 1988. "Ethnic Identity of Transethnically Adopted Hispanic Adolescents." *Social Work* 33: 531–535.

Baden, Amanda. 2002. "The Psychological Adjustment of Transracial Adoptees: An Application of the Cultural-Racial Identity Model." *Journal of Social Distress and the Homeless* 11, no. 2: 167–191.

Bartholet, Elizabeth. 1991. "Where Do Black Children Belong? The Politics of Race Matching in Adoption." *University of Pennsylvania Law Review* 139: 1163–1249.

Benet, Mary Kathleen. 1976. *The Politics of Adoption.* New York: Free Press.

Bonilla-Silva, E. 2003. *Racism without Racists: Color-Blind Racism and the Persistence of Racial Inequality in the United States.* Lanham, Md.: Rowman and Littlefield.

Briggs, Laura. 2003. "Mother, Child, Race, Nation: The Visual Iconography of Rescue and the Politics of Transnational and Transracial Adoption." *Gender and History* 15, no. 2: 179–200.

Brodzinsky, David. 1987. Adjustment to adoption: A psychosocial perspective. *Clinical Psychology Review* 7: 25–47.

Brodzinsky, David, and Marvin Schechter. 1990. *The Psychology of Adoption.* New York: Oxford University Press.

Brooks, Devon, and Richard Barth. 1999. "Adult Transracial and Interracial Adoptees: Effects of Race, Gender, Adoptive Family Structure, and Placement History on Adjustment Outcomes." *American Journal of Orthopsychiatry* 69, no. 1: 87–99.

Carp, E. Wayne. 2000. *Family Matters: Secrecy and Disclosure in the History of Adoption.* Cambridge, Mass.: Harvard University Press.

Cederblad, M., B. Hook, M. Irhammar, and A. Mercke. 1999. "Mental Health in International Adoptees as Teenagers and Young Adults: An Epidemiological Study." *Journal of Child Psychology and Psychiatry* 40, no. 8: 1239–1248.

Chestang, Leon. 1972. "The Dilemma of Biracial Adoption." *Social Work* 17: 100–105

"Close Encounters with a Home Barely Known." 2004. *New York Times,* July 22, F1.

Dalen, Monica. 2005. "International Adoptions in Scandinavia: Research Focus and Main Results." Pp. 187–211 in *Psychological Issues in Adoption,* ed. D. Brodzinsky and J. Palacios. Westport, Conn.: Praeger.

Dalen, Monica, and Barbro Saetersdal. 1987. "Transracial Adoption in Norway." *Adoption and Fostering* 11, no. 4: 41–46.

Dorow, Sara. 2006a. "Racialized Choices: Chinese Adoption and the 'White Noise' of Blackness." *Critical Sociology* 32, nos. 2–3: 357–379.

———. 2006b. *Transnational Adoption: A Cultural Economy of Race, Gender, and Kinship* New York: New York University Press.

Fanshel, David. 1972. *Far from the Reservation.* Metuchen, N.J.: Scarecrow Press.

Feigelman, William, and Arnold Silverman. 1983. *Chosen Children.* New York: Praeger.

Fogg-Davis, Hawley. 2002. *The Ethics of Transracial Adoption.* Ithaca, N.Y.: Cornell University Press.

Freundlich, Madelyn. 2000. *The Role of Race, Culture, and National Origin in Adoption.* New York: Child Welfare League of America, Evan B. Donaldson Adoption Institute.

Frieldlander, Myrna. 1999. "Ethnic Identity Development of Internationally Adopted Children and Adolescents: Implications for Family Therapists." *Journal of Marital and Family Therapy* 25, no. 1: 43–60.

Gans, Herbert. 1979. "Symbolic Ethnicity: The Future of Ethnic Groups and Cultures in America." *Ethnic and Racial Studies* 2: 9–11.

Glenn, Evelyn Nakano. 2002. *Unequal Freedom: How Race and Gender Shaped American Citizenship and Labor.* Cambridge, Mass.: Harvard University Press.

Grow, Lucy, and Deborah Shapiro. 1974. *Black Children, White Parents: A Study of Transracial Adoption.* New York: Child Welfare League of America

Hollingsworth, Leslie Doty. 1997. "Effect of Transracial/Transethnic Adoption on Children's Racial and Ethnic Identity and Self-esteem: A Meta-analytic Review." *Marriage and Family Review* 25, nos. 1–2: 99–130.

Hubinette, Tobias. 2003. "International Adoption Is Harmful and Exploitative." Pp. 66–71 in *Issues in Adoption: Current Controversies,* ed. William Dudley. San Diego: Greenhaven Press.

———. 2006. "From Orphan Trains to Babylifts: Colonial Trafficking, Empire Building and Social Engineering." Pp. 139–149 in *Outsiders Within: Writing on Transracial Adoption,* ed. Jane Jeong Trenka, Chinyere Oparah, and Sun Yung Shin. Boston: South End Press.

"International Adoption Changes Family's Culture, Race." 2001. *Oregonian,* February 19A1.

Kallgren, Carl A., and Pamela J. Caudill. 1993. "Current Transracial Adoption Practices: Racial Dissonance or Racial Awareness?" *Psychological Reports* 72: 551–558.

Kaye, K. 1990. "Acknowledgement or Rejection of Differences?" Pp. 121–143 in *The Psychology of Adoption,* ed. D. Brodzinsky and M. Schechter. New York: Oxford University Press.

Kennedy, Randall. 2003. *Interracial Intimacies: Sex, Marriage, Identity, and Adoption.* New York: Pantheon Books.

Kim, Dong Soo. 1978. "Issues in Transracial and Transcultural Adoption." *Social Casework* 59, no. 8: 477–486

Kim, Wun Jung. 1995. "International Adoption: A Case Review of Korean Children." *Child Psychiatry and Human Development* 43, no. 4: 141–154.

Kirk, H. David. 1984 (1964). *Shared Fate: A Theory of Adoption and Mental Health.* New York: Free Press of Glencoe.

———. 1988. "Integrating the Stranger: A Problem in Modern Adoption, but Not in That of Ancient Greece or Rome." Pp. 14–20 in *Exploring Adoptive Family Life: The Collected Adoption Papers of H. David Kirk,* ed. B. J. Tansey. Port Angeles, Wash.: Ben-Simon Publications.

Ladner, Joyce A. 1977. *Mixed Families: Adopting across Racial Boundaries.* New York: Anchor Press/Doubleday.

Lee, Richard. 2003. "The Transracial Adoption Paradox: History, Research, and Counseling Implications of Cultural Socialization." *Counseling Psychologist* 31, no. 6: 711–744.

Lipsitz, George. 1998. *The Possessive Investment in Whiteness: How White People Profit from Identity Politics.* Philadelphia: Temple University Press.

Maldonado, Solangel. 2006. "Discouraging Racial Preferences in Adoptions." *University of California, Davis, Law Review* 39: 1415–1480.

Meier, Dani. 1999. "Cultural Identity and Place in Adult Korean-American Intercountry Adoptees." *Adoption Quarterly* 3, no. 1: 15–48

Melosh, Barbara. 2002. *Strangers and Kin: The American Way of Adoption.* Cambridge, Mass.: Harvard University Press.

Ngabonziza, Damien. 1988. "Intercountry Adoption: In Whose Best Interest?" *Adoption and Fostering* 12, no. 1: 35–40.

Omi, Michael, and Howard Winant. 1994. *Racial Formation in the United States: From the 1960s to the 1990s.* New York: Routledge.

Placek, Paul. 1999. "National Adoption Data." Pp. 24–69 in *Adoption Factbook III,* ed. C. Marshner and W. Pierce. Washington, D.C.: National Council for Adoption.

Shiao, Jiannbin Lee. 2005. *Identifying Talent, Institutionalizing Diversity: Race and Philanthropy in Post–Civil Rights America.* Durham, N.C.: Duke University Press.

Shiao, Jiannbin Lee, Mia Tuan, and Elizabeth Rienzi. 2004. "Shifting the Spotlight: Exploring Race and Culture in Korean–White Adoptive Families." *Race and Society* 7, no. 1: 1–16.

Simon, Rita J. 1994. "Transracial Adoption: The American Experience." Pp. 136–150 in *Culture, Identity, and Transracial Adoption,* ed. I. Gabor and J. Aldridge. London: Free Association Books.

Simon, Rita James, and Howard Altstein. 1987. *Transracial Adoptees and Their Families: A Study of Identity and Commitment.* Westport, Conn.: Praeger.

———. 2000. *Adoption across Borders: Serving the Children in Transracial and Intercountry Adoptions.* Lanham, Md.: Rowman and Littlefield.

Tessler, Richard C., Gail Gamache, and Liming Liu. 1999. *West Meets East : Americans Adopt Chinese Children.* New York: Bergin and Garvey.

U.S. Department of State. 2001. "Immigrant Visas Issued to Orphans Coming to the United States: Top Countries of Origin." Available online at http://travel.state.gov/orphan_numbers.html.

———. 2006. "Immigrant Visas Issued to Orphans Coming to the United States." Available online at http://travel.state.gov/family/adoption/stats/stats_451.html.

Volkman, Toby Alice. 2003. "Embodying Chinese Culture: Transnational Adoption in North America." *Social Text* 74 (Spring 2003): 29–55.

Waters, Mary C. 1990. *Ethnic Options: Choosing Identities in America.* Berkeley: University of California Press.

Yngvesson, Barbara. 2000. "'Un Niño de Cualquier Color': Race and Nation in Intercountry Adoption." Pp. 247–305 in *Globalizing Institutions: Case Studies in Regulation and Innovation,* ed. J. Jensen and B. D. S. Santos. Burlington, Vt.: Ashgate Publishing.

———. 2002. "Placing the 'Gift Child' in Transnational Adoption." *Law and Society Review* 36, no. 2: 227–256.

III

Negotiating Change: Group Interaction on the Ground

7

Multiracial Youth Scenes and the Dynamics of Race

New Approaches to Racialization within the Bay Area Hip Hop Underground

ANTHONY KWAME HARRISON

Anyone wandering through San Francisco's Haight-Ashbury district on a Monday night in 2000 would have likely encountered a crowd of aspiring underground hip hop emcees gathered outside Haight Street's Rockin' Java coffee shop. The Day-One Open Microphone, which occurred weekly from 1998 through 2003, began as a local deejay event intended to cater to "all the broke college kids" (and hip hop fans) in the area. With the introduction of freestyling emcees, what started as a turntable exhibition quickly grew into one of the most popular weekly underground hip hop showcases in the Bay. While the deejays continued to provide the musical backdrop for the evening, it was during the final forty-five minutes of the three-hour event, when upward of twenty emcees would take the stage, that audiences would congregate and the energy of the night would peak.

At first glance, the Day-One Open Mic would appear to be an excellent example of the multiracial harmony that some speculators have predicted for hip hop (Kleinfeld 2000; Stephens 1991; Strauss 1999). Collectively, the Day-One deejays have bloodlines extending back to Asia, Africa, and Europe. The group of emcees who take to the stage on any given night seem to represent the entire racial/ethnic spectrum of the Bay Area population. And among the affiliations and friendship circles that have formed around the event, racial and ethnic diversity appear to be the norm, while homogeneity is more the exception. But this is only part of the story. Although race doesn't limit any Bay Area underground hip hopper from being accepted as a legitimate hip hop performer, it certainly sets the terms through which such acceptance takes place.

This essay draws on insights gained through ethnographic research in "the Bay" to present what is occurring within its underground hip hop scene as an example of an emerging mode of racial understanding and identification that, I argue, is coming to typify the way many young Americans see and experience race.[1] To be more specific, within a growing number of multiracial, youth social spheres, traditional perceptions of racial identity and approaches to interracial interaction are giving way to nuanced, more malleable, and, at times, contradictory forms of racial being. Much of what is occurring within Bay Area underground hip hop can also be seen in other youth-oriented social settings across America. From the metropolitan Northeast to Southern California, and a growing number of places in between, young Americans participating within racially and ethnically diverse scenes are approaching race in a manner that is notably different from the generations that preceded them. This is particularly evident within scenes that are oriented toward activities like music, art, and in some cases recreational sports.

During the last several decades, cultural commodities such as music, television, film, magazines and now the Internet have become increasingly implicated in acculturating the young people who consume them toward new conceptions of race. As the architects and promoters of contemporary coolness,[2] these networks of media are vital in providing and promoting the fashion, linguistic, and behavioral templates through which various subcultural capitals (Thornton 1995) get defined. These same cultural industries are also implicated in shaping and circulating subcultural knowledge and values. Clearly the growing visibility and idealization of African American celebrities within sports, music, and other media fields has encouraged a desire among some non-African Americans to reorient their social performances of race. This, in and of itself, is nothing particularly new. Both Norman Mailer's "White Negro" (1957) and William "Upski" Wimsatt's "mackadocious" wigger (1993) self-fashioned social identities that were inspired by certain understandings of black cool. What is changing is the scope and manner of these new approaches to racialization, as well as the integrated social contexts in which they play out. Where both the wigger and White Negro were exceptional in their performed blackness, the modes of racialization that are taking place today among young urbanites who frequent multiracial social spaces—such as urban electronic music club scenes, progressive youth artist collectives, and metropolitan basketball courts—are accepted as common, natural, and everyday.

While the specific manifestations of this racialized identity construction will undoubtedly vary in accordance with immediate demographics and particular galvanizing themes, the broad strokes of this phenomenon are generalizable to many racially diverse, predominantly middle-class, youth-oriented settings, especially those that aspire to some degree of mutual participation regardless of race. One of the most notable aspects of this phenomenon is the persistence of a black–white racial dichotomy that continues in the face of the growing presence and visibility of people identifying (broadly) as Asian American, Latino/a, and of mixed-race descent. Another important development is the degree of racial accountability and self-conscious effort put toward generating authentic sentiments of belonging found among people having identities that have historically enjoyed the privilege of being located atop America's racial hierarchy (i.e., European Americans or "white people"[3]). In essence, this traditional American racial hierarchy is being challenged by an emerging counter-text taking the form of an alternative, inverted racial order. Drawing on connections between race, class, and perceived privilege, participants within these scenes aspire to arrive at new forms of race-based legitimation in their everyday encounters. The enduring association between hip hop and poor black communities accentuates the ways in which these dynamics play out within multiracial hip hop scenes; however, this phenomenon of felt exclusion on the basis of historical racial privilege extends beyond the realm of underground hip hop. This much seems apparent.

In this essay, the contours of this developing racial subtext are examined through an analysis of racial identity constructions and interactions within Bay Area underground hip hop. I begin by contextualizing the Bay Area scene through an overview of its mid-1990s emergence and current racial makeup. This background is necessary for establishing the Bay Area underground's participatory character—a quality that, I argue, makes it a particularly illuminating site for exploring these issues. I next present a framework of racial identity construction, or what I am calling *racial being*, which serves as a theoretical backdrop for my subsequent discussion of some of the particular dynamics that are observable within this scene. In describing these emerging forms of racialization, I identify three specific dynamics—*testimonials of accountability, narratives of placement*, and *critiques of whiteness*—used by individuals identifying as members of traditionally privileged racial groups (most notably European Americans) as a means of racially situating themselves. I then examine the other end of the racial hierarchy, and consider how this changing nature of racial understanding affects people identifying as African Americans or black. In the context of Bay Area underground hip hop, many African Americans' racial performances are reactions against (largely media driven) notions of essential black subjectivity (Hall 1996). Beyond merely describing what is occurring, part of my purpose here is to open a dialogue regarding the extent to which these experiences benefit or hinder the opportunities, life chances, and social outlooks of African Americans. The chapter also explores how underground hip hoppers identifying as neither white nor black (exclusively) struggle for visibility yet are afforded ample flexibility in their constructions of racialized selves. I conclude by presenting Roland Robertson's (1995) concept of *glocalization* as a model for examining how local specifics of identity formation relate to larger national and global trends. Acknowledging the interrelations between local and global processes further supports my contention that what is occurring within the Bay Area underground hip hop scene is significant to our conceptions of race in America more generally.

Underground Hip Hop in the Bay

Virtually all Bay Area hip hoppers trace the scene's origins back to the early 1980s when, as legend has it, a fourteen-year-old Oakland resident calling himself Too $hort began recording homemade tapes on "mismatched stereo equipment and a Radio Shack mixer," which he sold "out the trunk of an old, beat-up hooptie with no reverse" (Jam 1999, 220–221). Too $hort is credited with initiating a Do-it-Yourself (DiY) approach to career building that has influenced the creation and dissemination of local hip hop in the Bay ever since. The turn-of-the-century Bay Area underground hip hop movement described here embraced this local production and distribution tradition but differed substantively from "$hort Dog" (and his anthems of pimping and thuggery) in not only the character and content of its music but also the constituency of its fan base. Exemplifying what Andy Bennett calls "the contested space of the local" (Bennett 2000, 63), Bay Area underground hip hop broke from the more gangsta-rap-oriented hip hop traditions of local artists like Too $hort, E-40, and Dre Dog, and instead followed directly from progressive/socially conscious early-1990s collectives like Hieroglyphics, Hobo Junction, Bored Stiff, and Solesides. These groups are among those most credited with bringing forth an ultra-creative approach to local hip hop lyricism that served as a catalyst for a grassroots movement against the glorified violence, misogyny, and commercialism that, through artists like NWA, Snoop Dog, and Too $hort, had come to dominate West Coast rap music at the time (Arnold 2006). By taking advantage of advances and price reductions in music producing, recording, manufacturing, and distributing technologies, during the latter part of the 1990s underground hip hop, both in the Bay and elsewhere, flourished primarily through commodity driven scenes.

The confluence of factors that contributed to the independent/underground hip hop scene in the Bay's becoming one of the most vibrant in America include the Bay's longstanding history of local hip hop performers, its lack of major-label music industry presence, and a local entrepreneurial ethos that residents refer to as "the Bay Area hustle." According to local hip hop veteran Ayentee, since the early 1990s the number of hip hop recording artists in the Bay has grown from "twenty or thirty" to "two or three thousand." Yet even as early as 1992 some people estimated that there were over one hundred and fifty (independent) rap music labels in the Bay (Orr 1995, 175). Bay Area hip hop's independent renown has been the subject of several articles (see, e.g., Inoue 2003; Jam 1997; Keast 1999), video documentaries (Best 2000), and underground hip hop folklore the world over. By 1998, the year when I first traveled to the Bay, the scene was ripe with bedroom studios, curbside and performance-venue music sales, accommodating music retailers, upstart distribution companies, and active online spaces.

Bay Area underground hip hop is a valuable arena through which to examine the changing nature of racial performance first and foremost because of its tremendous diversity. This diversity needs to be understood in relation to a twenty-five-plus year history of hip hop during which, with a few notable exceptions, its authentic creation was associated exclusively with poor, urban African Americans (McLeod 1999), and to a lesser extent Latinos (i.e., those falling at the bottom of America's socioeconomic and racial hierarchy). Since the early 1990s, this authentic sphere of production has been juxtaposed against a white, middle-class consumer base that by that time had already become rap music's largest audience (Light 1992; Samuels 1991). The DiY entrepreneurial creed of underground hip hop shatters this race-based producer–consumer dichotomy by embracing a mode of music production and distribution that exists outside of the gatekeeping practices of the established music industry. Rather than shopping one's music (and image) to a record company, according to Bay Area deejay (and Various Blends emcee) Rasta Cue Tip, the independent hip hop hustle involves "putting something out yourself, shopping it yourself, getting people to play it" and retaining the majority of your revenues. Through underground hip hop, the avenue to becoming a hip hop recording artist was suddenly opened to anyone having the resources and drive to record and "put out" a cassette tape or CD-R of their music. In this way Bay Area hip hop anticipated many of the changes brought on by affordable recording studio software and online distribution means like Myspace.com.

As a genre of music founded on the sampling, repeating, and layering of previously recorded musical texts (Rose 1994), hip hop musicianship prioritizes music consumption and technological mastery over more traditional aspects of cultivated musical virtuosity. Thus, even the practice of hip hop music making is accessible to people with little to no previous musical training. In vibrant independent hip hop scenes like those found in the Bay, virtually anyone with the means and know-how can produce and sell a (subculturally) legitimate hip hop album. According to the head hip hop buyer at Ameoba Music's San Francisco store (at the time the largest independent music store in the country[4]), by 2001 an estimated 70–75 percent of all musical commodities—CDs, records, and cassette tapes—brought into the store by local musicians fell under the heading "hip hop."[5] As a reaction against the essentialized representations of spectacular blackness which dominated early 1990s (West Coast) gangsta and (East Coast) hardcore rap subgenres, underground hip hop in the Bay shifted its legitimizing criteria away from ascribed identity characteristics (for instance, being of a certain race, class, and socio-geographic background) and the experiences that follow from them, toward more voluntarily adopted values, ideologies, and artistic principles. Either by intention or as a consequence, an ideology of hip hop legitimacy became accessible to a wider range of racial subjects.

The result of all this was a fiercely independent music scene where the boundaries between producers and consumers were blurred, and the demographic makeup of the scene's constituents mirrored the local youth population.[6] Importantly, Bay Area underground hip hop is not a multiracial setting where different racial identities are accorded different roles and statuses: such as the Dupont Circle (Washington, D.C.) Starbuck's that I once ventured into in which all the employees were African American and virtually all the customers were white and Asian American; or for that matter, a hip hop show in which all the performers are black and the majority of the audience is white. From the scene's earliest days, influential groups like the Living Legends, Bored Stiff, Solesides, and Kemetic Suns were integrated with black, white, Asian American, Latino, and mixed-race members. This diversity is fully participatory, meaning that within the *core of the scene*—and here I'm referring specifically to the strata of "underground" artists who still attend open mics and largely release music informally rather than with an established record company (independent or otherwise)—an emcee or deejay is just as likely to be African American, Asian American, Latino, or white as an audience member. It is this racially democratic participation that underlies the scene's *colorblind ideal* (Frankenberg 1993)[7]—the notion that a person's race or ethnicity should have no bearing on his or her ability to emcee, deejay, or take part in any other recognized component of hip hop cultural production. Among the Bay Area underground hip hoppers with whom I spent time, there was no shortage of testaments to this principle:

> I think with hip hop, it has such a generational relation that, just as youth, we have a connection with each other. Maybe back in the day you had black youth in this part of town, doing this sort of thing, you know? You had your white youth, in this part of town doing this sort of thing. I think our generation is one of the first generations where you can put twenty different types of people (together), and they can be . . . all doing, living, and experiencing the same thing. So I think hip hop is something that anybody can entertain and enjoy and understand.
>
> There's kids that are incredible that are from the coast-side and have lived on the beach their whole life that are some of the dopest rappers . . . and there's kids from the suburbs that are equally as good as people that are getting paid millions. . . . I think that anyone that wants to rap and has the know-how and can write dope rhymes, so be it. You know? Anyone. Any creed or color.
>
> Where 90 percent of (mainstream) rap fans might (look at non-black rap groups and) be like, 'What are you doing?' . . . underground hip hop allows everyone to do it. (Kegs One, personal interview, February 1, 2001)

Within underground hip hop scenes like the Bay, the experience of participation becomes the galvanizing force around which the most salient subcultural identities form, and from which the strongest sentiments of belonging materialize. Such participation involves a performance of race that goes beyond mere posturing. It means not only donning the (underground) hip hop outfit, but also walking the (underground) hip hop walk, and talking the (underground) hip hop talk. Such racialized performances take place on open mics, in street-corner rhyme cyphers, at hip hop shows, and upon the various recordings that appear. As such, the construction of identity through these public hip hop performances involves a particularly meaningful enactment of race.

A Philosophy of Racial Being

Before discussing the specifics of how racialized identities play out within this scene, it is important to establish a framework for understanding racial identity construction—what I am calling a philosophy of *racial being*. Let me start by making an important distinction between social identities—the social expectations and norms that are set in accordance with visible characteristics (Giddens 1991, 82)—and self-identities as they relate to the concept of race. It is hardly news to announce that there are people self-identifying as of a given race who are not immediately recognized by others as such. When a person identifying as black chooses to conceal this aspect of his or her (at least partial African) ancestry it is commonly referred to as "passing" (Piper 1992). In such cases, there is a clear difference between how a person understands his or her own racial identity and how the surrounding world (at least until further information is available) chooses to racially designate him or her. In the same vein, to be racially classified as (for instance) black—that is, to have a social identity through which people see you, interact with you, and recognize you as black—does not necessitate a self-identification as black or a formulation of life choices and plans in accordance with such recognition (Gooding-Williams 2001). Although these qualities tend to appear in concert—the recognizably black individual who refuses to acknowledge this aspect of his or her being is destined to walk a troubled path—the point is that he or she need not. This, then, becomes the key difference between an ascribed racial designation and a self-concept as a person of a particular race, or to continue with the example of African-descended persons, the difference between being racially classified as black and being a "black person" (Gooding-Williams 2001, 242). Acknowledging that the fashioning of racial self-identity is distinct from, albeit usually impacted by, racial social identity allows for a better grasp of the multiplicity of racial subjectivities—involving distinct experiences, ideologies, and dispositions—that are emerging.

What is essential to *racial being* is having the self-recognition of being of a particular race impact one's sociality. The manner in which it has an impact is dependent on a number of factors, including culture, personality, immediate interests, and personal biographies, but race—being neither culture nor biology—is enacted first and foremost through self-recognition. To illustrate this, let's take the example of a person living in the interior of New Guinea at the start of the twentieth century (an individual who much of the outside world would have classified as racially black). For this person, having never encountered, been told of, or conceived of people racially different from herself, there would be no understanding of herself as of any particular race and, therefore, no racial identity. Yet virtually all twenty-first-century Americans recognize their own racial identity (even if that identity includes a combination of races). Within social setting such as those that make up the world of Bay Area underground hip hop this acknowledgement of race comes to affect experiences and outlooks in various and nuanced ways. The intensity, specific motivations, and implications of this type of racialism (Appiah

1990) may differ from context to context and group to group. The fact that *racial being* is a direct consequence of racial self-recognition is unwavering.

Dichotomies and Continuums of Racial Identification

The perpetuation of a black–white racial paradigm is perhaps the most telling aspects of Bay Area underground hip hop's racial politics. While the ideal of color-blindness is widely preached, discourses surrounding hip hop legitimacy are saturated with allusions to race in which groups falling outside the black–white binary struggle for voice and visibility. For instance, when encountering the music of an artist whom they had not heard before (and could not racially place), it was common for hip hop enthusiasts of all races to ask whether the emcee "is black or white?" This occurred even though virtually all Bay Area hip hoppers were aware of numerous emcees who were neither. Such inquiries seemed to take place as frequently among Asian American, Latino, and mixed-race hip hoppers as they did among African Americans and European Americans. The salience of race has always been most profoundly felt as a binary opposition. People align themselves with what they believe they are, but fortify this position largely through an awareness of who they are not. Standing at opposite ends of America's racial continuum, blackness and whiteness continue to frame the terms through which all people locate themselves. In the face of this enduring dichotomy, however, a simultaneous process of racial heterogenization is occurring both within and between racial categories. A clear illustration of this is the revival in ethnic consciousness that can be seen within almost all racial groups, but that is probably most conspicuous among people identifying as either white or black.

At the bottom of hip hop's inverted racial hierarchy, white hip hoppers feel the greatest onus to legitimate themselves by constructing identities which challenge the perception that they are just another "white boy" or "white girl." Ethnocentric notions of white normalcy have predisposed many Americans of European descent to see themselves as without race, culture, and/or ethnic heritage and privilege. Yet as the proportion of whites in this country decreases, the idea of whiteness as a particular point upon a racial landscape (i.e., a more developed sense of white racial being) is gaining favor.[8] In some cases there are impetuses toward reclaiming the very same ethnic distinctions that many European Americans once sought to lose. Such drives were powerful enough to lead a few (appearing to be) white hip hoppers that I met to self-consciously renounce their white social identity in favor of various ethno-racial self-designations—for example, "half-Latino" or "part-Native-American." When successful, such performances of self (Ferguson 1997) gave (these seemingly) white hip hoppers a degree of ethnic merit which allowed them to participate in a racial dialogue that they might have otherwise felt excluded from.

Since the 1965 changes in U.S. immigration laws, greater numbers of black immigrants from Africa, the Caribbean, and Latin America have arrived in United States. Their growing visibility is redefining notions of what it means to be black in America. No longer only the descendants of slaves, the racial category black has come to include multiple historical subjectivities. During my ethnographic travels within the Bay, I spent considerable time with black hip hoppers who identified as Ethiopian, Guyanese, Kenyan, and Haitian. Even among African Americans whose families had resided in the United States for hundreds of years, there were strong inclinations toward accentuating the diversity of black experiences and interests. One place where this was apparent was in African American emcees' discussions of their musical and extra-musical career goals. Oakland emcee Kirby Dominant, for example, in doing this made a point of stressing the breadth of his musical ambitions: "I've got too many things going on in my head. I can mold, I can be with anybody. I want a punk group. I want a fuckin' R&B group with some back-up singers."

There is a pervasive draw to distinction and pursuit of individual style (see Bennett 1999b, 605) that runs throughout underground hip hop's genuine embrace. The subcultural spaces I moved within featured black emcees who strongly identified as skateboarders, teachers, filmmakers, and drum-and-bass performance emcees just as readily as those who tended toward more (stereo)typical qualities that have come to be associated with an authentic rap identity—qualities which have been critically characterized as the celebration of street-coded spectacular consumption (Watts 1997; see also Patillo-McCoy 1999) and "anti-intellectualism, ignorance, irresponsible parenthood, and criminal lifestyles" (Kitwana 2002, xxi). In their performances of race, African American underground hip hoppers in the Bay show a keen interest in defying popular media's racial imagery surrounding urban black (hip hop inflected) youth. Where people having narrow conceptions of black authenticity might interpret much of this as signaling a weakened association with blackness, I mean to emphasize this refusal to conform to media driven images of black essentialism as an emerging mode of black being. Such a reaction against rap music's racial clichés is made all the more significant because of the presence of high numbers of recent black immigrants within the scene.

The black–white dichotomy has historically forced groups falling outside of it to choose between aligning themselves against whiteness (as a collective "people of color") or adopting an orientation toward white America that involves a simultaneous disposition away from blackness. A few groups—for instance, Filipinos and Puerto Ricans—have historically been marked more by their ethnic identities than by race. This appears to be more common among people hailing from nations with longstanding histories of racial mixing. An emphasis on ethnicity can be looked at as a response to racial ambiguity, a means of affirming solidarity and a sense of belonging, and/or a way of distancing a group from potentially divisive racial polarities (see Maira 2002, 67).

Advances in communications and travel technology have allowed immigrant families and communities to maintain strong bonds with the places they left. This fosters the continuation and fortifies the resiliency of strong national and ethnic identifications. Like their African diaspora counterparts, many of these (non-black) immigrants hail from nations that were subject to discriminatory U.S. immigration policies for the majority of the twentieth century. Both the time period and available tools of this recent wave of immigration have enabled people within these groups to choose alternatives to the traditional model of assimilation (Branigan 1998). Among circles of socially conscious youth, the maintenance of immigrant identities is further fueled by collective reflections on the colonial and neocolonial plights that caused them to leave their homeland, and the experiences with racism and prejudice they have been subject to since arriving in America.

For people identifying as being of mixed-race descent, multiple racial subjectivities are the standard. As a general rule, a greater degree of racial diversity, within both scenes and individuals, offers greater opportunities to experiment with and test the boundaries of racial malleability. One young hip hopper, who described herself as of Puerto Rican/Japanese/ Filipino/ Chinese/Spanish descent explained how having grown up in Hawaii has caused her to "identify as a Hawaiian the best," even though she technically had no Polynesian ancestry. "I find it incredibly difficult to pick just one ethnicity," she explained. The acceptance of mixed-race identities has transformed the question of "what are you?" from an imposition of a strict racial designation into an opportunity to narrate one's own racial/ethnic biography, and to seek out mutual lines of ancestry with others.[9] This increased recognition is perhaps best reflected by the "mark one or more" option on the 2000 U.S. Census (Perlmann and Waters 2002).

On the liner notes of his 2000 solo CD *From All Angles,* Bored Stiff emcee Professor Whaley identifies himself as an Ethiopian, Choctaw Indian, French, and English, artist, scientist, University of California, Berkeley, graduate (with a degree in mathematics), Oakland Unified School District math teacher, trumpet player, and researcher (Whaley 2000). Featured tracks on the album include a song advocating the virtues of international travel as a means of broadening one's perspectives, a song about soccer (the world's most popular sport), a mathematical poem by one of Whaley's students, and a song in which "P. Way" shares his aspirations of writing a new kind of math textbook. As the integrity of racial categorizations and notions of racial essentialism give way to new forms of racial being, the emphasis on defining oneself through personally chosen rather than ascribed attributes will come to dominate everyday identity constructions.

Situated Responses to Racial Privilege

European American emcees in the Bay Area underground scene are keenly aware of both their white identity and its historically privileged status. Accordingly, they follow what could be described as their own code of ethical racial responsibility. This includes self-reflexive sentiments of racial accountability, self-biographies that emphasize socialization and past experiences in majority non-white settings, as well as adopting critical outlooks toward (other) "white people." An important aspect of all these acts is that they stand in opposition to what (within a multiracial context) would generally be considered typical attributes of white identity— that is, blindness to racial privilege, a "sheltered" upbringing with little exposure to non-white settings, and (often) a critical outlook toward non-white people. In this way, emphasizing personal qualities works to disassociate white (and to a lesser extent other traditionally racially privileged) hip hoppers from the essentialized whiteness that all hip hop defines itself against (McLeod 1999; see also Cross 1993, 64). Still, because such acts are first and foremost a response to white self-recognition, they should be understood as a particular form of white being.

Displays of accountability, which involve developing an understanding of the experiences of people and groups who differ from oneself (Collins 1994, 492) are one of the principal means through which Bay Area underground hip hoppers engineer this alternative white identity. Such sentiments frequently include heightened displays of racial consciousness that fly in the face of the scene's articulated principles of colorblindness. "You have to be aware of how your role as a white hip hop artist is viewed by both the black community and the white community," was how one European American emcee put it.

Even with underground hip hop's racial inclusivity, among white hip hoppers particularly, importance is placed on not forgetting hip hop's African American (and Latino) roots:

> Hip hop is a youth culture more than anything. It's the voice of youth and that's it. It's also the voice of minorities. It originated from the voice of blacks and Latinos. You know what I mean? In the city. But now it's more than that.... Like you said, it's changing. But at the same time, that's *got* to be remembered. It's essential I think. Where did this shit come from and why is it affecting me? (Gamma Ray, personal interview, January 12, 2001)

For Day-One deejay Mizzo, this connection between hip hop and blackness presented a contradiction that he, as someone identifying as half-Asian (Chinese and Japanese)/half-white, struggled to position himself within:

> Anyone can be in hip hop now pretty much. It's just about your skill, you know? It's not about whether you're black or whether you're whatever you know? But at the same time, I think we have to come to grips that there is a split between underground and like the mainstream, and in the mainstream it's all black artists and in the underground it's really diverse.... Before it was just the black community, the black community created the music and the black community consumed it. Now it's like, sorta becoming like jazz.... I'm not sure what it's gonna become in the future. *If what we call hip hop is gonna be something else*... I'm not really sure if I'm part of the solution or part of the problem in the whole thing. I can only do what I feel and I definitely feel a connection to hip hop. (DJ Mizzo, personal interview, April 11, 2001)

Self-reflexive *testimonials of accountability* represent one way in which height-ened racial consciousness is used to establish underground hip hop legitimacy.

A second strategy for achieving this, which I am calling *narratives of place-ment,* involves offering self-biographies that recount either personal or (some-times) communal links with other racial groups. For underground hip hoppers, many of these narratives highlight time spent in predominantly African Ameri-can social contexts as profound identity-shaping experiences—these include temporary stays in "all-black" high schools, neighborhoods, and (quite fre-quently) "the (Caribbean) Islands." Such self-biographies aspired to be both statements of non-racism (enjoying being immersed in a black world) and accounts of racial empathy—arguing that the experience of being a racial minor-ity allows one to understand something about what it feels like to be non-white in America. Accordingly, such stories are often marked by a tension between demonstrating an empathy with non-white groups and simultaneously—through the first-hand experience of being a racial minority—acknowledging one's own white racial identity.

In the Bay Area underground scene, these orientations toward blackness involved more than just personal histories. They also informed non-black hip hopper's daily activities, many of which (at some level) coveted African American approval. Where there was no African American presence, distinctively non-black hip hop enclaves were often viewed with suspicion. "I feel that there's a big difference between groups that are mostly black with a few white members, and all white groups," one European American explained.

Critiquing whiteness is yet another strategy commonly used by European Americans to disassociate themselves from white racial privilege (see Ware 2002, 29). However, where both *testimonials of accountability* and *narratives of place-ment* involve confronting one's own whiteness, acts of criticizing other "white people" require no such reflexivity. In fact, such statements were often made as if to suggest that the speaker was not white. During one interview a European American deejay spoke a length about a "fat ass white girl" who attempted to take one of his mix tapes without paying for it; on several other occasions white emcees railed about the problem of "all these white kids" claiming to "be down with the Bay Area underground" without just due.

While Bay Area underground hip hoppers rarely spoke directly of "white privilege," within other progressive social arenas the phrase has come to be used quite regularly when discussing issues of race and racism. As more European Americans have started embrace the term, I fear that it has become a different sort of double-edged sword: sharp in its attack on existing norms regarding race-based social, economic, and political advantage; yet dull in the extent to which, without proper self-reflection, like other *critiques of whiteness,* it offers white people who use it a gateway into distancing their own subjectivities from the issue they profess to be concerned with.

As a condition of acceptance within these multiracial settings, people who identify as white are forced to use displays of heightened race consciousness as a means of constructing alternative forms of white being. At the other end of the racial dichotomy, Bay Area underground hip hoppers who identify as black are more compelled to adhere to the colorblind principles that are upheld throughout the scene. This was effectively illustrated during a 1999 episode where two emcees, one European American and the other African American, engaged in a highly publicized on-air "rhyme battle" during a local college radio broadcast. Keeping with hip hop tradition, the battle consisted of competitors alternating turns trying to best and belittle their opponent through displays of impromptu, off-the-top-of-the-head rhyming ability. Like most events of this sort, the defining thrust of the competition was an ongoing effort on the part of each emcee to call to question his opponents hip hop legitimacy. These frequently took the form of highly personal and at times tasteless (specifically hypersexual and homophobic) verbal attacks. In light of the current discussion, what was most fascinating about this verbal confrontation was the infrequency of allusions to race, and the way in which the few mentions of race that did occur dominated online discussions over who won the battle.

If nothing else, the nearly complete avoidance of race on the part of both emcees attests to the scene-wide conscription to an underground hip hop colorblind principle. Yet as the battle went on, either by choice or by mistake, the African American emcee broke this unspoken code by making a number of specific references to his opponent's white identity. This included asking the European American emcee if he "wanted a tan," and comparing him to (infamous early 1990s white emcee) Vanilla Ice.

In the days, weeks, and months that followed this battle, debates over which emcee won appeared on a number of online hip hop forums. In both these online discussions and the face-to-face conversations I was involved in or privy to, popular sentiment interpreted the black emcee's decision to "play the race card" as an act of desperation "because he was losing the battle." There was, therefore, a sizable body of commentators who insisted that the black emcee's allusions to race, his violation of the colorblind ideal, stood as evidence of defeat. While questions over who won the battle, and why the black emcee decided to bring up race can be forever debated, what this example shows is how within multicultural settings of this sort, those atop the racial hierarchy (even an inverted one) are discouraged from rehearsing the terms of their racially privileged status. If anything, African Americans within Bay Area underground hip hop are obliged to show a lack of racial awareness. Any African American who brings up race—as a matter of hip hop credentials—runs a greater risk of losing credibility for such an act than of gaining it.

The power of race is imposed on people's identities from all angles. In racially diverse social settings it affects people on the top of the racial hierarchy as much as those on the bottom. In all this, the perception of race-based privilege and how it impacts the social identities and self-identities of racial subjects is of key interest. In order to successfully negotiate the terrain of these multiracial worlds, individuals must be willing to adopt social orientations and embrace forms of racial being that account for both the master- and sub-text of racial hierarchy (i.e., both the traditional and the subcultural status of their racial identity). Understanding these sliding scales of privilege may be most central to making sense of this phenomenon. However, as long as the discussion involves race, it seems that it will continue to take place through references to blackness and whiteness.

Implications of This New Racialization

If these new approaches to racial identity construction are to have any significant bearing on issues of racial inequality, it will largely depend on the extent to which the ethical principles they engender pervade other aspects of life, particularly as members of these diverse youth scenes move into further adulthood. This will be partly contingent on these young Americans' abilities (or inabilities) to resist deep-rooted societal pressures that push all people to form the most meaningful ties within their own racial and ethnic groups. It will also be affected by the extent to which they continue to spend time within racially diverse social settings. For without continued exposure to racial diversity as a means of reflecting on their own racial situatedness and status, I fear that some of the greatest promises of this subcultural phenomenon—like the development of a non-essentialized racial outlook that compels white people (particularly) to adopt more critical orientations toward whiteness—risk being swallowed and contained within the existing hegemony of racial understanding.

Virtually all people come to formulate life plans that seek to improve on their quality of living by attempting to "recapture" or "rise up from" their historical memory of how their ancestors lived. In pursuing this, Americans have traditionally identified the greatest threats to this quality of life—the threat of competition for jobs, increased crime, economic instability, and the fear of difference—as embodied in other racial/ethnic groups. The new approaches to racial identity construction discussed here have the potential to erode these deep-seated beliefs and to alter and increase political alliances across all groups. The emergence of a strong cosmopolitan multiracial constituency with specific integrationist agendas is certainly worth contemplating. I am tempted to say that without drawing considerably from existing race-based political blocs it is questionable whether (in the immediate foreseeable future) any such group could grow large enough to impact "politics as usual" in any meaningful way. Yet all one has to do is look at the lobbying efforts that resulted in the "mark one or more" 2000 U.S. Census option (Williams 2006) to realize that such interests have already been loudly heard.

To what extent can these new negotiations of identity, in and of themselves, be understood as modes of social change (see Cohen 1993, 132)? I am speaking here about a change that begins at the everyday level; and specifically concerns how people reflect upon the integrity of their own race and the races of others around them, as well as how these understandings influence dynamics of racial interaction—most notably with whom people choose to interact, and how they construct their identities when doing so. In considering this, I am calling for a greater appreciation of how racial attitudes have the potential to influence social structure. For within the informal contexts of social spaces such as those which make up the Bay Area underground hip hop scene, integration would seem to be as much a consequence of these new forms of racialization as it is a cause.

People holding pessimistic views on race relations might dismiss Bay Area underground hip hop as a multiracial field of (extra-)adolescent play where fantasies of colorblindness are sheltered from more pressing economic and social realities. It is my contention that these social maneuverings in and around hip hop authenticity, and the politics of race that accompany them, are of considerably more consequence than such outlooks suggest. In their interactions and affiliations with hip hoppers of other racial/ethnic identities, participants in the Bay Area underground hip hop scene are exploring the contradictions and implications of essentialized race. The interests and experiences that shape their subcultural existence foster their recognition that racial identities are never as stable as their "invented histories, biologies, and cultural affinities" would leave us to believe (Appiah 1992, 174; also see Taylor 2005). These new understandings of race's integrity and ethics will undoubtedly continue to evolve as underground hip hoppers move beyond their immediate subcultural worlds. However, the profoundness of their experiences participating in a racially egalitarian arena (even one that is largely imagined) will have a lasting impact on how they approach race as a concept and issues surrounding racial difference.

In this essay, I have argued that the social dynamics of underground hip hop in the San Francisco Bay Area are on the leading edge of a national trend toward more situated and situational racialization. Despite its tremendous diversity, the Bay Area is not alone here. Within multiracial underground hip hop scenes across America, similar processes can be observed. Outside of hip hop, municipal basketball courts are another example of places where racially diverse crowds of "regulars" construct and engage in new modes of racializing their identities whenever they take the court. These dynamic outcomes of America's increasing recognition of its own diversity saturate the lives of many young people today and only look to become more cemented in the decades ahead.

Glocalized Racial Understandings

In closing this chapter, I want to point out how the dynamics of situational racial identity construction occurring within Bay Area underground hip hop are outcomes of larger global processes which stress simultaneous distinction and commonality between and within social groups. British sociologist Roland Robertson, in his efforts to develop a more sophisticated model of globalization, is credited with popularizing the concept of *glocalization* to reference the "construction of increased differentiation" and "expectation of uniqueness" that has emerged as a consequence of the world becoming a smaller place (Robertson 1995, 28–29).[10] Understanding Bay Area underground hip hop's racial dynamics as a product of glocal phenomena further emphasizes the scope and significance of what is occurring.

Glocalization appreciates how the adoption and embrace of cultural commodities vary in accordance with the local specifics that continue to hold meaning for people. This examination of situational racialization shifts the glocal paradigm from questions of how groups embrace commodities, to issues of individual identity constructions and how they take shape within local contexts of global racial awareness. Through global flows (Appadurai 1996) of media images, goods, and people, over the last quarter century, hip hop has spread from the specific New York City communities within which it originated to virtually every corner of America and most parts of the world. As a cultural commodity that travels through globalized pipelines of music media and fashion, yet also takes root within the politics of local dissatisfaction, hip hop has been hailed as a particularly animated example of glocalization (Bennett 1999a, 6).

In diverse and inclusive multiracial scenes such as Bay Area underground hip hop, where people aspire to achieve, and believe they have achieved, a level of colorblindness, there are strong sentiments toward celebrating the commonalities that all people share. Yet both between and within racial groups, this orientation away from race-based difference encourages people to construct identities that reclaim a sense of individual distinction. Glocalization of this sort involves simultaneous processes of homogenization and heterogenization (Robertson 1995, 27) that affect the formation of both community and individual identities.

The situational constructions of racial identity seen within Bay Area underground hip hop occur within a framework of marked racial categories. In spite of the scene's colorblind mantra, there are obvious orientations toward (certain understandings of) blackness and away from (certain understandings of) whiteness that continue to influence the ways in which racial politics play out. Yet, in their everyday activities, young underground hip hoppers participating within multiracial scenes put their greatest efforts and intentions toward more voluntary forms of identification, and non-essential ways of racial being. In attempting to situate themselves along hip hop's racial landscape, Bay Area underground hip hoppers who identify as white have to be more outwardly conscious of race, and its historical implications. This consciousness and how it influences the formation of white collective identifications is one of the developments that make these new approaches to racial identity construction so potentially momentous. The fact the African Americans are restricted in their racial politics of legitimation is certainly notable. It is, at the very least, intriguing in the extent to which it draws an unsavory parallel with conservative civil rights legislation, which seeks to remove all discussion of race from matters of social policy (Williams 2006). At the same time, the prospects for black hip hoppers attempting to navigate this racial terrain are by no means bleak. Rather than choosing between the promises and dreads that inevitably accompany any racially dichotomous outlook, I end with a more ambivalent prognosis—one that recognizes the potential to develop a more socially and racially aware citizenship but is cautious in respecting the lengths to which privilege in America has always been tied to the manipulation of racial understandings. The changing integrities of racial distinctions described here have powerful implications for how race operates as an organizing principle in society. It is this new mode of racialism that, I argue, those interested in understanding the future of race in America must recognize and begin to acknowledge.

Notes

1. This research involved over one year of fully immersed participant observation (and several subsequent visits), semi-structured interviews, and weekly focus group-like critical discussions.

2. This is well illustrated in the PBS *Frontline* report "Merchants of Cool" (2001).

3. I use the label "European American" somewhat facetiously to draw attention to the fact that Americans of European descent, as much as any other group, should have qualifications to explain their presence on this continent.

4. Amoeba has since opened a larger store in Hollywood.

5. This included not only underground hip hop but also music from the prominent Bay Area rap scene—which traces its legacy to artists like Too $hort and E-40, and has recently received attention for initiating the *hyphy* movement—as well as a variety of deejay mix tapes and CDs.

6. The San Francisco Bay Area is among the most racially and ethnically diverse regions in America. According to the 2000 Census, the nine-county region was home to a population that was 50 percent (non-Hispanic) white, 19.4 percent Latino (of any race), 19.3 percent Asian/Pacific Islander, 7.3 percent African American, and 3.3 percent people listing themselves as "of two or more races" (Bay Area Census 2000). This diversity becomes even more pronounced among young Bay Area residents.

7. Although I prefer the term "colorblind," Mica Pollock's notion of colormuteness (Pollock 2005) may be equally appropriate. For more than an inability to see race, what the colorblind ideal affects is Bay Area underground hip hoppers' refusal to talk about race as being significant in any way.

8. One example of this is the growing popularity of white studies programs in universities across America.

9. I personally had more than a half dozen experiences where someone of (at least partial) Asian descent inquired as to whether we shared this. My negative response seemed to always generate some disappointment.

10. According to Robertson, the concept is derived from the Japanese agricultural principle of *dochaku* (living on one's own land), which during the 1980s came to be used within Japanese economics (Robertson 1995, 28).

References

Appadurai, Arjun. 1996. *Modernity at Large: Cultural Dimensions of Globalization.* Minneapolis: University of Minnesota Press.

Appiah, Kwame Anthony. 1990. "Racisms." Pp. 3–17 in *Anatomy of Racism,* ed. David Theo Goldberg. Minneapolis: University of Minnesota Press.

———. 1992. *In My Father's House: Africa in the Philosophy of Culture.* New York: Oxford University Press.

Arnold, Eric. 2006. "From Azeem to Zion-I: The Evolution of Global Consciousness in Bay Area Hip Hop." Pp. 71–84 in *The Vinyl Ain't Final: Hip Hop and the Globalization of Black Popular culture,* ed. Dipannita Basu and Sidney J. Lemelle. London: Pluto Press.

Bay Area Census. 2000. Metropolitan Transportation Commission, Association of Bay Area Governments Library, Oakland, Calif. Available online at http://census.abag.ca.gov/bayarea.htm.

Bennett, Andy. 1999a. "Rappin' on the Tyne: White Hip Hop Culture in Northeast England—an Ethnographic Study." *Sociological Review* 47, no. 1: 1–24.

———. 1999b. "Subcultures or Neo-tribes? Rethinking the Relationship between Youth, Style and Musical Taste." *Sociology* 33, no. 3: 599–617.

———. 2000. *Popular Music and Youth Culture: Music, Identity, and Places.* London: Macmillan.

Best, Oliver, dir. 2000. *Return of the B-Boy.* Tapeworm, Valencia, Calif.

Branigin, William. 1998. "The Myth of the Melting Pot, Part Three: Immigrants Shunning Idea of Assimilation." *Washington Post,* May 25. Available online at http://www.washingtonpost.com/wp-srv/national/longterm/meltingpot/melt0525a.htm.

Cohen, Sara. 1993. "Ethnography and Popular Music Studies." *Popular Music* 12, no. 2: 123–138.

Collins, Patricia Hill. 1994. "Toward a New Vision: Race, Class, and Gender as Categories of Analysis and Connection." Pp. 478–495 in *The Social Construction of Race and Ethnicity in the United States,* ed. Joan Ferrante and Prince Brown Jr. New York: Addison Wesley Longman.

Cross, Brian. 1993. *It's Not about a Salary: Rap, Race, and Resistance in Los Angeles.* New York: Verso Press.

Ferguson, Kennan. 1997. "How Peoples Get Made: Race, Performance, Judgment." *Theory and Event* 1, no. 3.

Frankenberg, Ruth. 1993. *White Women, Race Matters: The Social Construction of Whiteness.* Minneapolis: University of Minnesota Press.

Giddens, Anthony. 1991. *Modernity and Self-identity.* Stanford, Calif.: Stanford University Press.

Gooding-Williams, Robert. 2001. "Race, Multiculturalism and Democracy." Pp. 237–259 in *Race,* ed. Robert Bernasconi. Malden, Mass.: Blackwell Publishers.

Hall, Stuart. 1996. "New Ethnicities." Pp. 441–449 in *Stuart Hall: Critical Dialogues in Cultural Studies,* ed. David Morley and Kuan-Hsing Chen. London: Routledge.

Inoue, Todd. 2003. "Mystik Journeymen: Bay Area Underground Hip Hop." *Metro,* January 23–29. Available online at http://www.livewire.com/reviews/mystik-journeymen-17.php.

Jam, Billy. 1997. "Dirt Hustlin'." *San Francisco Bay Guardian,* April 9. Available online at http://www.hiphopslam.com/articles/artic_dirthustle.html.

———. 1999. "Too Short." Pp. 220–221 in *The Vibe History of Hip Hop,* ed. Alan Light. New York: Three Rivers Press.

Keast, Darren. 1999. "Rhyme Schemes." *San Francisco Weekly,* November 3/ Available online at http://www.sfweekly.com/1999-11-03/music/rhyme-schemes.

Kitwana, Bakari. 2002. *The Hip Hop Generation: Young Blacks and the Crisis in African-American Culture.* New York: BasicCivitas Books.

Kleinfeld, N. R. 2000. "Guarding the Borders of the Hip Hop Nation." *New York Times,* July 6, A1, 18–19.

Light, Alan. 1992. "Ice-T." *Rolling Stone*, August 20, 28–32.

Mailer, Norman. 1957. "The White Negro." *Dissent* 4: 276–293.

Maira, Saunaina Marr. 2002. *Desis in the House: Indian American Youth Culture in New York City*. Philadelphia: Temple University Press.

McLeod, Kembrew. 1999. "Authenticity within Hip Hop and Other Cultures Threatened with Assimilation." *Journal of Communication* 49, no. 4: 134–150.

Orr, Jackie. 1995. "Re/sounding Race, Re/signifying Ethnography: Sampling Oaktown Rap." Pp. 441–482 in *Prosthetic Territories: Politics and Hypertechnologies*, ed. Gabriel Brahm Jr. and Mark Driscoll. Boulder, Colo.: Westview Press.

Pattilo-McCoy, Mary. 1999. *Black Picket Fences: Privilege and Peril among the Black Middle Class*. Chicago: University of Chicago Press.

Perlmann, Joel, and Mary C. Waters. 2002. "Introduction." Pp. 1–30 in *The New Race Question: How the Census Counts Multiracial Individuals*, ed. Joel Perlmann and Mary C. Waters. New York: Russell Sage Foundation.

Piper, Adrian. 1992. "Passing for White, Passing for Black." *Transition* 58: 4–32.

Pollock, Mica. 2005. *Colormute: Race Talk Dilemmas in an American School*. Princeton, N.J.: Princeton University Press.

Robertson, Roland. 1995. "Glocalization: Time-Space and Homogeneity-Heterogeneity." Pp. 25–44 in *Global Modernities*, ed. Mike Featherstone, Scott M. Lash, and Roland Robertson. London: Sage.

Rose, Tricia. 1994. *Black Noise: Rap Music and Black Culture in Contemporary America*. London: Wesleyan University Press.

Samuels, David. 1991. "The Rap on Rap: The Black Music That Isn't Either." *New Republic*, vol. 205, no. 20, November 11, 24–29.

Stephens, Gregory. 1991. "Rap Music Double-Voiced Discourse: A Crossroads for Interracial Communication." *Journal of Communication Inquiry* 15, no. 2: 70–91.

Strauss, Neil. 1999. "A Land with Rhythm and Beats for All." *New York Times*, August 22, sec. 2, 1, 28–29.

Thornton, Sarah. 1995. *Club Cultures: Music, Media and Subcultural Capital*. Cambridge: Polity Press.

Taylor, Paul C. 2005. "Does Hip Hop Belong to Me? The Philosophy of Race and Culture." Pp. 79–91 in *Hip Hop and Philosophy: Rhyme 2 Reason*, ed. Derrick Darby and Tommie Shelby. Chicago: Open Court.

Ware, Vron. 2002. "Otherworldly Knowledge: Toward a Language of Perspicuous Contrast." Pp. 15–32 in *Out of Whiteness: Color, Politics, and Culture*, ed. Vron Ware and Les Back. Chicago: University of Chicago Press.

Watts. Eric K. 1997. "An Exploration of Spectacular Consumption: Gangsta Rap as Cultural Commodity." *Communication Studies* 48 (Spring): 42–58.

Whaley, Professor. 2000. *From All Angles: The Sonic Legacy of Professor Whaley*. Compact disc, Soul Note Records, San Francisco.

Williams, Kim M. 2006. *Mark One or More: Civil Rights in Multiracial America*. Ann Arbor: University of Michigan Press.

Wimsatt, William. 1993. "We Use Words like 'Mackadocious' (and Other Progress from the Front Lines of the White Struggle)." *Source* (May): 64–66.

8

Toward Diversity That Works

Building Communities through Arts and Culture

Maria Rosario Jackson

Cities, neighborhoods, college campuses, and even businesses often herald diversity—the tolerance and celebration of difference—as a selling point, making the case that it broadens perspectives, enriches lives, promotes compassion and even leads to innovation. But just what does it take to have diversity, particularly racial and ethnic diversity, in a context where racial and ethnic groups have been divided by racism, discrimination, competition for resources, and fear of change? How can tolerance and celebration of difference that leads to compassion and innovation thrive in such a context? Within urban planning and related fields, concern for fostering racial and ethnic diversity has resulted typically in attention to eradicating housing segregation and redistributing wealth and economic opportunity (Cashin 2004; De Souza Briggs 2005; Rawlings et al. 2004). While these are areas that warrant analysis and action, not enough attention has been paid to understanding or affecting the actual processes by which people express or work to change racial ethnic dynamics within and among different groups. Much of this is being achieved through arts and cultural participation.

This chapter uses examples of arts and cultural activity in communities around the United States to discuss how arts and cultural activity—through which people affirm, preserve, challenge, and transform racial ethnic identity and dynamics—is a precondition for true diversity, the tolerance and celebration of difference, and how that precondition is being achieved on the ground. Based on these examples, the chapter also discusses important implications for urban planners and policymakers concerned with efforts to create more equitable and diverse communities. My ultimate argument is that, without consideration for and inclusion of arts and cultural activity, such efforts are inherently flawed.

I draw in my discussion from a decade of research on the presence and roles of arts and cultural activity in many different types of communities around the United States, including moderate- and low-income neighborhoods, communities of color, and immigrant communities. This research has included participant observation in cultural events, hundreds of interviews, and scores of focus group discussions with neighborhood residents, community leaders, artists, people who run cultural organizations and others involved in a range of community institutions. The research—which focuses always on the kinds of cultural activity that people value in their communities and the reasons why these are valued—is being done by the Arts and Culture in Communities Project (ACIP).[1] Before launching into a discussion about how cultural participation contributes to diversity in communities, a few words are in order about how we interpret arts and culture in our work.

Understanding Arts and Cultural Activity in Communities

Ask someone in just about any city where to find arts and cultural activity and typically one will be directed to large venues downtown or in designated cultural districts—museums, performing arts centers, and similar places. Ask a room full of residents from a typical neighborhood in a U.S. city about the arts and cultural assets in their communities and they will probably be quick to tell you there are none, pointing out that their community has no formally designated cultural centers, museums, theaters, or concert halls. Query the same group about the kinds of things they find moving, beautiful, inspiring, thoughtful, or challenging in their communities, however, and the range of things they list will be many and interestingly varied—festivals, community celebrations and traditions, parades, garage bands, murals, local ethnic dance troupes, drumming circles, quilting and gardening clubs, elders who are storytellers, and local eating fare. Ask them what they miss about their communities when they are away from home or what a postcard that represents their community would include if they had to create one, and the answers will be similar. Ask them why such things matter and one will hear many reasons—it is a form of civic participation, strengthens and creates new bonds among community members, improves the built environment, makes people proud of their place, helps improve public safety, preserves cultural heritage, transmits cultural values and history, creates group memory, and bridges boundaries among diverse racial and ethnic groups (Jackson and Herranz 2002; Walker and Scott-Melnyk 2002).[2] But follow up with a question on whether the activities they have been describing with such enthusiasm are "art" and there will typically be no agreed-on answer—some saying yes, others saying no, still others on the fence.

American communities are typically interesting, complex, and vibrant places filled with creativity and the cultural expressions of their diverse citizenry. All of the artistic activity taking place in parks, schools, churches, and community centers—as well as concert halls, theaters, museums, and community cultural centers—embody the history, fears, frustrations, triumphs, aspirations, and musings of young and old. But alas, the many cultural assets that exist in communities are frequently neglected in measures of a community's well-being and not fully captured even in assessments of its art and culture. Among most policymakers and planners, and among typical residents of communities around the United States, what is considered arts and culture has long been dominated by large cultural institutions—buildings and spaces—concerned primarily with the formal presentation of professional arts to audiences. The wealth of cultural assets that emerge from the grassroots and include nonprofessional artists or arts practitioners—not only as audiences at special events or consumers of artistic products, but also as creators, performers, teachers, students, critics and arts supporters—has been largely ignored.

For the purposes of this chapter, the activity in which we are interested is that broad range of creative practice—amateur and professional, formal and informal—taking place in explicitly cultural venues such as museums and cultural centers as well as in parks, schools, churches, and other spaces that are not arts-specific. This full range of activity is what constitutes a community's cultural vitality and provides an important indication of its ability to contribute to diversity (Jackson et al. 2006).

Even though a narrow concept of arts and culture still appears to prevail in many policy and other contexts, it is encouraging to note that concepts of arts and cultural activity have recently become broader and more inclusive, more consistent with a democratized notion of the arts and the demographic realities of U.S. cities. There is growing evidence, moreover, that arts and cultural activity can and do positively affect local economies, levels of civic engagement, social capital, collective efficacy, and tolerance (Florida 2002; Jackson and Herranz 2002; Putnam 2000; Taylor 2007; Wali et al. 2002). Even more encouraging, there is increasing evidence of planners and developers using artists and arts organizations in communities as catalysts for neighborhood revitalization, although it is their economic impacts that are mostly recognized (Jackson and Kabwasa-Green 2006). This tendency to restrict attention to the economic impacts of the arts is unfortunate, because it relegates to the sidelines other important arts impacts that are more difficult to quantify but may be the most important in changing racial/ethnic dynamics.

Effects of Arts and Cultural Activity on Racial Ethnic Dynamics

In our ACIP research on arts and culture in communities, three distinct but interrelated functions having to do with racial ethnic dynamics surfaced as important: (1) affirmation and preservation of cultural identity; (2) critical assessment of racial ethnic identity; and (3) building of bridges among diverse racial ethnic groups. Examples of arts and cultural activity contributing to one, two, or all three of these functions abound.

Racial Ethnic Affirmation and Preservation

The affirmation and preservation of racial ethnic identity surfaced as particularly important for minority groups who have been the target of forced assimilation and often have a history of having been colonized and subjugated. For these groups, the ability to assert and preserve their racial ethnic identity is a crucial signal of their perseverance and survival despite hostile forces. For example, the head of Search to Involve Pilipino Americans (SIPA),[3] a social service organization in Los Angeles that integrates Pilipino arts practice into much of its community programming, said that being able to express and celebrate Pilipino and Pilipino American identities that enable the retention of language, history, aesthetics, and other cultural values is a crucial quality-of-life issue.[4] This sentiment was echoed by many respondents whom we interviewed about the intents and impacts of integrating arts and cultural programming into social service delivery and community development. In some cases, the impetus for the integration of such arts and cultural activity has been organizational leaders and staff of community agencies. However, in other cases, the impetus for integrating ethnic specific arts and cultural activity has come from clients and community members themselves who have been vocal and proactive about the importance of affirming and preserving their identity. Many clients noted that such activity enhances leadership and youth development efforts as well as efforts to politically organize and mobilize communities.

The affirmation, preservation and transmission of cultural identity from one generation to the next is also often the mission of "Saturday Schools" and cultural enrichment programs organized by churches and temples, benevolent societies, hometown associations, social service organizations, ethnic-specific business associations, arts organizations, and combinations of all of these. Such programs are concerned with instruction on and retention of the cultural traditions and language of the historic country of origin. Music, dance, and literary arts typically play a key role in this. Greek and Ukrainian schools in Chicago, Chinese schools in Northern California, Hebrew schools in New York, and Freedom Schools throughout the United States connected with the Children's Defense Fund and focused on African American heritage are all examples of programming with this intent.[5]

Ethnic parades, annual events that exist in just about every major city, are other cultural activities through which racial ethnic identity is affirmed. In these events people participate as marchers, organizers, artists, musicians, dancers, spectators and supporters to celebrate their heritage—St. Patrick's Day Irish parades in Chicago, Puerto Rican Day parades in New York, Italian parades on St. Joseph's Day in New Orleans, Chinese New Year's Day parades in San Francisco, among many others. While the focus is on the ethnic group celebrated, these events are typically more public and permeable than many of the Saturday Schools and cultural enrichment programs just described—open to people from all backgrounds who participate to different degrees, as spectators and sometimes also as performers and supporters.

Arts organizations focused on a particular ethnic group are other important venues through which identity is affirmed. Often, these organizations collaborate with social service agencies, local schools, and other community institutions not primarily concerned with the arts. In New Orleans, for example, professional and non-professional artists gather at Ashe Cultural Arts Center, not only to commemorate African American contributions to New Orleans, but also to create new performing and visual art expressing the present conditions and aspirations of African Americans and other New Orleaneans. As a dimension of its cultural mission, Ashe is leading the redevelopment of vacant properties for community cultural uses and provides cultural programming, including storytelling, poetry, music, dance, photography, and visual art giving voice to African Americans in New Orleans. Post–Hurricane Katrina, Ashe has been a particularly active hub for many artists of color (African Americans and Latinos, primarily) whose work deals with race, ethnicity, and social justice.

Critical Assessment of Racial Ethnic Identity

The critical assessment of racial/ethnic identity, interestingly, is not necessarily at odds, as one might think, with the previously described desire to preserve and affirm identity. In fact, what came through in our research was that the ability to both preserve and innovate are crucial and often coexist (although not always peacefully). Here, too, some of the same players as before provide important mechanisms—arts organizations, festival organizations, social service agencies involved in cultural work, and community centers where people gather to practice their cultural art forms.

While I have described ethnic parades as entities through which identity is affirmed and preserved, in many U.S. cities, ethnic parades and festivals are venues through which group identity is also debated and challenged. The Puerto Rican Day parade in New York, for example, is an event that showcases the many facets of the Puerto Rican community, with entries representing the traditional culture of the island as well as the culture of Nuyoricans (people of Puerto Rican ancestry born or living in New York). The different cultural representations in the parade are not all unanimously supported by the population the parade celebrates. There are always debates about what is really Puerto Rican and what is not, with some participants supporting only the most traditional cultural expressions from the islands and not fully embracing Nuyorican innovations such as those related to hip hop and other dimensions of pop culture. "People are always really concerned about the line-up of the parade because it's long and only the first couple of hours are televised. So there's a feeling that what comes out first is what people really believe is Puerto Rican. That's what people are going to see on TV," one observer said. Because the parade is not only an opportunity to showcase Puerto Rican culture internally to the Puerto Rican community itself but also, very importantly, to the rest of the world, the content and order of the procession is often challenged. In the end, the traditional culture persists and there is also plenty of evidence of cultural fusion and evolution. The parade, with all its complexity, is a reflection of the community.

Reflection and debate happens in other cultural settings as well. In Oakland, California, for example, we observed Mien women gathering at a community center for weekly sewing circles. "We talk. We teach our children so they don't forget from where we come. It takes a long time [sewing] and we talk about here and also what it was like before," said a sewing circle participant. The functions of these gatherings were not only to keep alive the tradition of making beautifully embroidered garments, but also to find ways of adapting their art form in a new context. In the process these women often discussed what it is for them and their descendants to be Mien in Oakland, what it is to be "Asian," a new label that includes them and other groups with which they are not so familiar, and potentially what it means for their descendants to be American. In this context, racial ethnic identity was affirmed, questioned, and to some extent, it was being invented.

In Boston, we learned of a newly forming Haitian cultural center comprising professional and amateur artists. As the Haitian population grows, and Haitians seek to assert a presence, questions have arisen about what type of group identity Haitians in Boston want to assert within the Haitian community itself and also to the broader Boston citizenry. Should the main language be French? Creole? English? Is the center about traditional art forms from Haiti? New Haitian American art forms? Should the center be called Haitian or Haitian American? How or should the new organization connect to artists and publics in Haiti?

In Los Angeles, Pilipino Americans of different generations gather through SIPA, a social service agency, and FilAmARTS, a Pilipino cultural organization, to do and enjoy Pilipino performing and other art forms as part of regular community events as well as annual festivals. According to respondents, through these activities Pilipinos in Los Angeles both affirm differences within the Pilipino population, which comprises people from different regions and ethnic groups in the Philippines, and define a common Pilipino American identity that incorporates these distinct populations. Here, too, participants take part in shaping how Pilipinos and Pilipino Americans represent themselves among themselves and to the broader Southern California community.

In Denver, El Centro Su Teatro is a cultural arts center focusing on Chicano (American born people of Mexican ancestry) and Latino experiences in the United States, which often deals with the complexity of that history through the art it presents. Born out of the Chicano civil rights movement, the center has a strong focus on theatre arts but also presents music and poetry as well as film and visual arts, with a concentration on youth and leadership development.

At El Centro Su Teatro, racial ethnic identity and relations are often examined along with other historical and present-day socioeconomic issues.

The Asian Arts Initiative in Philadelphia engages in social activism through the arts and provides a space where professional artists and amateurs can express the diverse experiences of Asian Americans. The center deals with all artistic disciplines. It encourages pre- and post-performance discussions and workshops as a means of making the work more accessible and meaningful to audiences and artists alike. Here too, racial ethnic identity and relations are examined, as are socioeconomic and political conditions from historical and present-day perspectives.

Building Bridges among Diverse Racial Ethnic Groups

Of the three functions that arts and cultural activity can perform with regard to racial ethnic dynamics, bridge building among diverse groups sometimes at odds with each other is the activity by far the most often thought of, sought out, and supported by government and foundations concerned with improving race relations. Unfortunately, too often the idea of bringing diverse groups together is over-simplified and rushed. I argue that one cannot really expect diverse groups to fruitfully come together without first having had the chance to adequately engage in the first two processes (affirmation of their own cultural identity and critical assessment of it) on their own terms. These processes are essential in helping people to understand who they are individually and as a group within the context of the broader society, that is, to understand their social standing and history in relation to other groups within a U.S. context, and also globally. Affirming and critically assessing racial/ethnic identity also make it possible for people to step into a diverse cultural commons with a point of view and something to contribute. The following two examples are of cultural initiatives that embody affirmation of identity, critical assessment of identity, and bridge building among distinct groups with complicated relationships. These examples have ultimately led to more meaningful diversity in their respective communities.

In Chicago, the National Museum of Mexican Art (formerly the Mexican Fine Arts Center Museum)—an organization in the predominantly Mexican Pilsen neighborhood, with strong ties to the local community and a long and strong record of programming that has affirmed and celebrated Mexican and Mexican American culture—challenged conventional assumptions about the racial composition of Mexico with a landmark exhibit, "The African Presence in Mexico: From Yanga to the Present."[6] Through photography, paintings, music, film, and historical artifacts, the exhibit highlighted the significant role Africans have played in the history and culture of Mexico. The exhibition had two companion exhibits. "Who Are We Now? Roots, Resistance, Recognition" focused on relationships between Mexicans and African Americans in the United States over the past two hundred years, and the "Chicago Galley Exhibition: Common Goals, Common Struggles, Common Ground" focused on historical and contemporary issues common to both African Americans and Mexicans in Chicago. Also in conjunction with the exhibits, the museum designed and executed a series of public programs that included lectures, public discussions, and participatory cultural events (music, dance, food).

The public programs were specifically designed to catalyze critical analysis of racial and ethnic labels, as well as discussion about the conditions of African Americans and Mexicans or people of Mexican ancestry in Chicago and possible ways in which strategic alliances between the groups might be mutually beneficial. The participatory cultural events were opportunities to learn about and celebrate aesthetic and cultural similarities. A curriculum guide for sixth- through twelfth-grade students based on the main exhibit was also developed and distributed widely to Chicago schools. The exhibit and its public programs, although controversial, were extremely well received. Museum staff reported record attendance in general and noted a huge spike in the attendance of African Americans at the facility. There is also some initial evidence that African American attendance at the museum continues to be higher than was the case in years prior to the exhibit. The exhibits and programs generated a great deal of discourse about race relations in both print and electronic media as well as among museum visitors.

Reporters from the *Chicago Tribune* said, "The exhibition asks tough questions about racial identity and politics."[7] Also, "Much here is unfamiliar to the communities treated and will be an entirely new world to other viewers who should welcome the complex lesson in cultural history."[8] A person who attended the exhibit and programs said, "This exhibition is very honest. It's the beginning of something that is healing and very productive."[9] Through cards on which museum visitors could register their responses, a visitor wrote, "The African Presence was enlightening and tragic. So many lost opportunities because of the mental illness of racism. Teach the children the truth." Another response card read, "Very provocative. I'm black and I don't think my Mexican friends would like this." Yet another card read, "African Presence—*magnifica exposición, lástima que no vi a mis compatriotas mexicanos en ella, sino unicamente African-American audience* (magnificent exhibition, what a pity that I didn't see my Mexican compatriots inside it but only an African American audience)!!!" Finally, another respondent wrote, "African Mexican exhibition was incredible. I will be sure to tell everyone I know to come. Hopefully its knowledge will contribute to building a greater relationship between African-Americans and Mexicans."

More than 500 school groups totaling 15,000 K–12 students attended the exhibition. Admission to the museum is free, and most public programs were also free of charge. The exhibit went on to tour major cities in the United States and Mexico. Public programs were created to address local issues in the cities the exhibit visited. The effort has also led to the creation of an annual Martin Luther King–Cesar Chavez luncheon, which boasts attendance of six hundred participants, to bring attention to common issues between the African American and Mexican communities in Chicago and to catalyze alliances among leaders from both communities.

The "African Presence in Mexico" exhibit and related programming was several years in the making. The museum had organized trips in which African American cultural and civic leaders as well as local funders from Chicago and museum staff traveled to Veracruz and other regions of Mexico where Mexicans of African descent have lived for hundreds of years with many African cultural retentions intact. The trips were essential in getting Chicago African American leaders and Mexican American staff to come face to face with evidence of the African legacy in Mexico. This legacy, which is not emphasized in the Mexican or U.S. educational systems, is unknown to many Mexican Americans and was not, until the early 1990s, even, officially acknowledged by the Mexican government.[10] In 2004, two years prior to the exhibition, the museum organized a steering committee comprising mostly African American local leaders (some of whom had participated in the trips to Mexico) and museum staff to advise on creation of the exhibits and programs.[11] The committee and museum staff took pains to think through language choices on sensitive issues in exhibit didactics and in text for exhibit literature as well as the presentation of controversial or particularly significant imagery in the exhibits themselves. The committee also ensured that a key function of the public programs was providing opportunities for audiences to further explore new ideas, questions, and emotions that emerged from viewing the exhibits.

In the Central Valley region of California, the Tamejavi Festival is an event celebrating the diversity of the region, where different cultures, including Hmong, Cambodian, South Asian, Latino, Mixteco (indigenous people from the Oaxaca region of Mexico), Pakistani, African immigrants, African Americans, Native Americans and Anglos, meet.[12] The groups intentionally come together through art and cultural activity—including community theater, comedy, music, dance, film, crafts, and food—to share their individual cultures with other groups in the Valley. Plays about the origins of the groups in the Valley are often written and performed by Valley residents, with the involvement of professional playwrights and other theater professionals who facilitate the process. Performances have involved both amateur and professional artists, including youth dance troupes that perform traditional music and dances from the various ethnic groups as well as performance artists such as Tou Ger Xiong—a Hmong comedian and hip hop artist whose work deals with being Hmong, Hmong American and refugee experiences, as well as with building intergenerational, interethnic and interracial alliances.[13]

During these festivals, as part of and in addition to enjoying cultural exchange, participants have opportunities to engage in conversations and forums about important issues in the Valley, such as health, education, political mobilization, economic opportunity, and environmental issues, as well as needs and concerns in the different communities' places of origin. Occurring about every two years, the festivals are the result of ongoing grassroots community organizing efforts among various immigrant groups in the Valley. The festivals are free of charge and organized by the Central Valley Partnership for Citizenship Civic Action Network.[14] This network consists of more than one hundred grassroots groups from the Valley, plus the Pan Valley Institute of the American Friends Service Committee.[15] Over the years, Tamejavi has grown from a three-day event to a year-round learning community comprising people of all ages, "artists and organizers, chiefs and healers, educators and students."[16] Yearlong activities include workshops, forums, and exhibits, as well as cultural exchanges in which the different ethnic groups in the Valley make overtures to one another for fellowship and exchange. The idea of yearlong cultural exchanges emerged from Tamejavi participants' desire to learn more about each other's culture— history, music, dance, and food—as well as the ways in which they are dealing with key issues in the Valley. The festival and yearlong activities are supported in part by the City of Fresno, local businesses, radio stations, and community and national foundations.

The examples presented here do not represent an exhaustive review of the kinds of arts and cultural activity that contribute to diverse communities; nor do they pretend to be a detailed examination of the construction of racial and ethnic identity. [17] Rather, they provide planners and policymakers concerned with fostering and sustaining diversity with potentially new ways of thinking about how to go about their work.

Implications for Planners and Policymakers

So what are the implications of this kind of activity for planners and policymakers concerned with fostering and sustaining racial and ethnic diversity in American communities?

First, arts and cultural activity as described here is an essential component of a healthy diverse community. That is, cultural vitality—evidence of a community's capacity to create, disseminate and validate arts and culture as part of everyday life—matters and needs to be nurtured and sustained if diversity is to flourish (Jackson et al. 2006). On a related note, old concepts of arts and culture—that (1) limit the notion of participation to just audience participation rather than the full range of ways in which people engage; (2) have the idea that an artist is the anonymous producer of an artistic good rather than the catalyst that helps people make meaning out of their artistic experience; and (3) believe in art for art's sake only rather than art as an activity that can hold multiple meanings and value simultaneously—get in the way of revealing cultural assets in communities and the roles they play, particularly as they relate to fostering diversity. Such limited notions need to be traded in for new assumptions about cultural participation, the possible roles of artists, and the strong connections of arts activity to other community priorities and processes, including the construction of racial and ethnic identity and fostering genuine diversity—the creation of communities that celebrate difference and ultimately lead to intergroup understanding and compassion. Such diversity can contribute to important social changes and lead to more equitable distribution of resources and opportunity.

Second, for groups that are not of the dominant culture, ethnic-specific activities and spaces are essential to nurturing diversity. Planners and policymakers should ensure that this kind of activity is present and supported in communities.[18] Ethnic-specific activities and spaces are central to the process of fostering cultural vitality in communities for several reasons. There was consensus among many respondents that these types of entities made possible genuine cultural expression—on a community's own terms. They provide the context in which people make sense of who they are individually and as a group, and how they fit into history and into the broader society. These are the contexts in which people are able to challenge imposed labels (e.g., Black, White, Latino, Asian, Native American) and figure out how they relate to them. For many people from ethnic groups that have been historically oppressed within the U.S. context, involvement in ethnic specific cultural activity provides a means not only for commemorating their history but for repairing and rebuilding their roots in the United States, as well as strengthening or re-establishing their historic ties to nations and places of origin. These activities are often also connected to other interests including education, youth and leadership development, community organizing, economic development and even health. Ethnic-specific cultural activity and spaces also play another role, by making it possible for people to step out into a diverse world with a history and a strong core, with something special to bring to the table.[19]

Third, while ethnic-specific spaces and activities, which can be exclusive and private, are necessary for diversity to thrive, activities and spaces that are public and permeable by outsiders are also necessary. So, there is a need for common spaces where people can come together on an equal footing—a cultural commons where diverse groups can showcase what they have to offer and also sample what others bring, where diversity is publicly validated. The presence of such spaces—whether they are parks, civic centers, or other publicly accessible gathering places—take on more importance when this is kept in mind. In these contexts cultural exchange often happens, and fusion and innovation can be further stimulated. In many cities, examples of this take the form of world festivals held in parks or communal public spaces—as is the case for the culminating celebration of the first Tamejavi Festival, which took place at a downtown theater and an adjacent facility and subsequently in other accessible spaces. Other examples of common spaces include the Los Angeles County Music Center through its Active Arts initiative, an innovative effort where amateur arts practitioners are encouraged to participate in different kinds of dance or music in a common public, civic space that serves to validate amateur practice in a range of artistic expression that bridges and supports the diversity of the region.[20]

In addition to this neutral ground, which is important, there is a need for a different kind of communal space. This is the communal space that is periodically made available by invitation of the ethnically specific group hosting others—as was the case with the National Mexican Arts Museum in Chicago, the Tamejavi communities during their cultural exchanges throughout the year, and some of the ethnic-specific arts organizations mentioned earlier in this chapter.

Sometimes, it is only in such a context that deeper exchange can happen—like the exchange that happens when people meet at the host's home as opposed to meeting at a generic restaurant. Many groups, if not most, ultimately are willing and even desire to share culture with a broader public in terms that the host group can control. For example, many culturally specific arts practices culminate in festivals or events to which the wider public is encouraged to come, often on that community's home turf. Even in the preparatory activity leading to the public culminating event, there is in many cases room for "outsiders." In other cases, the preparatory activity is more private. Sometimes it involves intra-group fellowship and even spiritual renewal. For example, according to the head of the Fund for Folk Culture, which provides support to several Native American basket-making organizations, at most several daylong gatherings, while most of the time is private for members of the group, at least one day is open to the public and is very explicitly about engaging people who are not of the group hosting the event.[21]

A fourth implication for planners and policymakers is that the ways in which arts and cultural activity reveal differences in world view based on race, ethnicity, class, nativity, citizenship status, and other factors highlight the inadequacy of the binary black–white model, still prevalent in socioeconomic analyses of communities. The racial and ethnic makeup of U.S. communities is much more complicated and nuanced than the old paradigms take into account. Even pan-ethnic labels that go beyond the black–white paradigm—to include Asian and Latino—must be unpacked, and policymakers must be judicious about when differences *within* these groups matter a great deal and when they matter less. Group identity as revealed through cultural activity can provide crucial insights into this issue.

Last, while a diverse society that celebrates difference and promotes compassion is certainly something that we should strive for as a society, the quest for diversity and the state of being in a diverse society are not always comfortable. It is imperative to recognize that true racial ethnic diversity, which requires the affirmation and critical examination of racial ethnic identity and the building of bridges among groups that may be at odds with each other, takes time, will, focused intention, and resources.

Notes

The author thanks Josephine Ramirez, Betsy Peterson, and Florence Kabwasa-Green for their input and Felicity Skidomore for her thoughtful and invaluable editorial assistance.

1. The Arts and Culture Indicators Project (ACIP), an effort to document arts and culture in communities and integrate arts and culture data into quality-of-life measurement systems, is the main study from which this chapter draws. Field research for this project has included more than three hundred in-person interviews and forty focus group discussions around the United States. Participant observation of arts and cultural activity has included attendance at local festivals, school-based arts events, ongoing workshops at cultural centers, ethnic organizations, and community centers; park-based programming; and participation in community cultural events sponsored by a range of arts organizations. The project

has operated with partners in Boston; Providence, Rhode Island; Cleveland; Chicago; Washington, D.C.; Denver; and Seattle; and in Oakland, Los Angeles County, and the Central Valley region in California. ACIP-related research has also been conducted in New York, New Orleans, Minneapolis, and other U.S. cities. ACIP is based at the Urban Institute and has been supported by the Rockefeller Foundation since the project's inception in the late 1990s. Other Urban Institute research projects that have informed this work include *Investing in Creativity: A Study of the Support Structure for U.S. Artists* (Washington, D.C.: Urban Institute), available online at http://www.urban.org/publications/411311.html; *The Participation Project: Artists, Communities and Cultural Citizenship,* a study of art making in communities and the role that professional and amateur artists play in community arts and cultural practices conducted by the Getty Research Institute in collaboration with the Urban Institute (see Participation Project, available online at http://www.getty.edu/research/scholarly_activities/events/participation/partproj.html); and *Cultural Dimensions of Transnational Communities,* a study of cultural participation among immigrant populations with interests and presence in the United States and countries of origin, conducted in collaboration with the Center for the Study of Urban Poverty at the University of California, Los Angeles.

2. This is based on findings from field research that included interviews and focus group discussions that were part of ACIP. Findings from this field research were largely confirmed in survey research on arts and cultural participation undertaken as part of the evaluation of the Community Partnerships for Cultural Participation Project supported by the Wallace-Reader's Digest Fund.

3. The terms "Pilipino" and "Filipino" are currently interchangeable when used to refer to the group of people. In the remainder of this chapter I will use the former term, which is consistent with the name of the organization referenced--Search to Involve Pilipino Americans (SIPA).

4. Interview with Joel Jacinto, executive director, SIPA. 2006

5. Freedom schools, organized by a range of local sponsors, are summer and after school enrichment programs that include academic enrichment, social action, leadership development, and health services. Many of these programs have Afro-Centric cultural components that incorporate art and cultural practices often using music, dance and other art forms intended to instill racial ethnic pride.

6. The mission of the National Museum of Mexican Art is "to stimulate and preserve knowledge and appreciation of Mexican culture through sponsoring events and exhibitions that exemplify the rich variety of visual and performing arts in the Mexican culture; to develop a significant permanent collection of Mexican art; to encourage the professional development of Mexican artists; and to offer arts education programs."

7. Oscar Avila, "Africans in Mexico: A blunt history; Pilsen museum opens ambitious exhibition, asking tough questions about racial identity south of the border," *Chicago Tribune,* February 8, 2006.

8. Alan Artner, "Tracing African Role in Mexican Culture." *Chicago Tribune,* February 23, 2006.

9. Quoted in Dani Garcia, "Chicago museum explores Mexico's African ancestry." *Daily Northwestern.* Evanston, Illinois. February 16, 2006.

10. In 1992, the Mexican government recognized Africa as the "third root" heritage of Mexico, along with Spanish and Indigenous heritages. Africans began arriving in Mexico through forced immigration in the early 1500s: Mexican Fine Arts Center Museum, "The African Presence in Mexico Report," 2006.

11. I served on the steering committee in 2004–2006. The "African Presence in Mexico: From Yanga to the Present" exhibition ran from February to September 2006.

12. "Tamejavi" is a word that was created by Central Valley organizers, activists, and artists who put together the sounds and symbols of three different languages (Hmong, Spanish, and Mixteco) to represent a community *marketplace TAJ* Laj Tshav Puam, *MErcado, NunJAVI*: Temejavi Festival press release, March 13, 2002.

13. See Gohmongboy.com.

14. "The Central Valley Partnership for Citizenship (CVP) is a collaboration of community organizing, legal assistance, popular education, social service, media, youth empowerment, and applied research organizations spanning California's Central Valley. Since 1996, CVP partners have launched campaigns and implemented programs to assist migrants, immigrants, and refugees organizing to claim their rightful place in the civic, cultural, and economic life of the Valley. The CVP supports Valley communities working together to achieve social and institutional change—change that provides the opportunity for all who reside in the Valley to live in dignity and good health, participate fully in decisions that affect their lives, and assume the rights and responsibilities of citizenship in its broadest sense." Central Valley Partnership for Citizenship website, available online at http://www.citizenship .net/index.shtml.

15. "The Pan Valley Institute (PVI) creates a place for immigrants and refugees to gather, learn from each other, and rebuild their world. Inspired by the historic Highlander Institute in Tennessee, which served as an important training base for the civil rights movement of the mid-twentieth century, the Pan Valley Institute brings grassroots leaders together from many communities to work together for more immigrant participation in the life of the Valley and of our nation": Pan Valley Institute website, available online at http://www.afsc.org/pacificmtn/fresno.htm.

16. See the website at http://www.tamejavi.org/tamejavi-news.htm.

17. Scholarly work about the construction of identity appears in the fields of cultural studies and psychology. The field of cultural studies is concerned with the meanings and uses people attribute to various objects and everyday practices.

18. While the existence of such spaces and programs is important, it is worth noting that accurately monitoring the presence of these types of entities poses a particularly challenging methodological issue for people concerned with measuring community amenities and quality of life. The ethnic-specific activity discussed here takes place in a wide range of venues, and there is no comprehensive, centralized database on such entities. That said, efforts to identify some way of measuring the extent to which activity of this sort is present in communities continue through ACIP.

19. This is consistent with sentiments expressed in the Convention on the Protection and Promotion of the Diversity of Cultural Expressions of the United Nations, Educational, Scientific and Cultural Organization (UNESCO 2005).

20. Interview with Josephine Ramirez, vice president of programming, Los Angeles County Music Center, 2007.

21. Interview with Betsy Peterson, executive director, Fund for Folk Culture, 2007.

References

Cashin, Sherryll. 2004. *The Failures of Integration: How Race and Class Are undermining the American Dream.* New York: PublicAffairs Books.

DeSouza Briggs, Xavier. 2005. *The Geography of Opportunity: Race and Housing Choice in Metropolitan America.* Washington, D.C.: Brookings Institution.

Florida, Richard. 2002. *The Rise of the Creative Class.* New York: Basic Books.

Jackson, Maria Rosario, and Joaquin Herranz. 2002. *Culture Counts in Communities: A Framework for Measurement.* Washington, D.C.: Urban Institute.

Jackson, Maria Rosario, and Florence Kabwasa-Green. 2006. *Artists' Space Development: Making the Case and Assessing Impacts.* New York: Leveraging Investments in Creativity.

Jackson, Maria Rosario, Florence Kabwasa-Green, and Joaquin Herranz. 2006. *Cultural Vitality in Communities: Interpretation and Indicators.* Washington, D.C.: Urban Institute.

Putnam, Robert D. 2000. *Bowling Alone: The Collapse and Revival of American Community.* New York: Simon and Schuster.

Rawlings, Lynnette, Laura Harris, and Margery Austin Turner. 2004. *Race and Residence: Prospects for Neighborhood Integration.* Washington, D.C.: Urban Institute.

Taylor, Garth. 2007. "What Is Cultural Vitality? How Is It Measured?" Presentation at the Community Indicators Consortium Conference, Jacksonville, Fla.

United Nations Educational, Scientific and Cultural Organization (UNESCO). 2005. "Convention on the Protection and Promotion of the Diversity of Cultural Expression." Paris: UNESCO.

Wali, Alaka, Rebecca Severson, and Mario Longoni. 2002. *Informal Arts: Finding Cohesion, Capacity and Other Social Benefits in Unexpected Places.* Chicago: Center for Arts Policy, Columbia College.

Walker, Chris, and Stephanie Scott-Melnyk. 2002. *Reggae to Rachmaninoff: How and Why People Participate in Arts and Culture.* Washington, D.C.: Urban Institute.

9

Commonality in Values across the Racial Divide

PATRICIA GURIN, GERALD GURIN, JOHN MATLOCK,
AND KATRINA WADE-GOLDEN

The concept of integration, to the extent that is applicable at all in the twenty-first century, must be broadened and made more complex than it was when *Brown v. Board of Education of Topeka* (1954) reflected a growing national understanding of integration. Then, integration primarily meant desegregating previously segregated schools by court mandated busing and other mechanisms to put black and white students into the same schools. The rationale for integration that was laid out in *Brown v. Board of Education* focused almost exclusively on the academic and self-concept costs that African American children suffered because of segregation. There was practically no concern with expected benefits that white children might enjoy by going to school with African American children, nor a concern with possible benefits that other racial groups might receive from desegregated schooling. In contrast, the defendants and their *amici* in the University of Michigan's recent affirmative action court cases heard by the U.S. Supreme Court stressed a *societal-wide* benefit—namely, that democracy, national security, and the health of the nation's mainstream institutions would be strengthened by racial/ethnic diversity in higher education.

The *amicus* briefs in *Gratz et al. v. Bollinger et al.* (2003) and *Grutter et al. v. Bollinger et al.* (2003) represent a broad conception of integration—that all Americans benefit by interacting with each other, and that higher education is a critical institution for assuring this kind of integration because of widespread, and in many places increasing, racial/ethnic segregation in K–12 schools. Most students entering colleges and universities today have grown up and attended schools in racially segregated environments. The arguments that were made in the affirmative action cases moreover concerned many racial/ethnic groups rather than the exclusive preoccupation in *Brown v. Board* with black–white relationships. Students in K–12 and in higher education will learn to understand the perspectives of students from many groups and become better citizens who are able to interact with people from many racial/ethnic backgrounds.

It is evident in these two famous court cases that a major shift has occurred in what integration might mean in the twenty-first century—a more complex, nuanced picture of the relationships among many racial/ethnic groups in American society and not just an assimilationist depiction of one-way integration of African Americans into the white majority.

The large demographic shifts that were put in place by the 1965 immigration policy that has produced largely Asian, Latin American, and other non-white immigration, as well as by higher fertility rates among some of these groups as compared to white Americans, have rendered the old conception of integration grossly inadequate for contemporary America. In 1999, African Americans were 12.1 percent of the U.S. population; Hispanics, 11.5 percent; Asian or Pacific Islanders, 3.8 percent; American Indian or Alaskan Natives, less than 1 percent. The majority of the population, approximately 72 percent, was white. However, current projections are that the nation's Hispanic and Asian populations will triple by 2050, and that even by 2020 Hispanics will be 18 percent, Asian Americans or Pacific Islanders 7 percent, with African Americans remaining a similar proportion as at the turn of the century, while the white, non Hispanic population will decrease to approximately 61 percent (U.S. Bureau of the Census 2004). Whites already are no longer the majority in California, Hawaii, New Mexico, and Texas. Five other states—Maryland, Mississippi, Georgia, New York, and Arizona—will be next as "majority-minority states," as they already have minority populations of about 40 percent (Bernstein 2005). What integration means in the twenty-first century thus has to involve relationships among all of these groups. Integration clearly must be as much about white Americans living in integrated ways with members of other racial/ethnic groups as about the old conception of minority groups integrating *into* white America.

The central question that follows from these demographic shifts is what kind of society will the United States be? Will all of these new immigrants and the diverse population that make up the United States become transformed into "one America" where cultural identities no longer matter in how individuals live and relate to one another? Whatever the longing for this colorblind vision of the United States that is expressed by some critics of multiculturalism (Schlesinger 1998) and by the lawyers and *amici* opposing affirmative action in the University of Michigan cases, it is improbable that this vision is realistic because of the demographic diversification of the United States. A second vision for society depicts totally separate racial/ethnic communities that interact rarely; and when they do interact, their intergroup relationships are characterized by guardedness, distrust, and hostility. Despite widespread racial and ethnic segregation both regionally and residentially within regions and cities, this vision, too, is unlikely to characterize intergroup relations in the twenty-first century. Already there are many settings in the United States, especially work settings, where interaction across race and ethnicity has to take place.

A third vision, which lies somewhere between these two polar conceptions, is a complex, pluralistic America in which different racial/ethnic and immigrant groups share some core ideas about democracy and fundamental values about work and family even as they preserve distinctive cultural identities. This vision provides a picture that is consonant with the one that Bobo and Johnson (2000) paint of contemporary multiracial Los Angeles, in which interracial/interethnic conflict exists but so, too, do cooperation and integration across racial/ethnic lines. It is a picture of both conflict and cooperation varying at different times and in different settings. They (and many other analysts; see Stephan and Stephan 1996, 2001) stress the highly situational nature of ethnic and racial relations, differing for example between the coasts and the Midwest, and varying across urban, suburban and rural areas, across particular states, different economic circumstances, age groups, and immigrant generations.

The Importance of Perceived Commonality

Perceptions of commonality across racial/ethnic groups play a critical role in all of these visions of America. The colorblind ideal assumes that all groups share common, if not identical, values. The separatist conception emphasizes differences, and even where commonality might exist, class and racial hierarchies prevent people from discerning or expressing them. The pluralist vision, while complicating what commonalities might mean and what role they might play in different situations where racial/ethnic groups interact, assumes that both commonalities and differences can fit within a sustainable, vital democracy.

Commonality is also a central idea in most social psychology theories about intergroup contact. These theories (Brewer and Kramer 1985; Gaertner and Dovidio 2000; Hewstone and Brown 1986; Stephan and Stephan 2001) are indebted to Allport's (1954) arguments about intergroup contact—namely. that for contact to reduce prejudice and discrimination, groups must cooperate with each other toward *common goals*. Moreover, contact must involve groups with equal status in the situation and allow members to get to know each other individually and to discover their common *humanity*. Finally, contact must be supported by relevant authorities and must lead to a sense of *common interests*. Following Allport, these three kinds of commonality—goals, interests, and sense of humanity—are critical in explaining whether contact will be positive or negative.

Allport's theorizing and subsequent theories that have built upon his work involve *interpersonal commonalities*—how individual members of groups come to view other individuals within and between groups as a function of the particular conditions under which they interact with each other. In the social psychology of intergroup relations there has been practically no attention to how members of groups interacting with each other think of the commonalities that *their groups have with each other.* While we do not discount the importance of interpersonal commonalities, we have emphasized how members of groups think about *group-based commonalities in core values about family and work.*

In this paper, we focus on how four groups of former University of Michigan students—African American, Latino/a, Asian American, and white—during their senior year and again as graduates nine years later responded to a question about group-based commonalities: "Think about important values in life such as values about work and family. How similar or different are your group's values and those of the following groups (African Americans, Asian Americans, Hispanics/Latinos, and White Americans)?"

We first examine if the perceptions of group-based commonalities as seniors persist into the adult world. We then use the perceptions of group-based commonalities expressed by three groups—African Americans, Asian Americans, and whites—to predict two aspects of their lives nine years later after college. [1]

First, in what ways did the views of African American, Asian American, and white seniors predict how racially/ethnically integrated their lives actually are as adults—where they live, work, and worship; how integrated their community involvements are; and how much and what quality intergroup contact they have as adults?

Second, did their perceptions of group-based commonalities as seniors predict the political perspectives they hold as adults?

After addressing these questions, we turn to how perceptions of group-based commonalities are formed. We are interested in the role that college experiences with diverse peers played in increasing (or decreasing) their sense of commonality with different racial/ethnic groups over the four years in college.

Previous Work

We have already reported some analyses of the correlates and implications of the perceptions of commonality that these University of Michigan alumni hold (Gurin et al. 2007). In that work we dealt only with the alumni data, whereas in this article we focus on the *predictive* role of perceived commonalities in the senior year for later indicators of integration and political perspectives.

The most important conclusion from our previous work on group-based commonalities, and the work of other analysts and conclusions drawn from national opinion polls, is the crucial significance of the racial/ethnic fault line that distinguishes African Americans and Latinos/as from whites and to some extent Asian Americans on some critical viewpoints about inequality and other central features of American society. For example, Bobo and colleagues (Bobo 2001; Bobo and Johnson 2000; Bobo and Massagli 2001) have shown that the stereotypes that African Americans, Latinos/as, Asian Americans, and whites in Los Angeles hold about each other reflect the racial fault line. On a stereotype index that summarizes across six qualities that often represent group stereotypes (wealth, intelligence, preference for self-support versus living on welfare, English language ability, involvement in drugs and gangs, and tendencies to discriminate against other groups), all groups considered whites and Asian Americans to be reasonably close to each other and different from Latinos/as and African Americans, who in turn were considered fairly similar on this index.[2] The four groups also differed in their racial/ethnic political policy preferences along this same division, which Bobo and colleagues claim does not reflect only the Los Angeles political culture because national polls show similar differences.

In an interesting, recent example of these racial/ethnic differences, reactions to the response of government to Hurricane Katrina in the fall of 2005 confirm a huge division between African Americans and whites, the two groups that typically anchor the two sides of the racial divide in political opinions. A Pew Research Council poll of one thousand adults conducted in September 2005 revealed "a huge racial divide in perceptions of the disaster and lessons to be learned from Katrina's aftermath. For example, 71 percent of blacks say the disaster shows that racial inequality remains a major problem in the country, while a majority of whites (56 percent) feel this was not a particularly important lesson of the disaster. And while 66 percent of blacks think that the government's response to the crisis would have been faster if most of the storm's victims had been white, an even larger percentage of whites (77 percent) disagree."

The importance of the racial/ethnic divide was also evident in many of our previously reported relationships between the Michigan alumni's perceptions of group based commonalities and their political orientations that were also measured nine years after college (Gurin et al. 2007). The political meaning of perceptions of commonalities with the groups on one side of the divide differed greatly from the meaning of perceptions of commonalities with the groups on the other side. Perceived commonalities with African Americans and Latinos/as had a clear political meaning that was expressed *by all groups*. When Asian Americans, whites, and Latinos/as felt that their groups shared core values about work and family *with* African Americans, they more often viewed themselves as politically liberal; they more often attributed the causes of racial and income/wealth inequality to institutional and structural causes such as unequal quality of schooling and insufficient jobs paying more then poverty wages. They also more frequently approved of higher education policies and practices such as affirmative action and multicultural education.

This liberal and structural perspective also in general characterized the African American, Asian American, and white graduates who believed that their groups shared common values with Latinos/as (although these relationships were less consistently statistically reliable). Conversely, these results also mean that when these graduates felt that their groups had little in common with African Americans and Latinos/as, they considered themselves more conservative, and they more frequently attributed racial and economic inequality in our society to motivational, skill and other personal inadequacies of individuals. These analyses further indicated that perceived commonalities with groups on the other side of the racial/ethnic divide—commonalities with whites and to some extent Asian Americans—carried much less political significance.

In this paper, we look again at the connection between perceived commonalities and political perspectives, but this time we focus on a *longitudinal* analysis of senior perceptions as they affect adult political standpoints, instead of the cross-sectional correlations described in previous reports.

The Data

The data we analyzed come from responses of students as seniors and of those same students nine years later in the post-college world to questionnaires administered by the Michigan Student Study (MSS). The MSS was initiated to monitor students' responses to the university's major institutional commitment to racial/ethnic diversity. It surveyed all undergraduate students who entered the University of Michigan in 1990 and followed up all students of color and a large representative sample of white students as seniors in 1994. All students who answered the senior questionnaire and could be contacted (87 percent of the total) were then surveyed as alumni nine years later in 2003. The response rate to the extensive alumni questionnaire was 77 percent ($N = 1,148$).

In this paper we are using the data from the students as seniors whom we successfully contacted as alums so that conclusions we draw from analyses of both seniors and alums are based on the same people. The number in each of the three groups are: African Americans (104); Asian Americans (161); and whites (797).[3]

The graduates were equally divided between men (49 percent) and women (51 percent), and 58 percent were married. As would be expected of graduates of a major research university, the alumni, only nine years out of college, had demonstrated considerable educational and economic achievement. Three out of five had attained a master's degree, doctorate, or professional degree, and one third reported annual earnings of over $75,000 a year.

Perceptions of Group-Based Commonalities: Seniors and Alumni

Table 9.1 shows the percentages of students and alumni from the three groups who felt that their groups were more similar to than different from the other racial/ethnic groups in life values about work and family. It shows in general that both the seniors and alumni felt that there was considerable commonality in life values about work and family between their own groups and other groups. It also shows that the senior-level perceptions persisted into the adult world and actually in all but one instance *more* alums than seniors reported that their own groups were more similar than different with respect to the other groups. However, at both points in time there was a definite disparity in perceptions across the racial/ethnic divide.

TABLE 9.1   SENSE OF COMMONALITY WITH OTHER GROUPS AS SENIORS (1994) AND AS ALUMNI (2003) (percentage saying life values are "more similar than different")

	African Americans		Latinos/as		Asian Americans		Whites	
	1994, %	2003, %	1994, %	2003, %	1994, %	2003, %	1994, %	2003, %
Commonality with:								
African Americans	—	—	71	78	24	31	58	65
Latinos/as	84	84	—	—	40	51	61	69
Asian Americans	33	50	52	63	—	—	70	84
Whites	30	42	48	65	47	62	—	—

Source: Michigan Student Study.

Many more whites expressed a high level of commonality between whites and groups of color than African Americans, Latinos/as, and Asian Americans believed that their groups had with whites. The size of this effect was about the same when the respondents were seniors and when they were alumni. Whites seem to imagine a racial/ethnic situation in the United States that has considerably more value concordance than do members of these other groups, and this may reflect the greater conviction among whites than among others that the United States is basically a colorblind society (Richerson and Nussbaum 2003). Another indicator of the racial/ethnic divide shows that at both points in time African Americans felt the greatest amount of commonality in life values with Latinos/as, and who in turn felt the greatest commonality with African Americans. In contrast, whites expressed the greatest commonality with Asian Americans, and Asian Americans did as well with whites.

Adult Lives and Attitudes toward Cross-Racial/ Ethnic Interactions: How Integrated?

We examined many aspects of the alumni's adult lives. We focus here on five categories of adult involvements and attitudes/motivations that might reflect integration across racial/ethnic lines:

- How integrated were their neighborhoods, current friendships, work settings, places of worship, and social/community groups (for white graduates, less exclusively white people; for graduates of color, less exclusively people of color).
- How much interaction did they currently have with African Americans, Asian Americans, Latinos/as, and white people.
- How positive or negative were their interactions with the racial/ethnic group with which they had the most interaction.
- How motivated were they to consider multiple perspectives as reflected in responses to such items as, "I sometimes find it difficult to see things from

the 'other person's' point of view"; "I try to look at everybody's side of a disagreement before I make a decision."

- How motivated were they to bridge differences as reflected in responses to such items as, "I want to bridge differences between different racial/ethnic groups"; "I like to learn about racial/ethnic groups different from my own."

In their responses to these questions, the Michigan alumni indicate a considerable degree of racial integration in their lives. For example, in response to the question that asked them to rate how much interaction they have with people from different racial/ethnic groups, about three out of four white alumni reported at least "some" interaction with African Americans, Asian Americans, and Latinos/as, with between 30 percent and 40 percent indicating "substantial" interaction. Interracial interaction was even more extensive for African Americans and Asian Americans. Reflecting the fact that whites are still a majority in our society, 84 percent of the African Americans and 92 percent of the Asian American alumni reported "substantial" interaction with whites. Also, despite the much smaller proportion of the other groups in society and thus less opportunity for interaction, two out of three Asian Americans reported at least some interaction with African Americans, and two out of five African Americans indicated at least some interaction with Asian Americans.

The question on the racial/ethnic composition of different settings in their lives indicated considerable differences between racial/ethnic groups in the degree of integration they experienced in various arenas of their lives. Asian Americans live the most racially integrated lives: 90 percent of them live in integrated neighborhoods, 80 percent work in integrated work settings, 72 percent participate in social, political, and community organizations that are multiracial, 65 percent have multiracial friendship circles, and almost half attend places of worship that are either racially integrated or predominantly white.

At the other extreme, white alumni tend to live in predominantly segregated settings in all of the arenas of their lives: 90 percent attend places of worship, 88 percent have friendships, 80 percent participate in political and community organizations, 75 percent live in neighborhoods, and 65 percent work in workplaces where the people in the setting are predominantly white. Yet, despite the predominance of whites in all of these settings, many white alumni reported, as noted above, interaction across race and ethnicity. These findings on the racial/ethnic composition of these different settings should not be surprising since they reflect the greater presence of white people in our society. But given the common complaint that it is people of color, particularly African Americans, who tend to self-segregate themselves, it is important to remember that the greatest segregation in our society still occurs among white people.

The degree of integration in the lives of the African American alumni varies greatly across settings. Only 18 percent attend places of worship and 27 percent have friendships that are racially integrated or are predominantly white. In contrast, the majority (62 percent) live in neighborhoods and work in mostly white settings (75 percent), and about half of them participate in social, political, and community organizations where the setting is integrated or mostly white.

There is also some evidence that in the two most segregated groups—whites and African Americans—there is a significant intergenerational movement toward increasing integration in their lives. In the questionnaire given to them in 1990 when they were entering the University of Michigan, they were asked about the racial/ethnic composition of the neighborhoods where they grew up. Ninety-two percent of the white students grew up in predominantly white neighborhoods, but significantly fewer (75 percent) reported living in such neighborhoods as alumni. Fifty-two percent of the African American students grew up in predominantly homogeneous neighborhoods, but this was true for only 38 percent of the alumni's neighborhoods.

What Does Perceived Commonality Foretell about Integration after College?

We turn now to the second question guiding our analyses: what do the perceptions of commonality that white, African American, and Asian American seniors expressed on two sides of the racial divide foretell about how integrated their lives turned out to be as alumni nine years after leaving college? Do the perceptions of commonality with African Americans and Latinos/as, and the perceptions of commonality with whites, have different implications for the degree of integration in their post-college lives?

To address this question on one side of the racial divide, we used the perceptions of commonality that white (and Asian American) seniors believed that their groups had with both African Americans and Latinos/as. We formed an index of perceived commonality with these two groups, and regressed this index on the five categories of alumni integration. In these regressions we also controlled for pre-college characteristics that might still have effects later in life, namely their gender, the racial composition of the high school they attended and neighborhood they grew up in, and both SAT scores and high school grade point averages. (We also constructed the same regressions on perceptions of commonality that African American seniors felt with Latinos/as in order to assess whether commonalities on this side of the fault line carried the same meaning that it did for seniors in groups on the other side of the fault line[4]).

On the other side of the racial divide, we used the perceptions of commonality that African American (and Asian American) seniors believed that their groups had with whites in regressions that also included the same control variables in predicting adult integration. Thus, for Asian Americans, whom researchers typically find positioned somewhere between whites and African Americans and Latinos, we examined the implications of perceived commonality on both sides of the racial divide.

TABLE 9.2   SENIORS' PERCEIVED COMMONALITIES PREDICTING POST-COLLEGE INTEGRATION

Indicators of Post-college Integration	Seniors' Perceived Commonality with African Americans and Latinos/as			Seniors' Perceived Commonality with Whites	
	Whites	Asian Americans	African Americans	African Americans	Asian Americans
Integration in different settings:					
Friendships				.211[a]	
Community groups	.085[a]	.245[b]			
Neighborhood			−.249[b]		
Amount of interaction with other groups:					
Latinos/as	.090[b]	.126[c]			.137[b]
Quality of interracial interactions:					
Less tense/hostile	.108[b]				
Less guarded/cautious	.112[b]			.277[b]	
More personal sharing				.242[a]	
Motivation to consider multiple perspectives	.119[b]		.217[a]		
Motivation to bridge differences	.085[a]		.224[a]		

Notes: For African Americans, the combined perceived commonality with African Americans and Latinos index reflects only perceived commonality with Latinos/as, *not* perceived commonality with other African Americans. Figures (standardized betas) are presented only for statistically significant relationships. Because of the small number of respondents, results at the $p < .10$ level of significance are included for African Americans and Asian Americans.

[a] $p < .05$

[b] $p < .01$

[c] $p < .10$

As indicated in Table 9.2, the answer to the question of how much perceived commonality at the end of college predicted the degree of integration in the lives of these alumni depended on the racial fault line.

For whites, senior perceptions of commonality with African Americans/ Latinos/as was significantly related to the white alumni's involvement in interracial/interethnic community organizations and activities, more contact with Latinos/as, greater motivation to consider multiple perspectives, and greater motivation to bridge differences. Moreover, those white seniors who felt the most commonality with African Americans and Latinos/as had *less* negative experience in the relationships with the group with which they had the most contact as alumni. They reported that these relationships were less tense/hostile and less guarded/cautious than did other white seniors in talking about the quality of their relationships with the other racial/ethnic group they interacted with the most as alumni.

For African Americans, senior perceptions of commonality on their side of the fault line, namely with Latinos/as, predicted their later motivation to consider multiple perspectives and motivation to bridge group differences. At the same time, felt commonality with Latinos/as was related for African Americans to living in neighborhoods that were *more* exclusively comprised of people of color. Perceptions across the fault line, namely with whites, also had predictive significance for post-college integration but for different dimensions of integration. African American seniors who believed that their group had a lot in common with whites later as graduates had more friends who were less exclusively people of color. They also had more positive relationships with the group with which they had the most contact as alumni. Since about 80 percent of the African American alumni mentioned white people as the group with which they had the most contact nine years after leaving college, this finding indicates that their judgments of commonality with whites at the end of college predicted having more positive interactions with whites in the post-college world.

For Asian Americans, the primary significance of perceptions of group-based commonalities as seniors was the greater participation in integrated community organizations for those who felt as seniors that Asian Americans and African Americans and Latinos/as had a lot in common. More frequent contact with Latinos/as among Asian Americans was related to felt commonality as seniors with both African Americans and Latinos/as and with whites, a finding that reflects the middle position that Asian Americans often hold along the racial divide.

Political Implications of Senior Perceptions of Group-Based Commonalities

Did the level of commonality that Michigan seniors believed that their racial/ethnic groups had with other groups reverberate in their political perspectives nine years later in the adult world? From previous work, we have demonstrated a cross-sectional correlational connection in the alumni data between perceived group-based commonalities and political perspectives. The longitudinal data that represent following the same seniors into the post-college world demonstrates a long-term connection that generally confirms the correlations we reported earlier.

We conducted the same kind of analysis described above in assessing the predictive role of senior perceived commonalities on indicators of adult-world integration. In all of these analyses we controlled for pre-college factors that might still influence these alums many years later (high school and neighborhood racial/ethnic composition, SAT, high school grade point average, and gender), and regressed the senior level perceptions of commonality on six political outcomes.

We emphasized self-definition of liberal/conservative and four other ideological dimensions that tend to divide liberals and conservatives and often distinguish whites and people of color in this country. Two focus on the critical issue of how much inequality is believed to exist and what causes inequality, specifically: (1) the extent to which racial discrimination exists or not; and (2) an institutional/structural versus individualistic analysis of poverty and wealth. In general, members of minority groups in the United States believe more than whites do that racial/ethnic discrimination still operates and helps shape the successes and failures of people of color. They also more frequently believe that various kinds of inequality are based in structural arrangements that result in minority and poor children being educated in less effective schools, and minority and poor adults having less access to adequate health care and insurance, secure employment, and adequate wages (Kluegel and Bobo 1993; Kluegel and Smith 1986).

These two ideological dimensions and liberal/conservative identification were measured as follows:

- *Denial/acceptance of the existence of racial discrimination* was measured by asking respondents to agree or disagree with four items such as: "Most people of color are no longer discriminated against in this country" (reversed), and "In the generation since the Civil Rights Movement, our society has done enough to promote the welfare of people of color" (reversed)." The response scale ranges from 1 (strongly disagree) to 5 (strongly agree) (alpha = .81).
- *Structural analysis of poverty and wealth* was assessed using eight items from Feagin's (1972) measure of systemic and individual attributions for poverty and wealth in the United States. Examples of items assessing system causes for poverty are "failure of society to provide good schools for many Americans," and "failure of private industry to provide enough jobs." Items assessing system causes for wealth are "money inherited from families" and "political influence or pull." Items assessing individual causes for poverty are: "lack of thrift and proper money management" and "lack of effort by the poor themselves." Items assessing individual causes for wealth are: "hard work and initiative" and "personal drive and willingness to take risks." High scores indicate endorsement of system causes and rejection of individual causes. The response scale ranges from 1 (very important) to 3 (not important) (alpha = .67).
- *Self-definition as liberal/conservative* was measured using the approach developed by the Institute for Social Research National Election Study, in which respondents place themselves on a continuum anchored by conservative (1 representing extremely conservative) to liberal (7 representing extremely liberal).

Another issue has been stressed especially by critics of affirmative action and multicultural education—namely, that such university policies and curricular emphases cause racial/ethnic division by bringing together unequally prepared students from different backgrounds and by drawing attention to cultural differences that presumably would otherwise not be important in social life. In their view, any focus on difference is inimical to democracy because difference leads to divisiveness, which in turn threatens the public unity that is so necessary for a healthy democracy (Bloom 1987; D'Souza 1991; Schlesinger 1998). Others of a liberal bent and people whose own racial/ethnic experiences have sensitized them to exclusivity, isolation, and invisibility believe that exposure to multicultural texts and to faculty of many cultural backgrounds and experiences are critical for educating youth to be effective citizens in a diverse democracy. They are persuaded that experience with diverse peers also promotes education for leadership and citizenship, that these are legitimate and important goals for higher education, and that affirmative action is a necessary means to assure diversity. In this perspective, divisiveness is viewed as the consequence of racial/ethnic/class inequalities rather than the result of attention to difference. It is felt that an appropriate mission of universities is to help students understand and gain skills to work effectively with conflict and racial/ethnic divisions, which are bound to exist in societies with marked racial/ethnic inequalities. We measured such views with two indices:

- *Difference and divisiveness.* Two belief statements were assessed to measure beliefs about difference and divisiveness. Both began with the phrase "The focus on/commitment to diversity in our colleges and universities," which was followed by two consequences: (1) "puts too much emphasis on differences between racial/ethnic groups"; and (2) "fosters more division among racial/ethnic groups than intergroup understanding." (Both statements were phrased to represent the perspective of critics of multiculturalism on difference, and the scores were then reversed to provide a non-divisiveness index. The scores range from 1 (strongly agree that attention to difference is divisive) to 4 (strongly agree that attention to difference is not divisive). Even with just two items, the index is reasonably internally consistent (alpha = .75).
- *Attitude toward affirmative action in higher education.* These studies span the years that affirmative action was a prominent and contentious issue on the Michigan campus. In the alumni questionnaire, attitudes toward affirmative action were measured by a scale consisting of two questions. One asked for agreement or disagreement with the statement, "Colleges should aggressively recruit more students of color." The second asked for support or opposition to the policy of considering whether an applicant was from an "underrepresented racial or ethnic group" as a factor in the college admissions decision (alpha = .80 for the two-item index).

Finally, our sixth political measure was an indicator of traditional political involvement, voting in an off-year election, in this instance the election of 2002. Many research studies and opinion polls have demonstrated that the different racial/ethnic groups in our society are sharply divided on these types of political views. The responses of the Michigan alumni reflect these differences, with white graduates generally fairly equally divided between liberal and conservative political positions, the African Americans predominantly liberal in perspective, and Asian Americans positioned somewhere between. On their self-identifications on a liberal–conservative scale, the ratio of liberals to conservatives was 41 percent to 40 percent for the white graduates, in contrast to 59 percent to 19 percent for the African Americans and 46 percent to 29 percent for the Asian Americans. While the great majority of the alumni in all racial/ethnic groups felt that some racial discrimination still exists in our society, they differed greatly on the extent to which they viewed it as a significant national problem. Eighty percent of the African Americans, in contrast to 18 percent of the whites and 34 percent of the Asian Americans "strongly disagreed" that "Most people of color are no longer discriminated against in this country." Illustrative of their different views of the significance of systemic causes of income inequality, 75 percent of the African Americans, 57 percent of the Asian Americans, and 45 percent of the whites felt that the "failure of society to provide good schools for many Americans" was a "very important" because of poverty in the United States. In their views of affirmative action, 95 percent of the African Americans, 67 percent of the Asian Americans, and 52 percent of the white alumni supported giving consideration in college admissions "to applicants from underrepresented racial or ethnic groups."

Table 9.3 shows dramatically that perceived commonality across the racial divide had different political implications for these groups of graduates.

First, we focus on white graduates. When they as seniors believed that whites had a lot in common in fundamental values about work and family with African Americans and Latinos/as, nine years later they held distinctive political viewpoints. Compared to those white seniors who felt less commonality across the racial divide, these white seniors self-identified when they were alums with being liberal rather than conservative. They more often believed that focusing on differences was not inevitably divisive or threatening to the viability of democracy. They more often analyzed inequality as resulting from institutional factors and the structuring of society rather than from individual deficiencies of individuals from different racial/ethnic groups. They more frequently believed that racial inequality exists. And they more often approved of affirmative action in higher education institutions. They also were more politically active, as represented by voting more frequently than other white graduates did in off year elections.

Turning to the group that anchors the other side of the racial divide, Table 9.3 shows that the amount of commonality that African American seniors felt with Latinos/as and with whites had more limited political significance than did the commonality judgments that white seniors had made, and that the political meaning of commonality with Latinos/as was different from the meaning of commonality with whites. For African Americans, perceived commonality with Latinos/as as seniors related to support for affirmative action and to an analysis of income equalities that stressed the importance of institutional and structural forces. In contrast, commonality with whites had the opposite political meaning, namely a more individualistic analysis of income inequality.

These different political meanings of perceived commonalities across the racial divide were especially well demonstrated in the results of the Asian American graduates. Treating them first as located on the same side as whites, the results

TABLE 9.3   SENIORS' PERCEIVED COMMONALITIES PREDICTING POST-COLLEGE
POLITICAL PERSPECTIVES

Post-college Political Perspectives	Seniors' Perceived Commonality with African Americans and Latinos/as			Seniors' Perceived Commonality with Whites	
	Whites	Asian Americans	African Americans	African Americans	Asian Americans
Liberal identification	.180[a,b]	.186[a]			
Multiculturalism not divisive	.144[a,b]	.251[b]			
Support affirmative action	.139[a,b]	.160[a]	.182[c]		−.193[b]
Structural analysis of income inequality	.111[b]	.130[x]	.201[a]	−.228[b]	−.147[c]
Existence of racial discrimination	.156[a,b]				−.204[b]
Voted in off-year election	.117[b]	.179[a]			

Notes: For African Americans, the combined perceived commonality with African Americans and Latinos index reflects only perceived commonality with Latinos/as, *not* perceived commonality with other African Americans. Figures (standardized betas) are presented only for statistically significant relationships. Because of the small number of respondents, results at the $p < .10$ level of significance are included for African Americans and Asian Americans.

[a] $p < .05$
[b] $p < .01$
[c] $p < .10$

for Asian Americans show nearly identical results as for white graduates. Those Asian American graduates who as seniors felt the most commonality with African Americans/Latinos/as later considered themselves more liberal. They more often viewed differences as non-divisive. They offered more structural/institutional explanations for poverty and wealth. They more often approved of affirmative action. They more often voted in off-year elections. In contrast to this liberal perspective of those who perceived commonality with African Americans and Latinos/as, Table 9.3 shows that Asian Americans' perceived commonality with whites predicted *less* support for affirmative action, more individualistic analyses of inequality, and greater denial of the existence of race discrimination.

Overall, these results show that all groups who believed that their groups had a lot in common with African Americans and Latinos (and just Latinos for African Americans) expressed a political ideology that included all or part of the following elements: awareness of the presence of racial discrimination; liberal identification; structural/institutional explanations for income/wealth inequalities; belief that multiculturalism is not necessarily divisive or inimical to democracy; and support for affirmative action. In contrast, although less dramatically, the results for the two groups of color showed that felt commonality with whites represented a quite different perspective, one that emphasized individual deficiencies as the primary cause of inequality, denial of discrimination, and disapproval of affirmative action.

Effects of College Experience on Perceptions of Group-Based Commonalities

Thus far, these analyses have demonstrated that senior perceptions of group-based commonalities did have import for racial/ethnic interactions, attitudes, and political perspectives nine years after these seniors left the University of Michigan. While some measures of alumni behaviors and attitudes were not related to their perceptions of commonality at the end of the college years, there were numerous significant findings across these groups of alumni.

We turn now to the question of how these senior year perceptions were formed. We focus on the impact of experience with diverse peers during the college years. We examined the effect of measures of diversity experience that were also used in the analyses that produced the expert testimony (Gurin 1999) that was part of the materials submitted by the University of Michigan to the courts in defense of its admissions policies (*Gratz et al. v. Bollinger et al.* 2003; *Grutter et al. v. Bollinger et al.* 2003). Here those measures were combined to form an index of amount and quality of cross-racial interaction during the college years. The index includes how much contact seniors reported that they had had with groups other than their own, the proportion of their six best friends at college that were from racial/ethnic groups different from their own, and how positive rather than negative their interactions were with the racial/ethnic group (other than their own) with whom they had the most contact.

Table 9.4 shows the impact of this summary index of experience with diverse peers during college on *increased* perceptions of commonality over the college years. Increased sense of commonality was determined by including in the regression analyses the freshman year perceptions along with the senior year perceptions. In addition, the pre-college control measures (neighborhood and high school diversity, SATs, high school grade point averages, as well as gender) were included in these analyses.

For whites and Asian Americans, diversity experience during college fostered greater perception of commonalities with African Americans and Latinos/as. For Asian Americans, diversity experience also resulted in greater sense of common-

---

TABLE 9.4. EFFECTS OF COLLEGE DIVERSITY EXPERIENCES ON INCREASED PERCEPTIONS OF COMMONALITY IN THE SENIOR YEAR (controlling for perceptions of commonality at college entrance)

	African Americans	Asian Americans	Whites
Seniors' perceptions of commonality with:			
African Americans and Latinos/as	.206	.165[a]	.115[b]
Whites	.201	.175[a]	—

Notes: For African Americans, the combined perceived commonality with African Americans and Latinos index reflects only perceived commonality with Latinos/as, *not* perceived commonality with other African Americans.

[a] $p < .05$

[b] $p < .01$

ality with whites. For African Americans, the effect of diversity experience was positive but not statistically reliable either in predicting an increased sense of commonality with Latinos/as or an increased sense of commonality with whites. (These relationships would have been reliable if the number of African American graduates had been as numerous as were the Asian Americans and whites.)

Overall, Table 9.4 shows that those graduates who had the most contact and the most positive and the least negative interactions with members of racial/ethnic groups other than their own became *more* aware over the college years of commonalities in work and family values with members of other racial/ethnic groups.

Conclusions

We have argued that the concept of integration must be broadened and made more complex in two ways: (1) by considering relationships for multiple groups of color and not merely for African Americans and whites; and (2) by considering relationships among these groups of color as well as between them and whites rather than merely looking at integration with whites. Our results support this argument in that associations between felt commonalities with racial/ethnic groups and integration and political perspectives of post-college life depended upon *which racial/ethnic group was being considered and on which side of the racial divide the judgments of commonality were drawn.* The impact of college experience on increasing perceptions of group-based commonalities over the college years also varied across racial/ethnic groups.

For whites, perceptions of commonalities with African Americans/Latinos/as as seniors in college predicted many aspects of more integrated and positive cross-racial relationships, and more liberal, structuralist political orientations nine years after leaving college. College experience with diverse peers, moreover, was influential in fostering felt commonalities with African Americans and Latinos/as during the college years.

For African Americans, perceptions of commonalities with whites as seniors in college was associated with friendships less exclusively with people of color as adults and also more positive and less negative cross-racial interactions. However, perceptions of commonality with whites also predicted a more individualistic analysis of inequality as alumni.

For Asian Americans, perceptions on neither side of the racial divide had much significance for adult cross-racial/ethnic interactions or attitudes, but perceptions of group-based commonalities did have political significance for the Asian American alumni. The results showed two different patterns across the racial divide, a liberal, structuralist one when Asian Americans felt commonality with African Americans and Latinos/as, and an individualistic one when they felt commonality with whites. Finally, college experience with diverse peers fostered greater sense of commonality with African Americans and Latinos/as over the college years, and with whites as well.

Does Any of This Matter?

What these seniors from different racial/ethnic groups thought about group-based commonalities at the end of their senior year in college does matter for integration. Their perceptions of commonality had implications for how much cross-racial interaction they had as alumni, how integrated their personal and public lives were as alumni, and how motivated they were to bridge differences and consider multiple perspectives. The consistency and reliability of the relationships between the senior-year group-based commonalities and these aspects of adult world integration varied as a function of the racial divide, particular groups, and across different settings, but as a whole the findings demonstrate a clear connection between group-based commonalities and some or all of these aspects of integration.

This connection was explicit in the arguments made by the many *amici* who came forward from mainstream institutions across many sectors of society on behalf of the University of Michigan in the affirmative action cases. In language reflecting their own institutional missions in society, they argued that college graduates need to consider multiple perspectives and have the cultural competence to bridge differences if they are to be effective leaders in corporations, the military, government, community organizations, and education.

The *amicus* brief submitted by the General Motors Corporation to the Supreme Court provides an example from a business perspective. To succeed in this increasingly diverse environment, American businesses must select leaders who possess cross-cultural competence—the capacities to interact with and to understand the experiences of, and multiplicity of perspectives held by, persons of different races, ethnicities and cultural histories (Brief of General Motors 2003, 4).

Second, the findings that reveal the political underpinnings of what these group-based commonalities mean have considerable import for intergroup interaction, especially when several members of two or more groups are brought together and where groups by necessity remain salient. In those situations, members of the two groups, and leaders working with the groups, need to be aware of and responsive to the different political perspectives and life experiences that are reflected in perceived group-based commonalities. Achieving interpersonal commonalities must not mask differences in group-based commonalities.

The emphasis upon commonality must not ignore power and hierarchy—the different political perspectives that are repeatedly demonstrated across the racial/ethnic divide in the United States, and the different organizational perspectives that arise because of different roles, status positions, or power within organizations. Such differences will inevitably produce conflicts even as individuals in intergroup situations learn to work cooperatively together. Commonality can be overstressed *if* political, power, and hierarchical features of commonality are ignored.

For example, the emphasis in all of the social psychological theories following Allport's classic work on intergroup contact on commonalities in goals, interests, and sense of humanity has at times resulted in too little attention to power and conflict (see Hewstone and Brown 1986 for a notable exception to this conclusion). Current work in complex systems similarly emphasizes commonalities— a common language, common world view, common commitment to solving a task—in accounting for when the presence of diverse perspectives in a work group results in greater productivity and robustness (Johnson 2005; Page 2005). Both of these disciplines use an individual framework in which individuals who hold diverse perspectives, have different roles in an organization, or come from diverse backgrounds are brought together, usually to solve a problem or complete a task, under conditions where groups are deliberately de-emphasized. Even in these conditions, however, individuals are likely to perceive others as members of groups, not *just* as individuals, and to be affected unconsciously if not explicitly by prejudices about groups and by implicit political theories that are aroused in intergroup situations.

A few examples may illuminate the problem. When individuals who work as higher education professionals in the division of students affairs are brought together with faculty in the division of academic affairs, their differences in status, power, and valuation within the academy always lurk just below the surface, potentially ready to erupt in conflict, despite both groups having a common language and worldview about the importance of the total college experience for student learning. Individuals in groups across the hierarchy of most corporations will bring some shared and some distinctive views about hierarchy, status differentials, and the position of various groups within the corporation. Those power- and hierarchy-based views need to be dealt with if the potential in diverse perspectives is to be maximally realized. Or, consider the challenge in higher education institutions of getting various student groups of color to work with each other, and with white students, on specific, common goals. Educators know that these groups often have different views of how higher education institutions respond to their groups and different perspectives on the role of race/ethnicity in the wider society. Effective intergroup collaborations and making diversity work require taking account of these different perspectives and developing skills for dealing with conflicts that may emerge because of them. Overall, our research results on the political nature of group-based commonalities support a conception of integration that, like the description Bobo and Johnson (2000) give of intergroup relations in Los Angeles, includes both conflict and cooperation and both interaction and separation at different times and in different situations.

Finally, college matters in shaping these judgments of commonality that then have implications for political views and aspects of adult lives for all of these groups. There is nothing "set" about the ways students of various groups evaluated commonalities. Instead, their interactions across race and ethnicity during college influenced how they ended up conceiving of commonalities. These findings on the impact of college support a now large literature showing positive benefits from interacting with diverse others. (Antonio 2001; Brief of the American Educational Research Association 2003; Chang et al. 2003; Hurtado et al. 2003; Nagda and Zuniga 2003; Orfield and Whitla 1999; Pettigrew 1998).[5]

Analyses of Inequality

The issue of individualistic/structural analyses of inequality is especially important in our results. When white and Asian American seniors express commonality with African Americans and Latinos/as, they also believe that discrimination continues to affect the lives of people of color, and that structural features in society, such as poor schools and problems in the labor market, are root causes of racial inequality and poverty. They also believe that wealth comes at least partly from advantages over generations. In contrast, when white and Asian American students feel that they have very little in common with African Americans and Latinos, they also more often negate the presence of structural problems that produce racial inequalities in our society. And so, too, do African American and Asian American students who feel an affinity in life values with whites. We emphasize these distinctions involving analyses of inequality because structural/ individualistic thinking is at the heart of the major divide among Americans.

Bobo (2001, 208) argues that "the centerpiece of the modern racial divide comes in the evidence of sharply divergent beliefs about the current level, effect, and nature of discrimination. Blacks and Hispanics, and many Asians as well, feel it and perceive it in most domains of life. Many Whites acknowledge that some discrimination remains, but they tend to downplay its contemporary importance." He further stresses that "minorities not only perceive more discrimination, they also see it as more 'institutional' in character. Many Whites tend to think of discrimination as either mainly a historical legacy of the past or as the idiosyncratic behavior of the isolated bigot. . . . Although many Whites recognize that discrimination plays some part in higher rates of unemployment, poverty, and a range of hardships in life that minorities often face, the central cause is usually understood to be the level of effort and cultural patterns of the minority group members themselves. For minorities, especially Blacks, it is understood that the persistence of race problems has something to do with how our institutions operate" (Bobo 2001, 281–282).

The connection between group-based commonalities and analyses of inequality is important, we believe, because this connection suggests possibilities for coalitions on both sides of the political spectrum. On the liberal side, we have learned that all groups who feel commonality with Latinos/as and African Americans—including whites—hold a structuralist perspective about both racial inequality and economic inequality that should provide a basis for a white, African American, and Asian American political coalition. *These* whites, African Americans, and Asian Americans could potentially work together with a sense of common fundamental values and a shared ideology about inequality. The opposite on the conservative side is also true. Whites who do *not* feel commonality with Latinos/as and African Americans are more conservative and more frequently hold an individualistic analysis of inequality. They could find political coalition with the much smaller group of African Americans and somewhat smaller group of Asian Americans who believe that they have much in common with whites and that inequality is largely produced by personal deficiencies of individuals. It is this inherently political meaning of group-based commonalities that we believe is most important in our results and most challenges many disciplinary conceptions of commonality as a non-political, necessary condition for positive intergroup contact.

Notes

1. We cannot use the same sense of commonality that Latinos/as have with the other three groups in these analyses because the number of Latino/a seniors and graduates in our sample is too small to generate reliable results.

2. The one exception to this conclusion is that African Americans differentiated among these four groups much less than the other groups did.

3. As mentioned earlier, the number of Latinos/as ($N = 57$) was too small to provide reliable results, and thus Latinos/as are not included in this chapter except as a group that the other three groups are asked to consider in judging group-based commonalities.

4. The survey question on perceived commonality did not ask for commonality with one's own group. Therefore, the perceptions of African Americans about Latinos/as could be used, although the index involving both African Americans and Latinos/as could not be used. It was also not possible to conduct analyses of the implications of white seniors' sense of commonality with other whites.

5. The work of Rothman and colleagues (2003) calls these studies into question. A national survey of higher education institutions shows that more diverse institutions, defined as including a larger percentage of African American students, up to 44 percent), was correlated with more negative views about the quality of education by students, faculty, and administrators. This study does not measure actual experience with diversity, however, and as we and others have stressed over and over, racial/ethnic diversity, like any other institutional resource, needs to be utilized. That is why we and most other scholars have studied the impact of actual interaction with diverse peers rather than merely whether or not campuses are diverse in their racial/ethnic composition, although it is also clear that students have more cross-racial/ethnic interaction on the most diverse campuses (Chang 2004).

References

Allport. G. 1954. *The Nature of Prejudice*. Cambridge, Mass.: Addison-Wesley.

Antonio, A. L. 2001. "The Role of Interracial Interaction in the Development of Leadership Skills and Cultural Knowledge and Understanding." *Research in Higher Education* 425: 593–617.

Bernstein, R. 2005. "Number of 'Majority-Minority' States Grows." CB05-118. Public Information Office, U.S. Bureau of the Census.

Bloom, A. 1987. *The Closing of the American Mind: How Higher Education Has Failed Democracy and Impoverished the Souls of Today's Students*. New York: Simon and Schuster.

Bobo, L. D. 2001. "Racial Attitudes and Relations at the Close of the Twentieth Century." Pp. 264–301 in *American Becoming: Racial Trends and Their Consequences*, vol. 1. Washington, D.C.: National Academy Press.

Bobo, L. D., and D. Johnson. 2000. "Racial Attitudes in a Prismatic Metropolis: Mapping Identity, Stereotypes, Competition, and Views on Affirmative Action." Pp. 81–163 in

Prismatic Metropolis: Inequality in Los Angeles, ed. L. D. Bobo, M. L. Oliver, J. H. Johnson, and A. Valenzuela. New York: Russell Sage Foundation.

Bobo, L. D., and M. P. Massagli. 2001. "Stereotyping and Urban Inequality. Pp. 89–162 in *Urban Inequality: Evidence from Four Cities,* ed. A. O'Connor, C. Tilly, and L. D. Bobo. New York: Russell Sage Foundation.

Brewer, M. B., and R. M. Kramer. 1985. "The Psychology of Intergroup Attitudes and Behavior." *Annual Review of Psychology* 36: 219–243.

Brief of General Motors Corporation as Amici Curiae in Support of Respondents. *Grutter v. Bollinger et al.,* no. 02-241 2003; *Gratz v. Bollinger et al.,* no. 02-516 2003.

Brief of the American Educational Research Association, the Association of American Colleges and Universities, and the American Association for Higher Education as Amici Curiae in Support of Respondents. *Grutter v. Bollinger et al.,* no 02-241 2003.

Chang, M. J., A. W. Astin, and D. Kim. 2004. "Cross-Racial Interaction among Undergraduates: Some Causes and Consequences." *Research in Higher Education* 45 (5), pp. 529–553

Chang, M. J., K. Hakuta, and J. Jones. 2003. *Compelling Interest: Examining the Evidence on Racial Dynamics in Colleges and Universities.* Palo Alto, Calif.: Stanford University Press.

D'Souza, D. 1991. *Illiberal Education.* New York: Free Press.

Feagin, J. R. 1972. "Poverty: We Still Believe That God Helps Those Who Help Themselves." *Psychology Today,* vol. 6, 101–129.

Gaertner, S. L., and J. F. Dovidio. 2000. "Reducing Intergroup Bias: The Common Ingroup Identity Model." Ann Arbor, Mich.: Sheridan Books

Gratz et al. v. Bollinger et al. 2003. Certiorari to the U.S. Court of Appeals for the Sixth Circuit, no. 02-516.

Grutter et al. v. Bollinger et al. 2003. Certiorari to the U.S. Court of Appeals for the Sixth Circuit, no. 02-241.

Gurin, P. 1999. "The Compelling Need for Diversity in Higher Education." Expert report prepared for *Gratz et al. v. Bollinger et al.,* no. 97-75231, B.D. Mich., and *Grutter et al. v. Bollinger et al.,* no. 97-75928, E.D. Mich., January.

Gurin, P., G. Gurin, J. Matlock, and K. Wade-Golden. 2007. "Sense of Commonality in Values among Racial/Ethnic Groups: An Opportunity for a New Conception of Integration." Pp. 115–132 in *Commemorating Brown: The Social Psychology of Racism and Discrimination,* ed. G. Adams, M. Biernat, N. Branscombe, C. Crandall, and L. Wrightsman. Washington, D.C.: American Psychological Association Books.

Hewstone, M., and R. Brown. 1986. "Contact Is Not Enough: An Intergroup Perspective on the Contact Hypothesis." Pp. 1–44 in *Contact and Conflict in Intergroup Encounters,* ed. M. Hewstone and R. Brown. New York: Blackwell.

Hurtado, S., E. L. Dey, P. Gurin, and G. Gurin. 2003. "The College Environment, Diversity, and Student Learning. Pp. 145–189 in *Higher Education: Handbook of Theory and Research,* ed. J. Smart. Amsterdam: Kluwer Academic Press.

Johnson, N. L. 2005. "Diversity: A Weapon of Mass Construction." Presentation at the Complexity of Diversity Colloquium, University of Michigan, Ann Arbor, November 10.

Kluegel, J. R., and L. Bobo. 1993. "Dimensions of Whites' Beliefs about the Black–White Socio-economic Gap." Pp. 127–147 in *Prejudice, Politics, and the American Dilemma,* ed. P. M. Sniderman, P. E. Tetlock, and E. G. Carmines. Stanford, Calif.: Stanford University Press.

Kluegel, J. R., and E. R. Smith. 1986. *Beliefs about Inequality: Americans' Views of What Is and What Ought to Be.* Hawthorne, N.Y.: DeGruyter.

Nagda, B. A, and X. Zuniga. 2003. "Fostering Meaningful Racial Engagement through Intergroup Dialogues." *Group Processes and Intergroup Relations* 61: 111–128.

Orfield, G., and D. Whitla. 2001. "Diversity and Legal Education: Student Experiences in Leading Law Schools. Pp. 143–174 in *Diversity Challenged: Evidence on the Impact of Affirmative Action*, ed. G. Orfield and M. Kurlaender. Cambridge, Mass.: Harvard Publishing Group.

Page, S. 2005. *A Logic of Diversity: Why Diversity May Trump Ability*. Ann Arbor: University of Michigan Press and Santa Fe Institute.

Pettigrew, T. F. 1998. "Intergroup Contact Theory." *Annual Review of Psychology* 49: 65–85.

Richerson, J. A., and R. J. Nussbaum. 2003. "The Impact of Multiculturalism versus Color-blindness on Racial Bias." *Journal of Experimental Social Psychology* 39: 233–239.

Rothman, S., S. M. Lipset, and N. Nevitte. 2003. "Does Enrollment Diversity Improve University Education?" *International Journal of Public Opinion Research* 151: 8–26.

Schlesinger, A. M. 1998. *The Disuniting of America: Reflections on a Multicultural Society*. New York: W. W. Norton.

Stephan, W. G., and C. W. Stephan. 1996. *Intergroup Relations*. Boulder, Colo.: Westview Press.

———. 2001. *Improving Intergroup Relations*. Thousand Oaks, Calif.: Sage.

U. S. Bureau of the Census. 2004. "U.S. Interim Projections by Age, Sex, Race, and Hispanic Origin." Available online at http://www.census.gov/ipc/www/usinterimproj.

10

Immigrant Political Empowerment in New York and Los Angeles

JOHN MOLLENKOPF

I n the decades after World War II, much of the white population moved to the suburbs, Southern blacks and Puerto Ricans moved northward, and the nation's population and employment shifted out of the old industrial heartland. In the large central cities, these trends led to a growing conflict between African Americans and the waning, but still dominant, white political elite. As a result, the literature on urban politics focused on analyzing how racial and ethnic minorities formed multiracial coalitions to challenge the old order (Browning et al. 2003; Reed 1988; Sonenshein 1994; Thompson 2005).

After 1965, however, a new trend emerged. A great wave of migration altered the nature of racial and ethnic succession in America's big cities, especially the "gateway" cities of California, New York, Texas, Illinois, Florida, and New Jersey (Frey 2003). Arriving from Mexico, Central and South America, the Caribbean, East Asia, South Asia, the Middle East, and former Soviet Union, the impact of these new residents has resembled that of the great wave of European immigration between the Civil War and 1924 and the northward migration of blacks and Puerto Ricans between 1940 and 1980. Though Mexicans predominate in Los Angeles, Cubans and Haitians in Miami, and Dominicans in New York, their arrival sets the stage for the "post–civil rights era" of urban politics. (This term does not mean that civil rights issues are no longer significant, only that they are taking new forms.)

Native-born whites with native-born parents now make up roughly a quarter of the central city population and less than half the *metropolitan* population in New York, Los Angeles, Chicago, San Francisco–Oakland, Dallas–Fort

Worth, Houston, and Miami. By themselves, metropolitan New York and Los Angeles hold two fifths of America's immigrant population. They thus make good laboratories for examining the political implications of the new urban diversity.

To be sure, these two cities differ in their racial and ethnic composition. In Los Angeles, almost three quarters of the population was born outside the United States or has at least one foreign-born parent.[1] First and second generation Mexicans make up 28 percent of the city's population, but other large groups include Central Americans (16.4 percent of the total), people from the former Soviet Union (3.4 percent), Filipinos (3.3 percent), and Koreans (3 percent). Native whites, by contrast, make up only 15.6 percent of the city's population and native African Americans another 7.8 percent. In New York City, just over half the population is first and second generation immigrants, with West Indians making up 11 percent of the total; Dominicans, 5.9 percent; Chinese, 4.4 percent; and the former Soviets and their children, 4.1 percent. (Mexicans and their children now make up 2 percent of the city's 8 million residents.) New York's immigrant population is thus more diverse, more likely to be black, more Asian, less Hispanic, and far less Mexican than that of the city of Los Angeles. Nevertheless, both cities have attracted new residents from virtually every part of the globe.

This massive demographic change is blurring traditional black–white racial distinctions in two ways. On the eastern seaboard, black and white immigrants are altering what it means to be "black" or "white." Nationally, nine out of ten whites are native-born people with two native-born parents; in New York City and Los Angeles, this is true of only just over half the whites. Similarly, almost nine out of ten of the nation's blacks are native stock, but fewer than half are in New York. Whiteness can have a Russian accent in New York, blackness a Caribbean lilt.

More fundamentally, many new immigrants, especially Latinos and Asians, are neither black nor white, but somewhere "in between." They do not fit easily into the black–white dichotomy and do not want to be pigeonholed in either category. (More that half of all Latinos told the 2000 Census that their race was "other" than black or white.) New immigrant ethnic groups like "Salvadorans," "Dominicans," "Chinese," and "Koreans" are seeking their own place in traditional urban racial geographies and are beginning to compete for influence in local politics (Falcon 1988). As a consequence, while big cities are still becoming less white, they are not becoming more African American (Frey 2003). Instead, they are becoming more diverse.

Earlier, the civil rights movement struggled to achieve political representation for African Americans, Puerto Ricans, and Chicanos. Their successes did not eliminate all demographic gaps between residents and elected officials, however. To the contrary, the gaps are reappearing in new forms. Once, native minorities faced off against the entrenched white political establishments. Today, ironically, new immigrant communities are emerging in areas represented not just by white ethnic office holders, but by African Americans, Puerto Ricans, or third generation Mexican Americans. So what do these two metropolitan areas teach us about political cleavages in urban America?

Diversity in New York City

New York has evolved from a predominantly white city in 1970 to a majority immigrant city in 2005. As native whites, blacks, and Puerto Ricans have all migrated out of the city, immigrant whites have moved in from the former Soviet Union, immigrant blacks from the Caribbean (Foner 2001; Kasinitz 1992; Waters 1999), immigrant Latinos from the Caribbean and South America (Pessar 1995; Ricourt 2002), and immigrant Asians (Kwong 1996; Zhou 1995, 2003) from China and South Asia. Barely 1 percent in 1970, the Asian population now exceeds 10 percent.

During the 1990s, these trends began to have an impact on political representation. Although native whites continue to hold more than half the seats, the City Council now includes two Dominicans, two West Indians, and one Chinese American among its fifty-one members. Given that political parties seek to shape their electorates so as to retain their hold on elective office, they have not tended to promote new immigrant candidates or mobilize new immigrant voters (Jones-Correa 2003; Shefter 1993). Nevertheless, immigrant candidates have managed to win office in New York City. On the City Council, both native whites and native blacks hold more seats than their shares of the eligible electorate (to say nothing of their even smaller shares of the total population), while the Latino share (10 of 51) lags well behind the city's Latino population (25 percent) and Asian representation (1 seat of 51) lags even farther behind the Asian population (11.3 percent).

The new immigrants have altered New York's racial and ethnic geography in several ways.[2] Russian immigrants moved into declining South Brooklyn Jewish neighborhoods like Brighton Beach. Afro-Caribbean immigrants did not settle in traditional black neighborhoods like Harlem and Bedford-Stuyvesant, but moved instead into adjoining areas like Crown Heights, Flatbush, and East Flatbush in Brooklyn; Williamsbridge and Wakefield in the Bronx; and Cambria Heights and Laurelton in Queens. Asian and Latino immigrants settled in between predominantly native white and black areas. The Chinese include not only poorly educated people from China who work in the city's restaurant and garment industries, but better educated people from Taiwan or Hong Kong who have settled in southern Brooklyn and Elmhurst and Flushing, Queens. The well-educated Koreans have gravitated to middle-class Queens neighborhoods like Bayside, while South Asians (including many Indo-Caribbeans from Guyana and Trinidad) can be found in Richmond Hill. Latino immigrants who come from countries with significant African ancestry have settled nearer black neighborhoods. While Dominicans sometimes live among Puerto Ricans, they have concentrated in Manhattan's Washington Heights, Sunset Park in Brooklyn, and Jackson Heights and East Elmhurst in Queens. (The recently arrived Mexicans now predominate in the formerly Puerto Rican neighborhood of East Harlem, or El Barrio, but are spreading rapidly through the city's other Latino neighborhoods.)

Diversity in Los Angeles

The trends that have had a profound impact on New York have even more thoroughly transformed Los Angeles (for a description, see Allen and Turner 2002). In 1970, non-Hispanic whites made up three quarters of Los Angeles County's population. By 2000, they were less than a third. Between 1970 and 2000, Los Angeles County's black population grew slightly, but its share of the total declined to less than 10 percent. Led by Mexican immigrants, the rapid rise of Los Angeles's Latino and Asian populations has prevented the city's population from shrinking. While Mexicans have long been present in Southern California, Mexican-born people made up only 3.2 percent of Los Angeles County's population in 1970, and only another 3.1 percent were natives with a Mexican father. But Los Angeles's Mexican population grew rapidly after 1970 (Acuña 1996; Gutiérrez 1995). Political turbulence also promoted migration to Los Angeles from El Salvador and Nicaragua. Finally, Chinese, Korean, Filipino, and other Asian immigrant groups have joined the small but well-established Japanese American community.

As in New York, native whites and blacks hold more Los Angeles City Council seats than their share of the population, while Latinos hold fewer and Asians hold none. Blacks are the most over-represented group, reflecting their long political history in the city, their high rate of citizenship, and the political achievements of the Tom Bradley mayoralty (Sonenshein 1994). Even as Bradley won a landslide third term in 1981, the fifteen-member Los Angeles City Council lacked a Latino member. Subsequent political struggle and litigation by Latino political activists has increased their council seats to four out of fifteen (Acuña 1996; Regalado 1998), and in 2005 Antonio Villaraigosa marked a tremendous political breakthrough by winning the mayoralty (Sonenshein and Drayse 2006). Asians are still absent from the council, however. (The City of Los Angeles is just one part of Los Angeles County. Of the five county supervisors, three are white, one is black, and one is Latina.)

New immigrant neighborhoods often stretch across the Los Angeles city line, which often seems arbitrarily drawn. (Indeed, freeways may be more important distinguishing features than the Los Angeles city border.) "West Los Angeles" includes independent cities like Santa Monica and Beverly Hills, while "East Los Angeles" extends well beyond the city line into independent municipalities like East Los Angeles and Monterey Park. Whites have lived near the beach on the West Side or north across a mountain range in the San Fernando Valley. Many have left the city, and even the Valley for Thousand Oaks and Simi Valley in Ventura County or Laguna Hills and Mission Vallejo in Orange County (Allen and Turner 2002, 13). African Americans have traditionally lived south of downtown in Crenshaw, Watts, and South Central, but they too have been moving to more suburban areas like Baldwin Hills, Hawthorne, and Lakewood, and eastward in San Bernardino County (Allen and Turner 2002, 17).

Latino populations have been growing rapidly throughout central and eastern Los Angeles County as well as the eastern end of the Valley, expanding into formerly black neighborhoods like Watts. Salvadorans have established a residential cluster in Pico-Union, just west of downtown (Allen and Turner 2002, 26–27). The rapid growth of Los Angeles's Asian population has taken place mainly outside its traditional Chinatown, Koreatown, and "Little Tokyo," moving eastward beyond the city line into Alhambra and Monterrey Park, northward to the eastern San Fernando Valley, southward toward Garden Grove and Westminster in Orange County, and in beach towns like Torrance and Palos Verdes (Allen and Turner 2002, 35–46).

As in New York, these trends have created many heterogeneous neighborhoods within a larger framework of black–white residential segregation. Once the home of Los Angeles's black community, South Central is now only a quarter black. Though blacks still form a plurality of the electorate, and African American legislators still represent the area, Latino immigrants are rapidly becoming the majority of the population in this area.

The Political Implications of Demographic Change

The white immigrants who arrived before World War I took as long as five decades to wield citywide political influence that was commensurate with their numbers. Post–World War II black migrants also took decades to begin to win mayoralties and City Council majorities. It is therefore safe to say that the new immigrants flowing into cities like New York and Los Angeles are taking their first steps on the long and sometimes difficult road to equal representation. Yet their political claims have already begun to change the nature of urban politics, especially at the neighborhood level.

Certain key factors will shape their progress:

- Their relative youthfulness and lack of citizenship restricts their weight in the electorate; new immigrant citizens may also be less likely to register, join a party, or vote, especially when living in new immigrant residential concentrations.
- The local political system may discourage immigrant candidates.
- Native white political incumbents and voters may not support new immigrant candidates.
- Native minority political incumbents and voters also may not support new immigrant candidates.

Demographic Barriers to Immigrant Political Empowerment: Age, Citizenship, Voter Registration

The citizenship among new immigrants clearly impedes their political advance. Tables 10.1 and 10.2 show the differences between their share of the general population, their share of voting age citizens, and their rate of representation on the City Councils in New York and Los Angeles.[3]

TABLE 10.1   POPULATION, ELECTORATE, AND CITY COUNCIL REPRESENTATION FOR
MAJOR ETHNIC FROUPS, NEW YORK CITY, 2005 (classified by background of head of
household)

	Popu-lation	Popu-lation, %	Voting Age Citizens	Voting Age Citizens, %	Voting Age Citizens/ Population	City Council Seats/ Voting Age Citizens, %
White natives	2,002,671	25.2	1,618,793	34.2	80.8	1.49
White immigrants	800,631	10.1	426,306	9.0	53.2	0
African Americans	1,046,158	13.1	742,028	15.7	70.9	1.25
Afro-Caribbeans	863,740	10.8	404,055	8.5	46.8	.69
Puerto Ricans	680,566	8.5	466,310	9.9	68.5	1.78
Dominicans	555,218	7.0	212,680	4.5	38.3	.87
Colombians, Ecuadorans, and Peruvians	287,359	3.6	98,672	2.1	34.3	0
Mexicans	206,752	2.6	24,530	.5	11.9	0
Chinese	403,481	5.1	214,949	4.5	53.3	.44
Indians	184,014	2.3	77,073	1.6	41.9	0
Koreans	86,167	1.1	39,007	.8	45.3	0
Total	7,962,148	100.0	4,730,788	100.0	59.4	

Source: 2005 American Community Survey.

TABLE 10.2   POPULATION, ELECTORATE, AND CITY COUNCIL REPRESENTATION FOR
MAJOR ETHNIC GROUPS, CITY OF LOS ANGELES, 2005 (classified by background of head
of household)

	Population	Population, %	Voting Age Citizens	Voting Age Citizens, %	Voting Age Citizens/ Population	City Council Seats/ Voting Age Citizens, %
White natives	812,878	21.8	637,491	48.8	78.4	1.09
White immigrants	282,789	7.6	29,714	2.3	10.5	0
African Americans	335,937	9.0	244,947	18.8	72.9	1.06
Mexicans	1,069,646	28.7	193,229	14.8	18.1	1.80
Salvadorans	204,849	5.5	17,226	1.3	8.4	0
Guatemalans	166,177	4.5	7,523	.6	4.5	0
Chinese	62,110	1.7	15,787	1.2	25.4	0
Filipinos	121,323	3.3	12,231	.9	10.1	0
Koreans	101,473	2.7	5,927	.5	5.8	0
Total	3,729,871	100.0	1,771,912	100.0	49.0	

Source: 2005 American Community Survey.

Looking at the columns in these tables that show how much of a given population is eligible to vote, it is clear that native whites and blacks enjoy a substantial
advantage over the new immigrant groups, which carries over into their greater
representation on the City Councils. In New York, this advantage helps all native-
born groups—particularly Puerto Ricans—to hold offices at much higher levels
than their presence in the population. In Los Angeles, third generation Mexican
Americans have a very substantial advantage over more recent Latino immigrant

groups. (Note, however, that Dominicans have done better in New York than the non-Mexican Latino groups in Los Angeles.) Finally, even though Asian groups have higher citizenship rates than the Latino immigrant groups in both cities, they have achieved less representation.

In both cities, white voters cast about half the 2004 presidential election ballots, despite being a small minority of the population. *Native stock* whites cast only a third of the votes, but white immigrants who have become citizens bolster their strength. Similarly, blacks cast far more of the votes (24.2 percent in New York and 18.4 percent in the city of Los Angeles) than their shares of the electorate, and far more than their shares of the population. Latinos and Asians cast less votes than their share of the eligible electorate.

Despite enjoying an electoral advantage, native whites and blacks are a diminishing political force in both cities because their share of the population has been declining rapidly. Meanwhile, the new immigrant groups are steadily growing older, becoming naturalized, and beginning to vote. Their native-born children are also reaching voting age. These demographic processes will inevitably continue to alter politics in both cities. (The November 2004 Current Population Survey measuring participation in the last presidential election suggests that first, second, and 2.5 generation voters cast 44 percent of the ballots in New York City and just over 50 percent in Los Angeles.)

Political Barriers to Immigrant Political Empowerment: The Political and Electoral Systems

While the local election machinery in New York and Los Angeles takes steps to provide information to voters in a variety of languages, the political parties of the two cities have not made any special efforts to encourage eligible immigrants to register and vote. Office-holders, political parties, labor unions, and issue advocacy organizations tend to focus on "prime voters" whose voting patterns they can predict, not new voters whose choices may not favor them. Since immigrant voters are typically new, often first time voters, and since many have not affiliated with a political party, incumbents often overlook them. (In both cities, however, non-partisan immigrant advocacy organizations, like the New York Immigration Coalition, have sought to mobilize immigrant voters.)

The political cultures of New York and Los Angeles differ greatly. Although New York elections have low turnout by national standards, more people vote in its partisan general elections than in Los Angeles's nonpartisan, "reformed" system. New York's strong public campaign finance program has drawn minority and immigrant candidates into local elections. Los Angeles has more expensive races for larger districts. Since Democratic nominees win most New York City elections, and since native-born and immigrant minority voters both make up a greater share of Democratic registered voters than total registered voters, New York's partisan system can also enhance the impact of minority voters, somewhat offsetting their relative youth and lack of citizenship. In Los Angeles, the non-

TABLE 10.3   VOTER PARTICIPATION, NEW YORK AND LOS ANGELES, 2001

	New York	Los Angeles
General election votes	1,519,517	469,037
Registered voters	3,737,533	1,537,787
Actual votes as a percentage of registered voters	40.7	30.5
Primary election votes[a]	780,401	394,998
Primary registered voters[a]	2,532,773	1,537,787
Actual votes as a percentage of registered voters[a]	30.8	25.7
Voting age population	6,040,079	2,712,172
Voting age citizens	4,671,332	1,851,325
Voting age citizens as a percentage of voting age population	80.0	83.1

[a] Democratic primary only for New York; 66,531 out of 475,058 registered Republicans (14 percent) participated in the Republican mayoral primary.

Source: Center for Urban Research, Board of Elections, U.S. Census 2000, 1% Public-Use Micro-data Samples file.

partisan electoral system may reinforce minority disadvantage by putting more weight on fundraising and access to mass media.

New York City government also delivers a vast array of public services, while the City of Los Angeles concerns itself with property related services, leaving the County of Los Angeles to deliver social services and the separately elected Los Angeles Unified School District to provide education. New York is one large, centralized, comprehensive jurisdiction. Since the vast majority of all funds for public services flows through its budget, City Hall is the seat of the action. Los Angeles, by contrast, is but one of eighty-eight municipalities in the county. Its charter gives the mayor less direct authority than in New York. Appointed boards stand between the mayor and many departments. The budgets of the Los Angeles Unified School District and the Metropolitan Water District both approach that of the City of Los Angeles. The County of Los Angeles, whose five supervisors each represent several million people, delivers health, welfare, and many other services. Its governments do not, as sometimes alleged, spend far less per capita than that of New York; these expenditures are just spread out across more levels of government. This may mean that property interests tune in to city politics, while those concerned with human services pay more attention to the county. These differences are illustrated in Table 10.3.

Multiracial Political Coalitions at the Citywide Level

Both cities have had difficulty sustaining the coalitions among blacks, Latinos, and liberal whites that elected David Dinkins and Tom Bradley. (In both cases, relatively conservative white mayors, both Republicans, succeeded black mayors.) The steady decline of the white population may have attenuated the differences (partisan, ethnic, or otherwise) among white voters and led them to consolidate behind white mayoral candidates in the face of a minority challenger, or even a white challenger with minority support. (This dynamic does not seem to apply to lesser city offices, such as comptroller in New York or city attorney in Los Angeles.) In New York City, many white Democrats defected from the Democratic nominees, African American David Dinkins in 1989 and 1993 and white liberals Ruth Messinger and Mark Green in 1997 and 2001. All of these nominees drew heavy support in minority areas. Instead, white Democrats joined white independents and Republicans in voting for Republicans Rudolph W. Giuliani and Michael Bloomberg.

Similarly, after Tom Bradley's retirement, white voters in Los Angeles supported Richard Riordan, a white Republican, against opponents with black and white liberal support, Michael Woo in 1993 and Tom Hayden in 1997. In 2001, James Hahn, a white Democrat, defeated Antonio Villaraigosa, a Latino Democrat (Sonenshein 2001), though Villaraigosa was able to turn the tables in 2005. In the 2001 primaries, relatively few white voters in New York or Los Angeles supported either Fernando Ferrer or Antonio Villaraigosa, the first Latino candidates widely perceived to have a good chance to win. As whites declined to half the electorate—decades after they became less than half the population—their voting patterns grew more racially polarized. "Race" per se may not have motivated their choices, since the candidates they favored shared their values, concerns, and interests. But these perceptions were strongly correlated with the race of the contending candidates (Arian et al. 1991; Kaufmann 2004).

Though African American voters were not part of the Giuliani or Riordan electoral coalitions, they still hold more City Council seats than their share of the electorate or population and hold other important positions in both cities. Like whites, their population share and electoral clout are gradually declining in the face of the new immigrant ethnic groups. In New York, however, blacks are a larger and more diverse group, including West Indians alongside African Americans. In Los Angeles, they are a smaller and more native group. Tom Bradley's long reign enabled them to forge links with the white political establishment; the prominence of African American officials as comptroller and Queens Borough president in New York has had a similar function in that city. In both cities, blacks are in an ambiguous position: only on the periphery of powerful white political elites, yet enough of a political establishment on their own to worry about challenges from newer, faster-growing immigrant minority groups.

Until recent elections in Los Angeles, the Latino and Asian populations have been the most under-represented ethnic groups in both cities. The victory of Antonio Villaraigosa in 2005 and the advent of several young Mexican American city councilors in Los Angeles have altered a long history of political under-representation. Like blacks, Latinos and Asians have a sense of racial minority status, but they do not have the same political advantages that African Americans have achieved through the civil rights movement, their command of English, high levels of citizenship, and even relatively good socioeconomic status. Though black–Latino political coalitions make political sense for both groups in both cities, and indeed were achieved in the 2001 Democratic mayoral primary in New York and the 2005 general election in Los Angeles, the black political establishments of both cities are not always comfortable with the Latino bid for greater representation, since the Latino immigrant population is growing in a number of districts currently represented by African Americans. Similarly, though Latino and Asian groups live near one another and share concerns derived from their immigrant status (Saito 1998, 2001), they differ sharply in language, socioeconomic position, and culture. Forging political coalitions across this boundary is not easy. Finally, Puerto Ricans are facing challenges from Dominicans and other new immigrant groups in New York, while the third generation Mexican American elites of Los Angeles are facing rapidly growing Salvadoran and Guatemalan populations, along with recently arrived Mexican immigrants with whom they have sometimes uneasy relationships.

The 2001 mayoral and City Council elections in the two cities gave evidence of both types of conflict. In both cities, no African American contender emerged for the mayoralty, despite both offices being open. Instead, several white candidates competed with a Latino contender.

In New York, two Jews, a white Catholic, and a Latino ran in a Democratic primary originally scheduled for September 11, 2001, but actually held on September 25. Bronx Borough President Fernando Ferrer came in first, followed by Public Advocate Mark Green. Ferrer campaigned on the need for greater attention to "the other New York" and forged an alliance between blacks and Latinos. Green had served as consumer affairs commissioner in the Dinkins administration and had previously received strong backing from African Americans. Between the first primary and an October 10 runoff primary, Ferrer increased his black support, which forced Green to search for support among more conservative white ethnic voters. This enabled Green to win a slim victory, but left the Democratic electorate deeply divided.

In the general election three weeks later, Republican Mike Bloomberg, a newcomer to politics, bested Green by a mere 35,489 votes out of 1.5 million cast. (In the same election, African American Democrat William Thompson handily won election as comptroller, the city's second highest office.) Bloomberg, who pioneered the provision of information to financial services firms, had changed his registration from Democratic to Republican in order to bypass the Democratic primary and ensure himself a place in the general election. He spent $73 million on his campaign, inundating the airwaves.

Compared to the previous highly racially polarized mayoral elections, Green did comparatively well in white neighborhoods, but Bloomberg also did better than Giuliani in black and Latino neighborhoods. The white neighborhoods that enabled Green to win the runoff primary against Ferrer shifted dramatically toward the Republican in the general election. Given that the high level of division among Democrats and the lingering disappointment among Latino voters, especially in the Bronx, the Bloomberg campaign's vast spending, and impact of

9/11 all helped Bloomberg, it is remarkable that Mark Green came so close to winning. Bloomberg succeeded in establishing a strong record as mayor. In his reelection campaign, former Borough President Ferrer once again ran to challenge him. In the primary, Ferrer faced two white candidates, Council Speaker Gifford Miller and Brooklyn Congressman Anthony Weiner, and Manhattan Borough President C. Virginia Fields, an African American. This time, Ferrer was not able to forge a black–Latino coalition, Weiner surged in the late running, and Ferrer barely emerged the victor in the primary. With incumbent mayor Bloomberg in a strong position and Ferrer in a weakened position, Bloomberg won a runaway victory in the 2005 general mayoral election, setting a new record in campaign spending.

The 2001 mayoral election in Los Angeles had different contours, but a similar outcome to the one in New York. Six white candidates, two Latinos, but no prominent African American ran in the initial non-partisan primary. The leading candidate, City Attorney James Hahn, a white Democrat, was the son of a former long-time Los Angeles County supervisor with strong roots in the city's Jewish and black communities. His main white competition was Steve Soboroff, a Republican from the San Fernando Valley endorsed by departing mayor Richard Riordan. (Some Valley political leaders were campaigning to secede from the city.) The Latino candidates were former California Assembly Speaker Antonio Villaraigosa and Congressman Xavier Becerra, representing competing wings of the East Side Mexican American political establishment. Villaraigosa assembled a vigorous grassroots campaign with strong support from the Los Angeles County Labor Federation and community-based organizations and also had support among West Side Jewish liberals.

In the April 10 primary election, Villaraigosa led with a third of the vote and Hahn got a quarter, with the others being eliminated. Positioning themselves for the general election, Hahn sought to add Soboroff's white base to his base of moderate whites and African Americans, while Villaraigosa sought to add enough black and white liberal support to make his Latino base into a new progressive majority. In the closely fought June 5 general election, Hahn won 53 percent to Villaraigosa's 47 percent. Hahn won a slight majority of the Jewish vote, especially those living in the Valley rather than the West Side (Sonenshein 2001). Many liberal whites, especially outside the San Fernando Valley, backed Villaraigosa, not Hahn. In the same election, Rocky Delgadillo, a Mexican American, won the city attorney's office by a wide margin.

Though Mayor Hahn was a Democrat with African American support, and thus in a position to consolidate a liberal coalition reminiscent of Mayor Bradley, he angered many black leaders by firing Los Angeles's African American police chief, Bernard Parks, and hiring former New York Police Commissioner William Bratton, who had led the Giuliani administration's charge to reduce crime rates in the early 1990s. He also vigorously opposed the Valley Secession movement. Former chief Bernard Parks and Antonio Villaraigosa subsequently won City Council seats in 2003 and proceeded to criticize the mayor from that platform.

Finally, Hahn's administration was dogged by charges of "pay to play" in connection with Los Angeles airport contracts. Weakened by these trends, Hahn once more faced off against Villaraigosa in the 2005 mayoral election. This time receiving widespread support from African Americans, Villaraigosa won the 2005 general election by a convincing margin

The 2001 and 2005 elections in both cities revealed the terrain of political mobilization. In both cities, white neighborhoods had relatively high turnouts and Asian neighborhoods low turnouts, with black and Latino neighborhoods in between. In New York, Ferrer's 2001 primary campaign elicited comparatively high turnout in both Latino and white neighborhoods in the runoff, but Latino turnout subsided in the 2001 general election and was not rekindled in the 2005 elections. In Los Angeles, the Villaraigosa and Becerra candidacies also elicited comparatively high turnout in Latino neighborhoods in 2001, which was sustained by Villaraigosa's strong position in 2005 (Sonenshein and Drayse 2006). Remarkably, Hahn's candidacy drew strong support and turnout in 2001, but not in 2005.

Both cities demonstrate the important but contingent nature of the black–Latino coalition. When conditions favored such an alliance, as in the 2001 Democratic primary in New York and the 2005 general election in Los Angeles, it has a major impact. Clearly, neither Ferrer in 2001 nor Villaraigosa in 2005 could have gone as far simply on the appeal to his own base. But conditions were as likely to work against such coalitions as in favor of them, particularly when the political interests of black and Latino elites diverged. Big city elections are normally marked by black–white racial polarization. While blacks and Latinos are generally both more likely than whites to vote Democratic, it cannot be taken for granted that they will form a coalition, especially if African Americans fear that a rapidly growing Latino population may put their political gains at risk.

Historically, the cleavage between whites and Latinos has received much less scholarly and public attention. In both cities in both mayoral elections, white voters strongly favored white candidates over Latino candidates. In New York, whites might have reacted against Ferrer's strategy for attracting strong black support. At the same time, former Borough President Ferrer had a squarely mainstream political career, and could hardly be described as a racial agitator or ideological firebrand. As a Catholic, he could potentially appeal to the white Catholic base "Giuliani Democrats." Yet both elections showed a substantial degree of white-Latino polarization. Similarly, though liberal Jewish voters on Los Angeles's West Side gave Villaraigosa strong support in both 2001 and 2005, white voters generally shied away from his candidacy. This underscores the ambiguous position occupied by Latino candidates. If they appeal too strongly for black votes, white voters may defect, but if they appeal too strongly for white votes, it may turn off black voters.

Where do emerging immigrant ethnic groups fit into this picture? In New York, Afro-Caribbean neighborhoods voted much like African American neighborhoods in both mayoral contests, though they were slightly less enthusiastic about the minority-backed candidates. They were also slightly more likely to turn out. Dominicans also voted much like their Puerto Rican neighbors, and were also more likely to turn out. Asian voters both were more likely to be evenly split between the two candidates and less likely to turn out. So far, they have not been a major factor in city elections. All in all, however, "new American" voters have become an important part of the New York City electorate, contributing roughly 30 percent of the general election vote. As Table 10.2 indicates, however, comparable groups play a much smaller role in Los Angeles, primarily because they are far less likely to be citizens and far more likely to live within concentrations of relatively recent immigrant arrivals.

Racial and Ethnic Competition at the City Council District Level

Dropping down from the citywide level to the neighborhood allows us to examine the extent to which candidates from different ethnic groups may be directly pitted against each other for local elected offices. The 2001 City Council elections in New York provide a particularly good cross section of this type of inter group competition. The following council elections were particularly interesting. (Since both cities have limits of two terms for incumbents on the council, the 2005 elections were less likely to feature challengers.)

- Alan Gerson's victory over several Asian American candidates in Manhattan District 1, which includes the traditional Chinatown. Asians are a plurality of this district, but whites make up the predominant share of the registered voters. Competition among multiple Asian American candidates undermined the ability of any one of them to win office.
- The victory of Maria Baez, a Puerto Rican, in District 14 in the Bronx, the heavily Latino area of the western side of the South Bronx shared by Dominicans and Puerto Ricans. The district has more Dominicans, but Puerto Ricans predominate in the electorate, which also has a substantial native black component. Here, support from regular Democratic Party organizations seemed decisive.
- The victory of John Liu, the council's first Chinese American, in Queens District 20. In this Asian American area of Flushing, Chinese make up a quarter of the population, but only 17 percent of the registered voters. The district also has substantial white and Latino populations. Support from the county Democratic organization and being a well-qualified candidate enabled him to prevail.
- The victory of Hiram Monserrate, a Puerto Rican, in Queens District 21. Puerto Ricans make up only 3.4 percent of this heavily Latino district, populated by Dominicans, Ecuadorans, Colombians, and Mexicans. A combination of county Democratic organizational support and competing candidates from other immigrant Latino ethnic groups helped him to win.

- The victory of Helen Sears, a white, in Queens District 25, which is 18.3 percent white, a third Latino, and a third Asian. It, too, covers part of the highly diverse area of Queens described earlier. It shows that a white incumbent can win with support from a dwindling group of white voters.
- The victory of Diana Reyna, a Dominican, in Brooklyn District 34, a mixed Latino area where Puerto Ricans substantially outnumber Dominicans. Here, Brooklyn County Democratic Leader Vito Lopez and his organization supported a second-generation protégée.
- The victory of Caribbean American Yvette Clarke in Brooklyn's District 40, where Afro-Caribbeans make up 41.6 percent of the population and African Americans, about 32.5 percent. Clarke succeeded her mother, the first West Indian woman elected to the City Council, on the basis of consolidating West Indian voters from many different backgrounds, and in 2006 went on to win a hotly contested Democratic primary to succeed long-serving African American Congressman Major Owens.
- The victory of Kendall Stewart, also an Afro-Caribbean, in Brooklyn District 45, which has an Afro Caribbean population of 46.2 percent and an African American population of 34.7 percent. His victory followed a similar pattern to that of Clarke.

Similarly, in Los Angeles, two council districts included heavily immigrant areas of interest:

- The victory of Ed Reyes, a Mexican American, against another Mexican American, David Sanchez, and a Japanese American candidate, Fumio Nakahiro, in the First District, which includes the heavily Latino and Korean areas of Pico Union west of downtown but stretches to Lincoln Heights and part of Mt. Washington to the east of Dodger Stadium. This contest shows that a plurality ethnicity can carry the day where other groups are fragmented.
- The victory of Jan Perry, an African American, who ran second in a six-candidate primary that included a Latino candidate, and later won a runoff election against Carl Washington, another African American, in the Ninth District, which includes part of South Central, the historically black neighborhood that is becoming increasingly Latino. This race also shows that, as in the Sears race in Queens, a declining but historically well-organized part of the electorate can prevail even though other groups are increasing.

Conclusion

What do these New York and Los Angeles elections tell us about new forms of intergroup competition or cooperation reflecting the arrival of new immigrant groups and their implications for empowering the new immigrant ethnic groups?

Barriers to Political Equality

The youthfulness and lack of citizenship among new immigrant groups clearly have made it more difficult for them to become politically active, win elected office, and influence citywide politics. In both mayoral elections in both cities, few Asian immigrants voted, their votes were somewhat divided, and the majority favored the relatively conservative white mayoral candidates. Asian candidates were also generally not successful in winning City Council seats. John Liu, the first Chinese American elected to the New York City Council, is a native-born Chinese American from a Taiwanese banking family who was supported by the Queens County Democratic Organization, enabling him to overcome the barriers that hobbled other Asian American candidates (Jones-Correa 2003). Such conditions are not yet widespread.

Though still substantially underrepresented, Latinos have become more influential in both cities, particularly Los Angeles. Latino voters provided an initial base of support for Latino mayoral candidates in both cities. In 2005, Antonio Villaraigosa was able to combine this base of support with that of white liberals and African Americans to create a new majority. Fernando Ferrer had no such success in New York. Among the differences between the two cities are the much larger Latino population of the City of Los Angeles, the unpopularity of the incumbent in Los Angeles (especially with black voters) as against the strong record compiled by Michael Bloomberg in New York, and differences in the two electoral systems that more or less guarantee that the Republican line will be available to a white candidate in New York if Democrats nominate a candidate white voters think is insufficiently attentive to their preferences. At the same time, the Latino populations and electorates are becoming more heterogeneous in both cities. In New York, Puerto Ricans make up a steadily declining share of the Latino electorate, and they are only a plurality of the Latino population. Any future Latino candidate will have to find a pan-ethnic way to mobilize this vote. Similarly, while Mayor Villaraigosa has succeeded in presenting himself as an advocate for a range of immigrant ethnicities, and Mexican Americans are destined to be the largest part of Los Angeles's Latino vote for some time to come, sooner or later the large Central American population will begin to seek ways to assert itself in electoral politics.

In New York, Dominicans broke into political office by winning a council seat in the 1991 elections, adding State Assembly seats, and winning a second council seat in 2001. This latter seat came not through ethnic mobilization, as in Washington Heights, but through old-fashioned ticket-balancing practices by the Vito Lopez political organization. (For an interesting comparison of the two political venues, see Marwell 2004.) Still, the goal of Dominican parity with Puerto Rican representation remains distant, and much will depend on how Puerto Ricans and Dominicans work out their political relationships. At the citywide level, Dominicans warmly embraced Ferrer as their mayoral candidate, but relations are less clear at the neighborhood level.

In Los Angeles, second and third generation Mexican Americans form the core of the Latino vote, but have marked cultural, language, and economic differences with both recent Mexican immigrants (see Acuña's 1996) and rapidly growing immigrant Latino groups, particularly Salvadorans. The Mexican American political leadership must manage tensions among different political factions within their community, forge pan-Latino links with recent Latino immigrants, and establish new coalitions with liberal whites, African Americans, and others who at times support non-Latino candidates (Chang and Diaz-Veizades 1999).

Immigrant ethnic groups must take the first step on the road to political incorporation by overcoming the lack of citizenship that lies at the foundation of their political inequality. Even after they become citizens, significant barriers remain. Because newcomers lack a history of participation and begin as small constituencies, incumbents' political mobilizing agents do not pay much attention to them, especially when they might upset their hold on office (Jones-Correa 2003). Campaigns to foster citizenship, allowing non-citizens to vote in municipal elections, and efforts to develop new leadership would all help remediate this situation. While anti-immigrant provisions in federal legislation and California ballot propositions of the 1990s produced a spike in applications for naturalization, many immigrants retain a bond with their home country. Acquiring American citizenship can sometimes seem to undercut their rights in their home counties. Ultimately, the children of immigrants now growing up in the United States, the new second generation, will have the biggest political impact.

Even when they are citizens, new Americans are less likely to register and vote than the native-born. This is partly because they are not "prime voters" targeted by candidates and parties. New citizens who live among many non-citizens also participate less than those who live among citizens (Mollenkopf et al. 2001). They are less likely to read campaign advertising in ethnic newspapers or hear news coverage in the English media. Many immigrants also come from countries with authoritarian or one party regimes, where parties and politics have a bad name. If they do not join a party when they register, party organizations will not seek to pull them to the polls. Finally, when native white or minority incumbents represent them, these incumbents are not likely to want to mobilize them. All this said, however, naturalized voters still make up a sizable and growing share of the electorates in both cities.

Finally, the party organizations have rarely made any real effort to mobilize immigrant voters or promote new immigrant candidates. These party establishments gained power with support from native-born constituencies and do not wish to put this power at risk. In New York, emerging Dominican and West Indian political leaders often see Puerto Rican and African American Democratic elected officials, who dominate the party machinery where they live, as being uninterested in—or even hostile to—accommodating their political advancement. (Here, Vito Lopez's support for Diana Reyna is an interesting exception.) Certainly, the York City and Los Angeles council races mentioned earlier suggest that Democratic incumbents have little liking for immigrant challengers.

In primary elections with candidates from many different ethnic backgrounds, support from New York's county party organizations enabled favored candidates to win small pluralities in low turnout elections (Jones-Correa 2003).

New York City offers two races that did not conform to this pattern, however. The Vito Lopez organization in Puerto Rican Bushwick supported its Dominican member, Diana Reyna, for the City Counci, while the Queens County Democratic Organization helped to make John Liu the first Chinese council member from Queens. In both cases, they chose candidates who were close to the organization. Both claimed not to be representing one immigrant ethnic group, but rather a broad array of interests. Both ran for open seats in districts where the pace of population change suggested that older racial and ethnic groups might have a difficult time maintaining power. While this offers evidence that regular party organizations can still perform their historic function of promoting ethnic succession, the infrequency of these examples and the declining efficacy of party organizations suggest they will not be much of a positive factor in promoting new immigrant empowerment. No immigrant ethnic group aside from Mexican Americans is currently represented on the Los Angeles City Council, and they are both a native minority group and an immigrant ethnic group.

Political Competition and Cooperation among Native and Immigrant Minority Groups

At the local level, immigrant political districts are bound to experience competition between immigrant and native minority candidates. This does not mean, however, that immigrant and native minority groups have fundamentally different interests that make them unwilling to vote for each other. While they sometimes square off against each other, the more frequent pattern is that multiple immigrant and minority candidates lose to a native white, as in New York's Chinatown, or multiple immigrant candidates cancel each other out, as in Los Angeles's First District.

Such neighborhoods may well become greenhouses for new kinds of alliances, not just battlegrounds for interethnic competition, however. The commonalities among immigrant and native minority groups can be substantial, and they have played out in some New York and Los Angeles elections. Whether they like it or not, native minority political leaders have a long term stake in capturing the growing immigrant vote within their communities, for this is the demographic destiny. And if they do reach out, rising immigrant political leaders will have good reason to respond to them.

Some immigrant minority groups occupy an ambiguous position in the larger balance between whites and blacks. South American immigrants have more education and higher incomes than those from the Caribbean. As a result, they have been more willing to support white Catholic candidates. They might ultimately align themselves with the last century's white immigrants rather than follow the racial minority path being taken by Afro-Caribbeans or Dominicans. Similarly, Chinese, Koreans, Indians, and Pakistanis may also be ambivalent about the Democratic Party. They, too, often have higher rates of education, income, property ownership, and self-employment than other immigrant groups. (For ambiguities in the Asian class position, see Espiritu and Omi 2000.) The council elections and mayoral races in New York and Los Angeles showed no evidence of Latino–Asian alliances, even though these groups often live intermingled with one another. Finally, white immigrants from the former Soviet Union or Iran also lean away from the Democratic Party. Not all immigrants, then, are good candidates for being incorporated into urban politics through the Democratic minority empowerment model.

The Larger Pattern of Racial Inequality

Persistent electoral polarization between white and minority candidates and voters may be the most important constraint on closing the immigrant representation gap. Even as the white share of the active electorate falls below a majority in both cities, white voters are still not inclined to support a bi- or multiracial coalition of the kind that once elected black mayors in both cities. (Villaraigosa was able to walk this tightrope more effectively than Ferrer.)

In both cities, white candidates repeatedly won the mayoralty after the departures of David Dinkins and Tom Bradley by mobilizing a white base against opponents identified with minority supporters. They added some minority support to their solid, if shrinking, white base. They appealed to these voters not on the basis of "minority empowerment," but in terms of navigating the complexities of intergroup competition, offering incentives to each group, and making appeals on the basis of class and religious affinities.

To counter this pattern, a multiracial coalition must promote immigrant political incorporation at the neighborhood level and consolidate the elusive Latino–black alliance, It seems unlikely that this can be done on the basis of racial or ethnic group membership or "identity politics." Instead, this alliance should articulate shared values and policy goals. To date, Antonio Villaraigosa has done the best job of setting forth such a vision.

Whites can sustain their hold on mayoral power in the two cities only by adding Latino or Asian support to their white base. Mayor Giuliani favored immigrants' rights, which undoubtedly helped him reach out to Latino and Asian immigrant communities, while Mayor Bloomberg campaigned in the Dominican Republic and Puerto Rico and invested heavily in the Spanish and Asian media during his campaigns. His 2001 and 2005 victories suggest that whites can find support among South Americans, East Asians, and South Asians. Whites are dwindling even more rapidly in Los Angeles, but they have a greater citizenship advantage. Certainly, Antonio Villaraigosa was able to forge a black–Latino coalition in 2005 despite the primary campaign of Bernard Parks, the African American former police chief. At the same time, African Americans are over-represented on the Los Angeles City Council and many hold local government jobs, and few come from immigrant backgrounds. Under the right circumstances, they might not continue to support Latino candidates

Next Steps

To get native political incumbents to accept greater immigrant political participation, more political challenges will be needed. Organizations with growing immigrant constituencies, such as labor unions and community organizations, can help to promote the emergence of new immigrant political leaders. To some degree, especially in Los Angeles, the county labor federation has already begun this process. Despite the barriers, new political leadership is being nourished by institutions like the public schools, the City University of New York, the California State University and University of California systems, the service sector labor unions, the Catholic parishes and Protestant churches, and the immigrant advocacy and social service networks. This leadership will be nourished by the coming of age of the second generation. Over time, from such people, a new, better-functioning, multiethnic urban democracy will emerge.

Notes

This chapter is based on Mollenkopf's section in Logan and Mollenkopf 2003. Mollenkopf alone is responsible for this version but thanks Logan for his stimulating partnership.

1. These figures are drawn from the March 2005 Annual Demographic Supplement of the Current Population Survey.

2. For further analysis, see John Logan's application of exploratory spatial data analysis with 2000 Census data (Logan and Mollenkopf 2003, 15–20).

3. These tables exclude people living in group quarters, like jails or hospitals, who rarely vote.

References

Acuña, Rodolfo F. 1996. *Anything but Mexican: Chicanos in Contemporary Los Angeles.* London: Verso.

Allen, James P., and Eugene Turner. 2002. *Changing Faces, Changing Places: Mapping Southern Californians.* Northridge: Center for Geographic Studies, California State University, Northridge.

Arian, Asher, Arthur Goldberg, John Mollenkopf, and Edward Rogowsky. 1991. *Changing New York City Politics.* New York: Routledge.

Browning, Rufus P., Dale Rogers Marshall, and David H. Tabb, eds. 2003. *Racial Politics in American Cities,* 3rd ed. New York: Longman Publishers.

Chang, Edward T., and Jeannette Diaz-Veizades. 1999. "Building Cross-Cultural Coalitions." Pp. 105–128 in *Ethnic Peace in the American City: Building Community in Los Angeles and Beyond.* New York: New York University Press.

Espiritu, Yen Le, and Michael Omi. 2000. "'Who Are You Calling Asian?': Shifting Identity Claims, Racial Classification, and the Census." Pp. 43–192 in *The State of Asian Pacific America: Transforming Race Relations*, ed. Paul M. Ong. Los Angeles: Leadership Education for Asian Pacifics, Asian Pacific American Public Policy Institute, and University of California, Los Angeles, Asian American Studies Center .

Falcon, Angelo. 1988. "Black and Latino Politics in New York City: Race and Ethnicity in a Changing Urban Context." Pp. 171–194 in *Latinos in the Political System*, ed. F. Chris Garcia. North Bend, Ind.: Notre Dame University Press.

Foner, Nancy. 2001. *Islands in the City: West Indian Migration to New York*. Berkeley: University of California Press.

Frey, William H. 2003. *Metropolitan Magnets for International and Domestic Migration.* Washington, D.C.: Brookings Institution Center on Urban and Metropolitan Policy.

Gutiérrez, David G. 1995. *Walls and Mirrors: Mexican Americans, Mexican Immigrants, and the Politics of Ethnicity.* Berkeley: University of California Press.

Jones-Correa, Michael. 2003. "Term Limits and Openings for New Political Actors in Urban Settings: The Case of New York City." Unpublished ms., Department of Government, Cornell University, Ithaca, N.Y.

Kasinitz, Philip. 1992. *Caribbean New York: Black Immigrants and the Politics of Race.* Ithaca, N.Y.: Cornell University Press.

Kaufmann, Karen. 2004. *The Urban Voter: Group Conflict and Mayoral Voting Behavior in American Cities.* Ann Arbor: University of Michigan Press.

Kwong, Peter. 1996. *The New Chinatown,* rev. ed. New York: Farrar, Strauss and Giroux.

Logan, John, and John Mollenkopf. 2003. *People and Politics in America's Big Cities.* New York City: Drum Major Institute. Available online at http://www.s4.brown.edu/cen2000/2003newspdf/People%20&%20Politics%20report.pdf.

Marwell, Nicole. 2004. "Ethnic and Post-ethnic Politics in New York City: The Dominican Second Generation." Pp. 257–284 in *Becoming New Yorkers: The Second Generation Comes of Age,* ed. Philip Kasinitz, John Mollenkopf, and Mary Waters. New York: Russell Sage Foundation.

Mollenkopf, John, David Olson, and Timothy Ross. 2001. "Immigrant Political Participation in New York and Los Angeles." Pp. 17–70 in *Governing Urban America: Immigrants, Natives, and Urban Politics,* ed. Michael Jones Correa. New York: Russell Sage Foundation.

Pessar, Patricia R. 1995. *A Visa for a Dream: Dominicans in the United States.* Boston: Allyn and Bacon.

Reed, Adolph. 1988. "The Black Urban Regime: Structural Origins and Constraints." Pp. 138–189 in *Power, Community, and the City,* ed. Michael Peter Smith. New Brunswick, N.J.: Transaction Books.

Regalado, Jaime A. 1998. "Minority Political Incorporation in Los Angeles: A Broader Consideration." Pp. 381–410 in *Racial and Ethnic Politics in California.* vol. 2, ed. Michael Preston, Bruce Cain, and Sandra Bass. Berkeley: Institute for Governmental Studies, University of California.

Ricourt, Milagros. 2002. *Power from the Margins: The Incorporation of Dominicans in New York City.* New York: Routledge.

Saito, Leland. 1998. *Race and Politics: Asian Americans, Latinos, and Whites in a Los Angeles Suburb.* Urbana: University of Illinois Press.

———. 2001. "Asian Americans and Multiracial Political Coalitions: New York City's Chinatown and Redistricting, 1990–1991." In *Asian Americans and Politics: An Exploration,* ed. Gordon H. Chang. Stanford, Calif.: Stanford University Press.

Shefter, Martin. 1993. *Political Parties and the State: The American Historical Experience.* Princeton, N.J.: Princeton University Press.

Sonenshein, Raphael J. 1994. *Politics in Black and White: Race and Power in Los Angeles.* Princeton, N.J.: Princeton University Press.

———. 2001. "The Prospects for Latino–Jewish Coalition in Los Angeles." In *Governing American Cities: Inter-ethnic Coalitions, Competition, and Conflict,* ed. Michael Jones-Correa. New York: Russell Sage Foundation.

Sonenshein, Raphael J., and Mark Drayse. 2006. "Urban Electoral Conditions in an Age of Immigration: Time and Place in the 2001 and 2005 Mayoral Primaries. *Political Geography* 25: 570–595.

Thompson, J. Phillip. 2005. *Double Trouble.* New York: Oxford University Press.

Waters, Mary. 1999. *Black Identities: West Indian Immigrant Dreams and American Realities.* Cambridge, Mass.: Harvard University Press.

Zhou, Min. 1995. *Chinatown: The Socioeconomic Potential of an Urban Enclave.* Philadelphia: Temple University Press.

Zhou, Min, and Rebecca Kim. 2003. "A Tale of Two Metropolises: Immigrant Chinese Communities in New York and Los Angeles." Pp. 124–149 in *Los Angeles and New York in the New Millennium,* ed. David Halle. Chicago: University of Chicago Press.

IV

The Road Ahead?

11

To Be Continued?

*The "Problem of the Color Line"
in the Twenty-First Century*

DAVID ROEDIGER

Almost two centuries after the French Revolution of 1789, Chinese leader Chou En-lai declined to pronounce on its historical impact. "It is," he remarked, "too soon to say."[1] Most historians, of whatever political stripe, will sympathize with this reticence, which almost perfectly resonates with my profession's hesitancy to analyze the recent past. It is therefore unsurprising that a historian like myself would approach this invitation to predict the future—let alone the global future—with much trepidation. What follows here thus seeks to be bold, but bold for a historian. It hopes to provoke by resituating the brilliant 1903 prediction of the African American W. E. B. Du Bois regarding the importance of the "color-line" in the twentieth century within Du Bois's broader commentary on the United States and the world. It then considers how Du Bois's prediction might apply to the century we have just entered, offering less a firm prognostication than a caution against dismissing out of hand the possibility that this new century too might feature color lines, and struggles against them, as a central feature. It challenges "race is over" triumphalism by considering perhaps the two most portentous U.S. events yet to occur in this century—the September 11 attacks and the Hurricane Katrina disasters—and placing them in a racialized nation and world.

Two points regarding Du Bois's most celebrated formulation of his position on the color line deserve initial emphasis. The passage most frequently quoted from his *Souls of Black Folk,* the book's second sentence, is straightforward enough: "The problem of the Twentieth Century is the problem of the color-line." But how Du Bois introduces and follows this statement complicates its meanings and its relations to national and global histories. In the prefatory "Forethought" of *Souls,* he frames the prediction first with a plea for the "Gentle Reader" to show patience as the book attempts to divine "the strange meaning of being black here in the dawning of the Twentieth Century." The signal importance of this strange meaning for the reader, who is implicitly cast as white, hinges on the role of race in the lives of everyone. What we would now call black studies is "not without interest to you," Du Bois tells his audience, because the color line so structures life on both of its sides.

When Du Bois returns to his "color-line" prediction, at the outset of the second chapter of *Souls,* the lyrical and historical "Of the Dawn of Freedom," he immediately moves on to a second reason why the reader must be engaged by his book. Writing during the bloody U.S. occupation of the Philippines, he finishes his point by defining the color line *globally:* "the relation of the darker to the lighter races of men in Asia and Africa, in America and the islands of the sea." Thus, from its very inception the color line was both specifically about the white-on-black brutalities of the United States and about what the African American intellectual Ralph Bunche would soon call "worlds of race." The Civil War and emancipatory dramas on which the chapter concentrates are but a "phase" of a world problem.

We now regularly read and hear that even in the race-saturated United States the new century will look nothing like Du Bois's prediction regarding the last one. By about the middle of the twenty-first century, journalists and social scientists tell us—usually seizing on some specific year—the U.S. population will no longer have a white majority. Somehow, we are told, this demographic change will supposedly cause race to lose its importance. Mixing projection with reporting, the resulting articles carry present-tense headlines like, "RACE IS OVER," although their contents muse on the future. *Time* produced the classic instance of this sort of reporting in a lavish 1993 special issue titled "The New Face of America." Its striking cover featured Eve, created by loosely feeding images and statistics on patterns of immigration and intermarriage into a computer, as the reassuring face of what a nonwhite-majority United States will look like. The ads and text of the issue, excepting a tart dissent from Toni Morrison, emphasized how passé race would be, and therefore already was, even as they emphasized the more-or-less unrelated matter of global trade as the key to new post-racial cosmopolitanisms on offer.

The intellectual perhaps most given to post-racial soothsaying is the great Harvard sociologist Orlando Patterson. His fullest manifesto on the subject, a 2000 article in *New Republic* titled simply "Race Over," explicitly revisited and critiqued Du Bois's earlier prediction. To regard the color line as important in the twentieth century was, Patterson allowed, perhaps "half-right." To carry concern with that line into the new century, Patterson continued, was "altogether wrong." Migration, "cultural and somatic mixing," and biotechnologies letting African Americans change their hair texture and skin color in pursuit of "hybridities" would certainly make race go "the way of smallpox" by 2050. Only in "the old Confederacy," he reckoned, could the allegedly traditional pattern in which "everyone knows who is white and who is black and needs reckon no in-between" continue to apply as an oddball "Atlanta System," exceptional in a nation and world without a color line.

We should keep Du Bois's prediction, in its fuller form, and Patterson's challenge to it in mind as we try to address the question of what's new in this new century by asking when the twenty-first century actually started in the United States. Surely it is far "too soon to say" when that century symbolically began, but two possible starting points have dramatically presented themselves. The first is, of course, the attack on the World Trade Center and the Pentagon on September 11, 2001. Such a possible point of departure would seemingly lead us well away from imagining the color line as anything like a dominant divide in the new century. Indeed in the wake of the 9/11 carnage the essential unity of everyone in the United States, regardless of race, quickly became a favorite theme for politicians and editorialists. The War on Terror and in particular the occupation of Iraq following the 9/11 attacks offered a spectacular display of "black (and brown) faces in high places" as policymakers and as military leaders. In any case, transnational dramas, not domestic inequalities, took center stage.

However, the longer aftermath of 9/11 has strongly challenged the division between global realities where race matters little and national/regional ones where it looms larger. Almost from the outset of the War on Terror, the racial profiling of Arab Americans and of Arab and Islamic travelers became a concern. Initial jokes from black comedians played on their relief at getting to take a rest from being the subjects of such suspicion and profiling. But such lines proved less funny as the broadcast faces of terror often looked like those of the "darker races" generally and not simply like the imagined Arab (whom the United States officially counts as white) stereotype, as African-origin and Puerto Rican prisoners became the most publicized of those incarcerated under extraordinary anti-terror provisions, and as communities of color literally suffered at the expense of war budgets that necessitated austerity in social spending.

The second candidate for the inaugural event of the twenty-first century in the United States apparently moves us in a very different direction. If we begin with the coming of Hurricane Katrina to the Gulf Coast in late summer of 2005, and specifically with the broadcast miseries of the devastated city of New Orleans after levees broke in the hurricane's wake, the color line moves back to center stage. Indeed, the city had scarcely suffered for a week when the rapper Kanye West told a prime-time television audience watching *A Concert for Hurricane Relief* that the main lesson of the disaster, and of the lack of disaster relief, could be easily summed up: "George Bush doesn't care about black people."

There were plenty of alternative explanations for the disastrous disaster relief—federal ineptitude, foot dragging by state and local officials, a president on vacation, and alleged looting by African American youth impeding relief efforts—but it proved hard to shift the controversy away from race and indeed from white institutional racism. The unraveling of scare stories regarding roving black youths particularly showed the persistence of the color line when accounts of wholesale rapes in New Orleans were quickly revealed to be based only on rumor and stereotype and when bloggers showed how mainstream photojournalism labeled black kids as looters when showing them gathering supplies from abandoned stores and captioned whites doing just the same thing as survivors. The great urban historian and journalist Mike Davis raised a series of questions three months into the rebuilding process of New Orleans and perfectly captured the continuing color line:

> Why is there so much high-level talk about abandoning the Ninth Ward as uninhabitable when no one is proposing to turn equally inundated Lakeview back into a swamp? Is it because Lakeview is a wealthy white community? And/or is it because the 30,000 reliably Democratic Black votes in the Ninth Ward hold the balance of power in Louisiana politics?[2]

To what extent, Davis wondered, did "ethnic cleansing" and rebuilding coincide?

Nor can post–Katrina New Orleans simply be written off as the "Atlanta System" oddity, soldiering anomalously on in its anachronistic nineteenth-century ways, for which Patterson leaves room in his otherwise raceless twenty-first century world. New Orleans's history as a strikingly multiracial city—not simply a white and black one—is in fact far older than the history of the United States. This history includes not just the city's complicated partial incorporation of mixed race elites but also its place as part of an area with a rich native past. A port opening onto the complex figurings of race in the Caribbean and Latin America, the city and its hinterlands had such a diverse working class a century ago that Covington Hall, a leading labor organizer then and there, sometimes divided the workforce into black, white, and "Latin" races. Hall counted Italians as well as Mexicans and Canary Islanders in the last category, reminding us that who falls on what sides of which color lines is a historical, social, and political matter, not a biological one.

Indeed, the politics of rebuilding after Katrina has immediately shown that both global capitalism and multiracialism are present, and have been so, at every turn in New Orleans, just as they were present in Du Bois's formulation of the color line. That the city is a shipping center and intimately connected to international marketing of Gulf of Mexico oil sets sharp limits on any plan to simply abandon New Orleans. These interests have also structured reconstruction policies with Davis pointing, for example, to the specific roles of

> lobbyists for energy utilities, oil refiners, and the shipping interests in drafting the Louisiana Reconstruction Act. Provisions of rebuilding policies have made the city even more multiracial. The temporary suspension of Davis-Bacon Act protections of the wages of workers involved in federally-supported cleanup and reconstruction efforts, for instance, dis-

couraged some black and white union and relatively high-wage workers from returning to the city even as the easing of enforcement of immigration laws opened the ways for Texas-based and Bush-connected contractors to bring large numbers of Latino workers into low-wage jobs on the Gulf Coast. The results already threaten to pit groups within what Du Bois called the "darker races" tragically against each other. New Orleans Mayor Ray Nagin, so tied to the labor policies and limitations on residents' ability to return to the city structuring black–Latino tensions, now seems to want to exploit the black/brown color line, warning that the city is about to be "overrun" by Mexican workers[3]

The increasingly visible interconnections between the War on Terror and the surrender to Hurricane Katrina's destructive force suggest that 9/11 and the storm might *together* mark the beginning of the twenty-first century in the United States—a century still largely defined by color lines, but not just by simple, binary, U.S.-centered ones. Together the two events, and their aftermaths, point to a world in which racial positions are multiple and show that global and local realities mix promiscuously in determining where color lines will be drawn. Whether war spending directly led to the shelving of critical levee repairs prior to the New Orleans disaster or only contributed to a general atmosphere of austerity in expenditure on repairing domestic infrastructure has occasioned spirited debate. The tardiness of the National Guard's response to Katrina similarly revealed that much of the Guard was better poised to respond to tragedies in the Persian Gulf than to those in the Gulf of Mexico. The global dimension of local crises also surfaced when the Bush administration found reasons not to welcome aid to hurricane victims proffered by "enemies" in Cuba and Venezuela.

Nor was the ability of the global to influence the local the whole story. The debacle in the Gulf region has greatly weakened the Bush presidency domestically and limited its ability to stay in Iraq, much less to intervene in Iran and elsewhere. Kanye West's remarks, and the black popular wisdom that they bespoke, coincided with further plummeting of Bush's popularity among and beyond the African American population and with an increasing inability to recruit the African American volunteers critical to war planning in the Mideast.

In large recent antiwar demonstrations, the most fascinating sign has read: "NO IRAQI HAS EVER LEFT ME TO DIE ON A ROOF." Its words recall haunting post–Katrina images and also sample the celebrated antiwar dictum attributed to Muhammad Ali: "No Vietnamese ever called me 'nigger.'" The latter line counts perhaps the quintessential late-twentieth-century example of Du Bois's insight regarding how the color line in the United States existed in systems of racialized global inequality. We should allow that the twenty-first-century "NO IRAQI" sign's variant of the earlier slogan is considerably more complex and expansive. Poor whites, and indeed the large numbers of Vietnamese resettled in the Gulf region and abandoned in Katrina's considerable wake, could conceivably march under the "NO IRAQI" sign. But the variant's echoing of its predecessor also captures the continuing resonance of the black–white color line as the most sustained demarcation of the racism practiced by what is now the world's lone imperial superpower.

Such resonance is "not without interest," as Du Bois had it, to Brazilians now attempting to implement race-based affirmative action programs in a society that figures race far differently than the United States, to South Africans who learned long ago that a white majority is not necessary for the functioning of white supremacy, and to Venezuelans whose expressions of popular power and of solidarity with the poor of the United States are so often challenged along racial lines by a self-consciously white national economic elite. Similarly the struggles of these nations and of the rest of the world with very different but intimately related color lines can hardly be without interest or impact in the United States in the century to come.

Notes

1. Slavoj Žižek, "Robespierre or the 'Divine Violence' of Terror," available online at http://www.lacan.com/zizrobes.htm.

2. Mike Davis, "Who Killed New Orleans? Questions for an Autopsy," *International Socialist Review* 44 (November–December 2005), available online at http://www.isreview.org/issues/44/whokilledNO.shtml.

3. Ibid.

Color Lines, the New Society, and the Responsibility of Scholars

GARY ORFIELD

The United States is a vast nation of enormous diversity that is undergoing revolutionary demographic changes that are certain to change its society and its institutions in many ways, some predictable, and others deeply dependent upon decisions to come and upon the ability of a creative country with fragmented and complex institutions and enduring prejudices to successfully adapt. The United States has been not only a land of opportunity for many peoples but also a land of intense and harmful racial and ethnic separation and inequality for African Americans, Indians, and Latinos. How it will function and will react to the most rapid change in its history is very much an open question.

This book suggests the range of vitally important and intellectually challenging issues to be addressed in studying twenty-first century U.S. race relations, revealing the inadequacy of existing models and introducing the talented scholars in a number of disciples ready to do the hard work that we badly need done in order to understand the shifting patterns of color lines and stratification. Rather than to try to tie together all of the interesting and provocative cuts that the scholars have provided to challenge existing assumptions and broaden our vision, I will take this last chapter to talk about the social, political, and intellectual challenges we face as unprecedented transformations sweep over the society. We need to understand why so little serious discussion takes place about these issues in our public life and to think about the potentials revealed by this book and all the other studies produced for the Color Lines conference and how that interest and energy might be the first step in the great work of understanding the historic transformation that the United States is now passing though.

We are in the midst of huge intergenerational changes that are operating with a force and depth and speed that makes them very difficult to understand. The dominant response has been a politics of racial and class polarization, reassertion of tradition, and denial of the need for change. We are a country that is deeply individualistic, where whites typically want to avoid issues of race, not dealing with today's reality of a profoundly multiracial society with stunning inequalities of opportunity across the new color lines and stratification systems. In the last half century we have built a civilization unique in world history— a vast predominantly suburban society in which each little suburb has the right (and the incentives) to try to extract resources from the city and other communities and to screen out though zoning and housing policies not only poor people but anyone who does not have a relatively high income. The wealthy suburbs are almost always white. It is a society in which location in certain sectors of suburbia and certain high schools and colleges confers enormous advantages, but where those are rarely available to the growing Latino and African American populations.

The existing trends are toward a society strikingly divided and declining in dangerous ways, as the majority becomes non-white and average education drops. That means that doing nothing is accepting an unacceptable result. In this situation, the country needs to reconstruct its basic understanding of the present and future of American society and to reframe the American story to cope with the vastly increased diversity. Research is an important part of what is needed, but the government and the major institutions have done little, in good measure because of the politics of fear and denial that has been dominant. Government is not supporting this research and often attacks proposals for change. Private resources have not been adequately mobilized. This creates a tremendous challenge to the intellectual community. Until government seriously addresses the issues, scholars have a deep responsibility to use their knowledge and their ability to analyze official data and collect new information to build an understanding of what is happening and what can be done to produce a more viable society and political community. Professors in professions dominated by increasingly narrow and specialized research need to take on these larger questions.

Intergenerational Change

Obviously the changes have already come faster than many can understand, and each generation is experiencing a society significantly different from the last. A World War II veteran who came to California was part of a massive, largely white migration from the Midwest and the South to the Golden State where a significant black population only arrived during the war and where the Mexican American population was still relatively small with many concentrated in the rural areas and thought of as migrants not residents. That veteran, who bought a tract suburban home with the GI Bill's help and settled into a community that was white and middle class, now finds himself with a home that is worth thirty times as much but in a neighborhood that may be full of immigrants from Mexico, and maybe some from Asia, where he often does not hear English when he goes out to shop with his senior citizen group. His grandchildren, who are now in their forties, grew up in a world of greatly increased diversity, where the region was no longer securely white but their neighborhood was. Their children, who are now in school, are part of a statewide enrollment that was only 31 percent white by 2005, and where they face diminishing chances to enter the leading public universities, which are now becoming very heavily Asian. Many public schools are struggling with majorities of entering students who understand no English, while their teachers are struggling with a state referendum that forbids them to use the children's own language. Blacks in urban California, who were at the center of much of the politics of the 1960s and 1970s, now find themselves falling behind Asians as the state's fourth largest minority group, but their problems persist. No one should be surprised that changes of this magnitude, speed, and complexity are hard to understand and accept. Nor should anyone be surprised that that uneasiness and those fears are a very tempting target for politicians willing to attain power though playing on fear and prejudice. There is a very dangerous point during sweeping demographic changes in a democratic society when those locked in the past and fearful of the changes have the power to systematically undermine the chances of the groups making up the future majority. We are at that point.

Politics of Polarization and Denial

Why, in the face of a trend of rapid change that has been apparent for at least a quarter century, have we done so little about it in a positive sense and taken so many actions that are likely to make a difficult transition much worse? Part of the answer is found in the way Americans govern themselves through two major political parties, each competing to win a majority of the electorate in a winner-take-all electoral system, where one party gets the presidency and the other gets nothing. Campaigns are directed toward registered voters only and especially the swing voters, usually giving lower-middle income white suburbanites the balance of power in a nation with a suburban majority. This system offers very little incentive for proposals for positive policies to address the racial transformation. One side tends to exploit the fears of change and demand a return to tradition. The other party, a tenuous coalition of minorities, suburban and Southern whites, labor, liberals, and working class urbanites, generally tries to avoid talking about race and demographic transition explicitly for fear of driving its white swing voters over to the other side whose policies play on their fears. Neither party is initiating new positive policies or pushing for new research, so it is unsurprising that government has done almost nothing to adequately understand and deal with the massive racial change.

There have been no positive federal policy initiatives for decades to deal with race relations or even to conduct serious research on the issues. Since the 1960s five of the seven presidents have been active civil rights opponents and the other two, Southern pro-business moderates. Social policy and educational policy have been in the hands of those who deny that there need be any changes outside the schools, support cuts in what was already the most limited system of social provision in the first world, and tend to blame groups which have less success for their own problems. Poverty is not the enemy as it was in the War on Poverty period; it is seen as the result of the laziness of the "welfare queens." Democratic President Bill Clinton supported a welfare reform more conservative than President Ronald Reagan's. The problem is not defined as finding resources for urban institutions but pursuing private and market solutions that tend to produce systematic advantages for those with better connections and networks and to produce increased inequality for those who were already excluded or far behind. Policy initiatives from the courts to end racial injustice have ended as opponents of these changes have taken over the courts and are cutting back on existing civil rights policy, holding that too much civil rights law was unfair to whites and unnecessary for minorities in what, they say, is now a society cleansed of its racial history. Older whites have supported tax cuts and retirement benefits that benefit them and have elected leaders who cut services to the young, who are a far more diverse population.

The dominant political movement of the past forty years has been anti-intellectual and anti-research. Virtually nothing has been done to study or invent solutions for the new problems of race relations or to generate new urban policies in a society where four fifths of the people and nine tenths of the non-whites live in metropolitan areas. The dominant politics has been a politics of denial in spite of evidence that individualistic assimilation is not working well for many millions. People wish to see society as a stable settled structure, but it is much more like a powerful, fast flowing river that may be spilling over its banks that had seemed secure. The floods and dangers of much worse to come are not being studied, and the potential solutions are not being implemented.

At present, the United States is a country still burdened with the parts of the legacy of slavery and rigid subordination of blacks that never have been overcome but where it is considered tiresome and ideological to mention that—a country where there is a widely accepted but untrue assumption that the passage of time heals intergenerational racial inequality. This assumption, of course, shifts the burden of the remaining inequalities from the society to the group that is subordinated. Conservative policies assume that misguided efforts to produce equal opportunity have gone too far and have been unfair to whites while also hobbling minorities. The only hope, they suggest, is the reassertion of what are described as traditional values and expectations and trusting the efficacy of private efforts and markets to provide opportunities and mobility. But those policies have little or no positive effect.

Why Haven't Researchers Filled the Void?

Though racial transformation is a risky issue for politicians, that should not hold true for researchers who could be a major resource. Since massive stores of many kinds of data are readily available, and many researchers possess the skills to use them, scholars could use their tenure and academic freedom to illuminate the transformation. Usually, though, they are constrained by the priorities of agencies giving grants, the fashions and priorities of the leading journals and scholars in their discipline, by the tiny representation of scholars of color in the major research institutions, and by the fact that they often have little direct personal understanding. In the academic world, theoretical contributions, and the products of elaborate statistical manipulation of certain kinds of data get the most rewards and practical contributions, especially those addressing controversial public policy issues or using secondary data are often considered to be of little scholarly value. The kind of work that gets the most academic attention in the social sciences is based on very expensive collection of new data, work requiring big grants. Government, particularly in conservative times, tends not to fund independent work on race relations and racial equality and to very actively communicate selective data and ideology supporting its goals, directing its research funding to researchers aligned with those objectives and then publicizing their findings. The corruption of the process within government took hold during the Reagan years when the long independent U.S. Civil Rights Commission was politicized, and independent research on these issues ended. So, although academics could be a major force in informing the country, there are serious barriers and limited rewards for them. This made the incredible response to the Color Lines conference all the more surprising.

Why Race Always Matters

The issues of color, race, and ethnicity have divided and challenged American society from its earliest beginnings. The dominant culture of what would become the United States was profoundly racist and, in a society with millions of slaves almost totally stripped of basic rights, law and tradition developed for many generations around systems of caste and suppression. In contrast to the history of the Spanish in the Americas or the French in Canada and Louisiana, the dominant forces in the settler communities in the British colonies had a more intense and absolute sense of racial hierarchy and a striking aversion to interracial social contact. The extreme nature of American slavery and the racial concepts that supported it are often noted. Color does, of course, matter in Latin societies, but it is simply not as absolute a barrier and there was massive intermarriage and cultural synthesis in major regions. In the United States we are living in a society forged on slavery, conquest, destruction of indigenous communities, and a deeply embedded ideology of white supremacy from the 1600s for more than four centuries to the middle of the twentieth century. We are also, on the other hand, a society that fought a horribly vicious civil war against slavery, had a civil rights movement whose message resounded across the world, and now has sets of laws and legal principles that have, at times, supported real and substantial expansions of rights of subordinated groups. But, because our dominant ideology is individualistic, all efforts to mobilize powerful public interventions on these issues are always subject to attack and possible reversal. Many of the accomplishments of the civil rights revolution of the 1960s have been undermined by a long succession of conservative governments. Most of the time, the United States is a society with a general denial of racial problems by those on the white side of the color line who usually believe that there already is a fair chance for everyone on an individual basis.

The United States has a story of equal rights gradually extended, of real progress—first across ethnic and religious lines among the widely disparate and often hostile groups that would eventually be defined as mainstream whites—and then fitfully across the color lines. These efforts sometimes brought a lasting expansion of rights, but sometimes only a surge of reform where rights were extended, only to be taken back. Many of the reforms came only well into the twentieth century, and much of the period since the civil rights era in the 1960s has been dominated by a politics of reaction and denial, through the coalition of white Southerners and suburbanites forged by Richard Nixon. As this book is going to press the Supreme Court's 2007 prohibition of voluntary school integration policies was a striking limitation of the *Brown v. Board of Education*. Although many of the most overt barriers are gone there has never been consistent support for deep institutional change or for giving historically excluded groups the extra resource they usually need to take advantage of new opportunities. The key problems of metropolitan America, based on residential segregation, fragmentation of communities and school districts, and forms of discrimination that are much harder to detect but devastatingly effective, still remain. The United States in the 1960s embraced its most generous vision of racial and ethnic equality in its history and the most comprehensive strategy for realizing it, but the consensus underlying those reforms was brief and the angry reaction against them was swift and has lasted for decades.

The Black–White Paradigm

Race in the United States has usually been dualistic—people of European origin, who dominated the society and all its major institutions, and people of other colors, defined as comprehensively inferior. At the first, in the colonies that would become the Eastern United States, the dualism was white versus Indian, which continued to be the most important division in some areas until the frontier closed. In spite of sporadic efforts to "civilize" the Indians, their racial and cultural inferiority was almost uniformly accepted. As the Indian issue was largely ended in the East though removal and destruction, it was replaced by the fundamental division established very early with the importation of African slaves, who became vital parts of the economy and a fundamental source of white wealth in the South where slavery was justified by a deeply held doctrine of inherent black inferiority.

Americans have dealt with a variety of forms of racial conflict, but the black–white vision of race remained dominant from the time of the abolitionist movement through the civil rights era. The issue of race for more than a century was largely defined in national politics and in scholarship as an issue of the status of blacks in a white society. The fact that the great research centers and the leading writers and politicians were long concentrated in the East, the South and the Midwest where Indians had been largely excluded, where Latinos were usually few in number and Asians fewer still, meant that for most of its history U.S. society defined itself around a black–white dualism, especially after the great migrations of blacks from the rural South to the urban North in the twentieth century created a national crisis. As great American cities seemed to be irreversibly changing from white to black majorities and the civil rights movement and the urban riots produced an intense national focus on the issue, that framework became ever more dominant. In 1968 in the report of the Presidential Commission addressing hundreds of urban riots, the commission concluded that we were becoming "two societies, separate and unequal" even as the 1965 Immigration Act was beginning to make us something a good deal more complex.

It was not surprising that the nation's political and intellectual energy overwhelmingly focused on the issues of African Americans, particularly on the fate of the apartheid laws of seventeen Southern and Border states and the conditions of the burgeoning urban ghettos. The black issue was a question of a relatively small minority in a nation committed in the 1920s to making itself continuously whiter by limiting immigration largely to Northern Europeans until 1965. The nation's history had a much deeper focus on the black–white division than any other social problem. In fact the issue of the position of blacks in American society had infected the U.S. Constitution with racism and split the country apart in a violent civil war. The fact that the civil rights movement had its roots in the black South and that its target was ending Southern apartheid deepened this focus.

Toward a Multiracial Vision

Now we have a confusing array of new color lines and color blends that our national history has not prepared us for, though they have deep historic roots. As the United States pressed into northern Mexico, the white settlers found and warred against a civilization with a high culture, which they defined as an inferior race and subjugated after the Mexican–American War made a vast expanse of Mexico part of the United States. When Asians surged into the West at the time of the Gold Rush and the great drive to build railroads across the continent, a fierce and angry racism erupted in California, which resulted in virtually total exclusion of immigration from the leading countries of Asia until 1965. Those stories, however, were of mostly regional interest until recently.

In just a few decades, we have become a society where the school age children will soon be majority non-white and where Americans of European descent are entering their last generation as the nation's majority. This society has more diversity, more color lines, and more complex patterns of persisting inequality. Black–white problems are far from resolved but are now occurring, not in a white society with a black minority, but in a multiracial society where blacks are extremely important in some regions and are a relatively small presence in others, and where huge new non-white communities are emerging from great movements of peoples across national borders, even as the white population ages and fails to reproduce itself.

America is now changing in ways few understand and many fear, changing much faster than either research or the policy discourse. Now, in the world's first predominantly suburban society, we sometimes face three or four-way racial separation and polarization spreading out into suburbs of tiny, highly divergent, local governments and school systems, almost none of which really understand or have plans to manage the social transformation that is well under way. Millions of people are coming into the country to take jobs that are far better than what they can find at home but that are dead ends in the U.S. context, providing insufficient resources to successfully launch their children into the American mainstream, and the society is cutting back on efforts to help such children. The growing non-white youth population faces service and education cutbacks while the older white population expects that its retirement costs will be borne by the new workers, many of them paying Social Security with no prospect of ever receiving aid since they are not legally present in the nation. Massive social and legal fictions and intergenerational injustices abound.

The three major responses to these changes are to do nothing, assuming that things will work out (or that nothing can be done), to try to restrict or reverse the change, or to extend rights and support. None of these alternatives has worked very well so far. Doing nothing has not prevented deepening problems. Trying to stop immigration has been highly popular but a massive failure. Instead of extending support, civil rights policies have been reversed and rights to social programs slashed.

The unanswered questions about the changes shaping our future are very basic. We really don't know, for example, what are the fundamental lines of cleavage in the society that will carry into the future. In the mid-twentieth century the color line had obvious meanings and the targets for legal reform seemed clear. In the early twenty-first century, none of these things is true and no young person really knows what kind of society there will be as the decades pass. We don't even know how we will classify ourselves and name our groups. A half century ago, African Americans were Negroes and almost all had been born in the United States. They became blacks in the late civil rights movement, and then African Americans, a name without great meaning to new immigrant blacks from Haiti, the Dominican Republic, or Jamaica. Latinos were not even counted as a category in mid-century, and there was very little data about them. Asians were small aging communities, certainly not thought of as a substantial cross-national group with some kind of common identity. Color, long considered an immutable characteristic in the United States, is different for Latinos and, in Latin societies, can sometimes be altered by social and economic mobility. Caste-like barriers to intermarriage long existing between blacks and whites in America have become less rigid for blacks and do not hold for other racial groups in the United States in the same way. It is far from certain what kinds of consciousness and groupings will emerge as mixed race status increases or whether the center, the mainstream, will broaden as it did for previously excluded groups like Catholics and Jews. Will there be a political and cultural movement about this issue parallel, perhaps, to that which occurred in Mexico after the revolution to give a positive image to mixed racial background?

There is, obviously, an extremely important role for accurate information and good research in this situation. When basic social issues become highly polarized and racial and ethnic scapegoating exacerbates social divisions, scholars are in a position to offer data and interpret changes free of political considerations. They have the capacity to characterize and interpret large social changes. Unfortunately they often do not explore these vital issues. Since these are highly political and ideological issues, government often either does not fund independent research or supports only work expected to support its position. Second, minority scholars are often discouraged from studying the problems of their own group because of claims from white scholars that they are biased, and white scholars are seldom interested in work that is rarely considered cutting edge in their discipline. Without money to stimulate interest, too little work is done. Third, the academic journals that so strongly shape academic careers value theoretical work and cutting edge statistical models much above descriptive or policy work and the studies intelligible by a broad audience that are needed to inform the public debate. Fourth, seriously engaging in controversial social issues exposes researchers and institutions to political and community attacks that are often uncomfortable for academics.

The issues raised in this book, and the enthusiastic participation in the Color Lines conference that stimulated its creation, show that there are many exciting research projects to be done and that a great many scholars, including many young scholars of color, are eager and ready to explore them. The questions are huge, some of the largest in American history and, since the public discussion has been so impoverished, the contributions can be very large both in terms of research and public understanding.

The questions begin with the most basic: what is race? Do the existing categories make sense? If not, how can we best describe the structure of the society as it goes through transformation? What is continuous and what is new about the situation of the nation's original inhabitants and its black population? Will the meaning of whiteness change as whites become conscious of their minority situation in more and more contexts? Will there be a fragmentation into national origin or religious identities? Will some non-white groups such as the successful

Asian and Latino nationality groups be incorporated into a larger "mainstream" population? Will the categories of Latino and Asian, which are basically conventions of counting, not coherent groups, become real pan ethnic identities? As cross-racial marriages increase, how will the families and children identify themselves, and what will their social situation be?

Suppose the United States grows to more than 400 million people by 2050, becoming a little less than half of European origin with 100 million Latinos, 80 million blacks, 40 million Asians, and 4 million American Indians. If that happens, as the census now predicts, the school age population would be a third white, about a sixth black, a tenth Asian, more than 30 percent Latino, with the rest mixed race and American Indian. Children would be growing up in an overwhelmingly non-white world in which each generation to come would likely be less white. The old black–white definition of race would have been supplanted by something more complex and fluid, and color and language would work in different ways in markets, popular culture, politics and many aspects of life. The inequalities might have deepened or been diminished depending on the wisdom of the policies adopted as the racial transition took place, the economy, the changing culture and values, or other dimensions not now foreseen. If the trends now in place were merely projected, we would be living in a society with a shrinking minority comprised of many whites and Asians and some members of other groups dominating the educational, economic, political, and cultural institutions. In every likelihood a society of this nature would be experiencing serious internal conflict and have an uncertain and difficult future.

Up to the present there has been an astonishingly broad acceptance of the "American dream" ideology among both the privileged and excluded groups in the society. Much of the discussion about the future of race relations in the nation assumes that this basic consensus will remain and that the only risk of racial polarization will be from the political strategies of whites. The experience of other societies, however, suggests that latent cleavages can give way to deep division and political polarization and hostility, and that this can be triggered not only among the dominant groups but also among subordinated majorities. The existing demographic trends in regions of the country suggest that such opportunities and possibilities will be more present in the future and that it may not be safe to simply extend assumptions from a quite different past. It may be essential now, while there is time, to consider the mistakes of other societies, the consequences, and the possible alternatives. It may be important to search for better analogies and probabilities from elsewhere than to assume continuity in a society that is changing very rapidly and has shown, not increased, but sharply diminished commitment to strategies to try to incorporate and integrate the non-white emerging majorities.

The reality is that policies forged during the civil rights revolution four decades ago, primarily to deal with the problems of overt discrimination against blacks in seventeen southern and border states, are being dismantled, and there are no initiatives of significance to deal with issues of multiracial inequality and separation in the nation's metropolitan areas where more than 80 percent of the people live. Each generation of Latino and black children after the 1980s will have less contact with white children if the existing trends continue.

Before we can possibly solve the problems we must better understand them. It was relatively easy to understand the deepest form of segregation and oppression practiced in the South (at least for those outside the South) because it was basically a polarized black–white world with the clearest of officially imposed social and governmental boundaries. Even in this extreme case there were generations of denial and inattention and passive acceptance until the Supreme Court and a great social movement led by the most eloquent speaker of twentieth-century America forced it into the center of public attention and two presidents chose to make it a dominant issue of their administrations. At least it was about a cleavage that had been a central reality of American society from the beginning and there was a tradition of legal and ethnical reasoning about it.

When a Southern sheriff beat up peaceful civil rights marchers it was not hard to separate the victims from the villains or to think about how the situation could be changed. What, however, is the way to understand liquor stores owned by Koreans being attacked by refugees from civil wars in Central America, or to think about whether or not it is discriminatory to teach a new immigrant only in English or to educate her at first in a language she understands? If a Chicano is denied entry to a school or college dominated by Chinese American students, is that discrimination, the result of a superior culture, or what? Do refugees have a right to claim discrimination in American society when their group had no significant presence in the United States until very recently and was not subject to a history of discrimination here? How should we understand and try to deal with the millions of people who have ancestors from more than one racial or ethnic group? Since race is far more a social than a biological construct, should their own identity and context be decisive or should there be some effort to measure degrees of ancestry?

There are no simple answers to these questions. Nor is it possible to easily project the future form of race and ethnicity in America. There was probably more continuity of understanding of the society from the foundation of the United States to the late twentieth century than there has been from decade to decade in the recent path. Since the 1960s the impact of the 1965 Immigration Act, of the plummeting white birth rate, and of the unprecedented tide of immigration from Mexico have made us a different nation. In fact, each generation of Americans is living in a country very different from that of the last generation.

Much has been made of the fact that race is not a sensible biological concept and ethnicity is even more confusing. Racial populations in the United States today are the products of widespread mixing, both informal and formal. Thomas Jefferson's black descendants, the black daughter of segregationist Senator Strom Thurmond, the mixing between slaves and Indians and between Indians and whites on the frontier, the success of many blacks in "passing" into the white community, the war brides, the huge intermarriage rates of some Asian groups and the immigration of a vast mestizo population from Latin America have made many statements that suggest a biological basis to lines of race and ethnicity absurd.

At the same time, the vast majority of Americans can tell you immediately what race and/or ethnicity they belong to, and less than 3 percent claimed mixed race background in the 2000 Census. Almost any set of social statistics or study of social relationships will quickly reveal strong relationships between the situation in the society and the race or ethnic group. Although some of these patterns change dramatically, many of these relationships are surprisingly durable over very long periods of time in dramatically changing conditions.

Understanding Social Construction

Since race and ethnicity are socially constructed but very important, governmental decisions about defining race and measuring relationships may be very important in the construction. The "white" race is itself a social construction, since it is really not strictly based upon color and is not limited to Europe and has incorporated groups not previously defined as white. Whites who come to the United States often define themselves initially as Italians or Hungarians, not seeing much in common with other groups in the "white" category, but quickly understanding the importance of this classification in the United States, something that has lead some groups of Latinos who have significant black heritage to classify themselves as whiter and whiter in successive censuses.

We now have two large groups, one of which is defined as a race and the other as an ethnicity—Asians and Latinos—which are the product of the American statistical system. Mexicans, a largely mestizo population with a predominantly Indian background have very little in common with Argentinians, who are of largely Spanish and Italian background and very different from nearby Bolivians, where large parts of the country do not speak Spanish and much of traditional Indian culture is intact. Puerto Ricans, Cubans, Dominicans, and Brazilians have a much stronger African heritage. Brazilians and Haitians and many in the Caribbean area don't even have Spanish as an official language.

The term "Latino" or "Hispanic" did not even exist in any coherent way within the U.S. data system until the late twentieth century, and much of the data has been collected for less than three decades. Within Latin America there is a great deal of stratification and difference within and between nations. Yet this statistical concept has emerged as a basic fact of American life, politics and community organizing. The synthetic category, created to aggregate data for immigrants from mostly Spanish-speaking countries of the Americas is becoming a real social and political category being built into the basic description of American reality. As the various Latino groups interact with each other more, especially in the largest cities and colleges, this category may spur increasing pan-ethnic consciousness and the concept may be becoming a social reality, taking on more race-like characteristics though it is profoundly interracial. In fact millions of Latinos tell the census they are part of an "other" race, not white, black, or Indian. The concept of Asian or Asian/Pacific Islander is even more improbable. For most Latinos and most Latin countries there is at least a common historic language and a history of conquest and settlement by the Spanish empire as well as a common widely shared religious tradition, traditional structure of cities, and much else. For Asians there are none of those. There are many languages, many cultures, many distinct histories and very wide differences of religious beliefs and traditions. Filipinos probably have less in common with Pakistanis than with Spaniards; Indonesians or Malaysians more in common with Moroccans than with Mongolians, and the list could go on. The social and economic and educational characteristics of the category are the products of the categories in U.S. immigration law and in the special provisions made for refugees after the Vietnam War—policies producing an extremely selective immigration from most countries and an extremely disadvantaged population from a few others—producing a strikingly bimodal category in which the smaller severely disadvantaged groups tend to be lost in the general story of success, integration, mobility and positive stereotypes of cultural superiority. Since the largest Asians groups are, on average, highly integrated with whites, have high socioeconomic status and intermarriage rates, this category seems particularly weak and, possibly, unstable.

The problem, first for researchers and then for those working for racial justice, is to come up with reasonable ways to deal with issues of discrimination and rights in the short run and then achieve ever deepening understandings of the many realities of a society in tumultuous change. Anti-discrimination policy and affirmative action should clearly focus on the groups most intensely affected by discrimination and still far behind. The basic premise of civil rights law is to end and, to the extent possible, compensate for the unresolved historic discrimination experienced by entire groups of people. Clearly African Americans and American Indians have the most dramatic claims followed by Latinos from Mexico and Puerto Rico, peoples first incorporated in the nation by conquest. No other group but blacks experienced centuries of slavery and apartheid. No other group but Indians faced the massive extermination, involuntary displacement and systematic destruction of economies and cultures that Indian tribes faced. Those from lands won by conquest from Mexico and Spain were then subject to either legal institutions that dispossessed them of their properties and rights or colonialized and subjected them to systematic discrimination as a group for long periods. All of these groups have always been far behind whites in American society and always the subject of serious stereotypes and discrimination.

Groups such as Chinese and Japanese who were once the subject of vicious discrimination but now are, on average, more successful educationally and economically than whites and well accepted in American society, have a far less pressing claim. Vast proportions of the nation, including, for example, Catholics and Jews, were victims of severe historic discrimination, but are doing well now. There must be present effects of the history of discrimination to sustain a claim of special rights. What, on the other hand, should be the status of a racial or ethnic minority driven out of their country as the result of U.S. intervention in a war who are experiencing persisting inequality within the United States? Groups who were not present during times of overt discrimination but are doing poorly in American society probably have less of a moral and legal claim than groups of poor whites long resident in the society unless, perhaps, they can demonstrate that they have been subsumed into a group subject to continuing overt discrimination on the basis of race. How should white subgroups experiencing severe intergenerational poverty concentrated in places like Appalachia be treated?

Obviously these are profound problems for legal and social research. Our legal structure and our concepts of discrimination were built for a far less complex society than the one we now possess. Neither the nation's founders nor the authors of the Fourteenth Amendment had any notion of the kind of society we now find in Queens, in South Los Angeles, in Miami, or on the North Side of Chicago. We have to invent sensible ways to extend the existing legal principles into the new contexts or invent ones that will serve them better. That legal work, if it is to be successful, must, in turn, rest on an updated understanding of the social realities. The fairness and effectiveness of policy depends upon understanding the social and historical realities.

Creating an Informed Policy Agenda

The basic emphasis in recent decades has been on policies that simply ignore divisions of race, ethnicity, class, and immigrant status and assume that the problem is nothing that relates to those facts but one of laxity in the institutions serving certain groups of people or the lack of appropriate market incentives, which are assumed to have provided for the mobility and incorporation of previous groups into the mainstream. So since the early 1980s, as poverty and civil rights policies have been reversed, there has been a tidal wave of requirements and tests and accountability measures, insistently rooted in the belief that the principal causes of remaining inequality are laxness of teachers and of students and that they can be cured by more demands and harsh sanctions, such as the denial of a diploma or the dissolution of a "failing" school. On the welfare side the emphasis has been to push very hard to force welfare moms to take any kind of a job without providing a guarantee of services such as child care and health care for their children. The success in lowering welfare payments has been taken as success of the policy. At the same time the assumption that laxness by police, the courts and the penal system has been responsible for the growth of crimes, committed overwhelmingly by virtually unemployable young high school dropouts, has been responsible for a massive expansion of the policy of incarceration to levels far above those in other advanced societies. The facts that long-term welfare and high dropout rates tend to be issues primarily of families of color living in areas of concentrated poverty, and that crime is concentrated there as well, have been treated as merely incidental or as a sign that there is something wrong with black and Latino communities.

Problems of race and ethnicity cannot be solved without understanding them, facing up to them, and learning how to resolve them. If they are connected to deep cleavages but simply ignored, it is virtually certain that the groups on the privileged side of the color lines will assume that there is something wrong with the groups which have fallen behind and add insult to injury with policies that both stereotype them and totally excuse those who control most of the opportunities from any responsibility for curing the inequalities.

The Future

The reality of the future is a society where the nation will not have any dominant racial or ethnic character but where race and ethnicity will still be very strongly related to patterns of opportunity, attitudes, and social and economic polarization. All groups, including whites, are going to be minorities in the nation, though there will be many localities and some states and regions with a dominant group. In this situation, particularly if there are high levels of segregation and racial polarization, each group is likely to have grievances toward others and to compete for resources, and there will be leaders trying to exploit fears and stereotypes. Since most students of color are likely to have poor educational preparation, there is a very serious risk of falling average educational levels for the entire society. At worst, we could face a society that comes apart, as have many other societies deeply divided along lines of race, ethnicity or religion.

What to do? First, we have to recognize and understand the changes of kinds unknown in American history. The computer experts and medical professionals coming into the country will find a relatively easy and mutually beneficial transition, but the economy that has a vast hunger for young, hard-working, powerless and very poorly paid workers, at the same time, wants to punish and expel them. This migration is bringing a young population into metro areas with aging and declining white populations, but it is a population that is increasingly separate both educationally and residentially, producing some areas with severe social pathologies. We must understand the triumphs and the crises, avoid stereotyping, look at economic and social causes, and devise strategies that work to provide genuine opportunity and stability.

The Research Challenge

Before anyone can figure out what needs to be done, we need a great deal of fundamental intellectual work on the many unanswered basic questions about opportunity, discrimination, cultural assimilation or pluralism, intergenerational mobility, and creation and transformation of communities defined by race. Is our democracy developing politics that are racially polarized or creating successful interracial coalitions? What kind of immigration policy, among feasible alternatives, would be most beneficial? Most issues of obvious significance for the future have received far too little serious research attention either from the government or the universities. The challenge now is to give the county a view of the vast multidimensional changes and develop understanding of the patterns of transformation in the society and its institutions. The work is as basic for the future as the research that was done on the situation of American blacks before the civil rights revolution or on the transformation of urban communities, with the emergence of urban sociology in the 1920s. It will give the nation an updated understanding of itself and its trajectory and options.

I strongly believe that there are hugely important and feasible studies of many sorts that can be done for relatively modest costs and that academics in this generation have both the opportunity and the responsibility to use their skills and university resources to paint a much richer portrait of the nature of contemporary American society and the basic trends that are changing it. There is much more basic descriptive and trend work that can be done at low cost because of the easy and convenient access to a great deal of Census data and many national, state, local and research data sets. With the tremendous expansion of educational data produced by the No Child Left Behind Act and related state educational reforms, for example, it is possible to describe much more fully than in the past the achievement and completion of students of different racial and ethnic groups in schools of different race and poverty levels and locations. Many important studies can be done of individual cities and metropolitan areas. Minority communities, elected officials, and civil rights organizations rarely have resources to do this work but are intensely interested in it if it is written clearly and researchers reach out to communicate with them. Small qualitative studies that explore the varieties of cultural and institutional changes and help to build theories about the kind of society that is emerging can be done with limited resources. Studies of the incorporation or exclusion of new and historically excluded groups from community life and politics are badly needed. Studies on the transformation of American literature, music, and mass media would be invaluable. Legal studies attempting to interpret provisions of law that have provided civil rights for blacks and translate to the wide range of circumstances of the new communities will be essential in a society founded by lawyers and deeply influenced by extremely powerful courts. Needless to say, policy studies analyzing the conditions under which various public services and educational institutions either effectively serve or tend to disserve non-white people could have large impacts. The basic reality is that we are very far into a transformation that has no precedent in American history and no one knows how to maximize the positive outcomes and minimize those that are harmful to the groups and to the society. The needs for research and reliable information are immense.

Those of us who worked on the Color Lines conference had no idea what the response of the academic world would be to our request to think boldly about new areas of research and propose new paradigms. We were thrilled when more than five hundred researchers and research groups from every part of the country sent us proposals and offered to do substantial studies for very little. When the event arrived and there were many hundreds of people who came from many locations at their own expense to hear more than 110 new studies, the atmosphere was one of discovery and intense excitement. Some of this work was cosmic in its ambition; other studies offered tantalizing vignettes full of suggestions about how we should understand an aspect of what is happening. That experience showed that there were many people, particularly young scholars, who had observed and were thinking creatively about intriguing and important aspects of the change. Many discovered that they were part of a potential community of scholars determined to understand a new social reality. That conference and this book are contributions to that movement. When more than a million people turn to the Civil Rights Project's website in a month, that is another sign of the hunger for data and policy ideas. There are many scholars who will respond to an opportunity to do serious research on aspects of racial transformation. It is very important that government and foundations provide funding to support major projects and studies and that there be a great national conversation. Until that happens, scholars must carry this work to the next stages, however they can, and share what they learn as broadly as they can. Universities and scholarly fields must recognize the importance of this work and realize that scholarship can help the society avoid the severe risks of these massive changes and reap many more of the potential gains. We are far along the path to a new society, with no coherent road map, and there is no time to wait.

Contributors

Luis A. Avilés is an associate professor at the University of Puerto Rico, Mayagüez Campus (UPRM). He obtained a B.S. in Mathematics at the University of Puerto Rico, Rio Piedras Campus, a M.S. in Biostatistics at the University of California Los Angeles, and a Ph.D. in Health Policy from the John Hopkins University. After being a University of California President's Postdoctoral Fellow at the Center for Iberian and Latin American Studies at the University of California, San Diego, he joined the Sociology Section of the Department of Social Sciences of the UPRM, where he teaches courses on medical sociology and social planning. His current areas of interest are health and socioeconomic development, critical epidemiology, and critical medical geography.

Juan Carlos Martínez-Cruzado is a Professor of Genetics at the University of Puerto Rico, Mayagüez campus. While there, he has contributed to the field of Genetics with respect to the study of Population History and Anthropology in Puerto Rico.

Nilanjana Dasgupta is an Assistant Professor of Psychology at the University of Massachusetts at Amherst. She received a Ph.D. in Psychology from Yale University in 1998 and an A.B. in Psychology and Neuroscience from Smith College in 1992. Her research is on intergroup relations, with special emphasis on the ways in which beliefs and attitudes about social groups are shaped by culturally shared stereotypes and prejudices that operate unconsciously—without perceivers' awareness, intention, or control. Her projects, supported by the National Science Foundation, the National Institute of Mental Health, and the American Psychological Foundation, currently focus on the behavioral manifestations of unconscious prejudice and stereotypes, and on the development of interventions aimed at prejudice reduction.

Christina Gómez is an associate professor of Sociology and Latino and Latin American Studies at Northeastern Illinois University. She received her Ph.D. in Sociology from Harvard University in 1998. Her research focuses on the construction of identity, specifically race and ethnicity as well as social inequalities and immigration. She has been published widely in various scholarly journals on these subjects, and her most recent article "Assimilation vs. Multiculturalism: Bilingual Education and the Latino Challenge" co-authored by J. Burdick-Will was published in *Journal of Latinos and Education* in July 2006.

Andrew Grant-Thomas is Deputy Director at the Kirwan Institute for the Study of Race and Ethnicity at The Ohio State University. Before assuming that position, he was Senior Research Associate at The Civil Rights Project at Harvard University, where he directed the Project's Color Lines Conference: Segregation and Integration in America's Present and Future, held over Labor Day weekend, 2003, at Harvard Law School. Most of the essays in *21st Century Color Lines* derive form papers initially developed for and presented at the conference. He is currently working on several writing projects, including essays on the nature of structural racism in the 21st century and on the meaning and trajectories of racial and ethnic integration in the United States.

Gerald Gurin is a Professor Emeritus of Higher Education and Research Scientist Emeritus of the Institute for Social Research at the University of Michigan. His research using the population survey methodology, has focused on a broad array of issues: Americans' political behavior and electoral choices, peoples' subjective mental health and coping strategies, socialization impacts of the college experience, motivational and opportunity issues in manpower training programs, psychological, social, and vocational implications of being members of racial/ethnic minorities in American society. He was actively involved in the Michigan Student Study since its inception in the years immediately preceding his retirement in 1993, and has continued this involvement since his retirement.

Patricia Gurin is the Nancy Cantor Distinguished University Professor Emerita of Psychology and Women's Studies at the University of Michigan. She is a Faculty Associate of the Research Center for Group Dynamics at the Institute for Social Research and of the Center for African and Afro-American Studies. She directs the research program of the Program on Intergroup Relations. A social psychologist, Dr. Gurin's work has focused on social identity, the role of social identity in political attitudes and behavior, motivation and cognition in achievement settings, and the role of social structure in intergroup relations. She is the author of eight books and monographs and numerous articles on these topics. She was an expert witness in the University of Michigan's defense of its admission policies that was recently decided by the Supreme Court.

Anthony Kwame Harrison teaches Sociology and Black Studies at Virginia Tech University and holds a Ph.D. in Anthropology from Syracuse University. His doctoral research explored issues of identity, power, and commodification among West Coast underground hip-hop enthusiasts living in the San Francisco Bay Area. He has also recorded and released two full-length albums as a member of the San Francisco–based hip-hop group Forest Fires Collective.

Maria Rosario Jackson is a senior research associate and director of the Urban Institute's Culture, Creativity and Communities Program. Dr. Jackson's research focuses on urban policy, urban poverty, community planning, and the role of arts and culture in community building processes and the politics of race, ethnicity and gender in urban settings. Dr. Jackson earned a master's degree in public administration from the University of Southern California and a doctorate in urban planning from the University of California, Los Angeles.

John Matlock is Associate Vice Provost in the Office of the Provost and Executive Vice President for Academic Affairs at the University of Michigan. He also directs the university's Office of Academic Multicultural Initiatives (OAMI). OAMI coordinates the largest commemoration of Martin Luther King Jr. programs in the country with some 90 campus-wide activities. Under his leadership, OAMI has served as a national model for using diverse groups of staff, faculty and students to advance campus diversity initiatives.

Nancy McArdle is a Senior Research Analyst at the Joint Center for Political and Economic Studies in Washington, D.C. She is a former researcher at Harvard University for the Civil Rights Project where she examined residential segregation in the metro Boston Area.

John Mollenkopf is Distinguished Professor of Political Science and director of the Center for Urban Research at the City University Graduate Center. He has authored or edited ten books on urban politics and policy and New York City. With Philip Kasinitz and Mary Waters, he is currently writing a book about educational attainment, labor market outcomes, and political and civic involvement among young adults from immigrant and native minority family backgrounds in the New York metropolitan area. With Gary Gerstle, he co-edited *E Pluribus Unum? Historical and Contemporary Perspectives of Immigrant Political Incorporation.* He also recently analyzed Latino voting patterns in the 2001 New York City mayoral election and co-authored "People and Politics in America's Big Cities" for the Drum Major Institute with John Logan.

Gary Orfield is Professor of Education, Law, Political Science and Urban Planning at The University of California, Los Angeles, and Co-Director of the Civil Rights Project. He received the American Political Science Association's Charles Merriam Award awarded to a scholar "whose published work and career represents a significant contribution to the art of government through the application of social science research" and the Gustavus Myers award for an outstanding book on race relations. He is the author or editor of numerous books on civil rights, education policy, urban policy, and minority opportunity, including, most recently, *Dropouts in America: Confronting the Graduation Rate Crisis,* in 2004.

john a. powell is an internationally recognized authority in the areas of civil rights, civil liberties, and issues relating to race, ethnicity, poverty and the law. He is the executive director of the Kirwan Institute for the Study of Race and Ethnicity at Ohio State University. He also holds the Williams Chair in Civil Rights and Civil Liberties at the Moritz College of Law. He has written extensively on a number of issues including racial justices and regionalism, concentrated poverty and urban sprawl, the link between housing and school segregation, opportunity based housing, gentrification, disparities in the criminal justice system, voting rights, affirmative action in the United States, South Africa and Brazil, and racial and ethnic identity and the current demographic shift.

Doris Ramírez is a Professor of Chemistry at the University of Puerto Rico, Mayagüez campus. She received her Ph.D. in 1989 from Rutgers University.

David Roediger is a professor of History at the University of Illinois at Urbana-Champaign (UIUC). His research interests include the construction of racial identity, class structures, and the history of American radicalism, on which he has written a number of articles and books. His most recent book is *The Colored White: Transcending the Racial Past* (University of California Press, 2002). In 1999, Roediger won the Carlton C. Qualey Memorial Award for his article "Inbetween Peoples," which was co-authored with James Barrett. The award is given by the Immigration and Ethnic History Society for the best article in the *Journal of American Ethnic History.*

Anayra O. Santory-Jorge is an associate professor in the Department of Humanities at the University of Puerto Rico, Mayagüez campus. She received her Ph.D. in 1994 from Indiana University, Bloomington.

Jiannbin Lee Shiao is an associate professor of sociology at the University of Oregon and the Assistant Director of the Ethnic Studies Program. His scholarship examines the dialectical relationship between demographic heterogeneity and race relations in the post–civil rights era, or in other words, between the quantity and quality of diversity. His research, which has received funding from the Russell Sage Foundation, has employed primarily qualitative methods. He has published extensively on these topics and has recently co-authored the book *International Korean Adoption: A Fifty-Year History of Policy and Practice* (Hayworth Press, 2007) with Mia H. Tuan.

Mia H. Tuan is an associate professor and Director of Teacher Education at the University of Oregon. Tuan's research interests include: racial and ethnic identity, racial reconciliation/mediation work, and immigrant adaptation. Along with her research on these topics, she has authored numerous books on these subjects, most recently *International Korean Adoption: A Fifty-Year History of Policy and Practice* (Hayworth Press, 2007) with Jiannbin Shiao. She is also one of the founding members of the Center on Diversity and Community, which is a "learning organization committed to promoting research and best practices on issues of cultural diversity, equity, and access."

Katrina Wade-Golden is a research coordinator for the University of Michigan in the Office of Academic Multicultural Initiatives and is currently a doctoral candidate in the Industrial/Organizational Psychology program at Wayne State University. She received her B.A. from the University of Michigan in Psychology with an emphasis in human resources and organizational development, and a Master of Science in Psychology (Industrial/Organizational) from Wayne State University. Her research interests include the impact of increasing diversity and affirmative action on organizations, conflict resolution, stress, and distance learning. She has presented at several national conferences on issues related to diversity and multiculturalism, gender, racism, and affirmative action.

Index